38 47

DATE DUE

MAY 13 '91		
NOV 25 '92		
GAYLORD		PRINTED IN U.S.A.

Artificial Intelligence &
Expert Systems Sourcebook

Artificial Intelligence & Expert Systems Sourcebook

V. DANIEL HUNT

President
Technology Research Corporation

CHAPMAN & HALL

New York   London

First published 1986
by Chapman and Hall
29 West 35th Street, New York, N.Y. 10001

Published in Great Britain by
Chapman and Hall Ltd
11 New Fetter Lane, London EC4P 4EE

© 1986 Chapman and Hall

Printed in the United States of America

Library of Congress Cataloging in Publication Data

Hunt, V. Daniel.
   Artificial Intelligence and Expert Systems Sourcebook

   Bibliography: p.
   Includes index.
   1. Artificial Intelligence Dictionary
   2. Expert Systems Dictionary   I. Title.
TJ2   1986
ISBN 0-412-012111

Dedication

To Audrey N. Hunt and Vernon E. Hunt for their continued help and support in establishing Technology Research Corporation. Both Jan and I appreciate their interest and participation in projects such as this book.

Table of Contents

Preface

Artificial Intelligence and expert systems research, development, and demonstration have rapidly expanded over the past several years; as a result, new terminology is appearing at a phenomenal rate. This sourcebook provides an introduction to artificial intelligence and expert systems, it provides brief definitions, it includes brief descriptions of software products, and vendors, and notes leaders in the field. Extensive support material is provided by delineating points of contact for receiving additional information, acronyms, a detailed bibliography, and other reference data.

The terminology includes artificial intelligence and expert system elements for:

- Artificial Intelligence
- Expert Systems
- Natural Language Processing
- Smart Robots
- Machine Vision
- Speech Synthesis

The Artificial Intelligence and Expert System Sourcebook is compiled from information acquired from numerous books, journals, and authorities in the field of artificial intelligence and expert systems.

I hope this compilation of information will help clarify the terminology for artificial intelligence and expert systems' activities. Your comments, revisions, or questions are welcome.

V. Daniel Hunt
Springfield, Virginia
May, 1986

Acknowledgments

The information in *Artificial Intelligence and Expert Systems Sourcebook* has been compiled from a wide variety of authorities who are specialists in their respective fields.

The following publications were used as the basic technical resources for this book. Portions of these publications may have been used in the book. Those definitions or artwork used have been reproduced with the permission to reprint of the respective publisher.

V. Daniel Hunt, *Smart Robots*, Copyright 1985, Chapman and Hall, New York, N.Y. Reprinted with permission.

Hayes-Roth, Waterman & Levot, *Building Expert Systems*, Copyright 1983, Addison-Wesley Publishing Company, Reading, Massachusetts. Reprinted with permission.

Donald A. Waterman, *A Guide to Expert Systems*, Copyright 1985, Addison-Wesley Publishing Company, Reading, Massachusetts. Reprinted with permission.

Armed Forces Communications and Electronics Association's Professional Development Center Course 110C entitled "Artificial Intelligence and National Defense: Applications to Command and Control and Beyond, 1985, AFCEA.

Patrick H. Winston & Berthold Horn, *LISP*, Copyright 1984, Addison-Wesley, Reading, Massachusetts. Reprinted with permission.

Patrick H. Winston & Prevdergost, *The AI Business: Commercial Uses of Artificial Intelligence*, Copyright 1985, The MIT Press, Cambridge, Massachusetts. Reprinted with permission.

Paul Harmon and David King, *Expert Systems—Artificial Intelligence in Business*, Copyright 1985, John Wiley & Sons, Inc., New York, N.Y. Reprinted with permission.

Henry C. Mishkoff, *Understanding Artificial Intelligence*, Copyright 1985, Texas Instruments Inc. Reprinted with permission.

Industrial Robots—A Summary and Forecast, Copyright 1985, Tech Tran Corporation, Naperville, Illinois. Reprinted with permission.

Machine Vision Systems—A Summary and Forecast, Copyright 1985, Tech Tran Corporation, Naperville, Illinois. Reprinted with permission.

Susan J. J. Scown, *The Artificial Intelligence Experience: An Introduction*, Copyright 1985, Digital Equipment Corporation, Massachusetts. Reprinted with permission.

The preparation of a book of this type is dependent upon an excellent staff, and I have been fortunate in this regard. Special thanks are extended to Janet C. Hunt, Audrey and Vernon Hunt, Donald W. Keehan, Kellie-Jo Anne Ackerman, James E. Wise, Jr., and Carla E. Wise for research assistance. Special thanks to Margaret W. Alexander for the word processing of the manuscript.

INTRODUCTION TO ARTIFICIAL INTELLIGENCE AND EXPERT SYSTEMS

Artificial intelligence, also sometimes referred to as machine intelligence or heuristic programming, is an emerging technology that has recently attracted considerable publicity. Many applications are now under development. One simple view of the field is that it is concerned with devising computer programs to make computers smarter. Thus, research in artificial intelligence is focused on developing computational approaches to intelligent behavior. That effort has 2 goals: making machines more useful and understanding intelligence.

The computer programs with which artificial intelligence is concerned are primarily symbolic processes involving complexity, uncertainty, and ambiguity. Those processes are usually those for which algorithmic solutions do not exist and search is required. Thus, artificial intelligence deals with the types of problem solving and decision making that humans continually face in dealing with the world.

This form of problem solving differs markedly from scientific and engineering calculations that are primarily numeric in nature and for which solutions are known that produce satisfactory answers. In contrast, artificial intelligence programs deal with words and concepts and often do not guarantee a correct solution—some wrong answers being tolerable, as in human problem solving.

Table 1-1 provides a comparison between artificial intelligence and conventional computer programs. A key characteristic of artificial intelligence programs is "heuristic search." In complex problems the number of possible solution paths can be enormous. Thus, artificial intelligence problem solving is usually guided by empirical rules—rules of thumb—referred to as "heuristics," which help constrain the search.

Table 1-1 Comparison of Artificial Intelligence with Conventional Programming

Artificial Intelligence	Conventional Computer Programming
• Primarily symbolic processes	• Often primarily numeric
• Heuristic search (solution steps implicit)	• Algorithmic (solution steps explicit)
• Control structure usually separate from domain knowledge	• Information and control integrated together
• Usually easy to modify, update and enlarge	• Difficult to modify
• Some incorrect answers often tolerable	• Correct answers required
• Satisfactory answers usually acceptable	• Best possible solution usually sought

Another aspect of artificial intelligence programs is the extensive use of "domain knowledge." Intelligence is heavily dependent on knowledge. That knowledge must be available for use when it is needed during the search. It is common in artificial intelligence programs to separate such knowledge from the mechanism'that controls the search. In that way changes in knowledge only require changes in the knowledge base. In contrast, domain knowledge and control in conventional computer programs are integrated together. As a result, conventional computer programs are difficult to modify, as the implications of the changes made in 1 part of the program must be carefully examined for the impacts and the changes required in other parts of the program.

The popular view that the study of artificial intelligence is difficult has been partly due to the awe associated with the notion of intelligence. It has also the result of the nomenclature used in artificial intelligence and the large size of some of the computer programs. However, the basic ideas are readily understandable, even though in complex applications, the "bookkeeping" associated with such programs can be arduous.

Before we go into details on these basic ideas, it is illuminating to review the history of artificial intelligence.

THE HISTORY OF ARTIFICIAL INTELLIGENCE

In 1956, 10 scientists convened a conference at Dartmouth College from which emerged the present field of artificial intelligence. The prediction made by those scientists was that in 25 years we would all be involved in recreational activities, while computers would be doing all the work. In 1981 at the International Joint Conference ·on Artificial Intelligence in Vancouver, Canada, a panel of 5 of those same scientists recalled that conference and their overoptimistic forecasts.

In 1956 it was assumed that intelligent behavior was primarily based on smart reasoning techniques and that bright people could readily devise ad hoc techniques to produce intelligent computer programs.

Fig. 1-1 lists some of the artificial intelligence activities during the first 15 years. The major initial activity involved attempts at machine translation. It was thought that natural language translation could be readily accomplished using a bilingual dictionary

---

ACTIVITIES

- Attempts at Machine Translation
- ELIZA—Key Word and Template Matching
- Symbolic Integration
- Game Playing—Checkers, Chess
- Pattern Recognition
- Computational Logic
- General Problem Solver

LESSONS LEARNED

- Artificial Intelligence Much More Difficult than Expected
- Heuristic Search Required to Limit Combinatorial Explosion
- Lack of Contextual Knowledge Severely Limits Capability
- Expectation Is a Human Characteristic of Intelligence
- Difficult to Handle a Broad Domain (e.g., Common Sense)

Fig. 1-1. A Condensed History of Artificial Intelligence—1965-70

and some knowledge of grammar. However, that approach failed miserably because of such factors as multiple word senses, idioms, and syntactic ambiguities. A popular story is that the saying "The spirit is willing, but the flesh is weak," when translated into Russian and back again into English, was rendered as "The wine is good, but the meat is spoiled." It was reported that "twenty million dollars of mechanical translation brought results so disappointing, that . . . by 1967 opinion had soured so dramatically that the National Academy of Sciences all but created a tombstone over the research." In fact, it has only been recently that substantial work in mechanical language translation has reappeared.

At The Massachusetts Institute of Technology a natural language understanding program was designed that simulated a nondirective psychotherapist. The program (ELIZA) bluffed its way through the interaction by picking up on key words and providing stock answers. When it did not find a recognizable key word, it would select a reply such as "Please continue." The program was written in part to show how difficult it was to expect true natural language understanding by a machine; the program nevertheless became popular, and some of its basic techniques are used in commercial Natural Language Interfaces today.

In 1961 a heuristic computer program was devised at M.I.T. to do symbolic integration. This proved to be the forerunner of a successful series of symbolic mathematical programs culminating in MACSYMA, in use at M.I.T. today and available over the "ARPANET" to other artificial intelligence researchers.

Game playing was also one of the early areas of artificial intelligence research, with work at IBM on machine learning in checkers proving to be one of the early successes. Solving puzzles was another area of early success in artificial intelligence, leading to the development of problem-solving techniques based on search and reducing difficult problems into easier subproblems. Early work in machine vision involved image processing and pattern recognition (which was concerned with classifying 2-dimensional patterns). Pattern recognition split off from artificial intelligence and became a field in itself, but now the 2 disciplines have become much more unified.

The pioneering work in computer vision was designed to understand polyhedral block scenes. The program found the edges of the blocks by using the spatial derivatives of image intensity and from the resulting edge elements produced a line drawing. It then utilized simple features, such as the numbers of vertices, to relate the objects in the line drawing to stored 3-dimensional models of blocks. The resulting candidate model was then scaled, rotated, and projected onto the line drawing so that one could see if the resultant match was adequate for recognition.

Another important area was computational logic. Resolution, an automatic method for determining if the hypothesized conclusion indeed followed from a given set of premises, was one of the early golden hopes of artificial intelligence for universal problem solving by computer. Using recognition, a general-purpose, question-answering system, QA3, which solved simple problems in a number of domains, such as robot movements, puzzles, and chemistry was developed. Unfortunately, resolution, though it guarantees a solution, devises so many intermediate steps which turn out not to be needed for the final solution that for large problems its use results in a combinatorial explosion of search possibilities.

Another approach, originally thought to have broad applicability, was the General Problem Solver (GPS) devised by Alan Newell et al. The generality resulted from the fact that GPS was the first problem solver to separate its problem-solving methods from knowledge of the specific task currently being considered. The GPS approach was referred to as "means-ends analysis." The idea was that the differences between the current problem state and the goal state could be measured and classified into types. Then appropriate operators could be chosen to reduce those differences, resulting in new problem states closer to the goal states. That procedure would then be repeated until the goal was reached. The series of operators used would then form the solution plan. Unfortunately, classifying differences and finding appropriate operators turned out to be more difficult than expected for nontrivial problems. In addition, computer running times and memory requirements rapidly become excessive for the more difficult problems.

Artificial intelligence proved much more difficult than had originally been expected. By 1970 it had had only limited success. Natural Language Translation had collapsed. "Toy" problems or well-constructed problems, such as games, proved tractable, but really complex problems proved to be beyond the techniques thus far devised or resulted in a combinatorially explosive search that exceeded the then current computer capabilities. Similarly, real world machine vision efforts tended to be overwhelmed by the noise and complexities in real scenes.

In 1971, the British Government called upon Sir Lighthill of Cambridge University to review the artificial intelligence field. The Lighthill report found that "in no part of the field have the discoveries made so far produced the major impact that was promised." Furthermore, he found that respected artificial intelligence scientists were then predicting that ". . . possibilities in the 1980s include an all-purpose intelligence on a human-scale knowledge base; that awe-inspiring possibilities suggest themselves based on machine intelligence exceeding human intelligence by the year 2000"—the same sort of forecasts that had been made 15 years earlier. Sir Lighthill saw no need for a separate artificial intelligence field and found no organized body of techniques that represented such a field. He felt that the work in automation and computer science would naturally come together to bridge whatever gap existed. The Lighthill Report eventually brought work in artificial intelligence in England to a virtual halt and cast a pall over such work in the United States.

However, the artificial intelligence of the 1950s and 1960s was not without merit. A great deal was learned about what really had to be done to make it successful.

It was found that expectation is a human characteristic of intelligence. That perception, both visual and in language, is based upon knowledge, models, and expectations of the perceiver. Thus it was found that communication via language is based upon shared knowledge between the participants and that only cues are needed to utilize the models from which to construct the complete message.

Thus in attempting communication or problem solving, lack of contextual knowledge was discovered to be a severe limiting capability. Reasoning techniques alone proved inadequate. Knowledge is central to intelligence. Lacking that knowledge, one will find it difficult to handle a broad domain. An example is "common sense," found to be elementary reasoning based upon massive amounts of experiential knowledge. Early on, artificial intelligence researchers discovered that intelligent behavior is not so much due to the methods of reasoning, as it is dependent on the knowledge one has to reason with. (As humans go through life, they build up tremendous reservoirs of knowledge.) Thus, when substantial knowledge has to be brought to bear on a problem, methods are needed to efficiently model that knowledge so that it is readily accessible. The result of the emphasis on knowledge is that knowledge representation is one of the most active areas of research in artificial intelligence today. The needed knowledge is not easy to represent, nor is the best representation obvious for a given task.

It was also found that heuristics are necessary to guide the search to overcome the combinatorial explosion of possible solutions that pervade complex problems—for each time one makes a decision, one opens up new possibilities. Much of the early work in artificial intelligence was focused on deriving programs that would search for solutions to problems. Note that every time one makes a decision, the situation is changed, opening up new opportunities for further decisions. Therefore there are always branch points. Thus, one of the usual ways of representing problem solving in artificial intelligence is in terms of a pyramid, starting at the top with an initial condition and branching every time a decision is made. As one continues down the pyramid, many different decision possibilities open up, so that the number of branches at the bottom can get to be enormous for problems requiring many solution steps. Therefore, some way is needed to efficiently search the pyramid.

Initially, there were "blind" methods for searching. They were orderly search approaches that assured that the same solution path would not be tried more than once. However, for problems more complex than games and puzzles, those approaches were inadequate. Therefore, rules of thumb (empirical rules), referred to as "heuristics," were needed to aid in choosing the most likely branches, so as to narrow the search. As an example, here is a simple heuristic to help choose which roads to follow when one is driving in the evening on back roads from Washington, D.C., to San Francisco: "Head for the setting sun." That may not produce the most optimum path, but it can serve to help advance one toward one's goal. Such heuristic rules can help guide search—reducing it enormously.

As indicated in Fig. 1-2, in the 1970s artificial intelligence researchers began to capitalize on the lessons learned. New knowledge representation techniques appeared. Search techniques began to mature. Interactions with other fields, such as medicine, electronics and chemistry, took place. Feasible approaches were demonstrated for language processing, speech understanding, machine vision, and computer programs that could perform like experts.

SHRDLU was a natural language program at M.I.T. devised by Terry Winograd to interface with an artificial "block world." It was the first program to successfully deal in an integrated way with natural language by combining syntactic and semantic analysis with a body of world knowledge.

From 1971 to 1976, the Advanced Research Project Agency now known as Defense Advanced Research Project Agency (DARPA) sponsored a 5-year speech understanding program. HEARSAY II at Carnegie Mellon University was successful; those enrolled were able to understand sentences, with 90% accuracy, from continuous speech based on a 1000-word vocabulary. (The "blackboard" system architecture, devised for HEARSAY II to deal with multiple knowledge sources, has since found use in other artificial intelligence applications.) A compiled network architecture system called HARPY, which handled the same vocabulary as HEARSAY II, was able to achieve a 95% accuracy.

ACTIVITIES

- Feasible Approaches Demonstrated:
  Language Processing
  Machine Vision
  Expert Systems
  System Understanding
- New Knowledge Representation Techniques Appear
- Search Techniques Begin to Mature
- Interaction with Other Fields Takes Place

LESSON LEARNED

- Knowledge Central to Intelligence
- Future Complex Systems Proved Feasible

Fig. 1–2. The Decade of the 70s

SRI developed the Vision Module as a prototype system for use in industrial vision systems. The system, which used special lighting to produce a binary image (silhouette) of an industrial workpiece, was able to extract edges by a simple continuous scan process and was to prove the basis for several sophisticated commercial vision systems.

In the 1970s, following an earlier successful effort called DENDRAL, a variety of prototype computer programs—called Expert Systems—designed to capture and utilize the expertise of a human expert in a narrow domain (such as medical diagnosis, crystallography, electrical circuitry, prospecting, etc.) made their appearance. MYCIN, a medical diagnosis and treatment consultant, devised by Edward Shortliffe (1976) at Stanford University, has been one of the most publicized.

Thus, in the 1970s the artificial intelligence research community was found developing the basic tools and techniques needed and demonstrating their applicability in prototype systems. Future complex systems were proved feasible. The emphasis on knowledge, as essential to intelligence, led to the subfield of "Knowledge Engineering" associated with the building of expert systems.

The 1970s set the framework from which the successes of the next decade emerged. In the 1980s expert systems proliferated. Dozens of prototype expert systems were devised in such areas as medical diagnosis, chemical and biological synthesis, mineral and oil exploration, circuit analysis, tactical targeting, and equipment fault diagnosis.

But the big news of the 1980s is that artificial intelligence has gone commercial. Artificial intelligence companies have formed to exploit applications. Computer, electronic, oil, and large diversified companies have set up artificial intelligence groups. The military has also joined the fray, setting up its own artificial intelligence groups and seeking early applications. The U.S. Defense Science Board views the field as one of the technologies that have the potential for an order of magnitude improvement in mission effectiveness.

In the expert system area, DEC reports that XCON/XCEL—a system designed to configure VAX computer systems—is already saving it some $20 million a year. MOLGEN—a system for planning molecular genetic experiments—is in regular commercial use. Schlumberger—a multi-billion-dollar oil industry advisory company— seeing artificial intelligence as a key to the company's growth in the 1980s, has established separate artificial intelligence groups.

In natural language front ends, some dozen systems are now commercially available. Highlighted by Texas Instruments' Speak and Spell system, many commercial speech output systems have appeared. Early speech recognition systems are also on the market, some using signal processing rather than artificial intelligence techniques. Many companies are now involved in machine vision systems, with dozens of commercial products already on the market for machine vision applications.

Personal computers that are specially designed to run LISP—the List Processing Language favored by the U.S. Artificial Intelligence community—are now commercially available from several companies.

The other indication that artificial intelligence has now emerged as a viable discipline is that the existing artificial intelligence technology is now becoming codified and therefore made broadly available to everyone, not just the core group of a hundred researchers of the 1970s.

DARPA sponsored a 3-volume *Artificial Intelligence Handbook,* which was published in 1982. Individual technology texts—in Machine Vision, Robotics, Natural Language, Expert Systems, and LISP—are beginning to appear in numbers.

Computer software tools for structuring knowledge and constructing expert systems are also becoming available.

In 1982 the Japanese officially began a 10-year, one-half-billion-dollar research project to create a Fifth Generation Computer. Its main features are that it is to have intelligent interfaces (speech, text, graphics, and so on), knowledge base management, and automatic problem solving and inference capabilities. All those capabilities are predicated on the use of artificial intelligence techniques. The machine itself is visualized as a non–Von Neumann computer featuring parallel processing and having the capability of 1 billion logical inferences per second.

The Japanese are using the European Artificial Intelligence language—PROLOG (Programming in Logic)—as the basis for their machine. Using PROLOG, logic problem-solving systems (heuristically guided) are reemerging (from the earlier failure of pure resolution) to handle complex problems.

With the advent of the Japanese Fifth Generation Computer Project, European nations, such as France and Britain, as well as the United States, are putting renewed effort into their artificial intelligence activities.

In summary then, we can conclude that artificial intelligence tools and systems are now available, and that artificial intelligence techniques are now sufficiently perfected for early applications. Furthermore, the importance of the concept is being recognized internationally, and substantial sums of money in the United States and abroad are now beginning to be committed to developing artificial intelligence applications.

THE BASIC ELEMENTS OF ARTIFICIAL INTELLIGENCE

The components of artificial intelligence can be characterized in terms of the integrated wheel shown in Fig. 1-3. The hub of the wheel depicts the basic elements from which the applications shown in the outer ring are composed.

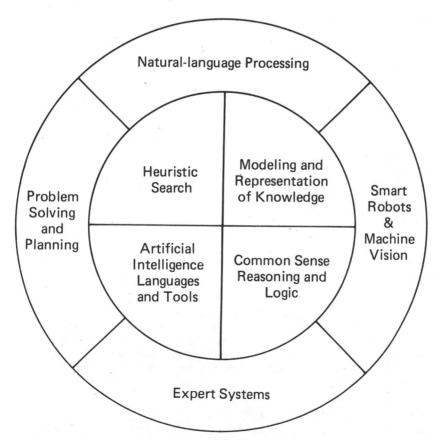

Fig. 1–3. Elements of Artificial Intelligence

In looking at the quadrant designated as heuristic search, one can often view artificial intelligence problem solving as a search among alternative choices. It is thus possible to represent the resulting search space as a hierarchical structure called a pyramid or a tree. The solution paths run from the initial state (root node) along the branches of the tree and terminate on the leaves (terminal nodes) called the "goal state."

For a large complex problem, it is obviously too cumbersome to explicitly draw such trees of all the possibilities and directly examine them for the best solution. Thus, the tree is usually implicit, the computer generating branches and nodes as it searches for a solution.

For fairly simple problems, a straightforward, but time-consuming approach is blind search, where we select some ordering scheme for the search and apply it until the answer is found. There are 2 common blind search procedures, breadth-first search and depth-first search. In breadth-first search, the nodes of the search tree are generated and examined level by level, starting with the root node. In a depth-first search, a new node (at the next level) is generated from the one currently being examined, the search continuing in this way deeper and deeper until forced to backtrack.

Blind search does not make any use of knowledge about the problem to guide the search. In complex problems such searches often fail, being overwhelmed by the combinatorial explosion of possible paths. Heuristic methods have been designed to limit the search space by using information about the nature and structure of the problem domain. Heuristics are rules of thumb, techniques of knowledge that can be used to help guide search. Heuristic search is one of the key contributions of artificial intelligence to efficient problem solving. It often operates by generating and testing intermediate states along a potential solution path.

One straightforward method for choosing paths by that approach is to apply an evaluation function to each node generated and then pursue those paths that have the least total expected cost. Typically, the evaluation function calculates the cost from the root to the particular node that is being examined and, using heuristics, estimates the cost from that node to the goal. Adding the 2 produces the total estimated cost along the path and therefore serves as a guide as to whether to proceed along that path or to continue along another, more promising, path among those thus far examined. However, that may not be an efficient approach to minimize the search effort in complex problems.

KNOWLEDGE REPRESENTATION

The purpose of knowledge representation is to organize required information into such a form that the artificial intelligence program can readily access it for making decisions, planning, recognizing objects and situations, analyzing scenes, drawing conclusions, and performing other cognitive functions. Thus knowledge representation is especially central to expert systems, machine vision, and natural language understanding.

Representation schemes are classified into declarative and procedural ones. Declarative refers to representation of facts and assertions, while procedural refers to actions or what to do. A further subdivision for declarative ("object oriented") schemes includes relational (semantic network) schemes and logical schemes.

The principal knowledge representation schemes are briefly discussed in the following paragraphs.

LOGICAL REPRESENTATION SCHEMES

The principal method for representing a knowledge base logically is to employ First Order Predicate Logic. In that approach a knowledge base (KB) can be viewed as a collection of logical formulas that provide a partial description of the world. Modifications to the knowledge base result from additions or deletions of logical formulas. Logical representations are easy to understand and have available sets of inference rules needed to operate upon them. A drawback of logical representation is its tendency to consume large amounts of memory.

Semantic Networks

A semantic network is an approach to describing the properties and relations of objects, events, concepts, situations or actions by a directed graph consisting of nodes and labeled edges (arcs connecting nodes). Because of their naturalness, semantic networks are very popular in artificial intelligence.

Procedural Representations and Production Systems

In procedural representations knowledge about the world is contained in procedures—small programs that know how to do specific things (how to proceed in well-specified situations). Classification of procedural representation approaches is based on the choice of activation mechanisms for the procedures and the forms used for the control structures.

The 2 common approaches consist of procedures representing major chunks of knowledge—subroutines—and more modular procedures, such as the currently popular "production rules." The common activation mechanism for procedures is matching the system state to the preconditions needed for the procedure to be invoked. Because of their modular representation of knowledge and their easy expansion and modifiability, production rules are one of the most popular artificial intelligence knowledge representations, and they are being chosen for most expert systems.

Analogical or Direct Representations

In many instances it is appropriate to use natural representations, such as an array of brightness values for an image, or a further reduced "sketch map" of the scene delineations in a computer vision system. Those natural representations are useful in computational vision, spatial planning, geometric reasoning, and navigation.

That form of representation has the advantages of being easy to understand and simple to update, and it often allows important properties to be directly observed so that they do not have to be inferred.

Property Lists

One approach to describe the state of the world is to associate with each object a property list, that is, a list of all those properties of the object pertinent to the state description. The state, and therefore the object properties, can be updated when a situation is changed.

Frames and Scripts

A large proportion of our day-to-day activities is concerned with stereotyped situations, such as going to work, eating, shopping, etc. Marvin Minsky conceived of "frames," which are complex data structures for representing stereotyped objects, events, or situations. A frame has slots for objects and relations that would be appropriate to the situation. Attached to each frame is information such as:

- how to use the frame
- what to do if something unexpected happens
- default values for slots.

Frames can also include procedural as well as declarative information. They facilitate expectation-driven processing—reasoning based on seeking confirmation of expectations by filling in the slots. Frames organize knowledge in a way that directs attention and facilitates recall and inference.

Scripts are framelike structures designed for representing stereotyped sequences of events, such as eating at a restaurant or a newspaper report of an apartment fire.

Semantic Primitives

For any knowledge representation scheme, it is necessary to define an associated vocabulary. For semantic nets there has been a real attempt to reduce the relations to a minimum number of terms (semantic primitives) that are nonoverlapping. A similar effort has emerged for natural language understanding, for which several attempts have been made to describe all of the world's aspects in terms of primitives that are unique, unambiguous representations into which natural language statements can be converted for later translation into another language or for other cognitive actions.

Roger Schank has developed a "conceptual dependency" theory for natural language in an attempt to provide a representation of all actions in terms of a small number of primitives. The system relies on 11 primitive physical, instrumental, and mental acts (propel, grasp, speak, attend, etc.) plus several other categories or concept types. There are 2 basic kinds of combinations or conceptualizations. One involves an actor doing a primitive act; the other involves an object and a description of its state. Attached to each primitive act is a set of inferences that could be associated with it.

Computational Logic

Logic is a formal method of reasoning. "Computational logic—doing logical reasoning with a computer—is based on what is traditionally known as symbolic logic, or mathematical logic. This, in turn, is divided into 2 (principal) parts, the simpler propositional logic and the more complex predicate logic."

Propositional Logic

In logic a "proposition" is simply a statement that can be true or false. Rules used to deduce the truth (T) or falsehood (F) or new propositions from known propositions are referred to as "argument forms."

Deduction involves deriving answers to problems based on a given set of premises. In mathematical logic deductive procedures are sometimes referred to as "formal inference." That type of reasoning can be represented as a mathematical form of argument called "Modus Ponens."

Predicate Logic

Propositional logic is limited in that it deals only with the true or false nature of complete statements. Predicate logic remedies that situation by allowing one to deal with assertions about items in statements and allowing the use of variables and functions of variables.

Propositions make assertions about items (individuals). A "predicate" is the part of the proposition that makes an assertion about the individuals. The predicate, together with its arguments, is a proposition. Any of the operations of propositional logic may be applied to it.

By including variables for individuals, Predicate Logic enables us to make statements that would be impossible in Propositional Logic. That can be further extended by the use of functions or variables.

LOGICAL INFERENCE

Resolution Method

Logical inference—reaching conclusions by using logic—is normally done by "theorem proving." The most popular method for automatic theorem proving is the resolution procedure. That procedure is a general automatic method for determining whether a hypothesized-conclusion (theorem) follows from a given set of premises (axioms). First, with the use of standard identities, the original premises and the conclusion to be proved are put into clause form. The conclusion to be proved is then negated. New clauses are then automatically derived using resolution and other procedures. If a contradiction is reached, then the theorem is proved.

Basically, resolution is the cancellation between clauses of a proposition in 1 clause with the negation of the same proposition in another clause.

Unfortunately, resolution has been unable to handle complex problems, as the search space generated by the resolution method grows exponentially with the number of formulas used to describe a problem. Thus for complex problems, resolution derives so many clauses not relevant to reaching the final contradiction that it tends to use up the available time or memory before reaching a conclusion. Several domain-independent heuristics have been tried to constrain the search but have proved to be too weak.

Factors That Affect the Efficiency of Deductive Reasoning

Paul R. Cohen and Edward Feigenbaum state that "one kind of guidance that is often critical to efficient system performance is information about whether to use facts in a forward-chaining or backward-chaining manner. . . . Early theorem-proving systems used every fact both ways leading to highly redundant searches."

Another factor that can greatly affect the efficiency of the deductive reasoning is the way in which a body of knowledge is formalized. "That is, logically equivalent formalizations can have radically different behavior when used with standard deduction techniques."

Nonresolution Theorem Proving

Paul R. Cohen and Edward Feigenbaum observe that "in nonresolution or natural deduction theorem-proving systems, a proof is derived in a goal-directed manner that is natural for humans using the theorem prover. Natural-deduction systems represent an ability to use uncertain facts and rules to arrive at useful conclusions about everyday subjects, such as medicine. A basic characteristic of such approximate reasoning seems to be that a conclusion carries more conviction if it is independently supported by 2 or more separate arguments.

Nondeductive Problem-Solving Approaches

All problems have certain common aspects: an initial situation, a goal (desired situation), and certain operators (procedures or generalized actions) that can be used for changing a situation. In solving the problem, one uses a control strategy to apply the operators to the situations to try to achieve the goal.

Problem Reduction

One simple form of problem solving is "divide and conquer," usually referred to as "problem reduction." Very often several subproblems (conjuncts) must be satisfied simultaneously in order to achieve a goal.

Problem reduction often fails without specific problem knowledge, as there is otherwise no good reason for attacking 1 interacting conjunct before another. Lack of such knowledge may lead to an extensive search for a sequence of actions that tries to achieve subgoals in an unachievable order.

Difference Reduction ("Mean-Ends" Analysis)

Difference reduction was introduced by the General Problem Solver (GPS) Program. It was the first program to separate its general problem-solving method from knowledge specific to the current problem.

The means-ends analysis first determines the difference between the initial and goal states and selects the particular operator that would most reduce the difference. If that operator is applicable in the initial state, it is applied and a new intermediate state is created. The difference between the new intermediate state and the goal state is then calculated, and the best operator to reduce this difference is selected. The process proceeds until a sequence of operators is determined that transforms the initial state into the goal state.

The difference reduction approach assumes that the differences between a current state and a desired state can be defined and that the operators can be classified according to the kinds of differences they can reduce. If the initial and goal states differ by a small number of features and operators are available for individually manipulating each feature, then difference reduction works. However, there is no inherent way in that approach to generate the ideas necessary to plan complex solutions to difficult problems.

More Efficient Tactics for Problem Solving

For more efficient problem solving it is necessary to devise techniques to guide the search by making better use of initial knowledge about the problem or the information that can be discovered or learned about the problem as the problem solver proceeds through the search.

Information relevant to planning that can be learned during the exploration process includes:

- order relationships among actions
- hierarchical links between actions at various levels of abstraction
- the purpose of the actions in the plan
- the dependence among objects (or states) being manipulated

There are 2 opposing ways to improve the efficiency (solution time) of a problem solver:

- use a cheap evaluation function and explore lots of paths that might not work out but in the process acquire information about the interrelationships of the actions and the states as an aid in efficiently guiding a subsequent search
- use a relatively expensive evaluation function and try hard to avoid generating states not on the eventual solution path

The following methods are attempts to achieve more efficient problem solving through employing various ratios of exploration and evaluation.

(a) *Hierarchical Planning and Repair.* As in planning by humans, one can start by devising a general plan and refine it several times into a detailed plan. The general plan can be used as a skeleton for the more detailed plan. If one uses that approach, generating rather complex plans can be reduced to a hierarchy of much shorter, simpler subproblems. As the detailed plans are generated, the results should be checked to see that the intended general plan is being realized. If not, various methods for patching up the failed plan can be applied.

Another approach is to observe that some aspects of a problem are significantly more important than others. By utilizing that hierarchical ranking, a problem solver can concentrate most of its efforts on the critical decisions or more important subgoals first.

(b) *Problem Solving by Creating and Then Debugging Almost-Right Plans.* That approach deliberately oversimplifies the problem so it can be more readily solved and then corrects the solution using special debugging techniques. An everyday example is the general tactic by which people use road maps: find a simple way to get to the vicinity of your destination and then refine the plan from there.

(c) *Special Purpose Subplanners.* That approach uses built-in subroutines to plan frequently occurring portions of a problem, such as certain moves or subgoals in robotics.

(d) *Constraint Satisfaction.* This technique provides special purpose subplanners to help ensure that the action sequences that are generated will satisfy constraints.

(e) *Relevant Backtracking (Dependency-Directed or Nonchronological Backtracking).* The focus here is on sophisticated post-mortem analysis gained from several attempts that failed. The problem solver then uses that information to backtrack, not to the most recent choice point, but to the most relevant choice point.

(f) *Disproving.* In this approach attempts are made to prove the impossibility of the goal, both to avoid further pursuing an intractable problem and to employ the resultant information generated to help suggest an action sequence to achieve the goal for a feasible problem.

(g) *Pseudo-Reduction.* For the difficult case where multiple goals (conjuncts) must be satisfied simultaneously, one approach is to find a plan to achieve each conjunct independently. The resultant solutions to those simpler problems are then integrated using knowledge of how plan segments can be intertwined without destroying their important effects. By avoiding premature commitments to particular orderings of subgoals, that tactic eliminates much of the backtracking typical of problem solving systems.

(h) *Goal-Regression.* The tactic regresses the current goal to an earlier position in the list of goals to be satisfied. The approach can be useful in cases where conjunctive subgoals must be satisfied, but where the action that satisfies 1 goal tends to interfere with the satisfaction of the others.

The basic automatic problem-solving relationships can be recast as a production system, as shown in Fig. 1-4. A production system consists of a knowledge base of production rules (consisting of domain facts and heuristics), a global data base (GDB) that represents the system status, and a rule interpreter (control structure) for choosing the rules to execute. In a simple production rule system, the rules are tried in order and executed if they match a pattern in the GBD.

However, in more complex systems, such as those used in expert systems, a very complex control structure may be used to decide which group of production rules (PRs) to examine and which to execute from the PRs in the group that match patterns in the GDB. In general, those control structures work in a repetitive cycle of the form:

- Find the "conflict set" (the set of competing rules that match some data in the GDB)
- Choose a rule from among the conflict set
- Execute the rule, modifying the GDB.

Production rule systems can be implemented for any of the problem-solving approaches discussed earlier. Thus, we may use a "top-down" approach, employing the rules to chain backward from the goal to search for a complete supportive or causal set of rules and data ("goal-driven," or "model-driven" control structure). Or we can use a "bottom-up" approach employing forward-chaining of rules to search for the goal ("even-driven" or "data-driven" control structure).

In complex systems (employing many rules) the control structure may contain meta-

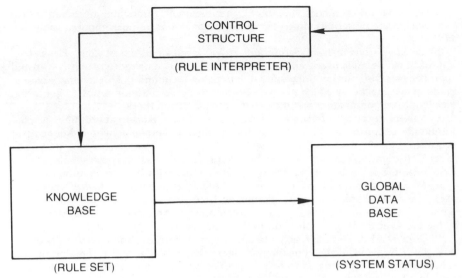

Fig. 1-4. A Production System

rules that select the relevant rules from the entire set of rules and also focuses attention on the relevant part of the data base. That reduces the search space to be considered. The control structure then employs further heuristics to select the most appropriate rule from the conflicting rules.

LANGUAGES, TOOLS, AND COMPUTERS

Programming Needs of Artificial Intelligence

Artificial intelligence has been an experimental science trying to develop computer programs that exhibit intelligent behavior. That has proved to be a difficult endeavor requiring the best programming tools. Artificial intelligence programs tend to develop iteratively and incrementally. As the programs are thus evolutionary, creating such programs requires an interactive environment with built-in aids, such as dynamic allocation of computer memory as the program evolves, rather than advance memory allocation as in most other programming domains. More important, the unpredictable intermediate forms of the data (as the program evolves) also influence the form of the programming languages and the management of memory.

Another unusual aspect of artificial intelligence programming is that researchers have found that expressing functions recursively (defined in terms of themselves) was a great simplification in writing programs. Thus, artificial intelligence programming languages tend to support recursive processing. Finally, artificial intelligence programs are primarily concerned with symbol manipulation, rather than numeric computation. Artificial intelligence languages thus support that feature.

Avron Barr and Edward Feigenbaum observe that, "Artificial Intelligence programs are among the largest and most complex computer programs ever developed and present formidable design and implementation problems. . . . Artificial Intelligence researchers in their capacity as language designers and programmers have pioneered an interactive mode of programming" in environments with extensive support: editors, trace and debugging packages, and other aids for the construction of large complex systems.

Two basic general artificial intelligence languages—LISP and PROLOG—have evolved in answer to these programming requirements.

LISP

(a) *Background.* Around 1960, John McCarthy at M.I.T. developed LISP as a practical list-processing language with recursive-function capability for describing processes and problems. Since then, LISP has been the primary artificial intelligence programming language—the one most used in artificial intelligence research.

(b) *Basic Elements of LISP.* All LISP programs and data are in the form of symbolic expressions (S-expressions), which are stored as list structures. LISP deals with 2 kinds of objects: atoms and lists. Atoms are symbols (constants or variables) used as identifiers to name objects that may be numeric (numbers) or nonnumeric (people, things, robots, ideas, etc.). A list is a sequence of zero or more elements enclosed in parentheses, where each element is either an atom or a list.

— Memory allocation is automatic.
— LISP expressions are very simple and regular. All expressions are made up of atoms and compositions of atoms.
— Control is normally applicative—the flow of control being guided by the application of functions to arguments, in contrast to the sequential control structure of most programming languages.
— Dynamic Scoping of Variables—usually a nonlocal variable will have its value locally assigned by the function evaluating it, unless it was assigned a value by the function calling the evaluating function.
— For real-time operation, LISP requires a sophisticated garbage collection system to recycle memory cells no longer being used.
— LISP is a huge package, and until the advent of the special personal LISP machines, the full capabilities of LISP could be implemented only on large computers.
— The use of nested parentheses in LISP can be confusing, but the confusion can be reduced somewhat by indenting expressions according to their level of nesting.

(c) *LISP Today.* There are several LISP dialects available today: MACLISP developed at M.I.T., INTERLISP developed by BBN, XEROX-PARC, and Common LISP, an attempt at standardization of the LISP dialects. Each offers very similar programming environments with editing and debugging facilities. Each offers many LISP functions. The emphasis in INTERLISP has been to provide the best possible programming environments, even at the expense of speed and memory space. MACLISP has had the most emphasis on efficiency, conservation of address space, and flexibility for building tools and embedding languages. Common LISP has optimized the language for broader use.

INTERLISP has been the much better-supported version, with complete documentation and many users. It runs on DEC and Xerox operating systems.

Out of the need to standardize the various MACLISP dialects has evolved "Common LISP" and "LISP Machine LISP" for personal artificial intelligence computers. The new dialect—Common LISP—is destined to be used on most of the new personal artificial intelligence machines and operating systems. Common LISP is intended to be efficient and portable, with stability a major goal.

Because of the rapid development of LISP features by the user community, other more local LISP versions (such as FRANZLISP at the University of California, Berkeley) exist at several university artificial intelligence labs.

PROLOG (PROgramming in LOGic)

(a) *History.* PROLOG is a logic-oriented language developed in 1973 at the University of Marseilles Artificial Intelligence Laboratory by A. Colmerauer and P. Roussel. Additional work on PROLOG has been done at the University of Edinburgh in Great Britain. Development of PROLOG in France has continued to the present, achieving a documented system that can be run on nearly all computers.

(b) *Nature of PROLOG.* PROLOG is a theorem-proving system. Thus, programs in PROLOG consist of "axioms" in First-Order Predicate Logic together with a goal (a theorem to be proved). The axioms are restricted to implications, the left- and right-hand sides of which are written in "Horn-clause" form. That consists of a set of statements joined by logical AND's.

A PROLOG program consists of a group of procedures, where the left side of a procedure is a pattern to be instantiated (an instance is found that satisfies it) to achieve the goals on the right side of the procedure.

PROLOG solves a problem by pattern-matching, which can be viewed as unification (the carrying out of instantiations) in the sense of First Order Predicate Logic. If the pattern-matching fails as PROLOG searches through its procedures, then it automatically backtracks to its previous choice point, resulting in a depth-first type of search.

The solution process starts with the system searching for the first clause whose right side matches (unifies with) the goal. Thus, the search process can be guided by the programmer by choosing the order for the procedures, the data, and the goals in the clauses.

PROLOG can be considered as an extension of pure LISP coupled with a relational data base query language that utilizes virtual relations. Like LISP, PROLOG is interactive and uses dynamic allocation of memory.

(c) *PROLOG Today.* PROLOG is a much smaller program than LISP and has now been implemented on a variety of computers, including microcomputers. The execution of PROLOG is surprisingly efficient and in its compiled version it is claimed to be faster than compiled LISP. PROLOG has proved very popular in Europe and is now targeted as the language for Japan's Fifth Generation Computer project. PROLOG's design is well suited to parallel search and therefore an excellent candidate for such powerful future computers incorporating parallel processing. Substantial interest in PROLOG is now arising in the United States, with some of PROLOG's features being implemented in LISP.

PROLOG was originally developed for natural language understanding applications but has since found use in virtually all artificial intelligence application areas.

Other Artificial Intelligence Languages

A number of artificial intelligence languages have been developed as extensions of, improvements upon (e.g., special features for knowledge organization and search), or alternatives to, LISP. They include:

- System Programming Languages (LISP-level)
  - SAIL (Stanford Artificial Intelligence Language) (1969)
  - QA4 and QLISP (at SRI 1968, 1972)
  - POP-2 (at U. of Edinburgh 1967)
- Deduction/Theorem-Proving Languages
  - PLANNER and MICROPLANNER (M.I.T., 1971)
  - CONNIVER (U. of Edinburgh, 1972)
  - PROLOG (U. of Marseilles, 1973)
  - AMORD (M.I.T., 1977)

LISP and POP-2 are designed to simplify the building of new languages within or on top of them—QLISP being embedded in INTERLISP, POPLER embedded in POP-2. POP-2 remains popular in England but has not caught on elsewhere.

Most of the above artificial intelligence languages are no longer supported and have fallen into disuse. However, they were experiments that helped pave the way for the modern artificial intelligence languages now in use, such as the LISP dialects and PROLOG. For instance, PROLOG's style of programming is similar to that demonstrated in QA3 and PLANNER.

Other special languages have been built for Knowledge Representation, Knowledge Base Management, writing rule-based systems, and special application areas.

Artificial Intelligence Computational Facilities

Good artificial intelligence people are still scarce, expensive, and dedicated. It therefore behooves an organization supporting an artificial intelligence group to provide the best facilities available (commensurate with cost) to maximize the productivity of their artificial intelligence people.

Fahlman and Steele state that desirable features of an artificial intelligence programming environment are as follows:

- Powerful, well-maintained, standardized artificial intelligence languages
- Extensive libraries of code and domain knowledge (a facility should support the exchange of code with other artificial intelligence research facilities)
- Excellent graphic displays: high resolution, color, multiple windows, quick update, and software to use all of those easily
- Good input devices
- Flexible, standardized inter-process communication
- Graceful, uniform user-interface software
- A good editor that can deal with a program based on the individual program structure.

They suggest that:

- Sticking with the hardware and systems that major artificial intelligence centers are using is important so that the time can be spent getting work accomplished, not reinventing the wheel.
- A salary of $60K to $100K per researcher for computing facilities is appropriate.
- Your artificial intelligence product can be developed in the best available environment. Once developed, it can be ported to other languages and machines, as appropriate.
- Isolated machines are nearly useless. Good network interfaces, internal and external, are critical.
- Artificial intelligence personnel spend roughly 80% of their time editing, reading, and communicating. Thus, facilities for that must be excellent.

Artificial Intelligence Machines

The computers used for artificial intelligence research in the early years have been primarily the DEC system-10 and DEC system-20 family of time-shared machines. These have now been superseded by the more economical DEC VAX and micro VAX computers and the newer personal artificial intelligence machines from Texas Instruments, Xerox, Sun, Tektronix, LMI, and Symbolics.

The newer machines tend to have 32-bit words, sorely needed for address space, as most artificial intelligence programs are huge.

Fahlman and Steel see the DEC VAX, with a UNIX operating system, as the best time-sharing machine today for artificial intelligence purposes. Several LISP dialects are available. The VAX is the current choice of many universities.

The new artificial intelligence personal machines represent unusually powerful interactive exploratory programming environments in which system design and program develop together. That is in sharp contrast to the more traditional structured programming approach in which software program specifications are first written, with the software development following in rigid adherence to the specifications.

To further enhance the exploratory programming approach, the user-friendly object-oriented programming languages have been devised. An object (such as an airplane or a window on a computer screen) can be encoded as a package of information with attached descriptions of procedures for manipulation of that information. Objects communicate by sending and receiving messages that activate their procedures. A class is a description of 1 or more similar objects. An object is an instance of a class and inherits the characteristics of its class. The programmer developing a new system creates the classes that describe the objects that make up the system and implements the system by describing messages to be sent. Use of object-oriented programming reduces the complexity of large systems. The notion of class provides a uniform framework for defining system objects and encourages a modular, hierarchical (top-down) program structure. "Smalltalk" is an object-oriented language available on the Xerox machines. "Flavors" is available on the MIT-based LISP machines. LOOPS developed at XEROX PARC is a further extension of the Smalltalk system.

The new artificial intelligence personal machines tend to come with interactive facilities for program development, editing, debugging, etc. For key portions of artificial intelligence programs, microcode allows key inner loops to be run very fast. That is especially important in graphics and vision programs. The efficiency of computers microcoded for artificial intelligence applications and supporting large memories makes these personal computers especially attractive.

ZETALISP derived from MACLISP is an integrated software environment for program development and program execution as the Symbolics 3600. ZETALISP has available nearly 10,000 compiled functions, making it an exceptionally powerful and functional form of the LISP programming language. Similar capabilities are available on the LMI Lambda machines.

Interlisp-D, used on the Xerox 1100 machines, provides a comprehensive programming environment particularly suited for the development and delivery of expert and other knowledge-based systems.

Future

It is expected that the price of good artificial intelligence personal computers that run LISP will rapidly drop below $40K as competition heats up and demand escalates. It is thus anticipated that one personal artificial intelligence machine per artificial intelligence person will be the standard.

Parallel architecture is now being considered for future artificial intelligence machines. That is especially attractive for PROLOG because its structure facilitates parallel search. Japan intends to build sequential PROLOG personal computers featuring 10K logical inferences per second. In the 1990 time frame, Japan's Fifth Generation Computer project is projected to yield an enormously powerful artificial intelligence parallel processing machine running PROLOG at 1 billion logical inferences per second (about 10,000 times more powerful than the DEC-KL-10 on which the artificial intelligence community grew up).

Summary and Forecast

It now appears that LISP dialects designed specifically for personal computers will become commonplace. It is also expected that software portability will improve substantially. PROLOG and its derivatives, now prevalent throughout Europe, will become integrated with LISP in the United States.

Powerful personal artificial intelligence computers costing less than $40K will appear and become the artificial intelligence standard for the next several years. In the longer term, powerful parallel computers, such as the Japanese Fifth Generation Computers, will probably become the standard as the number of artificial intelligence practitioners expands and more difficult problems are addressed.

The rapidly increasing capability and ease of development of VLSI chips promises to move artificial intelligence computing power for developed applications out of the laboratory and into the field and products as needed.

An emerging trend is the increased use of object-oriented programming to ease the creation of large exploratory programs. The use of objects is also a good way to program dynamic symbolic simulations, which will become more important as the quest for utilizing deeper knowledge accelerates and the demand for increased reliability of knowledge-based systems is pursued. Object-oriented programming also holds promise for distributed processing, as each object could be implemented on a separate processor in a linked network of processors.

Finally, it is anticipated that the artificial intelligence exploratory software development approach will slowly infuse conventional software practices.

APPLICATIONS OF ARTIFICIAL INTELLIGENCE

The potential range of artificial intelligence applications is so vast that it covers virtually the entire breadth of human intelligence activity. Generic applications are listed in Table 1-2. Examples of specific applications of artificial intelligence are listed in Table 1-3. Similar opportunities are available in many other public and private domains.

PRINCIPAL PARTICIPANTS

Originally, artificial intelligence was principally a research activity—the principal centers being Stanford University, M.I.T., Carnegie Mellon University (C.M.U.), SRI,

Table 1-2   Generic Applications of Artificial Intelligence

Knowledge Management

- Intelligent data base access
- Knowledge acquisition
- Text understanding
- Text generation
- Machine translation
- Explanation
- Logical operations on data bases

Human Interaction

- Speech understanding
- Speech generation

Learning and Teaching

- Computer-aided instruction
- Intelligent computer-aided instruction
- Learning from experience
- Concept generation
- Operation and maintenance instruction

Table 1-2   Generic Applications of Artificial Intelligence Cont'd.

Fault Diagnosis and Repair

- Humans
- Machines
- Systems

Computation

- Symbolic mathematics
- "Fuzzy" operations
- Automatic programming

Communication

- Public access to large data bases via telephone and speech understanding
- Natural language interfaces to computer programs

Operations of Machines and Complex Systems

- Factory automation
- Mechatronics

Autonomous Intelligent Systems

- Autonomous vehicles

Management

- Planning
- Scheduling
- Monitoring

Sensor Interpretation and Integration

- Developing meaning from sensor data
- Sensor fusion (integrating multiple sensor inputs to develop high-level interpretations)

Design

- Systems
- Equipment
- Intelligent Design Aids
- Inventing

Visual Perception and Guidance

- Inspection
- Identification
- Verification
- Guidance
- Screening
- Monitoring

Intelligent Assistants

- Medical Diagnosis, Maintenance Aids, and Other Interactive Expert Systems
- Expert System Building Tools

Table 1-3 Examples of Domain-Specific Applications of Artificial Intelligence

Medical

- Diagnosis and Treatment
- Patient Monitoring
- Prosthetics
  - Artificial Sight and Hearing
  - Reading Machines for the Blind
- Medical Knowledge Automation

Science and Engineering

- Discovering
  - Physical and mathematical laws
  - Determination of regularities and aspects of interest
- Chemical and Biological Synthesis Planning
- Test Management
- Data Interpretation
- Intelligent Design Aids

Industrial

- Factory Management
- Production Planning and Scheduling
- Intelligent Robots
- Process Planning
- Intelligent Machines
- Computer-Aided Inspection
- Mechatronics

Military

- Expert Advisers
- Sensor Synthesis and Interpretation
- Battle and Threat Assessment
- Automatic Photo Interpretation
- Tactical Planning
- Military Surveillance
- Weapon-Target Assignment
- Autonomous Vehicles
- Intelligent Robots
- Diagnosis and Maintenance Aids
- Target Location and Tracking
- Map Development Aids
- Intelligent Interactions with Knowledge Bases

International

- Aids to Understanding and Interpretation
  - Goals, aspirations, and motives of different countries and cultures
  - Cultural models for interpreting how others perceive
- Natural Language Translation

Table 1-3   Examples of Domain-Specific Applications of Artificial Intelligence Cont'd.

Services

- Intelligent Knowledge Base Access
  - Airline reservations
- Air Traffic Control
- Ground Traffic Control

Financial

- Tax Preparation
- Financial Expert Systems
- Intelligent Consultants

Executive Assistance

- Read Mail and Spot Items on Importance
- Planning Aids

Natural Resources

- Prospecting Aids
- Resource Operations
  - Drilling Procedures
  - Resource Recovery Guidance
- Resource Management Using Remote Sensing Data

Space

- Ground Operations Aids
- Planning and Scheduling Aids
- Diagnostic and Reconfiguation Aids
- Remote Operations of Spacecraft and Space Vehicles
- Test Monitors
- Real-time Replanning as Required by Failures, Changed Conditions, or New Opportunities
- Automatic Subsystem Operations

and the University of Edinburgh in Scotland. Research successes during the 1970s encouraged other universities to become involved.

In the 1980s, it became apparent that artificial intelligence had a large commercial and military potential. Thus, existing larger computer, electronic, and multinational corporations as well as some aerospace firms started forming artificial intelligence groups.

In response to a perceived market in natural language processing, computer vision and expert systems, new small artificial intelligence companies began to form, headed by former (and present) university researchers. Several dozen such companies now exist.

The computer science departments at major universities have also recently become involved, so that artificial intelligence courses and beginning artificial intelligence research now is evident at many universities.

Abroad, France and Great Britain have now joined Japan in sharing major interest. The largest major commitment to artificial intelligence has been by Japan, which has initiated a 10-year, one-half-billion-dollar program to develop a "Fifth Generation Computer." It will incorporate a parallel processing architecture, natural language interfacing, knowledge base management, automatic problem solving, and image understanding as the basis for a truly fast intelligence computer. In the United States a new cooperative organization—Microelectronics Computer Technology Corporation (MCC)—made up of U.S. computer and electronics manufacturers, has been formed to be a sort of American version of the Japanese Fifth Generation Computer research project.

Thus, the artificial intelligence research sponsored by DARPA, NIH, NSF, ONR, and AFOSR for the past 2 decades has now spawned such a burgeoning artificial intelligence community that it is no longer an easy task to list all those involved. However, Table 1-4 provides an indication of the current principal players. They are given by application area, as even most research efforts initially have a specific application domain as a focus, with the results of the research usually being generalized to cover a broader area.

Table 1-4   The Principal Participants in Artificial Intelligence

1. Universities

Expert Systems	Machine Vision	Natural Language Processing
Stanford	C.M.U.	Yale
M.I.T.	U. of Maryland	U. of California
C.M.U.	M.I.T.	(Berkeley)
Rutgers	Stanford U.	U. of Illinois
	U. of Rochester	Brown
	U. of Massachusetts	Stanford
		Rochester

2. Nonprofit

Expert Systems	Machine Vision	Natural Language Processing
SRI	APL/JHU	SRI
RAND	JPL	APL/JHU
APL/JHU	SRI	
JPL	ERIM	
MITRE		

3. U. S. Government

Expert Systems	Machine Vision	Natural Language Processing
NOSC, San Diego	NBS, Washington, D.C.	NRL AI Lab
NRL AI Lab, Washington, D.C.		

Table 1-4   The Principal Participants in Artificial Intelligence Cont'd.

4. Diversified Industrial Corporations

Expert Systems	Machine Vision	Natural Language Processing
Schlumberger	G.E.	BBN
Hewlett Packard	Hughes	IBM
Bell Labs	GM	TRW
Hughes	Technology Research	Burroughs
IBM	Westinghouse	SDC
DEC	Ford	Hewlett Packard
GM	Automatix	Martin Marietta
Martin Marietta	Cognex	Texas Instruments
Technology Research	Diffracto	Bell Labs
Texas Instruments	Machine Intelligence	Sperry Univac
TRW	Machine Vision Int.	Lockheed Electronics
Xerox PARC	Perceptron	Corp.
AMOCO	Robot Vision Systems	
United Technologies	View Engineering	
Corp.	Synthetic Vision	
Grumman Aerospace	AISI	
Corp.	ORS	
Lockheed Palo Alto		
Westinghouse Electric		
Corp.		
Advanced Decision		
Systems		
Carnegie Group		
Inference		
IntelliCorp		
Teknowledge		
Perceptronics		
Brattle Research Corp.		
B.B.N.		

5. AI Computer Manufacturers

LISP Machines, Inc.
Symbolics
Three Rivers Corp.
DEC
Xerox PARC
Daisy
BBN
Texas Instruments
Tektronix
IBM

6. Major Japanese Participants

Electromechanical-Technology Lab, Tsukiba	Fifth Gen. Computer
Fujitsu-Fanuc, Ltd., Kawasaki	Fifth Gen. Computer
Hitachi, Ltd., Tokyo	Fifth Gen. Computer
Mitsubishi Elec. Corp., Tokyo	Fifth Gen. Computer
Nippon Electric Co., Ltd., Tokyo	Fifth Gen. Computer
Nippon Tele and Tele Corp., Tokyo	

STATE-OF-THE-ART

The state-of-the-art of artificial intelligence is moving rapidly as new companies enter the field, new applications are devised, and existing techniques are formalized. The cutting edge of artificial intelligence today is Expert Systems, with some 100 demonstration systems having been built. With the advent of personal LISP machines and the general reduction in computing costs, development of commercial Artificial Intelligence systems is now under way. A number of Natural Language Interfaces and Machine Vision Systems are already on the market.

Japan has focused on artificial intelligence capabilities as the basis for its "Fifth Generation Computer" and has already initiated research toward this one-half-billion dollar, 10-year goal.

Britain's Industry Department has formed a study group to coordinate British artificial intelligence efforts. The European Space Agency (ESA) has published a substantial survey of artificial intelligence from a point of view of space applications. In the United States DARPA has been spending in the range of $20 million annually on artificial intelligence research and appears to be expanding its efforts. The U.S. Navy, Army, and Air Force are all initiating substantial artificial intelligence efforts.

INTRODUCTION TO EXPERT SYSTEMS

An "Expert system" is an intelligent computer program that uses knowledge and inference procedures to solve problems that are difficult enough to require human expertise for their solution. The knowledge necessary to perform at such a level plus the inference procedures used can be thought of as a model of the expertise of the best practitioners in the field.

Knowledge is a major factor in the performance of an expert system. That knowledge is in 2 forms. The first is common facts consisting of widely shared knowledge that is accepted by the professional and other accepted source of data. The second type of knowledge is called heuristic, which is the knowledge of good judgment and common good practice or "rules of thumb" in a field. Both facts and heuristic knowledge are required for development of an expert system.

The creation of that knowledge base is not just a data base, as in traditional information data bases. It includes facts, assumptions, beliefs, and heuristics; "expertise"; and methods of dealing with the data base to achieve the desired results, such as a failure diagnosis, interpretation of a situation, or the solution to the problem. The performance level of an expert system is primarily a function of the size and quality of the knowledge base that it possesses.

In the 1970s, it became apparent to the artificial intelligence community that data search strategies alone, even augmented by heuristic evaluations, were often inadequate for solving real world problems. The complexity of those problems was usually such that, without incorporating substantially more problem knowledge than had been brought to bear, either a combinatorial explosion occurred that defied reasonable search times, or the ability to generate a suitable search space did not exist. It became apparent that for many problems expert domain knowledge was even more important than the search strategy or inference procedure. That realization led to the field of knowledge engineering, which focuses on ways to bring expert knowledge to bear in problem solving. One important aspect of the knowledge-based approach is that the complexity associated with real-world problems is reduced by the more powerful focusing of the search that can be obtained with rule-based heuristics usually used in expert systems. The rule-based system is able to reason about its own search effort, in addition to reasoning about the problem domain. The resultant expert systems technology, limited to academic laboratories in the 1970s, is now becoming cost-effective and is beginning to enter into commercial applications.

The basic structure of an expert system as shown in Fig. 1-5 defines the basic system elements, which include:

- a knowledge data base consisting of facts and heuristic knowledge associated with the problem;
- a problem-solving inference and reasoning processor to utilize the knowledge base in the solutions of the problem;

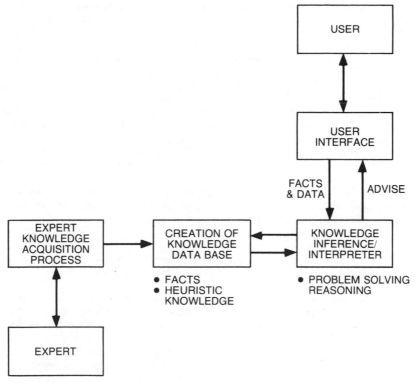

Fig. 1-5. Block Diagram of Expert System

• a user interface that provides a working memory for keeping track of the problem status, the input data for the specific problem, and the relevant history of what has thus far been done.

The expert system is developed through careful analysis of the knowledge of "experts" in a field. The experimental, judgmental knowledge, the knowledge underlying "expertise" and rules of thumb, the "heuristic" information, is the most difficult to obtain. Experts, rarely have the self-awareness to recognize the diverse extent and interaction of their knowledge. Knowledge engineers who study artificial intelligence and know how to represent knowledge in a computer are needed to develop the knowledge acquisition process, to create reasoning programs to utilize the knowledge, and to assure logical collection of "expert" knowledge for creation of an effective knowledge data base. That is called "knowledge engineering," defined as the art of designing and building expert systems and knowledge-based programs.

Facts and heuristic knowledge are collected in a data base consisting of information about objects and events on which the knowledge base will work to achieve the desired advice. Some systems use a relational data base in which the relationships between various objects and events are stored explicitly for flexibility of storage and retrieval.

The knowledge inference/interpreter consists of 2 main elements, which are the knowledge base management system and a symbolic inference processor. The knowledge base management system "manages" the knowledge base by automatically organizing, controlling, propagating, and updating stored knowledge. It initiates searches for knowledge relevant to the line of reasoning upon which the inference subsystem is working. The symbolic inference subsystem provides a process by which lines of reasoning are formed; for example, syllogisms and other common ways of reasoning step by step from premises. In the real world knowledge and data are often inexact. Therefore, some problem-solving inference procedures can use degrees of uncertainty in their inference making. In the expert system the inference subsystem works with the knowledge in the knowledge data base.

The user interface is another critical element of the expert system. Through the user access of the expert system, facts and data are entered into the problem-solving knowledge inference/interpreter. The user interface should be as "natural" as possible, employing language as close as possible to ordinary language and understanding and displaying images, all at speeds that are comfortable and natural for the user.

There are 3 different user modes associated with an expert system in comparison with the single mode of obtaining answers to problems characteristic of general computer application; they include:

- getting answers to problems—user as client;
- improving or increasing the system's knowledge—user as tutor;
- harvesting the knowledge base for human use—user as pupil.

It is desirable, though not yet common, to have a natural language interface to facilitate the use of the system in all 3 modes. In some sophisticated systems, an explanation module is also included, allowing the user to challenge and examine the reasoning process underlying the system's answers.

An expert system can act as a synergistic repository of knowledge obtained from a variety of "experts" on a particular problem. Therefore, the combined expert system knowledge could ultimately provide the user with a level of expertise exceeding the individual skills of the single "expert."

When the knowledge is stored as production rules, the knowledge base is often referred to as the "rule base" and the knowledge inference/interpreter as the "rule interpreter." In an expert system there is a separation of the general knowledge regarding the problem from information about the current problem and methods for applying the general knowledge to the problem. In a conventional computer program, knowledge pertinent to the problem and methods for utilizing that knowledge are all intermixed, so that it is difficult to change the program. In an expert system the program itself is only an interpreter for general reasoning mechanism, and the system can be changed by adding or subtracting rules in the knowledge base.

The integration of those functions produces an expert system, a computer-driven program that performs a specialized, usually difficult professional task at the level of a human expert. Because their functioning relies so heavily on large bodies of knowledge, expert systems are sometimes known as knowledge-based systems. Once the system has been developed, in addition to solving problems, it can also be used to help instruct others in developing their own expertise. Since they are often used to assist the human expert, they are also known as intelligent assistants.

EXPERT SYSTEM ARCHITECTURE

To build an expert system, the following prerequisites have been delineated:

- there must be at least 1 human expert acknowledged to perform the task well;
- the primary source of the expert's exceptional performance must be special knowledge, judgment, and experience;

- the expert must be able to explain the special knowledge and experience and the methods used to apply them to particular problems;
- the task must have a well-bounded domain of application.

Knowledge engineers believe that a good expert system application has these characteristics: it does not require common sense to solve, an expert will need a few minutes to a few hours to solve it, and it has an expert committed to system support. In other words, the problem should be significant for the expert system user but should not be deemed unreasonable to accomplish with the expert system.

Having found an appropriate problem and an accessible expert, one must then prepare realistic and incremental system design objectives. Major pitfalls to be avoided in developing an expert system are choosing a poor problem, excessive requirements, and inadequate technical and financial resources.

The stages of development of an expert system for robotic applications would follow the steps shown in Fig. 1-6. The system design based on the realistic objectives for the expert system would characterize the scope and goals of the system. The system would be defined and developed to meet those goals. The development of the expert system is an interactive process requiring formal evaluation of system performance by the real "experts" to assure accuracy. Those "expert" evaluations should be conducted until confidence in the output/results of the expert system are acceptable to the "expert." As in all computer projects, experience with the system and correction of problems further enhances the end product use. Demonstrations of the prototype system should enlist a broader group of evaluators to assure confidence in system performance in meeting the system design goals. All knowledge is changing, and the expert system must be configured to accept change, just as the "expert" must add new information and increase his capability through experience. Upon completion of that process, the expert system is ready for general release to the user community.

The time for construction of early expert systems was in the range of 20 to 50 man-years. Recently, breadboard versions of simple expert systems have been reported to have been built in as little as 3 man-months, but a complex system can still take as long as 10 man-months to complete. If present techniques are used, the time for development of complex systems appears to be converging toward 5 man-years per expert system. It takes 2 to 5 people to construct each unique expert system.

One way to classify expert systems is by function (e.g., diagnosis, planning, data interpretation, analysis, design, and instructional use). However, examination of existing expert systems indicates that, as shown in Fig. 1-7, there is little commonality in detailed system architecture that can be detected from this classification.

A more fruitful approach appears to be to look at problem complexity and problem structure and determine what data and control structures might be appropriate to handle those factors.

The knowledge engineering community has evolved a number of techniques that can be utilized in devising suitable expert system architectures. Those techniques are described in the following portions of this chapter.

To aid in the building of expert systems, special programming tools have begun to be developed. They are listed in Table 1-5.

AGE is an example of expert system programming tools that also guide people in the use of these modules in constructing their own individualized expert systems. AGE also provides 2 predefined configurations of components. One, called the "blackboard framework," is for building programs that are based on the blackboard model. The blackboard model uses the concepts of a globally accessible data structure, called a "blackboard," and independent sources of knowledge that cooperate in forming hypotheses. The other predefined configuration, called the "backchain framework," is for building programs that use backward chaining production rules.

Fig. 1-6. Basic Steps for Expert System Development

THE KNOWLEDGE BASE

The key bottleneck in developing an expert system is building the knowledge base by having a knowledge engineer interact with the expert(s). The first body of knowledge extracted from the expert is terms, facts, standard procedures, etc., as

Fig. 1-7 Expert System Structure Dissimilarities

Search Direction	Search Control	Search Transformation
EXPERT SYSTEM	FUNCTION	DOMAIN
ABSTRIPS	Planning	Robots
NOAH	Planning	Robots
MYCIN	Diagnosis	Medicine
DENDRAL	Data Interpreter	Chemistry
EL	Analysis	Elec. Circuits
GUIDON	C.A.I.	Medicine
KAS	Knowledge Acquisition	Geology
META-DENDRAL	Learning	Chemistry
AM	Concept Formulation	Math
VM	Monitoring	Medicine
GA1	Data Interpreter	Chemistry
R1	Design	Computers
MOLGEN	Design	Genetics
SYN	Design	Elec. Circuits
HEARSAY II	Signal Interpreter	Speech Unders.
HARPY	Signal Interpreter	Speech Unders.
CRYSALIS	Data Interpreter	Crystallography

one might find in textbooks or journals. However, that information is insufficient for building a high performance system. Thus, a cycle procedure is followed to improve the program—a sample case is run, with the expert disagreeing with its reasoning at some point. That forces the expert to introspect on what additional knowledge is needed. It often elicits a judgmental rule (heuristic) from the expert. As more and more heuristics are added to the program, the system incrementally approaches the competence of the expert at the task.

The most popular approach to representing the domain knowledge needed for an expert system is by production rules, which are also referred to as "SITUATION-ACTION rules" or "IF-THEN rules." A knowledge base can be made up mostly of rules that are invoked by pattern matching with features of the task environment as they currently appear in the knowledge data base.

The rules in a knowledge data base represent the domain facts and heuristics—rules of good judgment of actions to take when specific situations arise. The power of the expert system lies in the specific knowledge of the problem domain, with potentially the most powerful systems being the ones containing the most knowledge. Most existing rule-based systems contain hundreds of rules, usually obtained by interviewing experts for weeks or months. In any system the rules become connected to each other, by association linkages, to form rule networks. Once assembled, such networks can represent a substantial body of knowledge.

An expert usually has many judgmental or empirical rules, for which there is incomplete support from the available evidence. In such cases 1 approach is to attach numerical certainty to each rule to indicate the degree of certainty associated with that rule. In expert system operation, those certainty values are combined with each other and the certainty of the problem data, enabling one to arrive at a certainty value for the final solution.

The cognitive strategies of human experts in more complex domains are based on the mental storage and use of large incremental catalogs of pattern-based rules. Thus, human chess masters may be able to acquire, organize, and utilize as many as 50,000

Table 1-5 Programming Tools for Building Expert Systems

Tool	Organization	Nature
AGE	Stanford Univ.	A sophisticated expert system to aid users in building expert systems.
TEIRESIAS	Stanford Univ.	An expert system that facilitates the interactive transfer of knowledge from a human expert to the system via a (restricted) natural language dialog.
EMYCIN	Stanford Univ.	A domain independent version of MYCIN, which accompanies the backward chaining and explanation approach with user aids.
UNITS	Stanford Univ.	A knowledge representation language and interactive knowledge acquisition system. The language provides both for "frame" structures and production rules.
HEARSAY III	USC/Information Sciences Institute	A generalized domain-independent extension of HEARSAY II. Includes a "context" mechanism and an elaborated "blackboard" and scheduler.
ROSIE	RAND	A general rule-based programming language that can be used to develop large knowledge bases. Translates near-English into INTERLISP.
KAS	SRI	Supervises interaction with an expert in building or augmenting an expert system knowledge base in a network form implemented for PROSPECTOR.
OPS5	CMU	A programming language built on top of LISP designed to facilitate the use of production rules.
KRL	XEROX PARC	Knowledge representation language for frame-based processing.
SAM	Yale University	Computer programs utilized to analyze scripts.
FRL	M.I.T.	Frame representation language that provides hierarchical knowledge base format.
KL-ONE	BBN	Language for representation of natural language conceptual information.
DAWN	Digital Equip.	General programming and system description language.
OWL	M.I.T.	Semantic Network knowledge representation language.

pattern-based rules in achieving their remarkable performance. Those rules are so powerful that only some 30 rules are needed for expert system performance for a chess subdomain such as King and Knight against King and Rook, which has a problem space size of roughly 2 million configurations. For chess, the number of rules required grows slowly relative to the increase in domain complexity. Thus, in chess and other complex domains (such as industrial routing and scheduling), it appears that well-chosen pattern sets may maintain control over otherwise intractable explosions of combinatorial complexity.

The rule-based structure of expert systems facilitates acquisition by the system of new rules and modification of existing rules, not only by tutorial interaction with a human domain specialist but also by autonomous learning. A typical functional application is "classification," for which rules are discovered by induction for large collections of samples. DENDRAL is used for obtaining structural representations of organic molecules; it is a widely accepted expert system. As the knowledge acquisition bottleneck is a critical problem, a META-DENDRAL expert system models the processes of theory formation to generate a set of general fragmentation rules of the form used by DENDRAL. The method used by META-DENDRAL is to generate, test, and refine a set of candidate rules from data of known molecule structure-spectrum pairs.

DESIGN TECHNIQUES

There is little architectural design commonality based either on function or domain of expertise. Instead, expert system design may best be considered as an art form, like custom home architecture, in which the chosen design can be implemented using the collection of techniques discussed below.

Choice of Solution Direction

When data or basic ideas are a starting point, forward chaining is a natural direction for problem solving. It has been used in expert systems for data analysis, design, diagnosis, and concept formation. Backward chaining is applicable when a goal or a hypothesis is a starting point. Functional expert system examples include those used for diagnosis and planning. Combined forward and backward processing is used when the search space is large. One approach is to search both from the initial state and from the goal or hypothesis state and utilize a relaxation-type approach to match the solutions at an intermediate point. That approach is also useful when the search space can be divided hierarchically, so both a bottom up and top down search can be combined. Such a combined search is particularly applicable to complex problems incorporating uncertainties. Even driven problem solving is similar to forward chaining except that the data or situation is evolving over time. In that case the next step is chosen either on the basis of new data or in response to a changed situation resulting from the last problem-solving step taken. The event-driven approach is appropriate for real-time operations, such as monitoring or control, and is also applicable to many planning problems.

Reasoning in the Presence of Uncertainty

In many cases we must deal with uncertainty in data or in knowledge. Diagnosis and data analysis are typical examples. As discussed below, numeric techniques can be utilized or the uncertainties can be handled by incorporating a form of backtracking. Numeric procedures have been devised to handle approximations by combining evidence. MYCIN utilizes "certainty factors" (related to probabilities), which use the range of 0 to 1 to indicate the strength of the evidence. Fuzzy set theory, based on possibilities, can also be utilized. Often beliefs are formed or lines of reasoning are developed based on partial or errorful information. When contradictions occur, the incorrect beliefs or lines of reasoning causing the contradictions and all wrong conclusions resulting from them must be retracted. To accomplish that, a data-base record of beliefs and their justifications must be maintained. Using that approach, truth maintenance techniques can exploit redundancies in experimental data to increase system reliability.

Many straightforward problems in areas such as design, diagnosis, and analysis have small search spaces, either because the problem is small or the problem can be broken up into small independent subprograms. In many cases a single line of reasoning is sufficient, and so backtracking is not required. In such cases the direct approach of exhaustive search can be appropriate.

Techniques for Searching a Large Search Space

State space search is frequently formulated as hierarchical "generate and test"—reasoning by elimination. In that approach the system generates possible solutions, and a tester prunes those solutions that fail to meet appropriate criteria. Such exhaustive reasoning by elimination can be appropriate for small search spaces, but for large search spaces more powerful techniques are needed. A "hierarchical generate and test" approach can be very effective if means are available for evaluating candidate solutions that are only partially specified. In that case early pruning of whole branches (representing entire classes of solutions associated with these partial specifications) is possible, massively reducing the search required.

"Hierarchical generate and test" is appropriate for many large data interpretation and diagnosis problems, for which all solutions are desired, provided that a generator can be devised that can partition the solution space in ways that allow for early pruning.

In the "hierarchical generate and test" approach, when a line of reasoning fails and must be retracted, 1 approach is to chronologically backtrack to the most recent choice point. However, it is often much more efficient to trace errors and inconsistencies back to the inferential steps that created them, using dependency records. Backtracking that is based on dependencies and determines what to invalidate is called dependency-directed backtracking. Note the similarity to truth maintenance. When one is dealing with errorful information, backtracking is referred to as truth maintenance. Backtracking to recover from incorrect lines of reasoning is referred to as dependency-directed backtracking.

Multiple lines of reasoning can be used to broaden the coverage of an imcomplete search. In that case search programs that have fallible evaluators can decrease the chances of discarding a good solution from weak evidence by carrying a limited number of solutions in parallel, until the best solution is clarified.

Methods for Handling a Large Search Space by Transforming the Space

Breaking the problem down into noninteracting subproblems is an approach, yielding smaller search spaces, applicable for problems in which a number of noninteracting tasks have to be done to achieve a goal. Unfortunately, few real world problems of any magnitude fall into that class. For most complex problems that can be broken up into subproblems, it has been found that the subproblems interact so that valid solutions cannot be found independently. To take advantage of the smaller search spaces associated with that approach, a number of techniques have been devised to deal with these interactions:

- Find a fixed sequence of subprograms so that no interactions occur. Sometimes it is possible to find an ordered partitioning so that no interactions occur.
- Least commitment
  That technique coordinates decision-making with the availability of information and moves the focus of problem-solving activity among the available subproblems. Decisions are not made arbitrarily or prematurely but are postponed until there is enough information. In planning problems that is exemplified by methods that assign a partial ordering of operators in each subproblem and complete the ordering only when sufficient information on the interactions of the subproblems is developed.
- Constraint Propagation
  Another approach is to represent the interaction between the subproblems as constraints. Constraints can be viewed as partial descriptions of entities or as relationships that must be satisfied. Constraint propagation is a mechanism for moving information between subproblems. By introducing constraints instead of

choosing particular values, a problem solver is able to pursue a least commitment style of problem solving.
● Guessing or Plausible Reasoning
 Guessing is an inherent part of heuristic search, but it is particularly important in working with interacting subproblems. For instance, in the least commitment approach the solution process must come to a halt when it has insufficient information for deciding between competing choices. In such cases heuristic guessing is needed to carry the solution process along. If the guesses are wrong, then dependency-directed backtracking can be used to efficiently recover from them.

Hierarchical Refinement into Increasingly Elaborate Spaces—Top Down Refinement

Often the most important aspects of a problem can be abstracted and a high level solution developed. That solution can then be iteratively refined, successfully including more details. An example is to initially plan a trip using a reduced scale map to locate the main highways and then use more detailed maps to refine the plan. That technique has many applications, as the top-level search space is suitably small. The resulting high-level solution constrains the search to a small portion of the search space at the next lower level, so that at each level the solution can readily be found. That procedure is an important technique for preventing combinatorial explosions in searching for a solution.

Hierarchical Resolution into Contribution Subspaces

Certain problems can have their solution space hierarchically resolved into contributing subspaces in which the elements of the higher level spaces are composed of elements from the lower spaces. Thus, in speech understanding, words would be composed of syllables, phrases of words, and sentences of phrases. The resulting heterogeneous subspaces are fundamentally different from the top level solution space. However, the solution candidates at each level are useful for restricting the range of search at the adjacent levels, again acting as an important restraint on combinatorial explosion. Another example of a possible hierarchical resolution is in electrical equipment design, where subcomponents contribute to the black box level, which in turn contribute to the system level. Similarly, examples can be found in manufacturing, architecture, and in spacecraft and aircraft design.

Methods for Handling a Large Search Space by Developing Alternative or Additional Space

Sometimes the search for a solution utilizing a single model is very difficult. The use of alternative models for either the whole or part of the problem may greatly simplify the search.

It is possible to add additional layers of spaces to a search space to help decide what to do next. They can be thought of as strategy and tactical layers in which meta problem solvers choose among several potential methods for deciding what to do next at the problem level.

Dealing with Time

Little has been done in the way of expert systems that deal with time explicitly. The following are approaches to dealing with time in terms of time intervals.

Situational calculus was an early approach for representing sequences of actions and their effects. It uses the concept of situations that change when sufficient actions have taken place or when new data indicate a situational shift is appropriate. Situations determine the context for actions and, through the use of frames, can indicate what changes and what remains the same when an action takes place. A frame is a data structure for describing a stereotyped situation.

The method of least commitment and backward chaining initially produced a partial ordering of operators for each plan. When interference between subgoal plans was observed, the planner adjusted the ordering of the operators to resolve the interference to produce a final parallel plan with time-ordered operators.

The preceding shows some of the design techniques for developing expert systems. In the near term expert systems for robotics will primarily be university-derived efforts to utilize expert systems to solve robot planning and implementation requirements.

CURRENT EXPERT SYSTEMS

Table 1-6 is a list by source category of the principal players in expert systems.

Table 1-7 shows some of the existing major expert systems classified by function and domain of use. It can be observed that there is a predominance of systems in the medical and chemistry domains following from the pioneering efforts at Stanford University. From the list, it is also apparent that Stanford University dominates in number of systems, followed by C.M.U., M.I.T., and SRI, with a dozen scattered efforts elsewhere.

**Table 1-6   Source of Expert
System Knowledge**

Universities

Stanford
M.I.T.
C.M.U.

Nonprofit

SRI
APL/JHU
RAND
JPL
MITRE

Government

NOSC, San Diego, CA
NRL AI Lab, Washington, D.C.

Industrial

Advanced Decision Systems
Applied Expert Systems
Bell Laboratories
Carnegie Group
Computer Thought
DEC
Fairchild
General Research
GM
Hewlett Packard
Hughes

Table 1-6   Source of Expert
System Knowledge Cont'd.

Industrial con't.

IBM
Inference
IntelliCorp
IntelliGenetics
Machine Intelligence Corp.
Perceptronics
Schlumberger
Software A&E
Systems Control, Inc.
Texas Instruments
Technology Research Corporation
Teknowledge, Palo Alto, Calif.
Xerox PARC

Table 1-7   Existing Expert Systems by Functions

Function	Domain	System	Institution
Planning	Robotics	NOAH	U.C., Santa Cruz
	Robotics	ABSTRIPS	SRI
	Robotics	GIR	Tech. Research
	Planetary Flybys	DEVISER	SRI
	Errand Planning	OP-PLANNER	JPL
	Molecular Genetics	MOLGEN	Rand
	Mission Planning	KNOBS	Stanford U.
	Job Shop Scheduling	ISIS-II	MITRE
	Design of Molecular	SPEX	C.M.U.
	Genetics Experiments		Stanford U.
	Chemical Synthesis	SECHS	U.C., Santa Cruz
	Medical Diagnosis	HODGKINS	M.I.T.
	Tactical	TATR	Rand
Learning from	Chemistry	METADENDRAL	Stanford U.
Experience	Heuristics	EURISKO	Stanford U.
Diagnosis	Medicine	PIP	M.I.T.
	Medicine	CASNET	Rutgers U.
	Medicine	INTERNIST/CADUCEUS	U. of Pittsburgh
	Medicine	MYCIN	Stanford U.
	Medicine	PUFF	Stanford U.
	Computer Faults	DART	Stanford U./IBM
	Medicine	MDX	Ohio State U.
	Computer Faults	IDT	DEC
	Nuclear Reactor	REACTOR	EG&G Idaho Inc.
	Accidents		
	Telephone	WAVE	Bell Telephone Labs
Data Analysis	Geology	DIPMETER	M.I.T./Schlumberger
and Interpre-		ADVISOR	
tation	Chemistry	DENDRAL	Stanford U.
	Chemistry	GAI	Stanford U.
	Geology	PROSPECTOR	SRI

Table 1-7 Existing Expert Systems by Functions Cont'd.

Function	Domain	System	Institution
	Protein Crystallography	CRYSALIS	Stanford U.
	Determination of Causal Relationships in Medicine	RX	Stanford U.
	Determination of Causal Relationships in Medicine	ABEL	M.I.T.
	Oil Well Logs	ELAS	AMOCO
Analysis	Electrical Circuits	EL	M.I.T.
	Symbolic Mathematics	MACSYMA	M.I.T.
	Mechanics Problems	MECHO	Edinburgh
	Naval Task Force Threat Analysis	TECH	Rand/NOSC
	Earthquake Damage Assessment for Structures	SPERIL	Purdue U.
	Digital Circuits	CRITTER	Rutgers U.
Design	Computer System Configurations	R1/XCON	C.M.U. Digital Equip. Corp.
	Automatic Pro-gramming	PECOS	Yale
	Circuit Synthesis	SYN	M.I.T.
	Chemical Synthesis	SYNCHEM	SUNY Stonybrook
Concept Formation	Mathematics	AM	C.M.U.
Signal Interpre-tation	Speech Understanding	HEARSAY II	C.M.U.
	Speech Understanding	HARPY	C.M.U.
	Machine Acoustics	SU/X	Stanford U.
	Ocean Surveillance	HASP	System Controls Inc.
	Sensors on Board Naval Vessels	STAMMER-2	NOSC, San Diego/SDC
	Medicine—Left Ventrical Per-formance	ALVEN	U. of Toronto
	Military Analysis	ANALYST	Mitre
Monitoring	Patient Respiration	VM	Stanford U.
Use Adviser	Structural Analysis Computer Program	SACOM	Stanford U.
Computer Aided Instruction	Electronic Trouble-shooting	SOPHIE	B.B.N.
	Medical Diagnosis	GUIDON	Stanford U.
	Mathematics	EXCHECK	Stanford U.
	Steam Propulsion Plant Operation	STEAMER	BBN
	Diagnostic Skills	BUGGY	BBN
	Causes of Rainfall	WHY	BBN
	Coaching of a Game	WEST	BBN
	Coaching of a Game	WUMPUS	M.I.T.
Knowledge Acquisition	Medical Diagnosis	TEIRESIAS	Stanford U.
	Medical Consultation	EXPERT	Rutgers
	Geology	KAS	SRI

Table 1-7   Existing Expert Systems by Functions Cont'd.

Function	Domain	System	Institution
Expert System Construction	Expert System	ROSIE	Rand
	Expert System	AGE	Stanford U.
	Expert System	HEARSAY III	U.S.C./ISI
	Expert System	EMYCIN	Stanford U.
	Expert System	OPS5	C.M.U.
	Expert System	RAINBOW	IBM
	Medical Diagnosis	KMS	U. of Maryland
	Medical Consultation	EXPERT	Rutgers
	Electronic Systems Diagnosis	ARBY	Yale/ITT
	Medical Consultation Using Time-Oriented Data	MECS-AI	Tokyo U.
Consultation/ Intelligent Assistant	Battlefield Weapons Assignments	BATTLE	NRL AI Lab
	Medicine	Digitalis Therapy Advisor	M.I.T.
	Radiology	RAYDEX	Rutgers U.
	Computer Sales	XCEL	C.M.U.
	Medical Treatment	ONCOCIN	Stanford U.
	Nuclear Power Plants	CSA Model-Based Nuclear Power Plant Consultant	Georgia Tech
	Prompting	Reconsider	Univ. of Calif.
Management	Automated Factory	IMS	C.M.U.
	Project Management	Callisto	Dec./Carnegie Group
Automatic Programming	Modeling of Oil Well Logs	ΦNIX	Schlumberger-Doll Res.
		PECOS	Stanford Univ.
		LIBRA	Stanford Univ.
		SAFE	Univ. of Southern Calif.
		DEDALUS	SRI
		PA	M.I.T.
Image Understanding		VISIONS	U. of Mass.
		ACRONYM	Stanford U.

The list indicates that thus far the major areas of expert systems development have been in diagnosis, data analysis and interpretation, planning and design. However, the list also indicates that a few pioneering expert systems already exist in quite a number of other functional areas. In addition, a substantial effort is under way to build expert systems as tools for constructing expert systems.

The material in this chapter has provided an overview of artificial intelligence and expert systems. The balance of this book provides definitions of terms, product and vendor descriptions, points of contact for more information, and bibliography references.

A

AAAI. The American Association for Artificial Intelligence.

absolute address. An address in a computer language that identifies a storage location or a device without the use of any intermediate reference. An address that is permanently assigned by the machine designer to a storage location.

absolute coordinates. Location of point in terms of x, y, or z distance from established origin.

absolute indexed addressing. The effective address is formed by adding the index register (x or y) to the second and third byte of the instruction.

absolute order. In machine vision computer graphics, a display command in a computer program that causes the display devices to interpret the data bytes following the order as absolute data rather than as relative data.

absolute rule. An absolute rule is a purely deductive and assertive rule that is used to evaluate a situation. For instance, an absolute rule might detect that the diameter of a circle has become known in the database, and as a result, it might act to calculate the area and circumference of the circle.

absolute vectors. Line segment with endpoint expressed in x, y, and z coordinates.

ABSTRIPS. An expert system that solves diagnostic problems by developing an appropriate hierarchy to identify epistemologically appropriate diagnostic levels.

access-oriented methods. Programming methods based on the use of probes that trigger new computations when data are changed or read.

access time. The time interval between the instant at which data are called for from a storage device and the instant delivery is completed.

accumulator. A register that holds 1 of the operands and the result of arithmetic and logic operations that are performed by the central processing unit. Also commonly used to hold data transferred to or from input and or output devices.

accuracy. A measurement of the difference between the calculated point in space and the actual location reached by a robot arm.

ACE. ACE identifies trouble spots in telephone networks and recommends appropriate repair and rehabilitative maintenance. The system operates without human intervention, analyzing maintenance reports generated on a daily basis by CRAS, a cable repair administration computer program. Once ACE locates the faulty telephone cables, it decides whether they need preventive maintenance and selects the type of maintenance most likely to be effective. ACE then stores its recommendations in a special data base that users can access. The system makes decisions by applying knowledge about wire centers, CRAS maintenance reports, and network analysis strategies. It uses a rule-based knowledge representation scheme controlled by forward chaining. ACE is implemented in OPS4 and FRANZ LISP and runs on AT&T 3B-2 microcomputers located in the cable analysts' offices. It was developed by Bell Laboratories at Whippany, New Jersey.

ACES. ACES performs the cartographer's job of map labeling. The system takes as input an unlabeled map plus data describing points where objects are located and the text string and symbol type to be displayed at each point. The system produces a map containing the desired symbols and labels, all positioned to esthetically place the labels next to the symbols without overlap. The system chooses the symbol placement, type font, label size, and level of description that best fits the map in question. It uses an object-oriented knowledge representation scheme and is implemented in LOOPS for the Xerox Dolphin workstation.

achromatic color. One that is found along the gray scale from white to black.

achromatic region. The area of a chromaticity diagram in which acceptable "white" reference points can be located.

ACLS. ACLS is a system-building aid that induces rules for an expert system from examples of decisions provided by a domain expert. The user specifies the problem in terms of the set of attributes relevant to the decision and the possible decision classes. The user then gives ACLS examples of situation-decision pairs, from which it creates general rules that classify the examples and counterexamples interactively, thereby dynamically correcting or refining the rules. ACLS can output a rule either as a decision tree or as a PASCAL program. The rule induction is based on Ross Quinlan's ID3 inductive learning algorithm. ACLS is implemented in UCSD-PASCAL and operates on APPLE II+ and IBM PC microcomputers. ACLS was developed at the University of Edinburgh and is available from Intelligent Terminals Limited as a commercial system.

action. In a production system with a forward-chaining architecture, the right-hand side of a rule consists of a sequence of actions, each of which performs some activity such as creating, deleting, or modifying elements in data memory, performing input/output, modifying production memory, and halting the recognize-act cycle. When a rule fires, the actions that constitute the right-hand side are performed in sequence, using the bindings that were created when the rule was started.

activation. For each object in an activation network, the activation level is an associated number representing the degree to which that object is to receive attention. Activations are propagated between related objects in the network.

activation accommodation. Integration of sensors, control, and robot motion to achieve alternation of a robot's preprogrammed motions in response to sensed forces. Used to stop a robot when forces reach set levels or to perform force feedback tasks, such as insertions, door opening, and edge tracing.

activation cycle. In an activation network the activation cycle is the period of time during which activation is propagated among adjacent objects. Typically, during each activation cycle activation is propagated 1 arc farther from the source of activation. One or more activation cycles take place during a single recognize-act cycle.

activation mechanism. The situation required to invoke a procedure—usually a match of the system state to the preconditions required to exercise a production rule.

activation network. An activation network is a graph, each node of which represents an object, with each arc representing a relationship between 2 objects. If the arc is labeled, the label is a number indicating the strength of the relationship. When a node is processed, its activation level may change and the effects of that change are propagated along arcs to related nodes, resulting in changes to their activation level.

active illumination. Illumination that can be varied automatically to extract more visual information from a scene, e.g., by turning lamps on and off, by adjusting brightness, by projecting a pattern on objects in the scene, or by changing the color of the illumination.

active values. Often used with graphic images to allow the user to change the values in a system by simply altering an image on the computer screen.

actor. Procedure that does its work by generating new actors and by sending messages to other actors.

actuator. A motor or transducer that converts electrical, hydraulic, or pneumatic energy to effect motion of the robot.

ADA. Language developed by the U.S. Department of Defense, originally for internal use and now required programming language for all defense-mission-critical applications. Difficult language to work with, has received little commercial software support. Named for Lord Byron's daughter, Augusta Ada, who is referred to as the first programmer.

Ada-Plus. System Designers Software Inc. developed a unique software tool called Ada-Plus. Ada-Plus is an integrated set of software tools for the cross development of embedded systems in Ada using host target technology. Ada-Plus comprises: SD-Ada Compiler, Ada Compiler Tools, SD-Assembler, Builder System, Debug System, Target Runtime System and Prom Formatter. Host: Microvax, Vax II Family, Vax 8600. Target: MC68000, MIL-STD-1750A. The price is from $17,400.

adaptation. Adjustment of the pupil aperture and light-sensing sensitivity of the eye-brain system to a given ambient luminance level.

adaptive. The ability of a smart robot to "learn," modify its control system, and respond to a changing environment.

adaptive control. A control method in which control parameters are continuously and automatically adjusted in response to measured process variables to achieve better performance.

address. A number specifying where a unit of information is stored in the computer's memory.

address bus. A multiple-bit output bus for transmitting an address from the CPU to the rest of the system.

address format. The arrangement of the address parts of an instruction. The expression "plus 1" is frequently used to indicate that 1 of the addresses specifies the location of the next instruction to be executed, such as 1-plus-1, 2-plus-1, 3-plus-1, or 4-plus-1. The arrangement of the parts of a single address such as those required for identifying channel, module, track, etc., in a magnetic disk system.

address modification. The process of changing the address part of a machine instruction by means of coded instruction.

address register. A register in which an address is stored.

addressability. The characteristic of certain storage devices in which each storage area or location has a unique address. The address is then usable by the programmer to access the information stored at that location.

addressable point. Any position on a crt screen that can be specified by absolute coordinates, which form a grid over the display surface.

ADEPT. Used to aid battlefield situation assessment analysts by providing tactical interpretations of intelligence sensor reports. The system uses those reports to generate a display of combat locations on the battlefield. Military knowledge and expertise are encoded as rules concerning how and why enemy forces operate and the tactical significance of situation interpretations. The system is able to explain the reasoning behind its battlefield assessments. The expert reasoning component of ADEPT is implemented in ROSIE, and a Chromatics CGC 7900 color graphics system is used to display maps and military symbology. The system was developed at TRW.

adjacency. In character recognition a condition in which the character spacing reference lines of 2 consecutively printed characters on the same line are separated by less than a specified distance.

ADS. Developed by Aion Corporation as an expert system shell comprising two parts: the Application Building System (ABS) and the Application Execution System (AES). The program is written in PASCAL and is designed for IBM operating environments.

Advanced Decision Systems. Advanced Decision Systems (ADS) is a leader in military expert systems development. They have one of the finer staffs of AI/ES personnel.

ADVISE. A general-purpose, system-building aid consisting of an integrated set of development tools. They include support for multiple forms of knowledge representation (rules, semantic nets, and relational data bases), support for several certainty propagation schemes (probabilistic, approximate Bayesian, min/max logic, and weighting evidence), support for various control strategies (utility optimization, probabilistic network traversal, and forward and backward rule chaining), and the incorporation of inductive learning programs (GEM and CLUSTER) for inductively deriving decision rules and control information from examples. GEM generalizes examples of different concepts and creates formal logic rules for recognizing them. CLUSTER automatically constructs a classification of given entities using a conceptual clustering approach. In explanation mode, ADVISE paraphrases decision rules, allows simple interrogation of the knowledge base, and displays its reasoning steps. ADVISE is implemented in PASCAL and operates on DEC VAX computers under the UNIX operating system. ADVISE was developed at the University of Illinois.

ADVISOR. Assists novice users of MACSYMA by diagnosing their misconceptions and providing advice tailored to each user's needs. The user gives ADVISOR a sequence of user-entered MACSYMA commands and a statement of the overall goal, which was not met by the command sequence. The system infers the user's plan for achieving the goal, identifies the misconception, confirms it with the user, then generates advice. ADVISOR combines expertise about using MACSYMA with a model of novice user behavior that helps ADVISOR recognize users' plans and misconceptions. User plans and goals are represented as data-flow graphs and goal trees. ADVISOR was written in MACLISP at M.I.T.

advisory systems. Expert system that interacts with a person in the style of giving advice rather than in the style of dictating commands. Generally advisory systems have mechanisms for explaining their advice and for allowing their users to interact at an information detail level comfortable to the user.

AGE. A system-building design aid that helps the builder select a framework, design a rule language, and assemble the pieces into a complete expert system. It consists of a set of building blocks in the form of INTERLISP functions that support various expert system architectures. They include inference engines for forward and backward chaining and structures for representing a blackboard architecture, a framework where independent groups of rules called knowledge sources communicate through a central data base called a blackboard. AGE is implemented in INTERLISP and is designed for use by experienced INTERLISP programmers. It was developed at Stanford University.

agenda. An ordered list of actions. Some knowledge systems store and reason about possible actions as, for example, whether to pursue a particular line of reasoning. HEARSAY uses agenda-based control.

aggregate. The evaluation of an aggregate yields a value of a composite type. The value is specified by giving the value of each of the components. Either positional association or named association may be used to indicate which value is associated with which component.

AI/COAG. AI/COAG assists physicians in diagnosing diseases of hemostasis by analyzing and interpreting clinical blood coagulation laboratory tests. The system handles 6 types of coagulation screening tests, including those for platelet count and urea clot solubility. In addition, the system can evaluate a clinical hemostasis history of the patient to confirm the diagnosis suggested by the screening tests. AI/COAG was developed at the University of Missouri School of Medicine and was implemented on a DEC LSI-11 microcomputer.

AIMDS. AIMDS is a knowledge engineering language for frame-based representation, but it also supports procedure-oriented representation methods. Its principal characteristics include deductive and nondeductive reasoning, multiple inheritance, maintenance of belief contexts, automatic detection of knowledge-base inconsistencies, reasoning about hypothetical worlds, procedural attachment, and the use of expectations to guide actions and perform analogical inference. AIMDS is implemented in FUZZY, which is itself implemented in UCI-LISP, and provides access to all of the features and support tools of the LISP and FUZZY environments. AIMDS was developed at Rutgers University.

AI/MM. Analyzes behavior in the renal physiology domain and explains the rationale for its analyses. The system answers queries about the values of various parameters, such as the volume of body water, and interprets observations, such as abnormally high water intake. AI/MM's expertise includes the laws of physics and anatomy, fundamental principles of physiology, and empirical knowledge of physiological processes. That knowledge is represented as rules comprising a detailed causal model. Each rule also contains a description of its underlying principle for use in explaining the system's operation. AI/MM is implemented in MRS. It was developed at Stanford University.

AI/RHEUM. Assists physicians in diagnosing connective tissue diseases of clinical rheumatology by applying formal diagnostic criteria obtained from rheumatology experts. The system uses patient symptoms and laboratory findings to provide assistance with 7 diseases, including rheumatoid arthritis, progressive systemic sclerosis, and Sjoegren's disease. AI/RHEUM is a rule-based system implemented in EXPERT and accesses its rule through forward chaining. It was developed at the University of Missouri School of Medicine.

air motor. A device that converts compressed air into rotary mechanical force and motion. An air-servo-motor is one that is controlled by a servo mechanism.

AIRID. AIRID identifies aircraft on the basis of visually observed characteristics. The user enters observed features and the conditions under which the observation occurred (e.g., bad weather) from which AIRID determines the identity of the target aircraft. AIRID's expertise includes physical characteristics of aircraft, extracted from *Jane's All the World's Aircraft 1982–83*. The relevant features include wing shape, engine configuration (number and mounting position), fuselage shape, and tail assembly shape. The system is implemented in KAS and uses a combined rule-based and semantic network representation technique. AIRID assumes it has a successful identification when the certainty level in its network reaches 98% confidence. The system was developed at Los Alamos National Laboratory.

AIRPLAN. AIRPLAN assists air operations officers with the launch and recovery of aircraft on a carrier. The system analyzes current information (e.g., the aircraft's fuel level, the weather conditions at a possible divert site) and alerts the air operations officer of possible impending problems. AIRPLAN assesses the seriousness of a situation and manages its use of time by attending first to the most significant aspects of a problem. If time permits, it extends the analysis based on its initial conclusions. AIRPLAN is a rule-based system implemented in OPS7. It interfaces with the ship's officers through ZOG, a rapid-response, large-network, menu-selection system for human-machine communication. The system was developed at Carnegie-Mellon University and tested aboard the Carl Vinson.

AI Vaxstation. Digital Equipment Corporation developed the Vax hardware. The AI Vaxstation consists of a Microvax II processor with 9 Mbytes of memory, an RD53 71 Mbyte Winchester disk drive, a TK50 95 Mbyte tape subsystem, DECnet/Ethernet interface, 19-inch monochrome monitor, standard keyboard, and 3-button mouse. Disk storage can be expanded to 213 Mbytes. The price is $48,690.

ALADIN. Alloy design is a metallurgical problem in which a selection of basic elements are combined and fabricated resulting in an alloy that displays a set of desired characteristics (e.g., fracture toughness, stress corrosion cracking). The quest for a new alloy is usually driven by new product requirements. Once the metallurgical expert receives a set of new requirements for a new aluminum alloy, the expert begins a search in the literature for an existing alloy that satisfies them. If such an alloy is not known, the expert may draw upon experimental, heuristic, and theory-based knowledge in order to suggest a set of new alloys of which 1 may result in a successful combination. The search for a "successful" alloy may require many hypothesis and experiment cycles, spanning several years. Owing to the amount of information published each year, it is impossible for an expert to keep track of each new development in other labs and even in his own. Hence, some hypotheses might have been rejected if the expert had been aware of previous experiments performed in either the same lab or in other corporations or universities. If it were possible to provide more information in the alloy design phase, the number of false hypotheses would be reduced, allowing the search to converge more quickly and at a reduced cost. In addition, not all alloy design experts are created equal. Some are more expert than others, and their expertise covers different areas of knowledge. Capturing some of the knowledge used by a variety of experts to design alloys, in an accessible form, would extend the design powers of others. The goal of the ALADIN project is to perform research resulting in the design and construction of a prototype, AI-based, decision-support system for aluminum alloy design. In particular, to develop a knowledge bank of alloy knowledge and to construct a problem-solving capability that utilizes the knowledge bank to suggest or verify alloy designs.

algebraic language. An algorithmic language many of whose statements are designed to resemble the structure of algebraic expression—examples are ALGOL and FORTRAN.

algorithm. A step-by-step procedure that has a specific beginning and end and is guaranteed to solve a specific problem. A completely specified procedure for performing a computation in a finite amount of time. When contrasted with heuristic problem-solving methods, the term connotes a well-understood procedure that is guaranteed to find a solution if it exists or to determine that no solution exists.

aliasing. Undesirable visual effects in computer-generated images. The most common effect is a jagged edge along object boundaries.

ALICE. A knowledge engineering language for logic-based representation. Its principal characteristics include an extensive vocabulary for describing combinatorial problems in operations research and a process for achieving goals that involves finding any feasible solution, repeatedly building up better solutions, and giving the proof of the optimality of the solution. ALICE was developed as an experimental system at the Institut de Programmation, Paris.

allocator. The evaluation of an allocator creates an object and returns a new access value that designates the object.

allophone. A unit of speech that represents a particular sound as it actually occurs in a word.

alphabetic string. A string consisting solely of letters from same alphabet.

alphanumeric. Pertaining to a character set that contains both letters and numerals and usually other characters.

alphanumeric display (or alphameric display). A workstation device consisting of a crt on which text can be viewed. An alphanumeric display is capable of showing a fixed set of letters, digits, and special characters. It allows the operator to observe entered commands and to receive messages from the system.

alphanumeric keyboard. A workstation device consisting of a typewriterlike keyboard that allows the designer to communicate with the system using an English-like command language.

ALVEY PROJECT. Technology project formed in the U.K. in 1982 in direct response to the Fifth Generation Project and named for John Alvey, the British telecommunications expert who initiated it. The U.K. plans to spend approximately $300 million (U.S.) on research up until 1990, with matching funds from industry.

AL/X. AL/X is a knowledge engineering language for rule-based representation, but it also supports frame-based representation methods. Its principal characteristics include a combination backward and forward chaining control scheme, a semantic net that links rule components, certainty handling mechanisms, and automatic user querying. The support environment contains facilities for explaining the system's reasoning. AL/X closely resembles the KAS system, that is, PROSPECTOR stripped of its knowledge about geology. AL/X is implemented in PASCAL and operates on a PDP-11/34 running UNIX. Intelligent Terminals, Ltd., developed it as a research system.

AMORD. A knowledge engineering language for rule-based representation. Its principal characteristics include discrimination networks for assertions and rules, a forward chaining control scheme, and a truth maintenance system (TMS) for maintaining justifications and program beliefs. Each AMORD fact or rule has an associated TMS node. The TMS uses a nonmonotonic dependency system for maintaining the logical grounds for belief in assertions. An explanation facility provides both justification and complete proof of belief in aspecific facts. AMORD is implemented in MACLISP and was developed at M.I.T.

amplitude. Of an oscillatory signal, the measure of how large it is, e.g., the difference between positive and negative peaks of the signal, although other measures may be specified.

AMUID. Assists military commanders with land battlefield analysis. The system integrates information from intelligence reports, infrared and visual imaging sensors, and MTI (moving target indicator) radar. AMUID classifies targets and organizes them into higher-level units (e.g., battalions and regiments). It provides real-time analysis and situation updating as data arrive continuously over time. AMUID's expertise is encoded as rules that operate on domain knowledge (e.g., types of military equipment, deployment patterns for military units, and tactics) maintained in a semantic net. Certainty factors are employed to handle the uncertainty typically involved in the analysis of sensor data. The control structure is event driven, where events are new sensor reports, major decisions made by the system itself, or user queries. AMUID was developed at Advanced Information and Decision Systems.

analog. The use of physical variables, such as distance or rotation to represent and correspond with numerical variables occurring in a computation. In numerical control the term applies to a system that uses electrical voltage magnitudes or ratios to represent physical axis positions.

analog communications. Transfer of information by means of a continuously variable quantity, such as the voltage produced by a strain gauge or air pressure in a pneumatic line.

analog computer. A computer operating on the principle of physical analogy, usually electrical, to solve problems. Variables of a problem are represented as continuous physical changes in voltage and current and are manipulated by the computer according to mathematical expressions of the analogy.

analog data. Data represented by a physical quantity that is considered to be continuously variable and whose magnitude is made directly proportional to the data or to a suitable function of data.

analog-to-digital (A/D converter). A device that changes physical motion or electrical voltage into digital factors.

analog vector generator. A device that converts coordinate data into deflection signals for a crt.

ANALYST. Assists field commanders with battlefield situation assessment. The system generates displays of enemy combat unit deployment and does so in real time from multisource sensor returns. ANALYST aggregates information from those multiple sensor sources to (1) locate and classify enemy battlefield units by echelon, general function, and relative location, and (2) detect force movement. The system contains expertise obtained from intelligence analysts, including how to interpret and integrate sensor data. ANALYST is implemented in FRANZ LISP and represents knowledge using a combination of frames and rules. It was developed at the Mitre Corporation.

and/or tree. A proof tree in theorem proving and a goal tree in general problem solving are trees such that each node is labeled as either an and node or an or node. For and nodes, each of the child nodes specifies necessary subproofs or subgoals that must be achieved jointly if the parent node is to be achieved. For or nodes, each of the child nodes specifies a sufficient alternative subproof or subgoal, only 1 of which need be achieved if the parent node is to be achieved.

android. A robot that approximates a human in physical appearance.

ANGY. Assists physicians in diagnosing the narrowing of coronary vessels by identifying and isolating coronary vessels in angiograms. The system first processes digital angiograms of coronary vessels in order to extract initial line and region features. This information is then given to ANGY's knowledge-based expert subsystem, which addresses both low- and high-level stages of vision processing. The low-level image processing stage uses rules for segmentation, grouping, and shape analysis to develop the initial lines and regions into more meaningful objects. The high-level stage then uses knowledge of cardiac anatomy and physiology to interpret the results, recognize relevant structures (e.g., the aorta), and eliminate irrelevant structures or artifacts caused by noise. The low-level image processing routines are implemented in the C programming language and include the edge detector and region grower. The medical expertise is represented as rules implemented in OPS5 and LISP. ANGY was developed at the University of Pennsylvania.

ANNA. Assists physicians in administering digitalis to patients with heart problems, such as arrhythmia and congestive heart failure. The system uses patient symptoms and history to determine the appropriate dosage regimen, including the amount of digitalis to administer and the rate at which it should be taken. Once the system prescribes an initial dosage, it monitors the patient's response to the drug, adjusting the dosage appropriately when the demonstrated response fails to match the expected response. ANNA is implemented in LISP. It was developed at M.I.T.

antecedent. A statement of the conditions necessary for drawing a conclusion. In a production system the left-hand side of the rule encodes the antecedent conditions for the rule to fire, while the right-hand side encodes the consequent.

anthropomorphic. An adjesive with the literal meaning "of human shape." An anthropomorphic robot is one that looks more or less like a human being.

anti-aliasing. A filtering technique to give the appearance of smooth lines and edges in a raster image. The technique involves use of intermediate intensities between neighboring pixels to soften the "stair step effect" of sloped lines.

aperture. One or more adjacent characters in a mask that cause retention of the corresponding characters.

APES. A knowledge engineering language for logic-based representation. It provides a user interface for writing expert systems in the Micro-PROLOG logic programming language. Its principal characteristics include handling of uncertain information, an explanation facility, and extensions to PROLOG that provide interactive facilities for user interfaces. Rules and facts in the knowledge base are expressed as PROLOG clauses. APES supports MYCIN-style, Bayesian-style, and user-defined certainty handling modules. It is implemented in Micro-PROLOG and operates on a wide range of microcomputers including North Star Horizons and IBM PCs. APES was developed at Imperial College, London.

appearance. Primitive attribute specifying a display intensity level or color.

application program. A program that carries out tasks or solves problems directly related to an individual's or an organization's work.

applicative language. A programming language in which computations are expressed as nested function calls rather than sequences of statements. Typically, applicative languages have no program counter and may not allow side effects. LISP is a well-known applicative language.

APLICOT. APLICOT is a knowledge engineering language for logic-based representation. Its principal characteristics include a flexible control scheme utilizing both forward and backward chaining, certainty factor handling, and an explanation mode. The support environment consists of PROLOG utility packages such as an interactive clause/rule editor. APLICOT is implemented in DEC-10 PROLOG and oeprates on an ICOT DEC-2060 computer system. It was developed at the University of Tokyo.

ARAMIS. Helps physicians assess new patients with rheumatic diseases. The system retrieves data about previous rheumatic disease patients and performs statistical analyses of that data. Based on that activity, ARAMIS offers a prognostic analysis with respect to a variety of endpoints (e.g., death, pleurisy), recommends therapy, and generates a prose case analysis. ARAMIS's knowledge consists of a collection of statistical analysis methods plus a number of data bases containing detailed patients records. Patient data are stored in a tabular data base using TOD (Time-Oriented Databank System), a system able to follow relevant clinical parameters over time. ARAMIS is written in PL/X, a specialized form of PL/I. It was developed at Stanford University.

ARBY. ARBY is a knowledge engineering language for rule-based representation. Its principal characteristics include the use of predicate calculus notation for expressing rules, a backward chaining facility (HYPO) for hypothesis generation, and a human interface subsystem (IFM) that manages a set of interaction frames (IFs). IFs are invoked when the HYPO component needs to retrieve information that is not yet in the data base but could be obtained by asking the user. The support environment contains facilities for rule and IF editing, for explaining why a question is being asked, and for explaining why a given fact is currently believed. ARBY is implemented in FRANZ LISP and uses the DUCK general-purpose retriever. It was developed at Yale University.

ARCHES. A program developed by Patrick H. Winston as his thesis, which learned by example.

architecture. The organizing framework imposed upon knowledge application and problem-solving activities. The knowledge-engineering principles that govern selection of appropriate frameworks for specific expert systems.

archiving. Storage of computerized data on permanent memory medium for subsequent retrieval.

area fill processor. Device or board that shades or colors a delineated surface on CRT display.

argument form. A reasoning procedure in logic.

arithmetic logic unit. The part of the computer processing section that does the adding, subtracting, multiplying, dividing, and logical tasks.

arithmetic register. A register that holds the operands or the result of operations such as arithmetic operations, logic operations, and shifts.

arithmetic shift. A shift applied to the representation of a number in a fixed radix numeration system and in a fixed-point representation system, in which only the characters representing the absolute value of the numbers are moved. An arithmetic shift is usually equivalent to multiplying the number by a positive or negative integral power of the radix except for the effect of any rounding.

Arity Expert System Systems Development Package. Arity Corporation developed the Arity Expert Systems Development Package, which speeds the construction of expert systems and knowledge intensive programs. It provides 2 ways of representing knowledge, a taxonomy of frames and a rule-based system, and provides optimized backward chaining, ability to interface to other languages, a 2-directional interface, a 1-gigabyte capacity of virtual memory when accessing Arity/Prolog database, 4 megabytes of memory allocated for storage of up to 20,000 rules, and a built-in explanation and questioning facility for quick generation of user interfaces. IBM PC, XT, AT, or MS-Dos compatibles with 512K memory, and Arity/Prolog Compiler or Arity/Prolog Interpreter.

arm. An interconnected set of robot links and powered joints comprising a manipulator and supporting or moving a hand or end effector.

array. Data structure that stores the memory location of points by coordinates. A 2-dimensional array stores x and y coordinates. A 3-dimensional array stores x, y, and z coordinates, allowing for depth representation.

ARS. A knowledge engineering language for rule-based representation. Its principal characteristics include the representation of problem-solving rules as demons with pattern-directed invocation, an associative data base for maintaining assertions, and forward chaining with dependency-directed backtracking. ARS maintains complete records of all deductions it makes and uses the records for explanation and for processing contradictions during backtracking. ARS is implemented in MACLISP and operates under the MULTICS, TOPS-10, and ITS computer operating systems. ARS was developed at M.I.T.

ART. ART is a knowledge engineering language for rule-based representation. Besides providing rules, it also supports frame-based and procedure-oriented

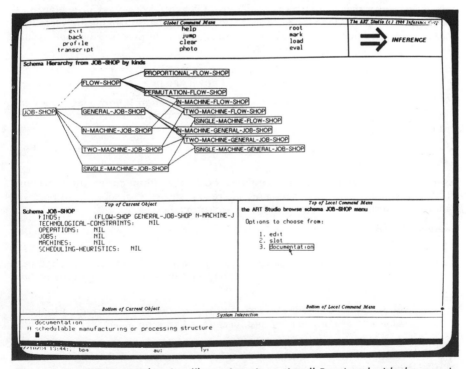

Figure A-1. ART screen showing "browsing viewpoints." *Reprinted with the permission of John Wiley and Sons, from "Expert Systems—Artificial Intelligence in Business" by Paul Harmon and David King.*

representation methods. Its principal characteristics include forward and backward chaining control schemes, certainty handling mechanisms, and hypothetical worlds—a way to structure the data base by defining the contexts in which facts and rules apply. The support environment includes standard debugging aids, such as trace facilities and break packages, that work in conjunction with a graphical monitor. ART is written in LISP and operates on CADR machines and the Symbolics 3600. Main features include:

- ART's Representation Language can model expert knowledge through the use of facts and schemata. Its language is rich with semantic features that ease the difficult task of encoding knowledge.
- ART's Viewpoint Mechanism support both the exploration of hypothetical alternatives and the modeling of situations that change with time.
- ART's flexible Rule Base (incorporating absolute rules, hypothetical rules, constraint rules and belief rules) helps the knowledge engineer capture human expertise.
- ART's Rule Compiler processes and compiles the rule base providing the speed for real time applications when seconds count.

articulated arm. A robot arm constructed to simulate the human arm, consisting of a series of rotary motions and joints, often powered by an air motor.

artificial intelligence. The subfield of computer science concerned with developing intelligent computer programs. That includes programs that can solve problems, learn from experience, understand language, interpret visual scenes, and, in general, behave in a way that would be considered intelligent if observed in a human. A growing set of computer problem-solving techniques that are being developed to imitate human thought or decision-making processes or to produce the same results as those processes. **(See figure on p. 53)**

artificial intelligence approach. An approach that has as its emphasis symbolic processes for representing and manipulating knowledge in a problem-solving mode.

ASCII. American (National) Standard Code for Information Interchange. The standard seven-bit code (a full eight bits with parity) for data processing, transmission, and communications.

aspect ratio. The ratio of width to height of a display surface. The standard machine vision aspect ratio is 4:3.

assembler. A program that translates symbolic operation codes into machine language, symbolic addresses to memory addresses, and assigns values to all program symbols. It translates source programs to object programs.

assembly directive. A mnemonic that modifies the assembler operation but does not produce an object code.

assembly language. A low-level language where each instruction is assembled into 1 machine-language instruction. The language result (object code) from the assembler is a character-for-character translated version of the original.

assembly robot. A robot designed, programmed, or dedicated to putting together parts into subassemblies or complete products. **(See figure on p. 54)**

assignment. Assignment is the operation that replaces the current value of a variable by a new value. An assignment statement specifies a variable on the left and on the right, an expression whose value is to be the new value of the variable.

associative memory. A sophisticated form of memory that combines logic circuitry with each item of memory. The feature departs from the tradition of separating processing from memory and can greatly accelerate memory searches.

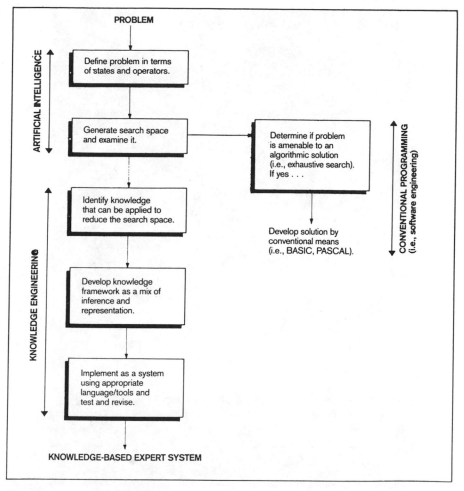

Figure A–2. Artificial Intelligence—The different concerns of AI and knowledge engineering. *Reprinted with the permission of John Wiley and Sons, from "Expert Systems—Artificial Intelligence in Business" by Paul Harmon and David King.*

ASTA. Helps an analyst identify the type of radar that generated an intercepted signal. The system analyzes the radar signal in light of general knowledge it has about the physics of radar and specific knowledge it has about particular types of radar systems. ASTA also helps the analyst by providing access to relevant data bases and explanations for the conclusions it reaches. Knowledge in ASTA is represented in the form of rules. The system was developed by Advanced Information and Decision Systems.

asynchronous. Not occurring at the same time or not exhibiting a constant repetition rate; irregular.

asynchronous computer. A computer in which each event or the performance of each operation starts as a result of a signal generated by the completion of the previous event or operation or on the availability of the parts of the computer required by the next event or operation.

Figure A–3. Assembly Robot—Control Automation Inc. Mini Sembler™ Robot for high precision assembly applications.

asynchronous operation. Describes machine operations that are triggered successively, not by a clock, but by the completion of an operation.

atom. An individual number or symbol. A proposition in logic that cannot be broken down into other propositions. An indivisible element.

ATR. ATR detects and classifies military targets from sensor images. The system integrates low-level image processing and high-level, domain-specific rules for object detection and identification. ATR first exploits contextual information (e.g., temporal, structural) to form hypotheses about the existence of certain objects in the image. It then seeks the evidence required to satisfy those hypotheses. Further hypotheses are generated by model-driven processing that redirects low-level image processing algorithms in order to gain new information from the image. The system uses frames and certainty factors together with an object-oriented control scheme to represent and access its knowledge. ATR is implemented in ZETALISP. It was developed at Hughes Aircraft Company.

ATTENDING. Instructs medical students in anesthesiology by critiquing their plans for anesthetic management. The system presents students with hypothetical patients about to undergo surgery and analyzes the management plans devised by the students. The system bases its analysis on an assessment of the risks involved in the context of the patient's medical problems. The critique produced by the system has the form of commentary, typically 4 or 5 paragraphs of English text. ATTENDING was developed at the Yale University School of Medicine.

attenuation. The reduction in the magnitude of a signal as it passes through a system. Opposite of gain or amplification.

attribute. A simple property attached to an object. In production systems the data memory may be represented as a set of attribute-value elements.

attribute-value element. A data structure for elements in data memory that encodes knowledge and objects in the form of a set of ordered pairs, the first element of which specifies the identity of an attribute and the second element of which specifies the value that the attribute assumes for that object.

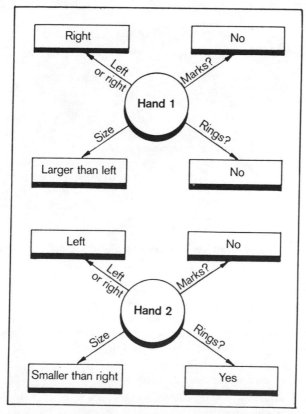

Figure A–4. Attribute-Value Element—Attributes and values of two obejcts (hands). *Reprinted with the permission of John Wiley and Sons, from "Expert Systems— Artificial Intelligence in Business" by Paul Harmon and David King.*

AUDITOR. Helps a professional auditor evaluate a client's potential for defaulting on a loan. The system uses information about the client's payment history, economic status, credit standing, and other knowledge to determine whether money should be held in reserve to cover a client's loan default. AUDITOR is a rule-based system implemented in AL/X, a derivative of KAS. It operates in a version of AL/X adapted for use in PASCAL systems on microcomputers. The system was developed at the University of Illinois, Champaign-Urbana, as a Ph.D. dissertation.

Augmented Transition Network. A grammar representation used in natural language systems to parse input. Augmented Transition Networks are strings representing legal sequences of parts of speech. Input text is compared with the strings. If the parts of speech represented by words in the input match the parts of speech in an Augmented Transition Network string, the system recognizes the input as legal. Actions to be performed on or with input may be associated with an ATN.

automated guided vehicle system. Vehicles that are equipped with automatic guidance equipment and follow a prescribed guide path that interfaces with workstations for automatic or manual loading and unloading. In FMSs guided vehicles generally operate under computer control.

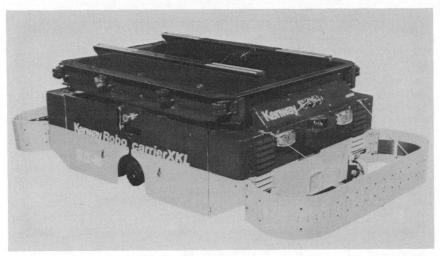

Figure A–5. Automated guided vehicle systems—Kenway Robo Carrier automated guided vehicle system.

automated storage and retrieval system. A high-density rack storage system with rail running vehicles serving the rack structure for automatic loading and unloading. Vehicles interface with automated guided vehicle system, car-on-track, towline, or other conveyor systems for automatic storage and retrieval of loads.

automatic controller. A device or system that measures a quantity, compares that with a desired value, and, if necessary, initiates a correcting action.

automatic error correction. A technique employed within a controlled system to detect errors and eventually correct them.

automatic program synthesis. The automatic computer construction of programs from rigorous and nonalgorithmic specifications describing what the programs should do.

automatic program verification. The use, by a computer, of mathematical techniques to show that programs behave according to their formal specifications, in order to prove the correctness of programs.

automatic programming. Several projects are under way to develop computer programs that will, in turn, write other computer programs from a programmer's specifications. If successful, such "higher level" programs will be used to "automate" major portions of computer programming. The application of artificial intelligence techniques to the general goals of automatic program construction and automatic program transformation.

automation. When a machine, process, or system, is operated by mechanical, or electronic devices and requires minimum human participation during the controlled operation, that is known as automation.

autonomous. A system capable of independent action.

AUTOVISION^R **II.** Machine vision system for smart robot applications. AUTOVISION^R II is a product of Automatix, Incorporated, of Billerica, Massachusetts.

auxiliary memory. The storage area that is supplementary to main memory. No manipulation of data can take place in auxiliary memory. That kind of memory is usually much slower than main memory.

auxiliary storage. Storage that supplements main memory devices, such as disk or drum storage.

axes. The directions of movements, for example, x, y, z, as in numerical machine tool control. A rotary or translational (sliding) joint in the robot. Also called degree of freedom.

azimuth. Direction of a straight line to a point in a horizontal plane, expressed as the angular distance from a reference line, such as the observer's line of view.

B

BABY. BABY aids clinicians by monitoring patients in a newborn intensive care unit (NICU). The system attempts to find clinically important patterns in the medical and demographic data about NICU patients. It monitors all on-line data in the NICU, keeps track of the clinical states of the patients, suggests further evaluation for important findings, and answers questions about the patients. BABY contains neonatology medical expertise for interpreting the clinical and demographic data. It is a forward chaining, rule-based system that uses rules embedded in a PROSPEC-TOR-like network. The system handles certainty by using a Bayesian probabilistic method similar to that used in PROSPECTOR. BABY is written in PASCAL and is situated within the ADVISE system, an integrated, rule-based software environment. It was developed at the University of Illinois, Champaign-Urbana.

back-chaining. A control procedure that attempts to achieve goals recursively, first by enumerating antecedents that would be sufficient for goal attainment and second by attempting to achieve or establish the antecedents themselves as goals.

background. Portion of a display not changed during an application.

background display list. Display list not requiring rapid refresh, different from foreground display list.

backtracking. A search procedure that makes guesses at various points during problem solving and returns to a previous point to make another choice when a guess leads to an unacceptable result. Returning the database, or conditions, in a system to a previous state in order to try an alternative solution path.

Backus-Naur Form. A formal language for expressing context-free grammars. A grammar consists of a set of rewrite rules, each of which has a left-hand side and a right-hand side, separated by the metalanguage symbol ::= . The left-hand side of each rule is a nonterminal symbol of the grammar, and the right-hand side is a sequence of nonterminal symbols and terminal symbols. Nonterminal symbols are usually surrounded by the angle brackets < and >. Extended versions of Backus-Naur Form include additional metalanguage symbols to denote repetition and alternation.

backward-chaining. A problem-solving method that starts with a goal to be achieved and recursively expands each unsolved goal into a set of simpler subgoals until either a solution is found or all goals have been expanded into their simplest components.

When a subgoal is solved, it backs up its solution to its parent goal. In production systems with backward-chaining architecture, the applicability of a rule is determined by examining its conclusions rather than its antecedent conditions.

Band-Pass Filter. Filter that allows only specific segments of the frequency to be passed.

bandwidth. Indicates the speed at which a monitor can accept data from the computer and is measured in megahertz. That number is the key to a monitor's overall performance. Video bandwidth constrains the screen refresh rate, active display area, pixel resolution, and image sharpness. Higher bandwidths allow steadier, sharper, more detailed images.

bang-bang-robot. A simple robot, often with only 2 or 3 degrees of freedom, which transfers items from place to place by means of point-to-point moves. Little or no trajectory control is available.

bar operators. Convolution masks to detect second derivatives of image brightness in particular directions.

base. The platform or structure to which a robot arm is attached, the end of a kinematic chain of arm links and joints opposite to that which grasps or processes external objects.

BASIC. An algebralike language used for problem solving by those who may not be professional programmers. BASIC stands for Beginner's All Purpose Symbolic Instructional Coded.

batch processing. The practice of running a stream of programs through the computer so that each is executed start to finish without interruption. As opposed to multiprogramming or time sharing.

BATTLE. Provides weapon allocation recommendations to military commanders in combat situations. The system improves the performance of the U.S. Marine Corps' Marine Integrated Fire and Air Support System by providing timely recommendations for the allocation of a set of weapons to a set of targets. To address the critical time aspect of real battle situations, the system uses a best-first strategy during consultations, considering first those propositions (battle conditions) likely to have the most cost-effective influence on higher-level propositions. BATTLE represents knowledge as rules with associated PROSPECTOR-like certainty values. BATTLE was developed at the Naval Research Laboratory in Washington, D.C.

baud. A unit of speed for data communications, equal to the number of times per second a signal is altered. Although baud usually is equivalent to bit rate, coding techniques make it possible to send more than 1 bit at a time in some systems. Thus, baud and bit rate may not always be the same.

BDS. BDS helps locate faulty modules in a large signal-switching network, an electronic device called a baseband distribution subsystem. The system uses test equipment readings to isolate faulty printed circuit boards or other chassis-mounted parts that could have caused the failure. BDS bases its diagnosis on both the strategies of the expert diagnostitian and knowledge about the structure, function, and causal relations of the components in the electronic device. BDS is implemented in the LES (Lockheed Expert System) language and uses a rule-based representation scheme with backward chaining. It was developed at the Lockheed Palo Alto Research Laboratory.

BEAGLE. Warm Boot Ltd. (UK)/VRS Consulting Inc. (USA) developed induction system. BEAGLE takes a database of examples and produces a set of decision rules from them. The rules can be dumped as Pascal and/or Fortran routines. (Basic and C are optional extras.) The induction method employs an evolutionary or "genetic" strategy, based on competition among proposed rules (which can be user- or machine-generated) and survival of the "fittest." IBM PC or compatibles with at least 12K RAM. A hard disc is recommended. (VAX/BEAGLE runs under VMS.) PC/BEAGLE $150; VAX/BEAGLE $1500. Educational discounts available.

beam penetration crt. Cathode ray tube that produces color by varying the electron beam penetration of a multilayer phosphor display surface.

belief. A statement that is not known or assumed to be true, as contrasted with a fact. The confidence in the reliability of a statement that is not known or assumed to be true. The degree of confidence may be indexed by a certainty or confidence factor.

beta site. A user's site or facility selected by mutual agreement between the user and the vendor for testing out a new system, application package, or hardware or software enhancement before its sale to other customers of the vendor.

bidirectional data bus. A data bus in which digital information can be transferred in either direction.

bilateral manipulator. A robot master-slave manipulator with symmetric force reflection where both master and slave arms have sensors and acutators such that in any degree of freedom a positional error between the master and slave results in equal and opposing forces applied to the master and the slave arms. A two-armed manipulator (can refer to 2 arms performing a task in cooperative movements or can refer to 2 arms in the sense of a master-slave manipulator).

binary code. Computer language made up of 1s and 0s arranged to represent words of computer instruction.

binary image. A black and white image represented as 0s and 1s, in which the objects appear as silhouettes.

binary number system. A number system using the base 2, as opposed to the decimal number system, which uses the base 10. The binary system is comparable to the decimal system in using the concepts of absolute value and positional value.

binary picture. A machine vision system picture in which objects are seen in silhouette only. A picture in which everything is either black or white.

binding. An association between a variable and a value for that variable that holds within some scope, such as the scope of a rule, function call, or procedure invocation.

Thomas O. Binford. Thomas O. Binford is a professor in the Computer Science Department at Stanford University. He holds a Ph.D. in Physics from the University of Wisconsin, 1965, and a B.S. in physics from Pennsylvania State University, 1957. He is a Leader of the Computer Vision and Robotics group at the Stanford Artificial Intelligence Laboratory. From 1967 to 1970 he was research associate at the Artificial Intelligence Laboratory at M.I.T. Research topics included artificial intelligence, computer vision, representation of shape, and LISP programming systems. Professor Binford has been a member of the NASA committees on Automation and Future Missions in Space and Machine Intelligence and Robotics and a member of IEEE Pattern Recognition Technical Committee. He has chaired 4 conferences on computer vision and has served as chairman or cochairman of other major conferences. He has contributed extensive written works to a variety of professional forums.

bit. An abbreviation of "binary digit" that is the smallest unit of data for a digital computer. A bit can be 1 or 0, the equivalent of yes or no, or on or off.

bit control. A means of transmitting serial data in which each bit has a significant meaning and a single character is surrounded with start and stop bits.

bit map. A grid pattern of bits (i.e., ON and/or OFF) stored in memory and used to generate the image or a raster-scan display. In a display bit map, each bit corresponds to a dot in a raster display image. Every bit map allows 1 logical bit of information (such as intensity or color) to be stored per dot (pixel) on the screen. The intensity or color of each point in the image can be represented as a group of bits, for example, as a pattern of 0s and 1s. The entire image, being an area of points, can be represented as an array of those groups in computer memory, on magnetic tape or any other storage medium.

bit map display. Display consisting of a large array of tiny, individually controllable dots that allows a programmer to turn each individual pixel on or off. Advanced types may have a million or more dots, each of which may be more or less bright, in color, or both.

bit plane. Hardware used as a storage medium for a bit map.

bit rate. The speed at which bits are transmitted, usually expressed in bits per second.

bit string. A string of binary digits (bits) in which the position of each binary digit is considered as an independent unit.

blackboard. A system architecture that employs a database or memory that is accessible to several processes, called knowledge sources. The memory that is common to all processes serves as a basis for communication of intermediate results among rules or knowledge sources. That architecture was introduced in the HEARSAY speech-understanding system.

blackboard approach. A problem-solving approach whereby the various system elements communicate with each other via a common working data storage called a blackboard.

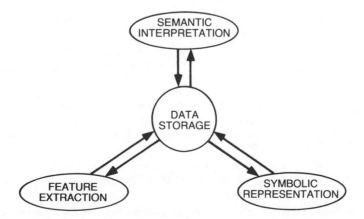

Figure B–1. Blackboard Approach—In blackboard approach the system elements communicate with each other via common working data storage.

blackboard architecture. An expert system design in which several independent knowledge bases each examine a common working memory, called a "blackboard." An agenda-based control system continually examines all of the possible pending actions and chooses the one to try next.

blanked area. Display space where display elements are not visible.

blanked vector. Vector instruction that produces no visible output but changes the beam position.

blanking. The process of decreasing (or increasing) the display-signal level so that no visible retrace will appear on the display screen.

BLAST. A knowledge-based design aid for the net-analysis task being implemented by the Carnegie Group. The net-analysis task covers those aspects of digital system design involved in bridging the ideal world of perfect wires and components to the real world of electrical noise and technology limitations. Net analysis keeps logic designers from being overwhelmed by such technology-specific details. BLAST performs an analysis on all possible types of interconnection structures that will be used in designing a specific system. The result is a set of abstract wiring-rules that will properly constrain the design. By designing a system that conforms to those rules, one can avoid most of the aforementioned problems.

blind search. An ordered approach that does not rely on knowledge for searching for a solution.

blinking. An operator aid that makes a predefined graphic entity blink on the cathode ray tube to attract the attention of the operator.

blob. Any group of connected pixels in a binary image. A generic term including both "objects" and "holes." A light or dark area in the image transmitted by a vision system's camera. A washer is a dark blob with a light blob in the middle.

block. A group of machine words considered or transported as a unit. In flowcharts, each block represents a logical unit of programming.

block statement. A block statement is a single statement that may contain a sequence of statements. It may also include a declarative part and exception handlers; their effects are local to the block statement.

blocks world. A small artificial world, consisting of blocks and pyramids, used to develop ideas in computer vision, robotics, and natural language interfaces.

BLUE BOX. Advises a physician on the selection of appropriate therapy for a patient complaining of depression. The system uses knowledge about the patient's symptoms and information about the patient's medical, psychiatric, drug, and family histories to diagnose the type and extent of depression and to suggest a management plan for controlling it. That plan includes decisions about hospitalization and drug treatments. BLUE BOX is a rule-based system implemented in EMYCIN and developed at Stanford University. The system was tested in the environment of the Palo Alto V.A. Mental Health Clinical Research Center.

body. Defines the execution of a subprogram, package, or task. A body stub is a form of body that indicates that this execution is defined in a separately compiled subunit.

Boolean algebra. A process of reasoning or a deductive system of theorems using symbolic logic and dealing with classes, propositions, or on-off circuit elements such as AND, OR, NOT, EXCEPT, IF, THEN, etc., to permit mathematical calculations.

Boolean logic/operation. Algebraic or symbolic logic formulas, adapted from George Boole's work, used to expand design-rules, check programs, and expedite the construction of geometric figures.

bootstrap. A technique for loading the first few instructions of a routine into storage and then using those instructions to bring the rest of the routine into the computer from an input device. That usually involves either the entering of a few instructions manually or the use of a special key on the console.

BORIS. Experimental, narrative-understanding natural language expert system developed by Roger Schank and his students.

bottom-up. A strategy of proceeding from the simple and concrete to the complex and abstract. As applied to a problem-solving strategy, it refers to the method of starting with the accumulation of results from simple observations or facts and proceeding to more complex combinations or hypotheses. Production systems with forward-chaining architecture often engage in bottom-up problem solving. As applied to a programming methodology, the term refers to a style in which simple program components are written before the more complex ones. The opposite strategy is top-down.

Figure B–2. Bottom-Up—A hierarchical bottom-up approach for expert systems.

bottom-up control structure. A problem-solving approach that employs forward reasoning from current or initial conditions. Also referred to as an event-driven or data-driven control structure.

bound. A variable that has been assigned a value by the process of binding is said to be bound to that value.

boundaries. Edge of a blob or object. Outside limits of a process or procedure.

bounding box. Rectangle with dimensions coinciding with width and height of a display entity to constitute limits.

boxing. Clipping test that uses a bounding box to check position of clipping boundaries.

J. Michael Brady. J. Michael Brady is senior research scientist in the Artificial Intelligence (AI) Laboratory of M.I.T. He has held that position since he joined the institution in March 1980. Before that he was on the faculty of the Department of Computer Science of the University of Essex, England. He is also the founding editor with Professor Richard Paul, Purdue University, of the *International Journal of Robotics Research*. Dr. Brady received a first-class honors B.Sc. degree in mathematics in 1966 and the degree of M.Sc. in 1968 from the University of Manchester, England. He completed his Ph.D. at the Mathematics Department of the Institute for Advanced Studies of the Australian National University, Canberra, Australia, in 1970. Michael Brady's research interests are in artificial intelligence and, more particularly, image understanding and robotics. In computer vision, his current research concerns the representation of 2- and 3-dimensional shapes, and he has developed a representation of 2-dimensional shape called smoothed local symmetries. In manipulation, Dr. Brady's robotics research is the application of techniques for depth perception to the problem of picking objects out of a bin. Dr. Brady is the author of *The Theory of Computer Science: a Programming Approach,* and he has edited several other books. He has had many articles published in professional journals, conferences, and other forums.

branch instruction. An instruction that causes a program jump to a specified address and execution of the instruction at that address. During the execution of the branch instruction, the central processor replaces the contents of the program counter with the specified address.

branching. Transfer of control program execution to an instruction other than the next sequential instruction. If the next instruction selected is predetermined, the branch is an unconditional branch; if the next instruction is selected on the basis of some sort of test, it is a conditional branch. A robot must possess the ability to execute conditional branches in order to react intelligently to its environment. The wider the variety of tests it can perform, the better it can react.

breadth-first search. An approach in which, starting with the root node, the nodes in the search tree are generated and examined level by level before moving to the next level. The approach is guaranteed to find an optimal solution if it exists.

breakpoint. Pertaining to a type of instruction, instruction digit, or other condition used to interrupt or stop a computer at a particular place in a program. A place in a program where such an interruption occurs or can be made to occur.

break package. A mechanism in a programming or knowledge engineering language for telling the program where to stop so the programmer can examine the values of variables at that point.

brightness. A psychophysiological attribute of visual perception in which a source appears to emit or reflect more or less light. Its psychophysical, photometric equivalent is luminance.

James R. Brink. James R. Brink, manager of Artificial Intelligence/Knowledge-Based Systems, has more than 7 years' experience in the field of computer science, including nearly 5 years in the area of artificial intelligence. His professional history includes establishing the AI technology thrust at Battelle-Columbus, managing software development projects, designing and implementing information systems, automating office procedures, and conducting statistical analyses. Currently, he conducts applied research in the field of artificial intelligence, principally in the development of knowledge-based expert systems and natural-language processing systems. He received M.S. degrees in mathematics (1975) and computer information science (1979) from The Ohio State University. He has a Ph.D. in mathematics from that institution.

bubble memory. Provides serial access nonvolatile memory storage of data in magnetic domains (or bubbles). Bubble memory is characterized by very low access times and high cost, but it is able to store data after power is removed. That nonvolatility makes it well-suited for portable applications in which disk storage is impractical.

Bruce G. Buchanan. Bruce G. Buchanan is professor of computer science research at Stanford University. He was a major contributor to the heuristic search model of scientific inference in the DENDRAL program, which provides explanations of analytic data in organic chemistry. He built on that with the METADENDRAL program, which finds regularities in large sets of data and proposes general principles to account for them. His interest in biomedical applications of artificial intelligence has led to interdisciplinary projects at the Medical School, including work in the MYCIN program that provides computer-assisted therapy consultation. MYCIN research is also being extended to intelligent computer-aided instruction.

buffer. A storage device used to compensate for a difference in rate of flow of data or time of occurrence of events when transmitting data from 1 device to another.

bug. A flaw in the design or implementation of a software program or hardware design that causes erroneous results or malfunctions.

BUILD. An expert system that solves problems by, in part, mimicking common-sense strategies.

bundled feature. A hardware or software module sold as part of a package and not available separately. It may consist of interrelated software programs or hardware or both.

burst. In data communication a sequence of signals counted as 1 unit in accordance with some specific criterion or measure.

bus. A means of distributing a set of signals so the computer can be interfaced with memory and external devices.

bye. A sequence of adjacent bits, representing a character that is operated on as a unit. Usually shorter than a word. A measure of the memory capacity of a system or of an individual storage unit.

C

C. C is a programming language for procedure-oriented representation. A relatively low-level and efficient language, it is often used for writing operating systems and has been called a system programming language. The UNIX operating system itself is written almost entirely in C. C deals directly with characters, numbers, and addresses rather than with character strings, sets, lists, or arrays, as a higher-level language might. It offers straightforward tests, loops, and subprograms but not more exotic control, such as parallel operations or coroutines. C was designed for use with UNIX operating systems and operates on a wide variety of computers (e.g., DEC VAXs). It was developed by Bell Laboratories and is available as a commercial system.

C-13. C-13 (Carbon 13) aids organic chemists in determining the structure of newly isolated, naturally occurring compounds. It helps the chemist analyze carbon-13 nuclear magnetic resonance spectra by using a constraint refinement search to determine the arrangement of atoms and bonds of complex organic molecules. The system's knowledge base contains rules relating substructural (bonding) and spectral (resonance) features, derived automatically from data for known structures. C-13 was developed as part of the DENDRAL project and follows DENDRAL's plan-generate-test paradigm. The system is implemented in INTERLISP. It was developed at Stanford University.

CAD/CAM. Computer-Aided Design/Computer-Aided Manufacturing.

CADHELP. CADHELP simulates an expert demonstrating the operation of the graphical features of a computer-aided design (CAD) subsystem for designing digital logic circuits. It explains to the user how to use the CAD subsystem, tailoring its explanations to fit the needs and desires of the user. It provides explanations in English when the user makes an error or asks for help and generates the text of the explanation from its knowledge base in a dynamic way, relying on scripts associated with the different features of the CAD subsystem. As the user becomes more experienced, the explanations created by CADHELP become more terse. Knowledge in the system is organized as a set of cooperating subsystems or "experts" controlled by a higher-level task manager program. The system is implemented in FRANZ LISP and runs on a DEC VAX 11/780 under UNIX. CADHELP was developed at the University of Connecticut.

CADUCEUS. Medical diagnosis expert system for internal medicine under development by Harry E. Pople, Jr., and Jack D. Myers, M.D., at the University of Pittsburgh. Formerly called INTERNIST.

CAI/CBI. Computer-Aided Instruction/Computer-Based Instruction.

CALLISTO. The CALLISTO project examines the extension and application of artificial intelligence techniques to the domain of large project management. Managing large projects entails many tasks. CALLISTO provides decision support and decision-making facilities. The ability to extend the capabilities found in classical approaches is due to CALLISTO's project model. Starting with the SRL knowledge representation language, a set of conceptual primitives including time, causality, object descriptions, and possession is used to define the concept of activities and product. The language is further extended by the inclusion of constraint language, representing the constraints among activities. The modeling language provides CALLISTO with the ability to model both products and activities in enough detail that inferential processing may be performed. CALLISTO's decision support and decision-making capabilities include: interactive change order management for products, multi-level scheduling of activities, rule-based analysis and maintenance of activities, and automatic generation of graphic displays of project models.

call. The action of bringing a computer program, a routine, or subroutine into effect, usually by specifying the entry conditions and jumping to an entry point. A special type of jump in which the central processor is logically required to "remember" the contents of the program counter at the time that the jump occurs. That allows the processor later to resume execution of the main program, when it is finished with the last instruction of the subroutine.

calling sequence. A basic set of instructions used to begin, initialize, or transfer control to and return from a subroutine.

CARGuide. Helps drivers find routes and navigate in city streets. The system uses the starting and destination locations, together with its map information, to calculate an optimum route from starting point to destination. Optimum route finding is accomplished using a combination of a divide-and-conquer method, precomputed routes, and Dijkstra's shortest-path algorithm. Once found, the route is displayed and highlighted on a graphical display of a street map. During the trip the car's position along the route is updated and displayed. Before each intersection, the system pronounces a direction (straight, left, or right) and the name of the street to take. The street map data base contains information relating street names to intersections and intersections to routes. It also contains pictorial information for picture generation. CARGuide was developed at Carnegie-Mellon University.

Carnegie Group, Inc. The Carnegie Group specializes in the applications of artificial intelligence to manufacturing. It produces interactive knowledge-based systems to solve complex problems inherent in industrial scenarios and also software tools to increase the productivity of engineers engaged in artificial intelligence applications. The Group's expertise combines synergistically to develop AI systems that: enhance productivity, decision making from engineering to production management, process control and diagnosis; provide user-friendly, natural language interfaces to expert systems and other complex software products; provide intelligent building blocks that aid the knowledge engineer. The group's expertise is in 3 major areas: automated engineering design—CAD/CAM/CAE expert systems; production management—"intelligent, reactive" management of the complete floor of the factory and project/product Management; and knowledge-based management of engineering and software products and activities. Founded in 1983 by 4 Carnegie-Mellon University computer scientists, the group has initiated and directed a variety of successful projects for large industrial sponsors. Its products include: language craft, knowledge craft, and manufacturing applications software for production management, scenario exploration and simulation, project management, process diagnosis/remote sensor analysis, natural language access to data bases, and natural language access to expert systems.

Cartesian coordinates. A set of 3 numbers defining the location of a point within a rectilinear coordinate system consisting of 3 perpendicular axes (x, y, z).

Cartesian robot. A robot in which there are linear motions arrayed in mutually perpendicular directions, i.e., east-west, north-south, and up-down, as well as rotary motions to change orientation.

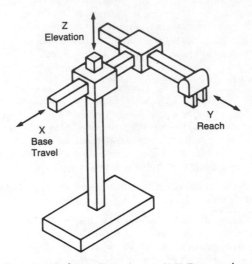

Figure C–1. Cartesian Robot—Cartesian or X-Y-Z arm robot manipulator.

cascade. An arrangement of 2 or more similar circuits in which the output of 1 circuit provides the input of the next.

CASNET/GLAUCOMA. CASNET/GLAUCOMA diagnoses disease states related to glaucoma and prescribes plans or therapies for treating them. The system bases its decisions on knowledge about the relations between patient symptoms, test results, internal abnormal conditions, disease states, and treatment plans. The system provides a narrative interpretation of the case and can retrieve literature references to support its conclusions. Knowledge is represented in a particular type of semantic net known as a causal-association network. The system is implemented in FORTRAN and was developed at Rutgers University.

cathode ray tube. A type of graphic display that produces an image by directing a beam of electrons to activate a phosphor-coated surface in a vacuum tube. The cathode ray tube (crt) is the most common type of monitor used in interactive graphics systems.

causal model. Model in which the causal relations among various actions and events are represented explicitly.

cell. The structure used in a computer to represent a list. Each cell has 2 fields for storing data and pointing to other cells in the list.

CENTAUR. Assists pulmonary physiologists in diagnostic interpretation of pulmonary function tests. The system uses measurements of the amount of gas in the lungs and the rates of flow of gases into and out of the lungs to determine the presence and severity of lung disease in the patient. The expertise contained in CENTAUR includes pulmonary physiology and prototypical lung test results for each pulmonary disease or subtype. Knowledge is represented as a combination of frames and rules, and certainty measures similar to EMYCIN's certainty factors are used to indicate how closely the actual data match the expected data values of the prototype. In addition, CENTAUR has an explanation capability that provides justifications from an underlying model of pulmonary physiology. CENTAUR is implemented in INTERLISP. It was developed at Stanford University.

certainty. The degree of confidence one has in a fact or relationship. As used in artificial intelligence, it contrasts with probability, which is the likelihood that an event will occur.

certainty factor. A numerical weight given to a fact or relationship to indicate the confidence one has in the fact or relationship. Those numbers behave differently than probability coefficients. In general, methods for manipulating certainty factors are more informal than approaches to combining probabilities. Most rule-based systems use certainty factors rather than probabilities.

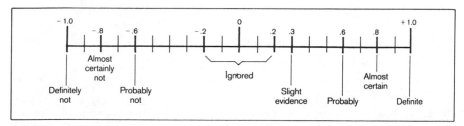

Figure C–2. Certainty Factor—Confidence represented by the certainty factors used in MYCIN. *Reprinted with the permission of John Wiley and Sons, from "Expert Systems—Artificial Intelligence in Business" by Paul Harmon and David King.*

chain code. A boundary representation that starts with an initial point and stores a chain of directions to successive points.

chaining. Process by which expert systems link together information and steps during problem solving. Forward chaining is the model used to arrive at the solution; back or backward chaining explains the steps taken to arrive at that solution.

character. An alphabetical, numerical, or special graphic symbol used as part of the organization, control, or representation of data.

character recognition. The identification of characters by automatic means.

character set. A set of unique representations called characters, such as the 26 letters of the English alphabet or the decimal digits 0 through 9.

characters per screen. The maximum number of characters that can fit—or that the manufacturer recommends placing—into the display area. For comparison, a standard

25-line-by-80-column display contains 2000 characters. That measure of resolution should be of greatest interest to those seeking alphanumeric or test displays.

characters per second. A measure of the speed with which an alphanumeric terminal can process data.

chip. The commonly used name for an integrated circuit.

chroma. A dimension of the Munsell color system that corresponds most closely to saturation. A distinction is sometimes made that saturation is relative, whereas chroma is absolute.

chromaticity. Dominant wavelength and purity of a color as objectively measured; corresponds to hue and saturation of the color without regard to brightness.

chrominance. The colorimetric difference (dominant wavelength and purity) between any color and a reference "white" of equal luminance. In 3-dimensional color space, chrominance is a vector that lies in a plane of constant luminance.

chunk. A collection of facts stored and retrieved as a single unit. The limitations of working memory are usually defined in terms of the number of chunks that can be handled simultaneously.

CICS. A mainframe operating system and program product for IBM mainframes. It allows for concurrent processing of information from individual terminals using customer-designed parameters. Used extensively for creating databases and maintenance systems.

clause. A syntactic construction containing a subject and a predicate and forming part of a statement in logic or part of a sentence in a grammar.

clear. To replace information in a storage unit by zero (or blank, in some machines).

clip boundary. Display space boundary beyond which graphics display is blanked.

clipping. The process of removing portions of an image that are outside the boundaries of the display screen.

clock. A device or a part of a device that generates all the timing pulses for the coordination of a digital system. System clocks usually generate 2 or more clock phases. Each phase is a separate square-wave pulse train output.

clock rate. The speed (frequency) at which the processor operates as determined by the rate at which words or bits are transferred through internal logic sequences.

clocking. A technique used to synchronize a sending and a receiving data communications device. Permits synchronous transmission at high speeds.

closed loop. A control system in which output data are measured and fed back to the control for comparison with the input data, so that information flows back and forth.

CLOT. Assists physicians with the evaluation of evidence for disorders of the blood coagulation system. The system diagnoses a bleeding defect by identifying which of the two coagulation subsystems, the platelet-vascular or the coagulative, might be defective. The primary motivation for implementing CLOT was to study knowledge acquisition tools and techniques; thus its medical expertise was not refined or fully tested. CLOT is a backward chaining, rule-based system implemented in EMYCIN, making use of EMYCIN's knowledge acquisition, explanation, and certainty factor mechanisms. The system was developed at Stanford University.

CMOS Technology. The current state-of-the-art technology for silicon chips used in computers. It will probably be replaced by GaAs (Gallium Arsenide) technology when the latter becomes cost effective.

code. The text of a computer program readable either by people or by machine.

CODES. Helps a data base developer who wants to use the IDEF1 approach for defining the conceptual schema of a data base. While IDEF1 is useful as an approach, its intricate rules often hamper its application. The developer describes the features and relationships desired in the data base under the interactive guidance of CODES. The system then uses its knowledge of IDEF1 rules and heuristics to generate a conceptual schema of the data base. Knowledge in CODES is represented as rules that use a backward chaining control strategy. Codes is implemented in UCI LISP. It was developed at the University of Southern California.

coding. The process of preparing a program from the flow chart defining an algorithm.

cognition. An intellectual process by which knowledge is gained about perceptions or ideas.

cognitive intelligence. Ability to plan and establish goals and to model the environment based upon sensory input.

cognitive modeling. The simulation of human cognition (i.e., perception, skilled action, memory, and thinking) in terms of information processing. Cognitive models often take the form of computer programs.

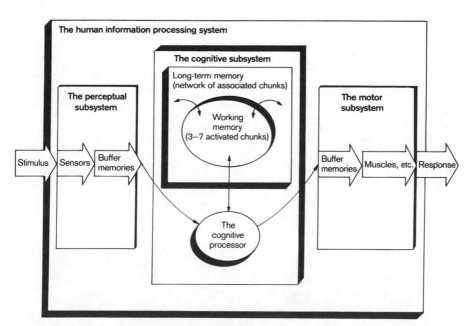

Figure C-3. Cognitive Modeling—An overview of the human information processing system. *Reprinted with the permission of John Wiley and Sons, from "Expert Systems—Artificial Intelligence in Business" by Paul Harmon and David King.*

Cognitive Science. The field that investigates the details of the mechanics of human intelligence to determine the processes that produce intelligence in a given situation.

coherence. Assumption used in raster scan technology that attributes the same value of an individual pixel to its adjacent pixel.

collection. The entire set of objects created by evaluation of allocators for an access type.

Allan Collins. Allan Collins is a principal scientist at Bolt Beranek and Newman Inc., a research firm in Cambridge, Massachusetts. He is a specialist in the fields of cognitive science and human semantic processing and also in the use of computers in education. He is one of the founders and served as the first chairman of the Cognitive Science Society, and he is widely known for his work with Dr. M. R. Quillian on semantic memory. He was also one of the original editors of the journal *Cognitive Science.* He received his doctorate in psychology at the Human Performance Center of the University of Michigan. His work there was in human information processing with Dr. P. M. Fitts and then in language and memory with Drs. E. Martin and A. W. Melton. Before that, he received a master's degree in communication sciences, where he acquired a background in artificial intelligence, mathematical logic, and linguistics. From 1970 to 1973 Dr. Collins directed a project with the late Dr. Jaime Carbonell on the SCHOLAR CAI system, where knowledge was structured like human memory so that it could be used in a variety of ways. From 1975 to 1979 Dr. Collins directed a project to develop an intelligent CAI system (the WHY system) that used a Socratic (or case) method for tutoring causal knowledge and reasoning. In conjunction with this project he developed a formal theory of Socratic tutoring in computational form, derived from analyses of a variety of inquiry teaching dialogues.

color contrast. The ratio of the luminance values of 2 colors.

color look-up table. Table providing a limited color selection from a large theoretical color range. Also called color map.

color purity. A psycho-physical measurement of the degree to which a color is free of white light. Its psycho-physiological equivalent is saturation. The term is also used to define the absence of color contamination in the operation of a 3-color cathode ray tube display.

colorimetric purity. The relative luminances of the spectrum and "white" components of a color.

colorizing. A method for arbitrarily assigning colors to image data. For instance, a different color can be assigned to each gray level in a black-and-white image.

combinatorial explosion. The rapid growth of possibilities as the search space expands. If each decision branch point has an average of n branches, the search space tends to expand as n^d, as the depth of search, d, increases.

COMMON LISP. The LISP (LISt Processing) language is a major programming language that has been successfully used to develop expert systems, natural language processors, and other artificial intelligence applications. LISP is a programming language for procedural representation. The new LISP dialect is designed to provide a standard LISP that is compatible with a wide range of computers. It incorporates an extensive and complex set of data types and control structures into a portable system. It was developed at Carnegie-Mellon University. COMMON LISP is available as a commercial system from a number of companies, e.g., from Gold Hill Computers as GCLISP and from Digital Equipment Corporation as VAX LISP. In contrast to conventional programming languages, LISP is a "symbolic" language—it uses symbols and lists rather than numbers or characters to develop applications for processes that are characterized by complex rules and relationships. Common LISP is a new standard LISP dialect, designed to provide compatibility across a wide range of computers. Widely endorsed by industry and funded and supported by the Defense Advanced Research Projects Agency (DARPA), Common LISP standardizes the proven features of several major implementations of LISP.

common sense. The ability to act appropriately in everyday situations based on one's lifetime accumulation of experimental knowledge.

common sense reasoning. Low-level reasoning based on a wealth of experience.

communications link. Any mechanism, usually electrical, for the transmission of information. It may be serial or parallel, synchronous or asynchronous, half duplex or full duplex, encrypted or clear, or point-to-point, multidrop, or broadcast; it may transmit binary data or text; it may use standard character codes to represent text and control information, such as the ASCII, EBCDIC, or BAUDOT (tty) codes; or it may use a handshaking protocol to synchronize operations of computers or devices at opposite ends of the link, such as BISYNC, HDLIC, or ADCCP.

Communications-Oriented Production System Language. CPSL is a LISP-based production system language, which was designed to expedite the development of expert systems. While CPSL has been used to develop an expert system for the design of fiber optic-based communications circuits, it is certainly not limited to such applications.

COMPASS. COMPASS analyzes telephone switching systems maintenance messages for GTE's No. 2 EAX Switch and suggests maintenance actions to perform. The system examines maintenance messages describing error situations that occurred during the telephone call-processing operation of the switch. It then identifies groups of messages that were probably caused by a common fault, determines the possible specific errors in the switch, and suggests maintenance actions to verify and remedy them. The system embodies the expertise of a top switch expert and integrates knowledge about individual switch structure, switch faults, maintenance messages, and possible maintenance actions. COMPASS is implemented in KEE and INTERLISP-D for use on Xerox 1108 workstations. It was developed by GTE Laboratories, Inc.

compatibility. The capability of using an instruction, program, or component on more than 1 computer with the same result.

compilation unit. The declaration or the body of a program unit, presented for compilation as an independent text. It is optionally preceded by a context clause, naming other compilation units upon which it depends by means of 1 or more with clauses.

compile. To prepare with a compiler an object language program from a symbolic language program by substituting machine-operation codes for the symbolic operation codes.

compiled knowledge. As a person acquires and organizes knowledge into chunks and networks, the knowledge becomes compiled. Some individuals compile knowledge into more and more abstract and theoretical patterns (deep knowledge). Others compile knowledge as a result of practical experience (surface knowledge). Most people begin by acquiring theoretical knowledge, and then, when they finish their schooling, they recompile what they have learned into practical heuristics. Expertise consists of large amounts of compiled knowledge.

compiler. A program that translates a source program written in a high-level language into an object program in a lower-level machine language. When a program is compiled, it usually runs faster than when the same program is interpreted.

compiler language. A computer language, more powerful than an assembly language, that instructs a compiler in translating a source language into a machine language. The machine-language result (object) from the compiler is a translated and expanded version of the original.

complement. To reverse all binary bit values (1s become 0s, 0s become 1s).

complementary color. A color that, when combined with another color, produces a reference "white" (black, gray, or white).

complex sensors. Vision, sonar, and tactile sensors that will enable a smart robot to interact with the work environment.

component. A value that is a part of a larger value or an object that is part of a larger object.

composite color. Color information encoded in a single video signal.

composite type. A composite type is one whose values have components. There are 2 kinds of composite type: array types and record types.

composition. A learning mechanism that combines 2 or more rules that fire in sequence to produce a single rule that has the net effect of the component rules. The name is derived by analogy to the mathematical concept of function composition.

compressed speech. A representation of speech in which some redundant features of the digitized representation have been removed.

computational logic. A science designed to make use of computers in logic calculus.

computed path control. A control scheme wherein the path of the manipulator end point is computed to achieve a desired result in conformance to a given criterion, such as an acceleration limit, a minimum time, etc.

computer architecture. The manner in which various computational elements are interconnected to achieve a computational function.

computer network. An interconnected set of communicating computers.

computer program. A sequence of instructions or statements necessary for achieving a certain result.

computer vision. Perception by a computer, based on visual sensory input, in which a symbolic description is developed of a scene depicted in an image. It is often a knowledge-based, expectation-guided process that uses models to interpret sensory data. Used somewhat synonymously with image understanding, scene analysis, and machine vision. **(See figure page 75)**

computer word. A sequence of bits or characters treated as a unit and capable of being stored in 1 computer location.

concatenate. To place end to end or link together. The result of concatenating "dfdfdf" with "abab" is "dfdfdfabab."

concept. A descriptive schema for a class of things or a particular instance of the schema with some of its general properties specialized to characterize the specific subclass or element that instantiates the class description.

conceptual dependency. An approach to natural language understanding in which sentences are translated into basic concepts expressed as a small set of semantic primitives. A conceptual dependency translates input into an internal representation usable by the system. A conceptual dependency makes use of a small number of

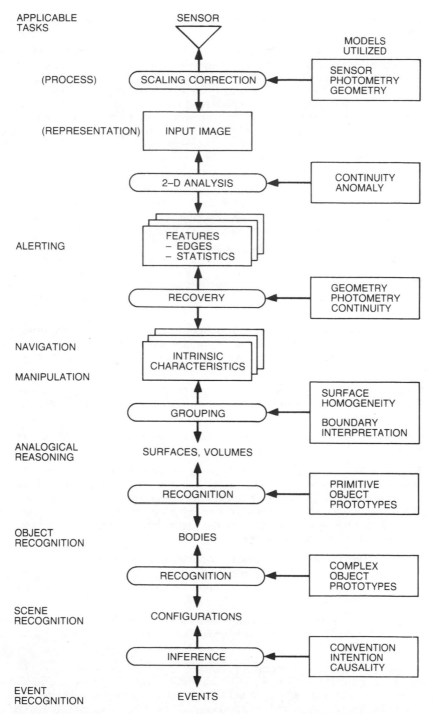

Figure C-4. Computer Vision—Computational architecture for a general purpose vision system.

basic components signifying meaning that can be combined to represent more complex meanings.

CONCHE. CONCHE is a system-building aid that helps check the completeness and consistency of domain knowledge and theory formation in the context of organic reaction mechanisms. Using examples presented during an interactive dialogue with a chemist, CONCHE derives a set of rules related to the relative strengths of organic acids. The essential domain theory is represented as MYCIN-like rules with additional domain knowledge encoded as facts in a semantic net. CONCHE uses a standard backward-chaining inference mechanism with MYCIN-like certainty factors. Explanations are presented in terms of rule chaining, facts accessed, and unsatisfied/unsatisfiable conditions. CONCHE is implemented in a combination of LISP and FUZZY. It was developed at the University of Leeds.

condition element. The left-hand side of a rule in a production system is sometimes expressed as a set of patterns or templates that are to be matched against the contents of data memory; each pattern is called a condition element. When a rule is instantiated, each condition element has been found to match 1 element of data memory.

conditional. In a computer, subject to the result of a comparison made during computation.

conditional breakpoint instruction. A conditional jump instruction that causes a computer to stop if a specified switch is set. The routine then may be allowed to proceed as coded, or a jump may be forced.

conditional jump. Also called conditional transfer of control. An instruction to a computer that will cause the proper 1 of 2 (or more) addresses to be used in obtaining the next instruction, depending on some property of 1 or more numerical expressions or other conditions.

confidence factor. The degree of confidence one has in a fact or relationship. As used in artificial intelligence, it contrasts with probability, which is the likelihood that an event will occur.

configure. To specify how the various parts of a computer system are to be arranged.

conflict resolution. The technique of resolving the problem of multiple matches in a rule-based system. When more than 1 rule's antecedent matches the data base, a conflict arises since every matched rule could be executed next, and only 1 rule can actually be executed next. A common conflict resolution method is priority ordering, where each rule has an assigned priority and the highest priority rule that currently matches the data base is executed next.

conflict resolution strategy. A specific principle that can be applied to partially order the instantiations in the conflict set. Each instantiation that is found to be dominated by another instantiation according to that principle is discarded from the conflict set, precluding it from firing on that cycle.

conflict set. The set of all instantiations generated by the match process during a recognize-act cycle. The process of conflict resolution selects 1 instantiation from the conflict set and fires it.

CONGEN. Helps structural chemists determine a set of possible structures for an unknown compound. The chemist provides CONGEN with spectroscopic and chemical data and a set of required and forbidden constraints on the possible interconnections among the atoms in the compound. CONGEN finds all possible ways of assembling the atoms into molecular structures that satisfy the specified constraints, and it presents the chemist with a set of structural drawings describing that exhaustive list of candidate structures. The system generates candidate structures by using a variety of graph-theoretic algorithms. CONGEN is implemented in INTERLISP. It was developed at Stanford University as part of the DENDRAL project and serves as Heuristic DENDRAL's hypothesis generator.

conjunct. One of several subproblems. Each of the component formulas in a logical conjunction.

conjunction. The Boolean operation whose result has the Boolean value 1 if and only if each operand has the Boolean value 1. A problem composed of several subproblems. A logical formula built by connecting other formulas by logic ANDs.

connected-speech system. A system that can understand a stream of speech in which the speaker does not pause between words to emphasize the beginnings and ends of words.

connected word recognition. An approach to speech recognition that recognizes words spoken in normal context.

connectives. Operators (e.g., AND, OR) connecting statements in logic so that the truth-value of the composite is determined by the truth-value of the components.

CONPHYDE. CONPHYDE helps chemical engineers select physical property estimation methods. The system handles the selection of vapor-liquid equilibrium coefficients for setting up a process simulation, given information about required accuracy and the expected concentrations, temperatures, and pressure ranges. Knowledge in CONPHYDE is represented in a combined rule-based and semantic net formalism, similar to PROSPECTOR. Its inferences are based on the use of certainty factors and Bayesian decision theory for propagating probabilities associated with the data. The system is implemented in KAS and uses the KAS explanation facility. CONPHYDE was developed at Carnegie-Mellon University.

consequent. The right side of a production rule. The result of applying a procedure.

CONSIGHT. Industrial machine vision object-recognition system, which was developed by General Motors and uses special lighting to produce silhouettelike images.

consistent bindings. A set of bindings of values to variables that satisfy the conditions of each pattern taken singly and simultaneously satisfy all constraints that apply between all patterns in a set.

constraint. A constraint determines a subset of the values of a type. A value in that subset satisfies the constraint.

constraint propagation. A method for limiting search by requiring that certain constraints be satisfied. It can also be viewed as a mechanism for moving information between subproblems.

constraint rule. A type of rule that applies limits to a search by specifying that its associated pattern is never allowed to occur in a valid solution. Constraint rules provide a means to reduce the number of unproductive searches.

consultation paradigm. Consultation paradigms describe generic types of problem-solving scenarios. Particular system-building tools are typically good for 1 or a few consultation paradigms and not for others. Most commercial tools are designed to facilitate rapid development of expert systems that can deal with the diagnostic/persriptive paradigm.

contact sensor. A device capable of sensing mechanical contact of the hand or some other part of the smart robot with an external object.

content-addressable memory. Memory in which information is retrieved by specifying the data rather than the address at which the data are stored.

contents. The information in a storage location.

context. A state in a problem-solving process. In a production system the context may be represented by a special working memory element, which is often called a context element, control element, or subgoal. Often conceptually isolatable tasks that must be performed by production systems may be partitioned into subtasks that, once initiated, are expected to run to completion. The rules that constitute that task each have condition elements that must match the associated context element.

context element. A working memory element that signals the state of the computation (context) and is used for purposes of control. The element is an instance of a control element.

context-free grammar. A grammar for describing a context-free language. One metalanguage for expressing a context-free grammar is Backus-Naur Form.

context-free language. A formal language in which each sentence can be generated by a grammar wherein the left-hand side of each rewrite rule consists of a single nonterminal symbol.

context-parameter-value triplets. One method of representing factual knowledge; it is the method used in EMYCIN. A context is an actual or conceptual entity in the domain of the consultant (e.g., a patient, an aircraft, or an oil well). Parameters are properties associated with each context (e.g., age and sex of a patient or location and depth of an oil well). Each parameter (or attribute) can take on values; the parameter, age, could take the value "13 years."

context tree. A structured arrangement of the objects (contexts) or conceptual entities that constitute the consultation domain. There may be 1 or more contexts. A static context tree is an arrangement of context types (e.g., a patient for whom cultures have been prepared). In EMYCIN the context tree forms the backbone of the consultant program.

continuous path. Movement by a robot in which the points between the points specified by the programmer, and the speed of movement, are precisely controlled by the robot's computer controller. Such movement is important in welding and spray painting.

continuous path control. A control scheme whereby the inputs or commands specify every point along a desired path of motion.

continuous speech. A method of operation in a voice recognition system whereby the computer can understand sentences and phrases spoken together, as opposed to isolated words or utterances.

continuous speech recognition. An approach to speech recognition that understands speech in typical conversations of normal durations.

contouring. Controlling the path of the robot arm between successive positions or points in space.

contrast. The ratio between the maximum and minimum luminance values of a display.

contrast control. A manual gain control for a display monitor. It affects both luminance and contrast.

control. Any procedure, explicit or implicit, that determines the overall order of problem-solving activities; the temporal organization of subprocesses.

control element. A working memory element the sole purpose of which is to store control knowledge. A context element is an example of a control element.

control hierarchy. A relationship of sensory processing elements whereby the results of lower-level elements are utilized as inputs by higher-level elements.

control strategy. A method for choosing the next action given many alternative problem-solving steps. In production systems backward chaining is an example of a control strategy.

control unit. The part of a computer system that effects the retrieval of instructions in proper sequence, the interpretation of each instruction, and the application of the proper signals to the arithmetic unit and other parts of the system in accordance with the interpretation. The performance of those operations requires a vast number of "paths" over which data and instructions may be sent.

controlled production system. A production system in which the control regime is specified by a finite-state machine for each rule set rather than by the production-system architecture.

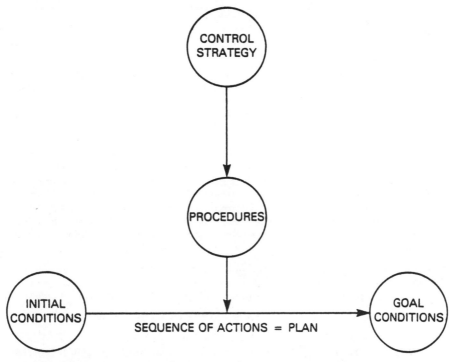

Figure C–5. Control Strategy—Control strategy problem solving procedure.

controller. The device that regulates a smart robot arm's movement and position by comparing the difference between the actual and calculated values and sending the signals necessary to make them match as much as possible.

convention. Standardized methodology or accepted procedure for executing a computer program.

convergency. The intersection of the 3 electron beams of an aperture-mask color cathode ray tube at the plane of the aperture mask.

converter. A unit that changes the representation of data from 1 form to another to make it available or acceptable to another machine, for example, from punched cards to magnetic tape.

convolve. Superimposing an operator over a pixel area in the image, multiplying corresponding points together, and summing the result.

cooperating knowledge sources. Specialized modules in an expert system that independently analyze the data and communicate via a central, structured data base called a blackboard.

coordinated axis control. Control wherein the axes of the robot arrive at their respective end points simultaneously, giving a smooth appearance to the motion. Control wherein the motions of the axes are such that the end point moves along a prespecified type of path (line, circle, etc.).

coordinates. An ordered set of absolute or relative data values that specify a location in a Cartesian coordinate system.

correlation. A correspondence between attributes in an image and its reference image.

counter. A digital device whose outputs count in binary each time a clock pulse occurs on their clock input.

COUSIN. The COUSIN (COoperative USer INterface) project is concerned with specifying graphical interfaces in an application-independent way. The COUSIN system allows application developers to specify the end-user interface for their application in a formal interface description language developed as part of the COUSIN project. Using that specification, COUSIN controls all interaction with the user. The application receives only complete and correct commands. That innovative approach to interface building is preferable in several ways to programming interfaces directly. It reduces the effort in interface construction by the application builder since the application descriptions are much shorter and easier to construct than the corresponding special purpose program. It improves consistency across applications since all interface details are provided through the same interface system. It allows for more iterative testing and for more involvement by human factors specialists since changing the description is much easier than changing code. That results in higher-quality interfaces. COUSIN is implemented on a PERQ workstation.

CP/M. Control Program for Microcomputers. Developed by Digital Research Incorporated (DRI) in 1976, used primarily for 8-bit microcomputers. Its dominance in the PC market was supplanted by the introduction of MS-DOS from Microsoft in 1981.

crash. The complete and often sudden failure of a computer system.

CRIB. Helps computer engineers and system maintainers locate computer hardware and software faults. The engineer gives the system a description of his or her observations in simple English-like terms. CRIB matches that against a data base of known faults. By successively matching larger and larger groups of symptoms with the incoming description, CRIB arrives at a subunit that is either repairable or replaceable. If a subunit is reached and the fault is not cured, the system backtracks automatically to the last decision point and tries to find another match. CRIB contains hardware and software fault diagnostic expertise as a collection of action-symptom pairs (called symptom patterns) where the action is designed to elicit the symptom from the machine. CRIB models the machine under diagnosis as a simple hierarchy of subunits in a semantic net. The system is written in CORAL 66. It was developed as a combined effort by Internationals Computers Limited (ICL), the Research and Advanced Development Centre (RADC), and Brunel University.

CRITTER. CRITTER helps circuit design engineers analyze the correctness, timing, robustness, and speed of VLSI circuit designs. The system accepts circuit schematics and I/O specifications from the engineer and builds a comprehensive model of the circuit's performance. CRITTER summarizes that information and presents it to the engineer with an assessment of the circuit's feasibility as well as diagnostic and repair information. The knowledge embedded in CRITTER includes information about circuit diagrams and circuit analysis techniques, such as subcircuit simulation and path delay analysis. Circuit diagrams are represented using frames, while other knowledge is in the form of algebraic formulas and predicate calculus. CRITTER is implemented in INTERLISP. It was developed at Rutgers University.

cross hairs. Cursor or 2 intersecting perpendicular lines to locate device coordinates.

cross-product. In set theory, the cross-product, or Cartesian product, of a set A and a set B is the set of all ordered pairs (a, b) so that a is a member of A and b is a member of B. In a discussion of the match process, the term is used to designate the set of all potential combinations of matches for a sequence of working memory elements.

CRYSALIS. CRYSALIS infers the 3-dimensional structure of a protein from an electron density map (EDM). The system interprets X-ray diffraction data composed of position and intensity of diffracted waves to infer that atomic structure. The system uses knowledge about protein composition and X-ray crystallography and heuristics for analyzing EDMs to generate and to test hypotheses about plausible protein structure. CRYSALIS uses a blackboard architecture, containing independent knowledge sources that build and test a multilevel hypothesis structure. The system is implemented in LISP. It was developed at Stanford University.

CSI Lisp Toolkit. Composition Systems, Inc. Lisp Toolkit consists of 11 modules that assist in building large distributed knowledge bases while minimizing "garbage" collection. Four modules link VAX Lisp with other DEC-layered products: RDB (Relational Database), GKS (Graphics Kernel System), FMS (Forms Management System), and DECnet (Digital's telecommunications network). The CSI Lisp Toolkit also ties Digital's CMS (Code Management System) and MMS (Module Management System) to the VAX Lisp Editor with the capability of operating over a network. Other enhancements are provided by a Natural Language Processor, a CSI Top Level, a CSI Lisp Optimizer, and CSI Lisp Window and Interprocess Communication modules. Runs on any VAX, Micro VAX II, VAX-station II, or DEC AI Workstation, running VMS 4.2 or later and VAX Lisp 1.2 or later. The price is from $6,000.

CSRL. CSRL is a knowledge engineering language for frame-based representation. It supports the representation of concepts in a diagnostic hierarchy as a collection of specialists. It also supports an establish-refine approach to diagnosis, implemented within CSRL via message passing among concepts. The support environment includes a syntax checker, commands for invoking any concept with any message, and a simple trace facility. CSRL is implemented in ELISP, uses a version of FRL, and operates on a DEC 20/60 computer system. It was developed at Ohio State University.

cursor. Recognizable display entity that can be moved about the display surface by a graphic input device.

cycle. A single iteration of a loop. In production systems an execution consists of iterated recognize-act cycles. In the Rete match algorithm, a match cycle occurs every time a working memory element is added to or removed from working memory. In spreading activation systems activation is propagated incrementally during a series of activation cycles.

cycle time. The time required for a robot to run through its programmed motions. A long cycle time may prevent a robot from doing a given job effectively, although it can perform all the necessary functions.

cylindrical coordinate robot. A robot whose manipulator arm degrees of freedom are defined primarily by cylindrical coordinates.

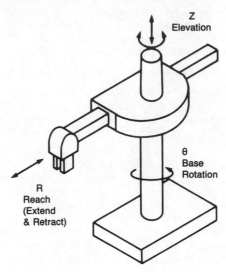

Figure C-6. Cylindrical Coordinate Robot—Cylindrical coordinate robot manipulator.

D

DAA. Assists VLSI designers by performing a hardware allocation from an algorithmic description of a VLSI system. The system (Design Automation Assistant) takes a data flow description of a VLSI system and produces a list of technology independent registers, operators, data paths, and control signals. The system's expertise consists of algorithms for hardware allocation collected from expert designers as well as knowledge found in the CMU/DA allocator (another VLSI design tool). DAA is a forward chaining, rule-based system implemented in OPS5. It was developed at Carnegie-Mellon University.

daisy chain. A method of propagating signals along a bus whereby devices not requesting service respond by passing the signal on. The first device requesting the signal responds by performing an action and breaks the daisy chain signal continuity. That permits assignment of device priorities based on the electrical position of the device along the bus.

DARPA. Defense Advanced Research Projects Agency. The primary organization for instituting advanced computer programs and projects within the United States military.

DART. DART assists in diagnosing faults in computer hardware systems using information about the design of the device being diagnosed. The system works directly from information about the intended structure and expected behavior of the device to help find design flaws in newly created devices. The system has been applied to simple computer circuits and the teleprocessing facility of the IBM 4331. DART uses a device-independent inference procedure that is similar to a type of resolution theorem proving, where the system attempts to generate a proof related to the cause of the device's malfunction. The system is implemented in MRS and was developed at Stanford University.

data. A collection of facts, numeric and alphabetical characters, etc., which is processed or produced by computer.

data base. A collection of data about objects and events on which the knowledge base will work to achieve desired results. A relational data base is one in which the relationships between various objects and events are stored explicitly for flexibility of storage and retrieval. The set of facts, assertions, and conclusions used to match against the IF-parts of rules in a rule-based system.

data base management system. A program that enables a data base to be organized to expedite the sorting, updating, extracting, or retrieving of information and the generation of reports or desired output.

data bus. A multiline, parallel path over which digital data are transferred from any of several destinations. Only 1 transfer of information can take place at any 1 time. While such transfer is taking place, all other sources that are tied to the bus must be disabled.

data directed. Controlled by changes in data rather than changes in goals. Used in contrast to goal directed.

data-directed inference. A problem-solving method that starts with initial knowledge and applies inference rules to generate new knowledge until either 1 of the inferences satisfies a goal or no further inferences can be made. In forward-chaining production systems, the applicability of a rule is determined by matching the conditions specified on its left-hand side against the knowledge currently stored in data memory. In an expert system, a forward-chaining rule detects certain facts in the database and takes an action because of them. For example: it is possible to solve problems such as "What will be the cost of new office furniture if I hire 3 more people?" In that case the program synthesizes an answer from pieces of knowledge.

data-driven. An expert system that employs forward-chaining techniques is also called a data-driven system. One of several control strategies that regulate the order in which inferences are drawn. In a rule-based system, forward chaining begins by asserting all of the rules whose if clauses are true. It then checks to determine what additional rules might be true, given the facts it has already established. The process is repeated until the program reaches a goal or runs out of new possibilities.

data file. A collection of related data records organized in a specific manner, e.g., a payroll file showing rate of pay, deductions, etc.

data filtering. Restricting the portion of data memory that participates in the match process to a subset for the sake of efficiency.

data link. Equipment that permits the transmission of information in data format.

data memory. The global database of a production system. The contents may be partially or totally ordered on the basis of their time of creation or most recent modification. Data memory of typically the most volatile part of a production system.

data structure. The form in which data are stored in a computer.

data tablet. A device for putting 2-dimensional information into the computer. The position of a stylus held by the user is digitized and continually fed to the computer as the user moves it about a special surface.

Randall Davis. Randall Davis is associate professor at M.I.T's Sloan School of Management and a member of the Artificial Intelligence Laboratory. His current research focuses on systems that work from descriptions of structure and function and hence are capable of reasoning from "first principles" to support a wider range of more robust problem-solving applications. Dr. Davis has been one of the leading contributors to the field of expert systems, having published some 40 articles and played a central role in the development of several systems. He serves on the editorial boards of *Artificial Intelligence* and *New Generation Computing* (the Japanese journal dealing with the Fifth Generation Project). He is the coauthor of *Knowledge-Based Systems in AI* and presented an Invited Lecture on expert systems at the 1981 International Joint Conference on AI. In 1984 *Science Digest* selected him as one of America's top 100 scientists under the age of 40. Dr. Davis has also lectured to numerous academic and industrial audiences, dealing with topics ranging from recent research results to tutorials on expert systems.

DEACON. An expert system that performs inferences on stored knowledge.

debugging. The process of determining the correctness of a computer routine, locating any errors, and correcting them. Also, the detection and correction of malfunctions in the computer itself.

declaration. Associates an identifier with an entity. That association is in effect within a region of text called the scope of the declaration. Within the scope of a declaration, there are places where it is possible to use the identifier to refer to the associated declared entity. At such places the identifier is said to be a simple name of the entity; the name is said to denote the associated entity.

declaration section. The section of a computer program in which constructs, such as data types, variables, procedures, and functions, are announced and sometimes defined. In OPS5 the declaration section defines working memory elements, indexes of attributes, vector attributes, and external functions.

declarative knowledge. Knowledge that can be retrieved and stored by cannot be immediately executed; to be effective, it must be interpreted by procedural knowledge. Representation of facts and assertions.

declarative part. A sequence of declarations. It may also contain related information, such as subprogram bodies and representation clauses.

decluttering. Selective erasure of display items when display details are too dense.

decoder. A matrix of switching elements that selects 1 or more output channels according to the combination of input signals present.

DEDALUS. An expert system that transforms program descriptions to aid automatic program generation.

dedicated. Designed or intended for a single function or use.

deduction. A process of reasoning in which the conclusion follows from the premises given. The process of reaching a conclusion by logical means.

deductive capability. Conclusions drawn from knowledge, rules, and general principles.

deep knowledge. Knowledge of basic theories, first principles, axioms, and facts about a domain. It contrasts with surface knowledge.

default. Computer programs often have prespecified values that they use unless they are given alternative values. Those assumed values are called default values. Knowledge systems often store default values that are used in lieu of facts. For example, a medical program may assume that a patient has been exposed to some common organism unless the user asserts that such exposure can be ruled out.

default value. A value that is used if no other value is specified.

degree of freedom. One of a limited number of ways in which a point or a body may move or in which a dynamic system may change, each way being expressed by an independent variable and all required to be specified if the physical state of the body or system is to be completely defined.

delimiter. A special character or word that enables a computer to recognize the beginning or end of a portion of a program or segment of data.

DELTA/CATS. General Electric Company's Corporate Research and Development division has applied expert system technology to the problem of troubleshooting and the repair of diesel electric locomotives in railroad running repair shops. The DELTA/CATS expert system uses production rules and an inference engine that can diagnose multiple problems with the locomotive and can suggest repair procedures to maintenance personnel. The prototype system was implemented in FORTH, running on a Digital Equipment PDP 11/23 under RSX-11M. That system contains approximately 530 rules (roughly 330 rules for the troubleshooting system and 200 rules for the help system), partially representing the knowledge of a senior field service engineer. The inference engine uses a mixed-mode configuration, capable of running in either the forward or backward mode. The help system, based on video disc storage technology, can provide the operator with assistance by displaying textual information, CAD diagrams, or repair sequences. The rules are written in a representation language consisting of 9 predicate functions, 8 verbs, and 5 utility functions.

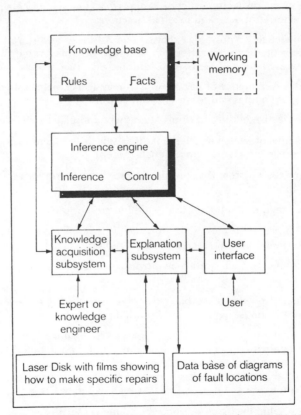

Figure D-1. DELTA/CATS—The overall architecture of the DELTA/CATS-1 system. *Reprinted with the permission of John Wiley and Sons, from "Expert Systems— Artificial Intelligence in Business" by Paul Harmon and David King.*

delta gun. Three electron guns grouped in triad for use with shadow mask to produce cathode ray tube color; each gun adds a color component to display.

demon. A procedure that executes whenever a particular predicate about a database becomes true. In a production system a rule that is not restricted to firing within any particular context or as part of a goal. A demon rule is permitted to fire as soon as it is instantiated, regardless of the presence of any partially completed goals. The name comes from the unit of a perception program called Pandemonium.

demultiplexer. A digital device that directs information from a single input to 1 of several outputs. Information for output-channel selection usually is presented to the device in binary weighted form and is decoded internally. The device also acts as a single-pole multiposition switch that passes digital information in a direction opposite to that of a multiplexer.

DENDRAL. DENDRAL (DENDRitic ALgorithm) infers the molecular structure of unknown compounds from mass spectral and nuclear magnetic response data. The system uses a special algorithm developed by J. Lederberg to systematically enumerate all possible molecular structures; it uses chemical expertise to prune that list of possibilities to a manageable size. Knowledge in DENDRAL is represented as a procedural code for the molecular structure generator and as rules for the data-driven component and evaluator. The system is implemented in INTERLISP and was developed at Stanford University.

denote. A declaration associates an identifier (or some other notation) with an entity. That association is in effect within a region of text called the scope of the declaration. Within the scope of a declaration, there are places where it is possible to use the identifier to refer to the associated declared entity. At such places the identifier is said to be a simple name of the entity; the name is said to denote the associated entity.

dependency. A relation between the antecedents and corresponding consequence produced as a result of applying an inferential rule. Dependencies provide a record of the manner in which decisions are derived from prior data and decisions.

dependency-directed backtracking. A programming technique that allows a system to remove the effects of incorrect assumptions during its search for a solution to a problem. As the system infers new information, it keeps dependency records of all its deductions and assumptions, showing how they were derived. When the system finds that an assumption was incorrect, it backtracks through the chains of inferences, removing conclusions based on the faulty assumption.

depth cuing. Technique to suggest depth by varying light or color intensity or by use of perspective.

depth-first search. In a hierarchy of rules or objects, depth-first search refers to a strategy in which 1 rule or object on the highest level is examined and then the rules or objects immediately below it are examined. Proceeding in that manner, the system will search down a single branch of the hierarchy tree until it ends. That contrasts with breadth-first search.

derivative action. A control operation in which the corrective action is related to the rate at which a quantity is deviating from the desired value.

derivative control. Control scheme whereby the actuator drive signal is proportional to the time derivative of the difference between the input and the measured actual output.

derived type. A derived type is a type whose operations and values are replicas of those of an existing type. The existing type is called the parent type of the derived type.

description. A symbolic representation of the relevant information, e.g., a list of statistical features of a region.

desired value. The value of an output quantity that is desired or a signal representing that value, applied as input signal to a control system.

destination. Register, memory location, or Input/Output device that can be used to receive data during instruction execution.

detectability. Attribute that permits identification of display items by a pick device.

DETEKTR. A system-building aid that helps domain experts construct expert troubleshooting systems. DETEKTR contains a diagram manager, a communications manager, a rule processor, and a rule acquisition subsystem built upon GLIB. The expert communicates with the system by pointing. An object is referred to by pointing at its representation in a diagram displayed on the screen. DETEKTR supports multiple diagrams relating to the task at hand, manages the pointing relations between them, and handles other display requirements, such as waveform pictures, English rule text, and question-answering dialogues. DETEKTR is written in SMALLTALK-80 and operates on theTektronix 4404 Artificial Intelligence System. It was developed by Tektronix, Inc.

Development Tool. A program designed to assist programmers in the development of software. Intelligent tools incorporate artificial intelligence techniques.

device coordinate system. A device-dependent coordinate system whose coordinates are typically in integer units (e.g., raster lines and pixels).

device driver. The device-dependent part of a host-computer graphics software package. The device driver generates a device-dependent output and handles all device-dependent interactions with the host-computer software and hardware.

device independence. Quality of a software package that permits it to be used on more than 1 type of display device.

device intelligence. Local intelligence of graphics device; in graphics software the ability to take full advantage of local intelligence.

device select pulse. A software-generated positive or negative clock pulse from a computer that is used to strobe the operation of 1 or more input/output devices.

DFT. Helps VLSI designers check for DFT (design for testability) rule violations and transform the design to remove them. Once the system locates DFT-rule violations, it analyzes them and corrects the design, using expertise based on a technique called the level sensitive scan design method. DFT also extracts control and observation information from the design structure and uses it for automatic test pattern generation. Knowledge in the system is represented within a logic-oriented framework. A digital design consists of a set of logic assertions that describe the VLSI node interconnects and the functions of the nodes. DFT is implemented in PROLOG. It was developed at Syracuse University.

DIAGNOSER. Helps physicians identify congenital heart disease, specifically, the cardiac anomaly known as total anomalous pulmonary venous connection. The system was intended to help artificial intelligence researchers develop and test predictions about the nature of errors in diagnostic reasoning. Presented with auscultation and X-ray data, DIAGNOSER determines its diagnosis by hypothesizing diseases whose prototype fits the observations. DIAGNOSER contains knowledge about diagnostic reasoning as well as knowledge about cardiac physiology, anatomy, and the pathophysiology of the causal structures underlying congenital heart diseases.

The disease knowledge is represented using frames, the diagnostic reasoning knowledge using rules embedded in frames. DIAGNOSER is implemented in LISP 1.4. It was developed at the University of Minnesota.

diagnostic/prescriptive consultation paradigm. Consultation paradigms refer to generic approaches to common types of problems. The diagnostic/prescriptive paradigm is used for problems that require the user to identify symptoms or characteristics of a situation in order to determine which of several alternative solutions may be appropriate. Most expert systems and tools are designed to handle this paradigm.

diagnostic routine. A test program used to detect and identify hardware malfunctions in the computer and its associated input/output equipment.

DIALYSIS THERAPY ADVISOR. Helps physicians select an initial dialysis regimen for a patient about to begin maintenance hemodialysis treatment. The system is given the patient's sex, height, weight, urine volume, and urea nitrogen concentration, and it produces a list of acceptable therapies. Expertise in the system consists of rules corresponding to the reasoning of medical experts on how to specify initial hemodialysis prescriptions. The rules are accessed via forward and backward chaining. The system also incorporates equation solving, explanation handling, data base retrieval mechanisms, metarules for planning, and a communication facility for user interaction. The DIALYSIS THERAPY ADVISOR is implemented in FRANZ LISP. It was developed at Vanderbilt University.

difference reduction. An approach to problem solving that tries to solve a problem by iteratively applying operators that will reduce the difference between the current state and the goal state. "Means-ends" analysis.

differentiation. A mathematical procedure for finding the equation of a curve whose value at each point is equal to the slope of a given function.

digit. One of the n symbols of integral value ranging from 0 to $n-1$ inclusive in a scale of numbering of base n, e.g., 1 of the 10 decimal digits—0, 1, 2, 3, 4, 5, 6, 7, 8, 9.

digital computer. A computer in which discrete representation of data is mainly used. A digital computer uses 1 and 0 as symbols and operates on the fact of the direct relationship between those numbers and the on and off condition at a specific place in the computer circuitry.

digital image. The numerical representation of a picture seen by a television camera "eye." A robot's computer analyzes the digital image to enable the robot to recognize an object.

digital image analysis. A multistage process that leads to the "understanding" of a digital image, the recognition of certain objects, or the recognition of certain attributes in given objects in the image. Stages of the image analysis process may be image digitizing, image preprocessing, feature extraction, and pattern recognition.

digital switch. A solid-state device that routes information in digital form. The term is also used to describe a digital switching system.

digital-to-analog converter. Interface to convert digital data into analog data. Device for translating a digital quantity, represented as a number of binary bits, into a voltage or current whose magnitude is in some way equivalent.

digital transmission. A method of sending and receiving information as a code made up of on-and-off pulses of electricity or light.

DIGITALIS ADVISOR. Aids physicians by recommending appropriate digitalis therapy for patients with congestive heart failure or conduction disturbances of the heart. The system questions the clinician about the patient's history, e.g., age, cardiac rhythm, serum potassium level, and then produces a set of recommendations for beginning therapy. After the patient has received an initial dose, the program analyzes the reaction of the patient, as given by the clinician's responses to another set of questions, and produces a new dosage regimen. Digitalis therapy expertise is represented as a hierarchy of concepts in a semantic net. An interpreter executes plans in the knowledge base (e.g., checking for digitalis sensitivity owing to advanced age). The system contains an explanation facility that produces explanations directly from the executed code. DIGITALIS ADVISOR is implemented in OWLI. It was developed at M.I.T.

digitize. To convert an analog quantity into its binary equivalent.

digitized image. A representation of an image as an array of brightness values.

digitized speech. Numerical representation of speech in which the amplitude of the speech waveform has been recorded at regular intervals. Speech is typically sampled from 8000 to 12,500 times per second in voice recognition systems.

digitizer. A device, often called a graphics tablet, that gives the computer 2-dimensional data.

DIPMETER ADVISOR. DIPMETER ADVISOR inters subsurface geological structure by interpreting dipmeter logs, measurements of the conductivity of rock in and around a borehole as related to depth below the surface. The system uses knowledge about dipmeter patterns and geology to recognize features in the dipmeter data and relate them to underground geological structure. The system provides the user with a menu-driven graphical interface incorporating smooth scrolling of log data. The system uses a rule-based knowledge representation scheme controlled by forward chaining. It is implemented in INTERLISP-D and operates on the Xerox 1100 series workstations. The system was developed by Schlumberger-Doll Research.

direct addressing. The second and third bytes of the instruction contain the address of the operand to be used.

direct digital control. Use of a digital computer to provide the computations of the control functions of 1 or multiple control loops used in process control operations.

direct memory access. A method of transferring blocks of data directly between a peripheral device and system memory without the need for central processing unit intervention. The powerful input/output technique significantly increases the data transfer rate and therefore system efficiency.

direct view storage tube. Type of graphic display device in which the display device does not need to be refreshed, because low-level electron flood guns sustain the illumination of the phosphors activated by the directed beam.

directed activation. In an activation network directed activation is a method for propagating the activation from 1 object to another. The activation network is a directed graph, indicating that propagation is to proceed only in accordance with the directed arcs.

directed graph. A knowledge representation structure consisting of nodes (representing, e.g., objects) and directed connecting arcs (labeled edges, representing, e.g., relations).

disable. Command that ends operation of a graphic input or output device.

discrete components. Components with a single functional capability per package; for example, transistors and diodes.

discrete type. A discrete type is a type that has an ordered set of distinct values. The discrete types are the enumeration and integer types. Discrete types are used for indexing and iteration and for choices in case statements and record variants.

discriminant. A discriminant is a distinguished component of an object or value of a record type. The subtypes of other components, or even their presence or absence, may depend on the value of the discriminant.

discriminant constraint. A discriminant constraint on a record type or private type specifies a value for each discriminant of the type.

discrimination. A process of learning that distinguishes instances of a concept from noninstances. The act of refining an overgeneralization of a concept to be learned so as to exclude noninstances that were once mistakenly classified as instances of the concept. A particular learning mechanism that exploits feedback concerning erroneous classifications to refine an overgeneralization of a concept.

disk memory. A nonprogrammable, bulk-storage, random-access memory consisting of a magnetizable coating on 1 or both sides of a rotating thin circular plate.

disk pack. A removable assembly of magnetic disks. A portable set of flat, circular recording surfaces used on a disk storage device.

DISPATCHER. Knowledge-based software implemented in OPS5 by the Carnegie Group to control the dispatch of WIP (work in progress) on an automated network consisting of storage carousels, robots, conveyors, and workstations. DISPATCHER maintains a database of products, lists of manufacturing steps for products, and manufacturing operations able to be performed at each workstation. DISPATCHER tracks the progress of each WIP through the list of manufacturing steps assigned to it. When a workstation requests work, the system selects the optimal WIP to send to it, taking into consideration the operations the workstation is currently set up to perform, the priority and due date of available WIPs, and the overhead of storage operations by the robots. DISPATCHER is designed for development beyond this reactive dispatch capability. With the experience gained from the operation of this reactive system, and with data concerning transit times and dwell times of WIP in the factory, the system will be developed into a proactive scheduler capable of maximizing the through-put of a manufacturing facility.

display background. Static background against which dynamic displays are projected.

display command. Processor-generated instruction to the display device.

display console. In computer graphics, a console consisting of at least 1 cathode ray tube display device and usually 1 or more input devices such as an alphanumeric keyboard, function keys, a tablet, a joystick, a control ball, or a light pen.

display device. An output device that stores results from computer operations and translates them into graphic, numerical, or literal symbols to be seen by the computer user.

display elements. Points, line segments, characters, or markers that constitute graphics displays.

display entity. Group of output primitives forming a recognizable unit on the display surface.

display foreground. Portion of display accessible in interactive mode and responsive to operator's commands.

display instruction. Coded information passed to the graphics processor to specify display items to be drawn on the display surface.

display list. Sequence of display instructions that create, change, and refresh graphics display.

display menu. List displayed on monitor indicating program options available to operator.

display space. Space delineated by device coordinates to set area where graphics image can appear.

display surface. Surface such as cathode ray tube screen and plotter bed where graphics data are displayed.

disproving. An attempt to prove the impossibility of a hypothesized conclusion or goal.

distal. Away from the base, toward the end effector of the robot arm.

distributed control. A control technique whereby portions of a single control process are located in 2 or more places.

distributed processing. Performing a data processing task by performing the needed calculations in a distributed computer network. The efficiency of the data processing task is improved through the simultaneous performance of operations in several interconnected processors of a distributed computer network.

dithering. Varying raster color or intensity by illuminating and blanking pixels in patterns similar to those of newspaper photo reproduction; process reduces picture resolution.

document generation system. A system that synthesizes text by manipulating stored information in response to specifications for the output. A type of document understanding system.

document understanding system. A system that accepts textural input, stores and classifies it, and then utilizes the input in response to specifications for tasks. Some document understanding systems provide paraphrases, some answer questions, some perform translation, and some draw inferences.

documentation. A written description of a program that includes its name, purpose, how it works, and, frequently, operating instructions.

domain. A topical area or region of knowledge. medicine, engineering, and management science are very broad domains. Existing knowledge systems provide competent advice only within very narrowly defined domains. In mathematics the set of values that the argument to a function may assume.

domain expert. An expert in a specific field of endeavor or knowledge who works closely with a knowledge engineer to build knowledge-based systems. It is his expertise that imparts the "expert" to expert systems. **(See figure p. 93)**

domain knowledge. Specific knowledge about the problem domain, e.g., knowledge about geology in an expert system for finding mineral deposits. **(See figure p. 94)**

dominant. When a conflict-resolution strategy leaves 1 instantiation in the conflict set but removes a second instantiation, the first instantiation is said to dominate the second.

DOS. Disk Operating System. The accepted standard operating system for the IBM PC. Developed by Microsoft, the first incarnation appeared as a direct spinoff of CP/M, under the name MS-DOS (Microsoft Disk Operating System).

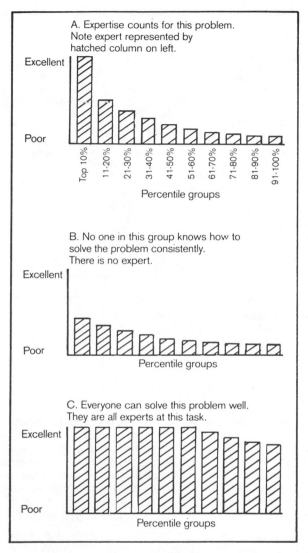

Figure D-2. Domain Expert—Finding expertise in a sample of problem solvers. *Reprinted with the permission of John Wiley and Sons, from "Expert Systems— Artificial Intelligence in Business" by Paul Harmon and David King.*

dot pitch. This is the distance between the holes in a video monitor's shadow mask. A smaller dot pitch produces closer pixels, higher resolution, improved character quality, and finer graphic detail. Most video monitors with dot pitches of 0.31 millimeter or less are billed as "high resolution."

double buffering. Technique that accelerates data display by alternately addressing each of 2 buffers; while 1 buffer is used to refresh the display, the other receives data for display during next access.

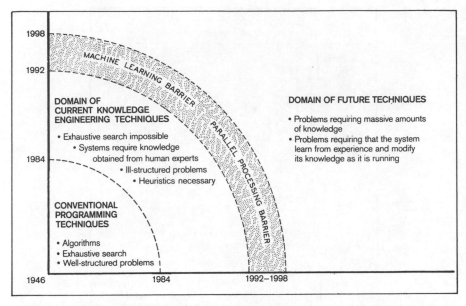

Figure D-3. Domain Knowledge—Problem domain of existing knowledge engineering techniques. *Reprinted with the permission of John Wiley and Sons, from "Expert Systems—Artificial Intelligence in Business" by Paul Harmon and David King.*

downtime. The time period during which a device or system is not functioning properly.

DPL. A knowledge engineering language for creating and manipulating frame-based representations of LSI designs. Its principal characteristic is the ability to represent both design and structure information in a single set of data structures. That uniform representation scheme can be used as a data base for answering questions about such things as the connectivity of the device and also can be used to simulate the device's behavior. The support environment includes an interactive graphics editor for creating LSI designs in the form of DPL procedures. DPL is implemented in ZETALISP and operates on Symbolics 3600 Lisp Machines. It was developed at M.I.T.

dragging. Moving a user-selected item on the cathode ray tube display along a path defined by a graphic input device such as an electronic pen and tablet.

drift. The tendency of a system's response to move gradually away from the desired response.

DRILLING ADVISOR. Assists an oil-rig supervisor in resolving problems related to the drilling mechanism sticking within the borehole during drilling. The system diagnoses the most likely causes of the sticking (e.g., conical hole, debris plugging the drill pipe) and recommends a set of treatments to alleviate the problem and lessen its chance of recurrence (e.g., jarring the drill string up or down or both). The system bases its decisions on knowledge of the geological formations at the drill site and the relation between observed symptoms and suspected causes of problems. Knowledge is represented as rules handled by a backward chaining control scheme. The system was originally implemented in KS300 and reimplemented in S.1. It was developed by Teknowledge in cooperation with Societe Nationale Elf Aquitaine.

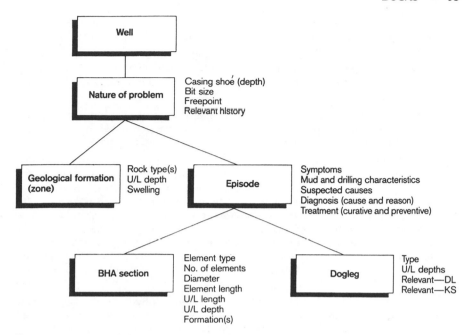

Figure D-4. DRILLING ADVISOR—The object hierarchy of the DRILLING ADVISOR system. *Reprinted with the permission of John Wiley and Sons, from "Expert Systems—Artificial Intelligence in Business" by Paul Harmon and David King.*

droop. A robot's tendency to hold a heavy load too low because of deflection in its "arm" members.

DRUG INTERACTION CRITIC. Helps physicians decide how to administer drugs in the presence of other drugs. The system identifies both adverse and beneficial interactions, explains why the interactions occur, answers questions about the interactions, and suggests corrective action for adverse effects. The knowledge base of drug types is arranged as a hierarchy of frames that includes information related to specific drugs, such as the drug's affinities, storage sites, and interaction characteristics. Knowledge about the mechanism of drug interaction is organized by frames according to one of the 4 mechanism types: chemicophysical, pharmacodynamic, pharmacokinetic, and physiologic. The system provides a limited natural language interface, including a spelling corrector, since drug names are commonly typed incorrectly. The system is implemented in PROLOG. It was developed at Virginia Polytechnic Institute and State University.

drum sequencer. A mechanical programming device that can be used to operate limit switches or valves to control a robot.

DSCAS. Helps contractors analyze the legal aspects of differing site condition (DSC) claims. A DSC claim is a contractually granted remedy for additional expenses incurred by a contractor because physical conditions at the site differ materially from those indicated in the original contract. DSCAS provides a contracting officer (CO) on a construction jobsite with the legal expertise needed to handle the DSC claim. If DSCAS determines there is a reason for not including the requested additional expenses, the analysis stops and an explanation is given. DSCAS contains a model of the decision process used by lawyers for analyzing DSC claims. That knowledge is represented in the form of forward chaining rules. DSCAS is implemented in ROSIE. It was developed at the University of Colorado.

dual-port. A dual-port device can be physically connected to 2 computer busses simultaneously. Access to the device by 1 bus does not required the loss of bus cycles on the other.

dual semantics. The idea that a computer program can be viewed from either of 2 equally valid perspectives: procedural semantics (what happens when the program is run) and declarative semantics (what knowledge the program contains).

DUCK. A knowledge engineering language for logic-based representation. Its principal characteristic is the combination of 4 AI paradigms: logic programming, rule-based systems, nonmonotonic reasoning, and deductive search. DUCK uses a notation based on first-order predicate calculus, where the conditions and actions of rules are logical predicates. DUCK achieves nonmonotonic reasoning through dependency directed backtracking that uses a truth maintenance system and data pools. DUCK supports forward and backward chaining control schemes. It is implemented in NISP, a portable dialect of LISP, and operates on DEC VAX's running UNIX or VMS and the Symbolics 3600 and Apollo workstations. It was developed by Smart Systems Technology as a commercial system.

Michael J. B. Duff. Dr. Michael J. B. Duff is a reader in physics in the Department of Physics and Astronomy at University College, London, where he heads the Image Processing Group. He is a fellow of the Institution of Electrical Engineers and honorary secretary of the British Pattern Recognition Association, which he founded in 1967. Dr. Duff's research interests have centered around parallel processing techniques applied to image analysis, and his research group has been responsible for the development of the CLIP series of image processors. He has published more than 50 papers on those and related topics and has organized and lectured at many international conferences and workshops promoting understanding in this field.

dump. To transfer all the data accumulated on the system during a given period between temporary storage, i.e., disk, and more permanent storage, i.e., magnetic tape, punched cards, listings, etc.

dynamic accuracy. Degree of conformance to the true value when relevant variables are changing with time.

dynamic knowledge base. In expert systems working memory is made up of all of the attribute-value relationships that are established while the consultation is in progress. Since the system is constantly checking rules and seeking values, all values that are established must be kept immediately available until all the rules have been examined. The dynamic portion of a production system's memory. Working memory contains the database of the system, which changes as rules are executed. Another name for data memory.

dynamic memory. A type of semiconductor memory in which the presence or absence of an electrical charge represents the 2 states of a storage element. Without refresh, the data represented by the electrical charge would be lost.

Dynamic RAM. A random access memory that uses a capacitive element for storing a data bit.

dynamic segment attribute. Segment attribute, such as visibility, highlighting, image transformation, or detectability, which can be altered after the segment is defined.

E

ECESIS. Provides autonomous control of an environmental control/life support subsystem (EC/LSS) for use aboard a manned space station. The system decides how to shift the modes of the various EC/LSS subsystems during the transition from shadow to sun. It also monitors the EC/LSS, triggering actions in response to various events. Although ECESIS is intended to operate autonomously, it has a simple explanation capability to facilitate system demonstration. ECESIS has a hybrid architecture involving both rule-based and semantic net formalisms, and it uses the Bayesian scoring model developed for PROSPECTOR to handle uncertainty. The system is implemented in YAPS. It was developed at Boeing Aerospace Company.

echo. Graphics display, such as text string or cursor, which provides visual feedback to the operator.

EDAAS. Helps information specialists decide which information concerning the manufacture and distribution of toxic chemicals may be released to the public. The system uses knowledge specifying when information must be released (from the Toxic Substances Control Act) together with knowledge about when sensitive information cannot be released (because it is classified as confidential business information). EDAAS is implemented in FORTRAN, but it uses a rule-based knowledge representation scheme as well as a modified linear programming algorithm to reach a decision. The system was developed by Booz, Allen, and Hamilton for use by the Environmental Protection Agency (EPA), which uses it on a regular basis.

edge. A change in pixel values (exceeding some threshold) between 2 regions of relatively uniform values. Edges correspond to changes in brightness that can correspond to a discontinuity in surface orientation, surface reflectance, or illumination. The transition from logic 0 to logic 1 or from logic 1 to logic 0 in a clock pulse.

edge-based stereo. A sterographic machine vision technique based on matching edges in 2 or more views of the same scene taken from different positions.

edge detection. A computer vision technique that helps the computer understand the visual images it receives by locating the edges of an object.

edge operators. Templates for finding edges in machine vision images.

EEG ANALYSIS SYSTEM. Analyzes electroencephalograms (EEGs) recorded from renal patients. The system analyzes EEGs fed to it directly from an EEG machine by using a fast Fourier transformation method. It then uses the resulting spectral features to classify the EEGs as either normal or abnormal. The system uses knowledge obtained from a professional electroencephalographer, represented in the form of rules with associated certainty factors. The system explains its results by simply displaying the outcomes of certain rules. A rule-editing program, written in C, helps system developers maintain and update the rules. The system is implemented in assembly language and the C programming language and embedded in a Motorola MC6801 single-chip microprocessor. The EEG ANALYSIS SYSTEM was developed at Vanderbilt University.

effective address. The actual address of the desired location in memory, usually derived by some form of calculation.

effector. An actuator, motor, or driven mechanical device.

efficiency. In machine vision applications, the ratio of a luminance flux to the power supplied to a radiant source. It is expressed as lumens per watt.

EL. Performs a steady-state analysis of resistor-diode-transistor circuits. Given a description of a circuit schematic, the system analyzes the circuit and determines the values of various circuit parameters, such as voltage or current values at given points. EL's expertise includes general principles of electronics (e.g., Ohm's law) and circuit component characteristics (e.g., the functional properties of transistors). The system uses a rule-based knowledge representation scheme with forward chaining and an indexed data base of facts and assertions. A limited explanation facility exists, built upon the property that EL remembers the justifications for new assertions. EL is implemented in ARS. It was developed at M.I.T.

elaboration. The elaboration of a declaration is the process by which the declaration achieves its effect, such as creating an object; the process occurs during program execution.

ELAS. Gives advice on how to control and interpret results from INLAN, a large-scale interactive program for oil well log analysis, and display developed by Amoco. ELAS assists the user by recommending analysis methods, warning of inconsistencies or unpromising directions of analysis and by summarizing and interpreting the results of the user-INLAN interaction. The user directs both the mathematical analysis of INLAN and the interpretive analysis of ELAS by changing parameters or invoking tasks through a sophisticated graphical display. The system is primarily rule-based and is implemented in EXPERT. It was developed at Rutgers University in cooperation with Amoco Production Research.

elbow. The joint that connects a robot's upper arm and forearm.

element. The most primitive unit into which a system can be decomposed. In OPS5, for example, the units of the left-hand sides of rules are called condition elements, and the units of working memory are called working memory elements.

element class. The data type of a working memory element.

element variable. The variable that is bound to an entire working memory element instead of to the values of that element's attributes.

ELIZA. A software product that has an individual converse with the computer, with the computer responding with typical response or questions. Not strictly an artificial intelligence program but much cited.

ellipsis. The omission of words so that a sentence is not grammatically complete but is still comprehensible to the intended audience.

embed. To write a computer language on top of another computer language, such as LISP.

EMERGE. Assists physicians in the analysis of chest pain in an emergency-room environment. The system decides whether an emergency-room patient who is suffering with chest pain should be admitted to the hospital. it also provides advice on possible treatments, together with an indication of the severity of the condition. EMERGE contains expertise derived from existing medical outlines, known as criteria maps, which reflect a collection of knowledge gained over a period of years from consultations with experts. The system represents that knowledge as rules organized in a hierarchy to improve performance. It also handles certainty calculations and provides explanations showing the logical paths taken by rule searches. EMERGE is implemented in standard PASCAL and operates on mainframes, minicomputers, and microcomputers. The system was developed at U.C.L.A.

emulate. Hardware imitation of another system's data-processing capabilities to initiate the same results or permit software compatibility.

EMYCIN. EMYCIN is a skeletal knowledge engineering language for rule-based representation. Its principal characteristics include a restrictive backward chaining control scheme suitable for diagnosis and consultation-type problems, certainty handling mechanisms, and automatic user querying facilities. The support environment contains sophisticated interface facilities for explaining the system's reasoning and for acquiring new knowledge. The system is implemented in INTERLISP and was originally designed to operate on a DEC PDP-10 under TENEX or TOPS20. EMYCIN was developed at Stanford University and is essentially MYCIN stripped of its domain knowledge. (Essential MYCIN)

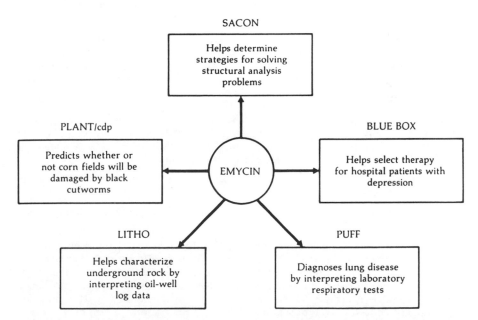

Figure E-1. EMYCIN—Applications of EMYCIN. *Reprinted with the permission of Addison-Wesley Publishing Company from "A Guide to Expert Systems" by Donald A. Waterman.*

enable. Activate a graphics device for input or output.

encoder. A transducer used to convert position data into electrical signals. The robot system uses an incremental optical encoder to provide position feedback for each joint. Velocity data are computed from the encoder signals and used as an additional feedback signal to assure servo stability.

end effector. A robot's "hand." It may be a welding gun, a paint spray nozzle, a pneumatic screwdriver, a gripper, or any other such device for doing work.

endpoint. End of a line segment expressed in terms of x, y, and z coordinates.

end-point control. Any control scheme in which only the motion of the robot manipulator end point may be commanded and the computer can command the actuators at the various degrees of freedom to achieve the desired result.

end-point rigidity. The resistance of the hand, tool, or end point of a robot manipulator arm to motion under applied force.

end-user. The person who uses the finished expert system, the person for whom the system was developed.

entry. An entry is used for communication between tasks. Externally, an entry is called just as a subprogram is called; its internal behavior is specified by 1 or more accept statements specifying the actions to be performed when the entry is called.

envelope. The set points representing the maximum extent or reach of the robot hand or working tool in all directions. The work envelope can be reduced or restricted by limiting devices that establish limits that will not be exceeded in the event of any foreseeable failure of the robot or its controls. The maximum distance the robot can travel after the limit device is actuated will be considered the basis for defining the restricted work envelope.

EPES. EPES assists F-16 pilots in handling in-flight emergency procedures, such as loss of canopy. The system uses knowledge about aircraft features (e.g., canopy, pilot) and mission goals (e.g., maintain the current state of the aircraft) to decide how to respond to emergencies. The primary goal of EPES is to maintain the aircraft at a constant airspeed, heading, and altitude. When emergencies arise, violating that goal, the system first warns the pilot and then takes corrective action, sending requests for changes to a robot-pilot. Knowledge in EPES is represented in both rule-based and semantic net form. The rules decide when to set new goals and are linked via semantic net to all parts and goals that affect their activation. EPES is implemented in ZETALISP. The system was developed at Texas Instruments.

error. The difference between the desired value and the actual or measured value of an output quantity.

error checking or error detection. Software routines that identify, and often correct, erroneous data.

ERS. ERS is a knowledge engineering language for rule-based representation. Its principal characteristics include a PROSPECTOR-like semantic network that links rule components, certainty handling mechanisms including Bayesian and Fuzzy logic techniques, automatic user querying, and the ability to call upon a set of application-specific primitive functions for the evaluation of evidence nodes. The primitive functions can consult various data bases for factual information. The support environment includes facilities for graphical display of the results of analysis and for explaining the system's reasoning. ERS is implemented in PASCAL and operates on an IBM PC-XT and a DEC VAX 11/780. It was developed by PAR Technology Corporation.

ESIE. Lightwave Consultants expert system shell, ESIE is a backward chaining inference engine. A "goal" statement tells ESIE what information the knowledge base is trying to learn. Production rules are used to guide the search for that information and are used to make conclusions based on previous knowledge. A legal-answers statement restricts the responses that the user can enter to a set of legal values. ESIE comes with a TRACE feature to help construct knowledge bases. Requires IBM PC or compatible, with 128 KB of memory. Color or monochrome monitors and fixed disks are all supported.

ESPRIT. European Strategic Program for Research in Information Technology. The Common Market's program for the development of new technologies; extraordinarily similar to Japan's Fifth Generation Project in the scope of what it hopes to achieve.

ethernet. Local network for sending messages between computers by way of a single coaxial cable that snakes through all of the computers to be connected.

ETS. A system-building aid that helps a domain expert construct and analyze OPS5 knowledge bases. ETS interviews a domain expert, helps the expert analyze an initial set of heuristics and parameters for the problem, and automatically produces a set of rules. ETS helps the expert express the problem in terms of a rating grid, using elicitation techniques based on George Kelly's personal construct theory work in psychotherapy. ETS generates rules with certainty factors that may be reviewed and modified by the expert. ETS is written in INTERLISP-D and operates on XEROX 1100 series workstations. It was developed by Boeing Computer Services.

EURISKO. Expert system used to design 3-dimensional electronic circuits, learns by discovery. EURISKO learns new heuristics and new domain-specific definitions of concepts in a problem domain. The system can learn by discovery in a number of different problem domains, including VLSI design. EURISKO has tackled the problem of inventing new kinds of 3-dimensional microelectronic devices that can be fabricated using laser recrystallization techniques and has designed new and interesting microelectronic devices. EURISKO operates by generating a device configuration, computing its input/output behavior, assessing its functionality, and then evaluating it against other comparable devices. The system is implemented in INTERLISP for the Xerox 1100 series workstations. It was developed at Stanford University and is more an artificial intelligence program for learning by discovery than an expert system.

evaluation function. A procedure used to determine the value of worth of proposed intermediate steps during a hunt through a search space for a solution to a problem.

event. Operator-prompted data collected through peripheral device.

event-driven. A forward-chaining problem-solving approach based on the current problem status. **(See figure p. 102)**

evolutionary development. The practice of iteratively designing, implementing, evaluating, and refining computer applications, especially characteristic of the process of building expert systems.

EXAMINER. Analyzes physicians' diagnostic behavior on cases in internal medicine. The system presents a hypothetical case, and the physician identifies the disease most likely to cause the manifestations present and indicates other diseases or problems that could be present. The system performs that analysis using (1) heuristic knowledge about how to relate diseases to their manifestations, and (2) medical knowledge obtained directly from the INTERNIST data base. The system produces a text commentary that evaluates the physician's diagnosis, acknowledging correct assumptions and explaining why incorrect ones are wrong. Knowledge is in the form of

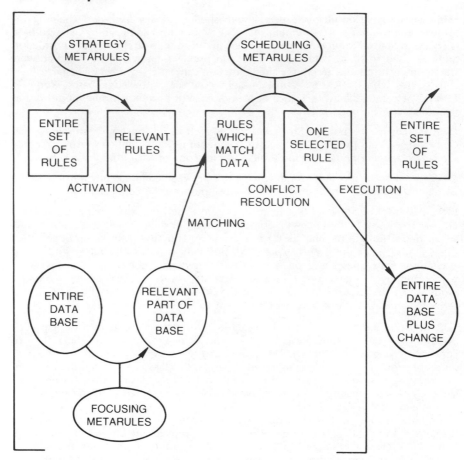

Figure E–2. Event Driven—Idealized event-driven control system.

procedures embodying principles of internal medicine. The system is implemented in LISP and was developed at the University of Pittsburgh.

exception. An exception is an error situation that may arise during program execution. To raise an exception is to abandon normal program execution to signal that the error has taken place. An exception handler is a portion of program text specifying a response to the exception. Execution of such a program text is called handling the exception.

EXCHECK. An expert system that teaches university-level courses in logic, set theory, and proof theory.

excitation. The driving signal to any speech model in humans, the movement of the vocal cords.

execute. Carry out the steps specified in a procedure or the actions in a rule.

executive control program. A main system program designed to establish priorities and to process and control other programs.

exhaustive search. A problem-solving technique in which the problem solver systematically tries all possible solutions in some "brute force" manner until it finds an acceptable one.

exit. An instruction in a computer program, in a routine, or in a subroutine after the execution of which control is no longer exercised by that computer program, that routine, or that subroutine.

expanded name. An expanded name denotes an entity that is declared immediately within some construct. An expanded name has the form of a selected component: the prefix denotes the construct (a program unit or a block, loop, or accept statement); the selector is the simple name of the entity.

expansion. The process of inserting a sequence of operations represented by a macro name when the macro name is referenced in a program.

expectation-driven. Processing approaches that proceed by trying to confirm models, situations, states, or concepts anticipated by the system.

expectation-driven reasoning. A control procedure that employs current data and decisions to formulate hypotheses about yet unobserved events and to allocate resources to activities that confirm, disconfirm, or monitor the expected events.

experiential knowledge. Knowledge gained from hands-on experience. It typically consists of specific facts and surface knowledge rules-of-thumb. This is in contrast with deep knowledge of formal principles or theories.

EXPERT. EXPERT is skeletal knowledge engineering language for rule-based representation. Its principal characteristics include a forward chaining control scheme designed for diagnosis or classification-type problems, mechanisms for handling certainty, and efficient and transportable code. The support environment contains sophisticated user interface facilities including those for explanation, acquisition, and consistency checking. EXPERT is implemented in FORTRAN and operates on both DEC and IBM equipment. It is one of the most widely used knowledge engineering languages for medical applications. EXPERT was developed at Rutgers University. **(See figure p. 104)**

EXPERT-2. EXPERT-2 is a knowledge engineering language for rule-based representation. Its principal characteristics include a backward chaining rule interpreter and support for analytic subroutines that allow full access to the underlying FORTH system. Those include routines for interfacing with the user or specialized data processing. EXPERT-2 is implemented in FORTH and operates on the Apple II microcomputer system. It was developed by Helion Inc.

EXPERT-EASE. EXPERT-EASE is a system-building aid that helps a domain expert construct an expert system. The expert defines the problem in terms of features or factors that lead to particular results, and the system queries the expert for examples describing conditions leading to each result. From the examples, the system learns a procedure for solving the problem and generates a decision tree representing that procedure. EXPERT-EASE is implemented in PASCAL and operates on an IBM PC or XT with 128K of memory. It was developed by Intelligent Terminals Ltd. of Great Britain as a commercial system.

Expert-Knowledge Systems, Inc. Expert-Knowledge Systems, Inc. (EKS), develops, packages and delivers expert knowledge to solve organizational problems, such as in business, health care, legal, intelligence, military, and human service settings. Typically the company goals are to increase productivity and reduce costs. The company has a 10-year history of acquiring expert knowledge and implementing programs that use the acquired knowledge.

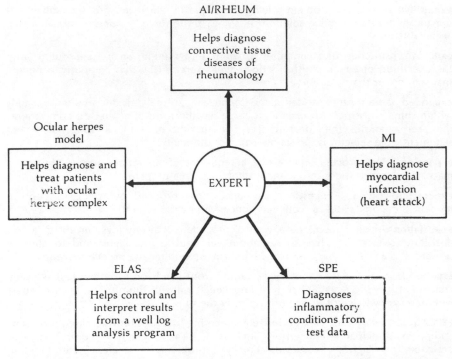

Figure E–3. EXPERT—Applications of EXPERT. *Reprinted with the permission of Addison-Wesley Publishing Company from "A Guide to Expert Systems" by Donald A. Waterman.*

EXPERT NAVIGATOR. Monitors navigation sensors on advanced tactical aircraft. The system manages and reconfigures the onboard navigation sensors (e.g., radio aids, inertial navigation systems, and digital terrain aids), monitors their ability to support the aircraft's primary mission, and suggests viable alternatives when the primary mission is threatened. Knowledge in the system is in the form of rules operating within a blackboard architecture. EXPERT NAVIGATOR is implemented in LISP for the Symbolics 3600 workstation. It was developed at the Analytic Sciences Corporation.

expert system. A computer program that contains both declarative knowledge (facts about objects, events, and situations) and procedural knowledge (information about courses of action) to emulate the reasoning processes of human experts in a particular domain. Two types of expert systems are rule-based and model-based. A computer system that embodies the specialized knowledge of 1 or more human experts and uses that knowledge to solve problems. By capturing in software the best knowledge and judgment available, it is possible to distribute expertise on a wider scale. An expert system generally consists of a knowledge base and an inference engine, both of which are continually modified and evaluated. It may also include a natural language interface that facilitates user communication with the system, an explanation facility and a knowledge acquisition subsystem that is used to enhance the knowledge base. A major strength of an expert system is that it can take the best insights of

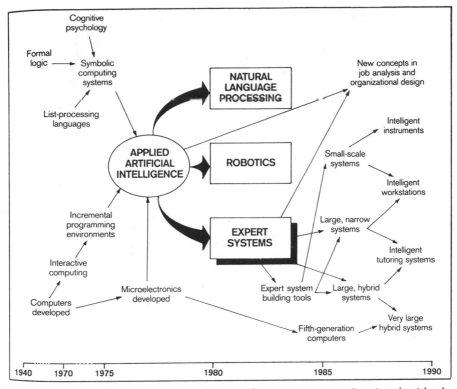

Figure E-4. Expert System—The evolution of expert systems. *Reprinted with the permission of John Wiley and Sons, from "Expert Systems—Artificial Intelligence in Business" by Paul Harmon and David King.*

several human experts and apply them to the same problem simultaneously. When human experts see the mistakes that an evolving expert system is making, they can determine what knowledge the system is lacking and continue to enhance it. These computer programs typically represent knowledge symbolically, examine and explain their reasoning processes, and address problem areas that require years of special training and education for humans to master.

expert-system-building tool. The programming language and support package used to build the expert system. **(See figure p. 106)**

expertise. Proficiency in a specialized domain. An expert system is said to have expertise in its domain if its performance is comparable to that of a human with 5 to 10 years of training and experience in the domain. Expertise often consists of massive amounts of information combined with rules of thumb, simplifications, rare facts, and wise procedures in such a way that one can analyze specific types of problems in an efficient manner.

explanation. The process of describing how an expert system reached its conclusions or why it asked particular questions of a user. Explanations may be used to justify decisions or problem-solving strategies or to teach those strategies to the user. Broadly, that refers to information that is presented to justify a particular course of

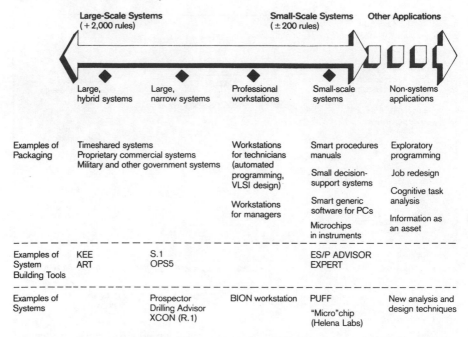

	Large-Scale Systems (+2,000 rules)			Small-Scale Systems (±200 rules)	Other Applications
	Large, hybrid systems	Large, narrow systems	Professional workstations	Small-scale systems	Non-systems applications
Examples of Packaging	Timeshared systems Proprietary commercial systems Military and other government systems		Workstations for technicians (automated programming, VLSI design) Workstations for managers	Smart procedures manuals Small decision-support systems Smart generic software for PCs Microchips in instruments	Exploratory programming Job redesign Cognitive task analysis Information as an asset
Examples of System Building Tools	KEE ART	S.1 OPS5		ES/P ADVISOR EXPERT	
Examples of Systems		Prospector Drilling Advisor XCON (R.1)	BION workstation	PUFF "Micro"chip (Helena Labs)	New analysis and design techniques

Figure E–5. Expert-System-Building Tool—A range of expert systems applications to expect in the 1980s. *Reprinted with the permission of John Wiley and Sons, from "Expert Systems—Artificial Intelligence in Business" by Paul Harmon and David King.*

reasoning or action. In knowledge systems it typically refers to a number of techniques that help a user understand what a system is doing. Many knowledge systems allow a user to ask "Why," "How," or "Explain." In each case the system responds by revealing something about its assumptions or its inner reasoning.

explanation facility. The component of an expert system that can explain the system's reasoning, such as how a conclusion was reached or why a particular question was asked.

exploratory programming. A set of techniques developed by the artificial intelligence community to deal with problems for which the design of a solution cannot be known in advance. A major premise of such programming is that, by exploring various techniques and attempting to rapidly prototype a solution to some small subset of the problem, it can be better understood. Supporting techniques include interactive editing and debugging, integrated programming environments, and graphics-oriented user interfaces.

EXPRESS. Sophisticated financial modeling expert system. EXPRESS is a product of Management Decision System.

expression. An expression defines the computation of a value.

EXPRS. EXPRS (EXpert PRolog System) is a knowledge engineering language for rule-based representation. Its principal characteristics include an Englishlike rule format, an attribute-object-value knowledge representation scheme, and a forward and backward chaining inference mechanism. The Englishlike nature of the rules facilitates the addition of complex rules and enables EXPRS to automatically generate answers to questions about why and how a rule fired. EXPRS has an automatic bookkeeping system that supports the explanation facility. PROLOG code can also be accessed directly using a rule clause form. EXPRS is implemented in PROLOG and operates on DEC-10 computer systems. It was developed by the Lockheed Palo Alto Research Laboratory.

exoskeleton. An articulated robot mechanism whose joints correspond to those of a human arm and, when attached to the arm of a human operator, will move in correspondence to his or hers. Exoskeleton devices are sometimes instrumented and used for master-slave control of manipulators.

extension. Orientation or motion toward a position where the joint angle between 2 connected bodies is 180°.

external sensor. A sensor for measuring displacements, forces, or other variables in the environment external to the robot.

F

facet. An element in a frame representation to be filled with designated information about the particular situation. Facets may correspond to intrinsic features, such as name, definition, or creator, or they may represent derived attributes, such as value, significance, or analogous objects. An attribute associated with a node in a frame system. The node may stand for an object, concept, or event; e.g., a node representing the object employee might have a slot for the attribute name and 1 for the attribute address. These facets would then be filled with the employee's actual name and address.

fact. Broadly, a statement whose validity is accepted. In most knowledge systems a fact consists of an attribute and a specific associated value.

fade. The gradual lowering of a signal amplitude.

fail-safe. Failure without damage or hazard. Robots are often provided with fail-safe brakes so their motions will "freeze" in the event of loss of power.

FAITH. FAITH is a general-purpose diagnostician whose initial application is the troubleshooting of spacecraft by monitoring the telemetry stream transmitted to earth. That stream contains test measurements from a wide variety of subsystems. FAITH uses its knowledge of the system under scrutiny to evaluate the data and to discover the most likely causes of the symptoms. FAITH represents declarative knowledge as frames that are expanded into logical assertions as required. Procedural knowledge is represented as production rules. FAITH's reasoning engine employs predicate logic and alternates between backward and forward chaining. FAITH was developed at the Jet Propulsion Laboratory.

FALCON. FALCON identifies probable causes of process disturbances in a chemical process plant by interpreting data consisting of numerical values from gauges and the status of alarms and switches. The system interprets the data by using knowledge of the effects induced by a fault in a given component and how disturbances in the input of a component will lead to disturbances in the output. Knowledge is represented in 2 ways—as a set of rules controlled by forward chaining and as a causal model in network form. The system is implemented in LISP and was developed at the University of Delaware.

fall time. The time required for an output voltage of a digital circuit to change from a logic 1 to a logic 0 state.

fan-out. The number of parallel loads within a given logic family that can be driven from 1 output mode of a logic circuit.

feature. Certain characteristics of a machine vision image, such as edges, contours, silhouettes, transitions from black to white, or vice versa, pixel amplitudes, edge-point locations and textural descriptors, or somewhat more elaborate image patterns, such as boundaries and regions.

feature vector. A set of features of an object (such as area, number of holes, etc.) that can be used for its identification.

feedback control. A guidance technique used by robots to bring the end effector to a programmed point.

Edward A. Feigenbaum. Edward A. Feigenbaum is professor of computer science at Stanford University. He is principal investigator of the Heuristic Programming Project at Stanford, a leading laboratory for work in knowledge engineering and expert systems. Dr. Feigenbaum also heads the national computer facility for applications of artificial intelligence to medicine and biology known as the SUMEX-AIM facility, established by NIH at Stanford. He is the past president of the American Association for Artificial Intelligence. He has served on the National Science Foundation Computer Science Advisory Board and the Defense Advanced Research Projects Agency (DARPA) Advisory Committee for the Strategic Computing Project. He is the co-editor of *The Handbook of Artificial Intelligence.* He also coauthored *Applications of Artificial Intelligence in Organic Chemistry: The DENDRAL Program.* His most recent publication (coauthored with Pamela McCorduck) is *The Fifth Generation: Artificial Intelligence and Japan's Computer Challenge to the World.*

fetch. One of the 2 functional parts of an instruction cycle. The collective actions of acquiring a memory address and then an instruction or data byte from memory.

FG502-TASP. FG502-TASP assists technicians in the diagnosis of malfunctioning Tektronix FG502 function generators. The system uses ad hoc rules about system behavior together with heuristics gathered from experienced technicians rather than a theoretical model of the FG502 operation, which would require advanced electronics principles. In addition to querying the technician to direct the diagnosis, the system provides a graphical display of the parts layout on the relevant circuit board and a picture of what the waveform should look like when measured at a given point on the board. FG502-TASP is an object-oriented system implemented in SMALLTALK-80. It was developed by Tektronix.

fiber optic image cable. A bundle of optical fibers that can transmit a real image through its length without distortion.

fiber optics. A communication technique where information is transmitted in the form of light over a transparent fiber material such as a strand of glass. Advantages are noise-free communication not susceptible to electromagnetic interference.

field. One of the 2 or more equal parts into which a display frame is divided in an interlaced scanning system. An area of an instruction mnemonic.

field frequency. The number of fields displayed per second. The United States standard is 60 fields/second. The European standard is 50 fields/second. Also called field-repetition rate.

Fifth-Generation Computers. The next generation of computing machines. It is assumed that they will be larger and faster and will incorporate fundamentally new designs. Parallel processing, the ability of a computer to process several different programs simultaneously, is expected to result in a massive increment in computational power. Since expert systems tend to be very large and involve a large amount of processing, it is assumed that expert systems will not reach maturity until these more powerful machines are available.

file. A collection of data records treated as a single unit.

file maintenance. The processing of a master file required to handle the nonperiodic changes in it.

fill. Solid coloring or shading of display surface made by a pattern of line segments.

filled surface. The transition surface that blends together 2 surfaces; for example, an airplane wing and the plane's body.

filter. Device to suppress interference that would appear as noise.

filtering. The exclusion of either data or rules from the match process for the sake of efficiency.

finite element model. Mathematical model of an object divided for structural analysis into an array of discrete elements.

fire. Execute the set of actions specified in the right-hand side of an instantiation of a rule. The term is derived from neurophysiology: When a neuron generates an action potential or spike, it is said to fire.

firmware. Computer programs, instructions, or functions implemented in user-modifiable hardware, i.e., a microprocessor with read-only memory. Such programs or instructions, stored permanently in programmable read-only memories, constitute a fundamental part of system hardware.

First Order Predicate Logic. A popular form of logic used by the artificial intelligence community for representing knowledge and performing logical inference. First Order Predicate Logic permits assertions to be made about variables in a proposition.

fixed-point part. In a floating-point representation, the number that is multiplied by the exponential implicit floating-point base to determine the real number represented.

fixed stop robot. A robot with stop point control but no trajectory control; i.e., each of its axes has a fixed limit at each end of its stroke and cannot stop except at 1 or the other of these limits. Such a robot with N degrees of freedom can therefore stop at no more than 2 locations (where location includes position and orientation). Often very good repeatability can be obtained with a fixed stop robot.

fixture. A device to hold and locate a workpiece during inspection or production operations.

flag. A status bit that indicates that a certain condition has arisen during the course of arithmetic or logic manipulations or data transmission between a pair of digital electronic devices. Some flags may be tested and thus be used for determining subsequent actions.

flag register. A register consisting of the flag flip-flops.

FLAVORS. A programming language for object-oriented representation within ZETALISP. It augments the ZETALISP environment, allowing it to support structured objects (much as STROBE provides object-oriented support for INTERLISP). Its principal characteristics include simple definition of abstract types, message passing, and generalization hierarchies. FLAVORS also allows property lists to be associated with objects. FLAVORS is implemented in ZETALISP and operates on the symbolics 3600 series workstations. It was developed by Symbolics.

flicker. A perceived rapid periodic change. Flicker disappears when the frequency of the stimulus change exceeds a rate called the critical flicker frequency.

flip-flop. A bistable logic device. A device capable of assuming 2 stable states. A bistable device that may assume a given stable state depending upon the pulse history of 1 or more input points and having 1 or more output points. The device is capable of storing a bit of information, controlling gates, etc. A toggle.

floating-point representation. A number representation system in which each number, as represented by a pair of numerals, equals 1 of those numerals times a power of an implicit fixed position integer base, where the power is equal to the implicit base raised to the exponent represented by the other numeral.

floor-to-floor time. The total time elapsed for picking up a part, loading it into a machine, carrying out operations, and unloading it (back to the floor, bin, pallet, etc.); generally applies to batch production.

floppy disk. Magnetic recording on a flexible magnetic disk.

flow chart. A graphical representation of a sequence of operations, using symbols to represent the operations, such as: compute, substitute, compare, GO TO, IF, read, write, etc. Flow charts of different levels of generality can be drawn for a given problem solution. Terms used are system flow chart, program flow chart, coding level flow chart, etc. A symbolic representation of the algorithm required to solve a problem.

FOLIO. Helps portfolio managers determine client investment goals and select portfolios that best meet those goals. The system determines the client's needs during an interview and then recommends percentages of each fund that provide an optimum fit to the client's goals. FOLIO recognizes a small number of classes of securities (e.g., dividend-oriented, lower-risk stocks, and commodity-sensitive, higher-risk stocks) and maintains aggregate knowledge about the properties (e.g., rate of return) of the securities in each class. The system uses a forward chaining, rule-based representation plan to infer client goals and a linear programming plan to maximize the fit between the goals and the portfolio. FOLIO is implemented in MRS. It was developed at Stanford University.

following error. If the input shaft velocity of a servo system is constant, the output shaft will rotate at the same speed but lag behind with an angle just sufficient to provide the error signal necessary to maintain the drive. That error is known as the following error.

force feedback. A sensing technique using electrical or hydraulic signals to control a robot end effector.

force sensor. A sensor capable of measuring the forces and torques exerted by a robot at its wrist. Such sensors usually contain 6 or more independent sets of strain gauges plus amplifiers. Computer processing (analog or digital) converts the strain readings into 3 orthogonal torque readings in an arbitrary coordinate system. When mounted in the work surface, rather than the robot's wrist, such a sensor is often called a pedestal sensor.

FOREST. Isolates and diagnoses faults in electronic equipment. The system supplements the fault detection and isolation capabilities of current automatic test equipment (ATE) diagnostic software. FOREST's knowledge includes experimental rules of thumb from expert engineers (e.g., if all pulse period measurements fail, then look for a pulse amplitude problem), knowledge of the use of circuit diagrams (e.g., the generation of the main pulse triggers the system clock reset), and general electronic troubleshooting principles (e.g., insufficient amplitude of a signal may result from excessive resistance along the signal path). That knowledge is encoded using rules with PROSPECTOR-like certainty factors and a MYCIN-like explanation facility. FOREST is implemented in PROLOG. It was developed at the University of Pennsylvania in cooperation with RCA Corporation.

format. The predetermined arrangement of characters, fields, lines, page numbers, punctuation marks, etc. Refers to input, output, and files.

FORUM. The FORUM environment is a set of modules that may be combined with an interface to provide decision support. The modules of which FORUM is made up provide knowledge representation and inference capabilities. The following are the modules under investigation: *BRUTUS:* A facility for the representation and manipulation of dependency networks in Knowledge Craft. BRUTUS provides standard relations and schemata to represent dependencies and new versions of slot and value creation/deletion functions that maintain those networks. For example, when a value is deleted, all values depending upon it are also deleted. *NERO:* A facility for the representation and manipulation of quantitative information in Knowledge Craft. NERO allows the user to construct multi-dimensional quantity spaces and relate points and subspaces by equations. It will evaluate those equations to determine the value of points in the space. NERO uses BRUTUS to represent dependencies between slots and values as defined by the equations. *CAESAR:* A facility for the representation and manipulation of production rule information in SRL+. CAESAR extends PSRL by allowing the user to construct a production-rule representation of deductive knowledge, interpret in either a forward or backward chaining mode, and use BRUTUS to represent dependencies between deduced information. *DIOGINES:* A facility for the explanation of dependencies represented by BRUTUS.

forward chaining. Problem-solving technique characterized by working forward from known facts toward conclusions. The method that starts with initial knowledge and applies inference rules to generate new knowledge until either one of the in-

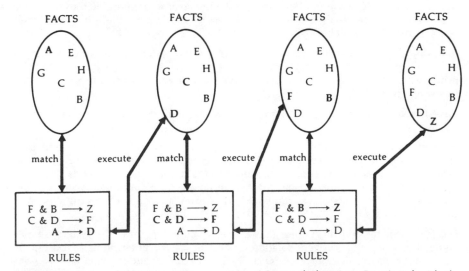

Figure F-1. Forward Chaining—An example of forward chaining. *Reprinted with the permission of Addison-Wesley Publishing Company from "A Guide to Expert Systems" by Donald A. Waterman.*

ferences satisfies a goal or no further inferences can be made. In forward-chaining production systems, the applicability of a rule is determined by matching the conditions specified on its left-hand side against the knowledge currently stored in data memory. In an expert system, a forward-chaining rule can detect certain facts in the database and takes an action because of them. An expert system that employs forward-chaining techniques is also called a data-driven system.

Mark S. Fox. Mark S. Fox Heads the Intelligent Systems Laboratory of The Robotics Institute and is an assistant professor of industrial administration at Carnegie-Mellon University. His primary interests in artificial intelligence is knowledge-based management and manufacturing systems. At present, his laboratory is extending artificial intelligence techniques to the design and construction of engineering, production control, and management systems for "flexible" factory organizations. Dr. Fox received a B.Sc. in Computer Science from the University of Toronto and a Ph.D. in Artificial Intelligence from Carnegie-Mellon University. Dr. Fox's publications include: "The Intelligent Management System: An Overview" in *Processes and Tools for Decision Support;* "A Knowledge-Based System for Factory Scheduling" in *International Journal of Expert Systems;* and "Artificial Intelligence in Manufacturing" in *Artificial Intelligence* magazine.

frame. A knowledge representation based on the idea of a frame of reference. A frame carries with it a set of slots that can represent objects that are normally associated with the subject of the frame. The slots can then point to other slots or frames. That gives frame systems the ability to carry out inheritance and simple kinds of inferencing. A knowledge representation method that associates features with nodes representing concepts or objects. The features are described in terms of attributes (called slots) and their values. The nodes form a network connected by relations and organized into a hierarchy. Each node's slots can be filled with values to help describe the concept that the node represents. The process of adding or removing values from the slots can activate procedures (self-contained pieces of code) attached to the slots. The procedures may then modify values in other slots, continuing the process until the desired goal is achieved. The total amount of instantaneous information (as perceived by the viewer) presented by a display. In 2-field interlaced raster scanning, a frame is the time interval between the vertical retrace at the start of the first field and the end of the second field.

frame-based CAI. A computer-assisted instruction technique based on the method used in a programmed instruction text. The material presented to the student depends on how the questions asked are answered.

frame-based methods. Programming methods using frame hierarchies for inheritance and procedural attachment. **(See figure p. 114.)**

frame buffer. Memory device that stores the contents of an image pixel by pixel. Frame buffers are used to refresh a raster image. Sometimes they incorporate local processing ability and can be used to update the memory. The "depth" of the frame buffer is the number of bits per pixel, which determines the number of colors of intensities that can be displayed.

frame frequency. The number of frames displayed per second. The United States standard is 30 frames/second. The European standard is 25 frames/second.

framework system. A type of artificial intelligence systems-building tool designed to reduce the amount of time required to develop an expert system. A framework system includes built-in knowledge representation and reasoning techniques, and may also include editors, translators, and debugging tools to simplify the coding of expert knowledge in a form that the computer can use. A knowledge engineer

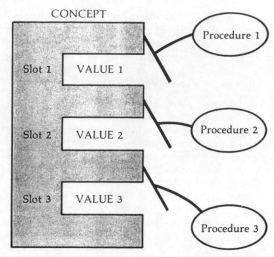

Figure F–2. Frame-based Methods—A node in a frame system. *Reprinted with the permission of Addison-Wesley Publishing Company from "A Guide to Expert Systems" by Donald A. Waterman.*

customizes a framework system for a specific application by building a knowledge base for the problem domain of interest.

FRANZLISP. The dialect of LISP developed at the University of California, Berkeley.

FRL. A knowledge engineering language for frame-based representation. Its principal characteristics include support for multiple inheritance, defaults, constraints such as requirements and preferences, abstraction, indirection, and procedural attachment that includes IF-ADDED, IF-NEEDED, and IF-REMOVED methods. FRL was developed at M.I.T.

frequency response. If a system is subjected to a sine-wave input whose amplitude is constant, but whose frequency varies, the amplitude of the output and its phase relative to the input sine wave will vary. This variation related to frequency is called the frequency response.

full-duplex mode. Allows 2 computers to transmit and receive data at the same time.

function. A standard, prepackaged set of coded instructions for carrying out a computer operation, such as finding the square root of a number.

functional application. The generic task or function performed in an application.

fusing. A machine vision operation that causes separate blobs to fuse into 1 larger blob.

fuzzy logic. An approach to approximate reasoning in which truth values and quantifiers are defined as possibility distributions that carry linguistic labels, such as true, very true, not very true, many, not very many, few, and several. The rules of inference are approximate, rather than exact, in order to better manipulate information that is incomplete, imprecise, or unreliable.

fuzzy set. A generalization of set theory that allows for various degrees of set membership, rather than all or none.

G

GAI. GAI analyzes DNA structure from restriction enzyme segmentation data. The system accepts enzyme digest data, topology, tolerance, and other constraints. After repeatedly generating and discarding possible candidate structures, it finally determines plausible DNA structures. The expertise contained in GAI is a textbook model of the mechanism involved in enzyme digestion analysis of DNA structures, augmented with knowledge of the nature of errors inherent in laboratory test environments. GAI follows the generate-and-test paradigm used in DENDRAL: Hypotheses are proposed by a generator based on a procedure for enumerating all possible solutions. The system provides a user-adjustable contradiction tolerance level to compensate for small amounts of erroneous data. GAI is written in INTERLISP. It was developed at Stanford University.

GALEN. GALEN diagnoses cases of congenital heart disease in children. The system uses data describing the patient's medical history, physical examinations, X rays, and EKGs to identify the disease present. GALEN hypothesizes a small set of possible diseases and then prioritizes them based on the degree of fit between its expectations for each disease and the actual patient data values. GALEN's expertise is based on models of pediatric cardiology diseases. Knowledge is represented as a combination of rules and frames, with the rules describing the conditions under which a hypothesis should be considered, accepted, rejected, or modified. GALEN uses the frames to collect information relevant to a particular disease hypothesis. The system was developed at the University of Minnesota.

GAMMA. GAMMA helps nuclear physicists identify the composition of unknown substances by interpreting gamma-ray activation spectra produced when the substance is bombarded with neutros. The system performs the identification by using knowledge about characteristic radiation energies and intensities emitted by different substances. Knowledge in the system is processed via the generate-and-test paradigm. The system was developed by Schlumberger-Doll Research.

gantry. A bridgelike frame along which a suspended robot moves. A gantry creates a much larger work envelope than the robot would have if it were pedestal mounted.

gap. An interval of space or time associated with an area of data processing activity (record) to indicate or signal the end of that record.

garbage collection. A technique for recycling computer memory cells no longer in use.

gate. A logic circuit with 1 output and several inputs designed so that the output is energized only when certain input conditions are met. An individual unit of logic such as an OR gate or an AND gate.

gate array. An integrated circuit characterized by a rectangular array of logic sites. The sites consist of identical collections of diffused or implanted transistors, diodes, and resistors. Surrounding the array are the input/output circuits for off-chips connections. The final process in creating the desired circuit is the custom metaleization of the logic sites and their subsequent interconnections. Gate-array design permits a standard set of logic elements to be used for a wide variety of integrated circuit applications.

Gaussian. A Gaussian distribution is a frequency distribution for a set of variable data, sometimes called a normal distribution and typically represented by a bell-shaped curve that is symmetrical about the mean.

Gaussian filtering. A convolution procedure in which the weighting of pixels in the template fall off with distance according to a Gaussian distribution.

GCA. GCA helps graduate students plan their computer science curriculum. The system gathers information about a student's academic history and interests and then acts as a faculty adviser by suggesting a schedule of courses. GCA's expertise includes departmental and university regulations regarding graduate degree programs, course descriptions, and sequences of courses frequently taken by computer science students. The knowledge in GCA is organized as 4 interacting subsystems under the direction of a manager program. Those subsystems determine (1) the number of courses the student should take, (2) the courses the student is permitted to take, (3) the best courses to take, and (4) the best schedule for the student. GCA's knowledge is encoded as rules with associated certainty factors. The system is implemented in PROLOG using a MYCIN-like inference engine. It was developed at Duke University.

GEN-X. A knowledge engineering language for rule-based representations that also supports frame-based and decision table representation methods. The GEN-X system consists of a knowledge manager that provides an interactive graphics facility for knowledge base creation and editing, interpreters for the various representations that drive consultation sessions, and code generators that translate the knowledge base and appropriate interpreters into programs written in C, ADA, PASCAL, and FORTRAN. GEN-X is implemented in the C programming language and operates on the IBM PC and a variety of minicomputers. It was developed at General Electric's Research and Development Center.

General Problem Solver (GPS). The first problem solver (1957) to separate its problem-solving methods from knowledge of the specific task being considered. The GPS problem-solving approach employed was "means-ends analysis."

generalization. An abstract principle that captures commonalities among a set of specific instances. The process of deriving an abstract principle, either deductively or inductively. The learning mechanism by which an abstract principle is derived by making a specific principle more abstract. In learning programs implemented as production systems, a learning mechanism that relaxes the constraints on a rule so that it can apply to a wider range of data.

generalized cone (generalized cylinder). A volumetric model defined by a space curve, called the spine or axis, and a planar cross section normal to the axis. A "sweeping rule" describes how the cross section changes along the axis.

generalized ribbon. A planar region approximated by a medial line (axis) and the perpendicular distances to the boundary. The 2-dimensional version of a generalized cone.

general-purpose knowledge engineering language. A computer language designed for building expert systems and incorporating features that make it applicable to different problem areas and types.

general purpose vision system. A vision system that is universally applicable. A system that is based on generic rather than specific knowledge. A system that can deal with unfamiliar or unexpected input.

generate and test. A problem-solving technique involving a generator that produces possible solutions and an evaluator that tests the acceptability of those solutions.

generative grammar. A formal grammar of a language expressed as a set of rules that can be applied to generate all the sentences of the language and no sentences that are not in that language. A generative grammar is not necessarily the best way to represent the grammar for purposes of classifying or parsing sentences in the language.

generic unit. A generic unit is a template either for a set of subprograms or for a set of packages. A subprogram or package created using the template is called an instance of the generic unit. A generic instantiation is the kind of declaration that creates an instance. A generic unit is written as a subprogram or package but with the specification prefixed by a generic formal part that may declare generic formal parameters. A generic formal parameter is either a type, a subprogram, or an object. A generic unit is 1 of the kinds of program unit.

GENESIS. Expert system that helps to plan and simulate gene-splicing experiments.

geometric processing. The process of taking measurements that are characteristic for the geometry of certain objects in an image. Examples: area, coordinates of center of gravity, orientation, perimeter, number and location of holes.

GETREE. A system-building aid for managing a knowledge base organized as a network that forms an AND/OR graph representation of rules. The AND/OR graph provides the mechanism for direct graphic documentation of the rules, for answering how, how not, why, and why not questions about conclusions and facts, for displaying execution traces of forward- or backward-chaining inferences, for modifying inference strategies, and for teaching the rules to a user. The support environment includes an interactive graphical interface that uses a VT100 alphanumeric terminal with graphics character set and spoken output via a speech synthesizer. GETREE operates on DEC VAX computers under the VMS operating system. It was developed by General Electric Company.

GLIB. GLIB is a knowledge engineering language for rule-based representation. It is used to acquire troubleshooting rules for electronic instruments. GLIB provides a vocabulary and syntax for expressing rules, specifications, and observations about the behavior of general analog devices. Menu-based rule acquisition is supported through the use of expectation tables the provide the alternative choices for each word in the rule as it is being constructed. GLIB is implemented in SMALLTALK-80 and operates on the Tektronix 4404 Artificial Intelligence System. It was developed by Tektronix, Inc.

global data base. Complete data base describing the specific problem, its status, and that of the solution process.

global method. A method based on nonlocal aspects, e.g., region splitting by thresholding based on an image histogram.

global operation. Transformation of the gray scale value of the picture elements according to the gray scale values of all elements of the picture. Examples are Fourier transform, correlation, etc.

goal. The solution a system attempts to reach using operations. Sometimes, in order to reach the goal, subgoals must first be achieved. The end to which problem solving aims. In a production system a goal may be represented in a separate memory or in a distinguished class of working memory elements.

goal directed. Another term for backward chaining. Used in contrast to data directed.

goal driven. A problem-solving approach that works backward from the goal. A top-down approach often referred to as "hypothesize and test."

goal regression. A technique for constructing a plan by solving 1 conjunctive subgoal at a time, checking to see that each solution does not interfere with the other subgoals that have already been achieved. If interferences occur, the offending subgoal is moved to an earlier noninterfering point in the sequence of subgoal accomplishments.

goal tree. A tree data structure in which the root node represents a goal to be achieved, and the children of each goal represent subgoals that when achieved suffice to achieve the goal represented by their parent. A goal tree may be an and/or tree.

Golden Common LISP. GCLISP, a state-of-the-art LISP training and development system for microcomputers, creates an inexpensive yet powerful environment for exploratory programming in artificial intelligence. Developed by Gold Hill Computers, GCLISP is the first implementation of Common LISP on microcomputers. GCLISP provides an intelligent software environment that makes it easy for programmers to learn both the LISP programming language and advanced development techniques. Yet it is comprehensive enough to give experienced LISP programmers the tools to create and deliver practical applications—all at a fraction of what it would cost to implement a LISP environment comparable in functions and features on special purpose hardware or larger general-purpose computers.

Golden Common LISP Interpreter. The GCLISP Interpreter implements 60% of the standard Common LISP primitives and significantly extends the functions of Common LISP. The interpreter includes advanced programming tools—including a symbolic debugger and an error-handling system—that make development efforts far more productive. Input/output functions are implemented as streams of data that can be redirected easily from 1 output device to another.

GPSI. GPSI is a system-building aid for the construction of rule-based systems. It consists of an integrated collection of tools that include: a monitor for supervising the interaction between different units in the system, a knowledge acquisition unit, an inference engine, a rule compiler, and a user interface. The knowledge acquisition unit provides both text and graphical editing facilities to help users construct rules. it also handles bookkeeping and answers user queries about the system's rules. GPSI contains mechanisms for certainty handling and automatic user querying. It can also execute the expert system by applying the inference engine to the compiled rules. GPSI was developed at the University of Illinois.

graded series. A scale of colors used in graphics to present change in a variable. A graded series may be composed of progressive change in either lightness or saturation of 1 hue, in hue steps around the hue circle, or along the gray scale.

gradient. A vector indicating the change of gray scale values in a certain neighborhood of a pixel. The gradient can be obtained by applying a difference operation on the neighborhood. Often only the magnitude is calculated as means to obtain the contour of an object.

gradient space. A coordinate system (p,q) in which p and q are the rates of change in depth (gray value) of the surface of an object in the scene along the x and y directions (the coordinates in the image plane). Thus (p,q,l) has the direction of the surface normal.

gradient vector. The orientation and magnitude of the rate of change in intensity at a point in the image.

granularity. The level of detail in a chunk of information, e.g., a rule or frame.

graph. An image representation in which nodes represent regions and arcs between nodes represent properties of and relations between those regions.

graphic system. A system that collects, uses, and presents information in pictorial form.

graphics. Using computer technology to create a drawing that is usually displayed on a terminal or plotter.

graphics processor. Controller that accesses the display list, interprets the display instructions, and passes graphics data to the vector generator.

graphics terminal. An "intelligent" terminal that receives data from a minicomputer or mainframe and can manipulate that data by means of its own processor; most minicomputers can be converted into graphics terminals by purchasing appropriate software or interfaces or both.

Grassmann's Law. The sum (or mixture) of 2 colors can be matched by summing the primary-color components of each color.

gray level. A quantified measurement of image irradiance (brightness) or some other pixel property.

gray-scale picture. A digitized image in which the brightness of the pixels can have more than 2 values, typically 128 or 256; requires more storage space and much more sophisticated image processing than a binary image but offers potential for improved visual sensing.

gripper. A clamp at the tip of a robot arm used for grasping an object. A gripper is 1 type of end effector. **(See figure p. 120.)**

GUESS/1. GUESS/1 is a knowledge engineering language for rule-based representation. It also supports relational tables, hierarchical trees, semantic nets, and frames. Control knowledge is encoded in frames and rules, which allow both backward and forward chaining. Frames can trigger rules, and rules can invoke frames. Multiple knowledge sources communicate via a blackboard mechanism. A multilevel security mechanism allows each table, tree, network, or frame to be labeled to control access on the basis of a user's security clearance. GUESS/1's support environment includes an explanation facility and a natural language and menu facility. GUESS/1 is implemented in PROLOG and runs under the VMS operating system on a DEC VAX 11/780. It was developed at the computer science department of Virginia Polytechnic Institute and State University.

GUIDON. GUIDON is an intelligent computer-aided instructional program for teaching diagnosis, such as medical diagnosis. Without reprogramming, the GUIDON program can interact with a student to diagnose those problems that it can solve on its own. Moreover, by substituting problem-solving knowledge from other domains, the program can immediately discuss problems in those domains. That power derives from the use of artificial intelligence methods for representing both subject material and knowledge about how to teach. They are represented independently, so the

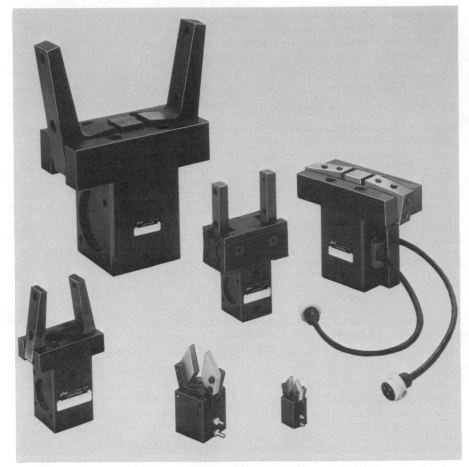

Figure G–1. Gripper—PHd Inc. Smart Robot Grippers.

teaching knowledge is general. There are teaching rules and procedures for: determining what the student knows, responding to his partial solution, providing hints, and opportunistically interrupting to test his understanding. Experience with GUIDON reveals the importance of separating out casual and strategic knowledge in order to explain diagnostic rules and to teach a reasoning approach. The lessons are now guiding the development of new representations for teaching. The program instructs students in the selection of antimicrobial therapy for hospital patients with bacterial infections. The system selects a case, solves it, presents it to the student to solve, and analyzes the student's responses and queries during the solution process. From that the system determines how closely the student's knowledge and reasoning match the diagnosis procedure it used to solve the case. The differences found are used to guide the system's tutoring and explanation mechanisms. GUIDON actually uses the MYCIN expert system to solve the cases; thus it teaches students the rules and procedures embedded in MYCIN. GUIDON is a rule-based system containing both rules and metarules (rules to decide how to use the rules). It is implemented in INTERLISP and was developed at Stanford University.

GUMMEX. GUMMEX is an expert system for generating process-plans for rubber products, which produces a document for the shop floor detailing the sequence of manufacturing operations, the machines involved, and the technical details of the manufacturing process, such as times, temperatures, weights, dimensions, etc. GUMMEX consists of a graphics package, a set of ancillary programs, an inference engine, and 3 rule-modules. The graphics package allows the interactive description of parts belonging to predefined families producing the corresponding drawings. The planning mechanism of GUMMEX is implemented as forward-chaining production systems. Its knowledge base comprises at present about 400 production rules.

H

Half-ASCII. A 64-character ASCII code that contains the code words for numeric digits, alphabetic characters, and symbols, but not keyboard operations.

half-duplex. A data transmission mode that provides both transmission and reception, but not simultaneously.

hand. A device attached to the end of a robot manipulator arm having a mechanism with closing jaws or other means to grasp objects.

handshake. Interactive communication between 2 system components, such as between the control processing unit and a peripheral; often required to prevent loss of data.

HANNIBAL. Performs situation assessment in the area of communications intelligence. It identifies enemy organizational units and their communication order of battle by interpreting data from sensors that monitor radio communications. The data include information about the location and signal characteristics (e.g., frequency, modulation, channel class, etc.) of the detected communications. Knowledge in HANNIBAL is represented within a backboard architecture using multiple specialists or knowledge sources. The system is implemented in AGE. It was developed by ESL.

hardware. The mechanical, magnetic, and electronic components of a system. Examples include computer processors and telephone switching equipment. The physical parts of a computer system, including printed circuit boards and wiring, in contrast to software, the programs and languages of a computer system.

hardware debugging. Process of finding and fixing malfunctioning electronic equipment, particularly digital equipment.

hardwired. An electronics programming technique using soldered connections; hence, not readily reprogrammable. Hardwired memories in early robots employed a wire matrix to register voltages from feedback potentiometers.

harmony. Subjective term referring to a systematic or orderly choice of colors, contributing to a balanced graphic image. On the color wheel, complementary colors, adjacent colors, and colors at equal intervals are typically considered harmonious. A color series that alters only 1 of the 3 dimensions of color (hue, lightness, saturation) is also thought to be harmonious.

HARPY. Simple experimental speech-understanding system intended to show what can be done without resorting to sophisticated techniques.

HASP Detects and identifies various types of ocean vessels using digitized acoustic data from hydrophone arrays. The data take the form of sonogram displays, which are analog histories of the spectrum of received sound energy. The system uses knowledge about the sound signature traits of different ship classes to perform the interpretation. HASP attempts to identify the vessels and to organize them into higher-level units, such as fleets. It provides real-time analysis and situation updating for continuously arriving data. Knowledge is represented as rules within a blackboard architecture using a hierarchically organized control scheme. HASP (also known as SU/X) was an initial investigation phase and formed the foundation for SIAP. The system is implemented in INTERLISP and was developed through a joint effort by Stanford University and Systems Control Technology.

Frederick Hayes-Roth. Frederick Hayes-Roth received his A.B. in applied mathematics from Harvard University, his M.S. in computer and communications sciences from the University of Michigan, and his Ph.D. in mathematical psychology from the University of Michigan. He has held faculty appointments at M.I.T., Stanford University, and Carnegie-Mellon University. Before joining Teknowledge, Dr. Hayes-Roth directed The Rand Corporation's research program in artificial intelligence and was a principal designer of Hearsay-II, one of the first 1000-word continuous speech understanding systems, the ROSIE system for programming knowledge systems, and many knowledge systems for military decision making.

HCPRVR. A logic-based programming language and interpreter. An HCPRVR program is an ordered list of axioms, each of which is either an atomic formula or an implication. An atomic formula is an arbitrary LISP expression beginning with a LISP atom, which is referred to as its predicate name. NCPRVR allows the use of LISP functions in place of predicate names, in which case the function is called instead of having the HCPRVR interpreter prove the formula. The interpreter is a Horn clause-based theorem prover. HCPRVR is implemented in LISP and was originally designed to operate on DEC PDP-10 computer systems. It was developed at the University of Texas at Austin.

HDDSS. Helps physicians determine and select appropriate treatment for patients with Hodgkin's disease. The system applies Bayesian estimation techniques to produce a priori probabilities of the extent of tumor spread. It then uses those probabilities to help select a diagnostic procedure or treatment. After it chooses a diagnostic procedure, it uses Bayes' theorem to revise the probabilities and the process continues. HDDSS finally produces an optimal diagnostic plan and a set of near optimal plans for the physician to study. The system contains radiotherapy knowledge in a hierarchical taxonomy and patient data in a relational data base. HDDSS is implemented in MACLISP. It was developed at M.I.T.

HEARSAY-III. HEARSAY-III is a knowledge engineering language for rule-based representation. It integrates rules with a blackboard architecture consisting of knowledge sources that communicate via a central blackboard or data base. Each knowledge source is a collection of rules that execute by matching data and knowledge in the blackboard. In HEARSAY-III the blackboard has 2 parts: a domain blackboard for reasoning about the problem domain, and a scheduling blackboard for reasoning about when and how to apply the domain knowledge. HEARSAY-III supports the design of systems requiring asynchronous processing of information and the design of control structures for handling multiple goals. HEARSAY-III is implemented in LISP. It was developed by the Information Sciences Institute. **(See figure p. 124.)**

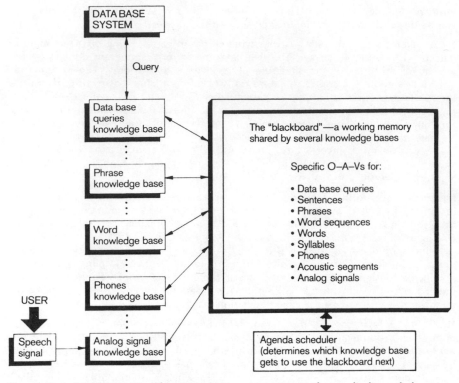

Figure H–1. HEARSAY-III—The HEARSAY system. (Note that only five of the nine knowledge bases are shown.) *Reprinted with the permission of John Wiley and Sons, from "Expert Systems—Artificial Intelligence in Business" by Paul Harmon and David King.*

HEART IMAGE INTERPRETER. Helps physicians perform a diagnostic interpretation of the motional behavior of the heart. The system analyzes 2-dimensional intensity distribution images of the heart produced by injecting the radionuclide substance Technetium 99-m into the patient's vein. A scintillation camera produces a sequence of 12 to 64 images for the system to analyze and interpret. Knowledge in the system includes the structural properties of the heart and left ventricle, the motional phases of a heart cycle, and rules for relating medical evidence to diagnoses. Image processing and medical diagnostic knowledge is encoded in a semantic net containing frames and associated rules that use certainty factors. HEART IMAGE INTERPRETER is implemented in RATFOR, a dialect of FORTRAN. It was developed at the University of Erlangen.

HEME. HEME helps physicians diagnose hematologic diseases. The system uses patient findings entered by a physician and a version of Bayes' theorem to compute the probability that the patient has each of the diseases currently registered in the system. HEME then displays a listing of differential diagnoses together with their probability of occurrence. Knowledge in HEME includes estimates of the frequency of occurrence of a given disease, the probability that a patient with the disease has a given finding, and the probability that a patient without the disease has a given finding. Those conditional probabilities represent the judgments of experienced hematology clinicians and include measures of how confident the clinicians are about their original probability estimates. HEME was developed at Cornell University.

heterarchical approach. An image interpretation control structure in which no processing stage is in sole command, but in which each stage can control other stages to its needs as required.

heuristic. Experiential, judgmental knowledge; the knowledge underlying "expertise"; rules of thumb, rules of good guessing, that usually achieve desired results but do not guarantee them. A process, sometimes a rule of thumb, that may help in the solution of a problem but that does not guarantee the best solution, or indeed, any solution. A rule of thumb or other device or simplification that reduces or limits search in large problem spaces. Because the success of a heuristic is not guaranteed, a problem that can be solved by 1 algorithm frequently requires many heuristics. The primary effect of heuristics is to eliminate the need to examine every possible approach. Knowledge derived from experience. Usually referred to as rules of thumb or acquired wisdom, it is an ambiguous term defining an ambiguous type of knowledge. It is not based on defined sets of facts, but rather inferences made from experience in similar or related situations. One of the major obstacles in providing machines with intelligence is the current inability to define and structure heuristics for computer programming.

heuristic problem-solving. The ability to plan and direct ordered problem solving actions to achieve higher order goals.

Heuristic Programming Project. The research group at Stanford University that principally pioneered the field of knowledge engineering and produced a large collection of expert systems.

Heuristic Rules. Rules written to capture the heuristics an expert uses to solve a problem. The expert's original heuristics may not have taken the form of if—then rules, and one of the problems involved in building a knowledge system is now to convert an expert's heuristic knowledge into rules. The power of a knowledge system reflects the heuristic rules in the knowledge base.

heuristic search techniques. Graph searching methods that use heuristic knowledge about the domain to help focus the search. They operate by generating and testing intermediate states along potential solution paths.

hexadecimal numbering system. A numbering system using the equivalent of the decimal number 16 as a base. Most third-generation computers operate on a principle that utilizes the hexadecimal system, as it provides high utilization of computer storage and an expanded set of characters for representing data. In base 16 (hexadecimal), 16 symbols are required. Because only a single character is allowed for each absolute value, the hexadecimal system uses the 10 symbols of the decimal system for the values, 0 through 9, and the first 6 letters of the alphabet to represent values 10 through 15 (A through F, respectively). The positional significance of hexadecimal symbols is based on the progression of powers of 16. The highest number that can be represented in the units position is 15.

hierarchical approach (vision). An approach to vision based on a series of ordered processing levels in which the degree of abstraction increases as we proceed from the image level to the interpretation level. **(See figure p. 126.)**

hierarchical planning. A planning approach in which first a high level plan is formulated considering only the important aspects. Then the major steps of the plan are refined into more detailed subplans.

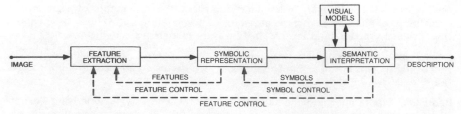

Figure H–2. Hierarchical Approach—Basic vision system image understanding hierarchical approach.

hierarchy. An ordered network of concepts or objects in which some are subordinate to others. Hierarchies occur in biological taxonomies and corporate organizational charts. Hierarchies ordinarily imply inheritance; and, thus, objects or concepts higher in the organization "contain" the objects or concepts that were beneath them. "Tangled hierarchies" occur when more than 1 higher-level entity inherits characteristics from a single lower-level entity.

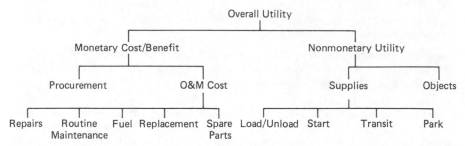

Figure H–3. Hierarchy—Hierarchical utility structure for sample problem. *Reproduced with the permission of AFCEA.*

higher levels. The interpretative processing stages such as those involving object recognition and scene description, as opposed to the lower levels corresponding to the image and descriptive stages.

high-level languages. A language in which the instructions more closely resemble English. One high-level language instruction often is converted into several machine-language instructions. Computer languages lie on a spectrum that ranges from machine instructions through intermediate languages like FORTRAN and COBOL to high-level languages like ADA and C. High-level languages incorporate more complex constructs than the simpler languages. **(See figure p. 127.)**

high-speed data. A rate of data transfer ranging upward from 10,000 bits per second.

histogram. Relative frequency of the gray scale value distribution in a digital image. The histogram of an image provides very important basic information about the image.

hither plane. Z-clipping plane nearest viewer defining front of view volume.

HODGKINS. An expert system that plans diagnostic procedures for Hodgkins disease.

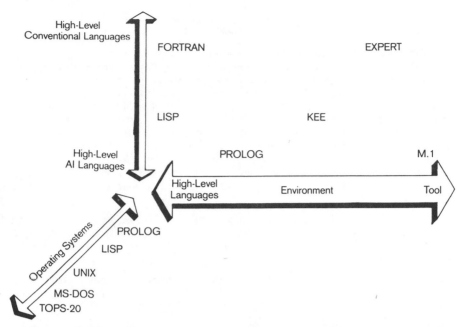

Figure H–4. High-Level Languages—A multidimensional language-tool spectrum. *Reprinted with the permission of John Wiley and Sons, from "Expert Systems— Artificial Intelligence in Business" by Paul Harmon and David King.*

Horn clause. In logic programming Horn clauses are expressions connected by "or" with at most 1 positive proposition. Thus, a Horn clause takes the form: "Not A or Not B or . . . or Not C or D." Logical programming is made more efficient by restricting the type of logical assertions to Horn clauses in much the same way that production systems insist on having knowledge stated in terms of if—then rules. Used in PROLOG.

host computer. The central processing unit which provides the computing power for terminals and peripheral devices that are connected to it.

HPRL. A knowledge engineering language for frame-based representation. It integrates a frame representation scheme with a rule-based representation. A core set of LISP functions perform rule execution under the supervision of a frame-based rule interpreter. HPRL supports forward- and backward-chaining control schemes and metarules that enable users to construct arbitrarily complex reasoning strategies. HPRL is an extension of FRL; it is implemented in PSL (a portable dialect of LISP) and operates on DEC VAX and HP-9836 computer systems. HPRL was developed by the computer research laboratory of Hewlett-Packard.

HSRL. A knowledge engineering language that provides logic programming capabilities. HSRL is embedded in SRL and effectively combines frame-based and logic-based representations. Logic programs are expressed as SRL frames. Atomic formulas can refer to information embedded in the frames; thus rules about properties of frames may use information from both the SRL knowledge base and the axioms in a logic-program schema. The support environment includes an interactive facility for creating, editing, and executing HSRL programs. The HSRL interpreter is a modified version of the HCPRVR logic program interpreter. HSRL is implemented in FRANZ LISP as an extension to SRL and operates under UNIX. It was developed at the Robotics Institute of Carnegie-Mellon University.

HT-ATTENDING. Critiques a physician's approach to the pharmacologic management of essential hypertension. The system helps physicians manage hypertensive patients and provides information about new drugs and treatments. It extends the approach used in ATTENDING to the domain of hypertension. HT-ATTENDING uses information about the patient (e.g., age, medical problems) together with information about the patient's present antihypertensive regimen and the proposed change to that regimen to critique the proposed change. The critique is generated as several paragraphs of English text. The system contains knowledge about antihypertensive agents used in outpatient treatment, treatment modalities, and conditions affecting hypertension management. It uses a frame-based knowledge representation scheme and is implemented in LISP. The system was developed at Yale University.

hue. Subjective term that refers to the objectively measurable dominant wavelength of radiant energy on the visible portion of the electromagnetic spectrum, the most basic attribute of color. Used loosely, hue can also refer to mixtures of different wavelengths, such as purple.

Hueckel operator. A method for finding edges in an image by fitting an intensity surface to the neighborhood of each pixel and selecting surface gradients above a chosen threshold value.

human information processing. A perspective on how humans think that is influenced by how computers work. That approach to pyschology begins by focusing on the information that a person uses to reach some conclusion and then asks how one could design a computer program that would begin with that same information and reach that same conclusion. Espoused by Herbert Simon and Allan Newell, the perspective currently dominates cognitive psychology and has influenced the design of both computer languages and programs.

human interface. One subsystem of an expert system with which the human user deals routinely. It aims to be as "natural" as possible, employing language as close as possible to ordinary language and understanding and displaying images, all at speeds that are comfortable and natural for humans. The other 2 subsystems in an expert system are the knowledge base management subsystem and the inference subsystem.

hunting. Occurs when a control system's output continuously searches for a final value. Very rapid hunting is usually termed oscillation.

HYDRO. An expert system that solves water resource problems. HYDRO helps a hydrologist use HSPF, a computer program that stimulates the physical processes by which precipitation is distributed throughout a watershed. The system assists in describing watershed characteristics to HSPF in the form of numerical parameters. The system estimates those parameters, using knowledge about soil type, land use, vegetation, geology, and their affect on the specific parameter in question. The system is patterned after PROSPECTOR; it uses a combination rule-based and semantic net formalism to encode its knowledge and bases its influences on the use of certainty factors and the propagation of probabilities associated with the data. The system is implemented in INTERLISP and was developed by SRI International.

hypothetical worlds. A way of structuring knowledge in a knowledge-based system that defines the contexts (hypothetical worlds) in which facts and rules apply.

I

I&W. I&W assists an intelligence analyst in predicting where and when an armed conflict will next occur. The system analyzes incoming intelligence reports, e.g., reports of troop location, activity and movements, using knowledge about common indicators of troop activity. Knowledge is represented within a blackboard architecture that uses both frames and forward chaining rules to organize the expertise. The system is implemented in INTERLISP-D for the Xerox 1100 series workstations. It was developed through a joint effort by ESL and Stanford University and reached the stage of a demonstration prototype.

icon. An imagelike symbol to which a computer user can point an interface device in order to select a function, such as "move window."

ICOT. Institute for New Generation Computer Technology. Formed by MITI to lead the Fifth Generation Project, it is composed of many of Japan's leading corporate and educational technology researchers.

identity. Two logic propositions that have the same truth value.

ideology machine. Stimulates conversational responses of committed ideologues.

IDT. IDT helps a technician locate the field replaceable units that should be replaced to fix faults in PDP 11/03 computers. The system uses knowledge about the unit under test, such as the functions of its components and their relation to each other, to select and execute diagnostic tests and interpret the results. The system is rule-based using forward chaining and is implemented in FRANZ LISP and OPS5. IDT was developed by Digital Equipment Corporation and reached the stage of a research prototype.

IF/Prolog Compiler. Translates Prolog programs into machine-code. Compiled programs into machine-code. Compiled programs are capable of performing 90 KLIPS on the SUN-3. The IF/Prolog compiler includes the compiler, an interpreter, a C-interface, and a Fullscreen BoxDebugger. Requires 512K minimum memory, VAX and Motorola 680xx systems. Sun, Cadmus 9000 price, $4,050; Venus 8800, $11,300.

IJCAI. The International Joint Conference on Artificial Intelligence. Held biannually, sponsored in the U.S. by AAAI.

if-then rule. A statement of a relationship among a set of facts. The relationships may be definitional (e.g., If female and married, then wife), or heuristic (e.g., If cloudy, then take umbrella).

Network of Rules

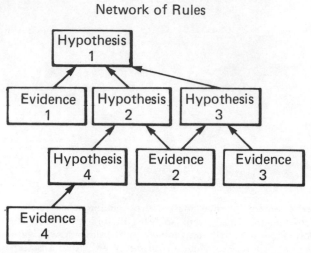

Figure I–1. If-Then-Rule—Expert systems may consist of hundreds of IF-THEN rules combined into networks like these.

IMACS. IMACS assists managers in a computer systems manufacturing environment with paperwork management, capacity planning, inventory management, and other tasks related to managing the manufacturing process. IMACS takes a customer's order and generates a rough build plan from which it can estimate the resource requirements for order. Just before the computer system in the order is built, IMACS generates a detailed build plan and uses it to monitor the computer system's implementation. IMACS is a forward-chaining, rule-based system organized as a set of cooperating knowledge-based subsystems. It is implemented in OPS5. IMACS was developed by Digital Equipment Corporation.

image. A projection of a scene into a plane. Usually represented as an array of brightness values.

image enhancement. The process of enhancing the quality of appearance of an image. Image enhancement operations may be noise filtering, contrast sharpening, edge enhancement, etc.

image plane. Z-plane on which an image is displayed.

image preprocessing. A computational step before the feature extraction step in an image analysis procedure. Preprocessing may serve the purpose of enhancing the features to be extracted or adjusting the image in other ways to certain conditions set forth by the subsequent feature extraction procedure.

image processing. Transformation of an input image into an output image with more desirable properties, such as increased sharpness, less noise, and reduced geometric distortion. Signal processing is a one-dimensional analog.

image transformation. Altering a display by clipping, scaling, rotating, translating, or shearing display elements.

image understanding. Employs geometric modeling and the artificial intelligence techniques of knowledge representation and cognitive processing to develop scene interpretations from image data. Image understanding has dealt extensively with 3-dimensional objects. Image understanding usually operates not on an image but on a symbolic representation of it. Image understanding is somewhat synonymous with computer vision and scene analysis.

imaging. Computer processing of graphics data to produce a display.

immediate addressing. The operand is the second byte of the instruction, rather than its address.

implementation environment. In the context of this book implementation refers to the overall environment in which an expert system will function. The implementation environment includes the hardware the system will run on, the operating system that will support the expert system, any higher-level languages that the system will depend upon, and any interfaces that the system will have with other computer systems or sensors. A small knowledge system, for example, might run on an IBM personal computer. The system would assume an operating system and need to have an expert system program installed before the knowledge system would work. So far, most expert systems and tools have been developed to run in very specific implementation environments, and one must consider the implementation requirements very carefully before deciding if one could use a system.

implied addressing. A 1-byte instruction that stipulates an operation internal to the processor. Does not require any additional operand.

implies. A connective in logic that indicates that if the first statement is true, the statement following is also true.

IMPULSE. A system-building aid that provides editing facilities for the STROBE knowledge engineering language. That display-oriented knowledge base editor provides 4 levels of editing: a top-level knowledge base manager, a knowledge base editor, an object/slot editor, and a facet editor. Each level has an editor window and associated command menus. IMPULSE also provides a graphical display of tree and graph hierarchies. Objects for editing may be selected from menus and from nodes in graphically displayed trees. IMPULSE is implemented in INTERLISP-D and operates on the Xerox 1100 series workstations. It was developed by Schlumberger-Doll Research as a research system.

IMS/VS. Information Management System/Virtual Storage. An IBM operating system, usually run with MVS and used primarily for transaction and batch processing.

INATE. Helps a technician troubleshoot a Tektronix Model 465 oscilloscope by analyzing symptoms and producing a decision tree of test points that the technician should check. The system applies 2 types of rules: those supplied by an expert diagnostician and those generated automatically from an internal model of the oscilloscope, which is a block diagram of the unit augmented with component failure rates. Knowledge is represented as rules incorporating probabilistic measures of belief about circuit malfunctions. As the rules are applied, the beliefs are updated through a procedure similar to minimaxing. The system is implemented in FRANZ LISP. It was developed at the Naval Research Laboratory.

IN-ATE/KE. A system-building aid for constructing fault diagnosis expert systems. Knowledge is represented as a high-level block diagram of the unit under test and includes information about component/test point connectivity. IN-ATE/KE supports a PROSPECTOR-like, rule-based semantic network and a data base containing component failure rates, accessible test points, test and setup costs, and component replacement costs. Semantic constraints on testing order are specified through rule preconditions. IN-ATE/KE generates an expert system in the IN-ATE framework and produces a testability report that includes a binary fault diagnosis decision tree. IN-ATE/KE (previously called IN-ATE/2) was developed at Automated Reasoning Corporation.

incident light. Light falling on an object. The color of an object is perceived as a function of the wavelengths of incident light reflected or absorbed by it.

increment. To increase the value of a binary word. Typically, to increase the value by 1.

index. An integer used to specify the location of information within a table or program.

index constraint. An index constraint for an array type specifies the lower and upper bounds for each index range of the array type.

index register. A memory device containing an index.

indexed address. A memory address formed by adding immediate data included with the instruction to the contents of some register or memory location.

indexed component. An indexed component denotes a component in an array. It is a form of name-containing expressions that specify the values of the indices of the array component. An indexed component may also denote an entry in a family of entries.

indexed indirect addressing. The second byte of the instruction is added to the contents of the index register, discarding the carry, to form a zero-page effective address.

indirect absolute addressing. The second and third bytes of the instruction contain the address for the first of 2 bytes in memory that contain the effective address.

indirect address. An address used with an instruction that indicates a memory location or a register that in turn contains the actual address of an operand. The indirect address may be included with the instruction, contained in a register, or contained in a memory location.

indirect indexed addressing. The second byte of this instruction is a zero-page address. The contents of this zero-page address are added to the Y index register to form the lower 3 bits of the effective address. Then the carry is added to the contents of the next zero-page address to form the higher 8 bits of the effective address.

individual. A nonvariable element in logic that cannot be broken down further.

induction system. A knowledge system that has a knowledge base consisting of examples. An induction algorithm builds a decision tree from the examples, and the system goes on to deliver advice. Induction systems do not facilitate the development of hierarchies of rules.

industrial robot. A reprogrammable, multi-functional manipulator designed to move material, parts, tools, or specialized devices through variable programmed motions for the performance of a variety of tasks. **(See figure p. 133.)**

industrial robot components. The 3 principal components of an industrial robot are 1 or more arms, usually situated on a fixed base, that can move in several directions;

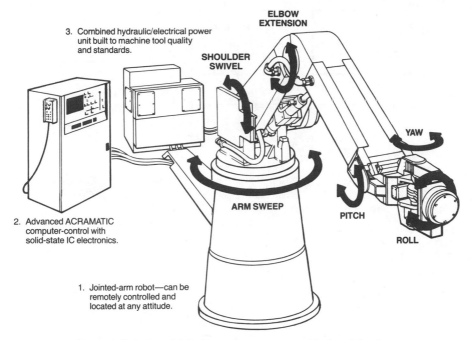

3. Combined hydraulic/electrical power unit built to machine tool quality and standards.

ELBOW EXTENSION

SHOULDER SWIVEL

YAW

ARM SWEEP

PITCH

2. Advanced ACRAMATIC computer-control with solid-state IC electronics.

ROLL

1. Jointed-arm robot—can be remotely controlled and located at any attitude.

Figure I–2. Industrial Robot—Components of industrial robot.

a manipulator, the working tool of the robot, the "hand" that holds the tool or the part to be worked; and a controller that gives detailed movement instructions.

infer. To derive by reasoning. To conclude or judge from premises or evidence.

inference. The process of reaching a conclusion based on an initial set of propositions, the truths of which are known or assumed. A process by which new facts are derived from known facts. A rule (e.g., If the sky is blue, then the time is day), combined with a rule of inference (e.g., modus ponens) and a known fact (e.g., The sky is blue) results in a new fact (e.g., The time is day). A complex series of inferences can be organized to proceed from antecedent propositions that are given to whatever consequent propositions are justified, in which case the forward-chaining process is called data-directed inference, or it can start from a specification of the desired consequence and proceed by trying to prove antecedents that will justify concluding the consequent, in which case the backward-chaining process is called model-directed or goal-directed inference.

inference chain. The sequence of steps or rule applications used by a rule-based system to reach a conclusion. **(See figure p. 134.)**

inference, data-directed. Inferences that are driven by events rather than by goals.

inference engine. The component of an expert system that controls its operation by selecting the rules to use, accessing and executing those rules, and determining when a solution has been found. That component is known also as the control structure or rule interpreter. That part of a knowledge-based system or expert system that contains the general problem-solving knowledge. The inference engine processes the

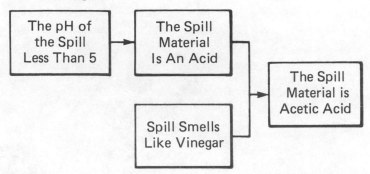

Figure I-3. Inference Chain—Inference chain for inferring the spill material. *Reprinted with the permission of Addison-Wesley Publishing Company from "A Guide to Expert Systems" by Donald A. Waterman.*

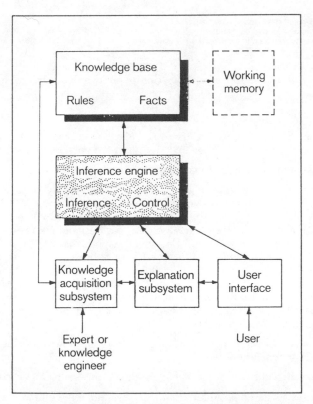

Figure I-4. Inference Engine—The architecture of a knowledge-based expert system. (The inference engine is shaded for emphasis.) *Reprinted with the permission of John Wiley and Sons, from "Expert Systems—Artificial Intelligence in Business" by Paul Harmon and David King.*

domain knowledge (located in the knowledge base) to reach new conclusions. It is a software framework or shell structure that is applied to the information in a knowledge base in order to make relationships and determinations about that information. An inference engine's program is designed to make logical assumptions, cross-references, and inferences about knowledge programmed into an expert system. That is done through the use of standard object rules inherent in the inference engine. Inference engines are characterized by the inference and control strategies they use. Thus, for example, the Inference engine of MYCIN uses modus ponens and backward chaining.

inference, goal-directed. Inferences that are driven by goals rather than data.

inference method. The technique used by the inference engine to access and apply the domain knowledge, e.g., forward chaining and backward chaining.

inference net. All possible inference chains that can be generated from the rules in a rule-based system.

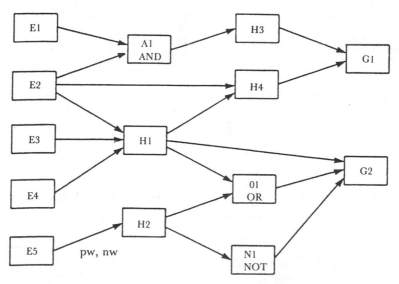

Figure I–5. Inference Net—Sample form of an inference network. *Reproduced with the permission of AFCEA.*

inferential rule. An association between antecedent conditions and consequent beliefs that enables the consequent beliefs to be inferred from valid antecedent conditions.

Information Processing Language. An artificial intelligence programming language and a forerunner of LISP.

inheritance. A process by which characteristics of 1 object are assumed to be characteristics of another. If we determine that an animal is a bird, for example, then we automatically assume that the animal has all of the characteristics of birds.

inheritance hierarchy. A structure in a semantic net or frame system that permits items lower in the net to inherit properties from items higher up in the net.

initialize. A program or hardware circuit that will return a program, a system, or a hardware device to an original state.

input. The date supplied to a computer for processing. The device employed to accomplish such transfer of data.

input/output. Pertaining to either input or output signals or both. A general term for the equipment used to communicate with a computer. The data involved in such communication. The media carrying the data for input-output.

instantiation. A pattern or formula in which the variables have been replaced by constants. In a production system an instantiation is the result of successfully matching a rule against the contents of data memory. It can be represented as an ordered pair of which the first member identifies the rule that has been satisfied, and the second member is a list of working memory elements that match the condition elements of the rule.

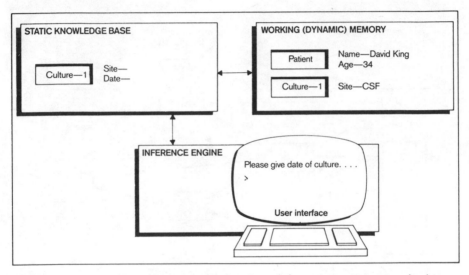

Figure I-6. Instantiation—Comparison of static and dynamic (or instantiated) objects, attributes, and values. *Reprinted with the permission of John Wiley and Sons, from "Expert Systems—Artificial Intelligence in Business" by Paul Harmon and David King.*

instruction. A set of bits that will cause a computer to perform certain prescribed operations. A computer instruction consists of an operation code that specified the operation(s) to be performed. One or more operands. One or more modifiers used to modify the operand or its addressee.

instruction code. A unique binary number that encodes an operation that a computer can perform.

instruction cycle. A successive group of machine cycles, as few as 1 or as many as 7, that together perform a single microprocessor instruction within the microprocessor chip.

instruction decoder. A decoder within a central processing unit that decodes the instruction code into a series of actions that the computer performs.

instruction register. A counter that indicates the instruction currently being executed. The register that contains the instruction code.

integer type. An integer type is a discrete type whose values represent all integer numbers within a specific range.

integrated circuit. An electronic circuit containing multiple electronic components fabricated at the same time in steps on a single slice or wafer of semiconductor material. When separated Into Individually packaged integrated circuits, they are known also as ICs or chips.

integrated data processing. A system that treats all data-processing requirements as a whole to reduce or eliminate duplicate recording or processing while accomplishing a sequence of data processing steps or a number of related data-processing sequences.

integrated optical circuit. The optical equivalent of a microelectronic circuit, it acts on the light in a lightwave system to carry out communications functions. Generates, detects, switches, and transmits light.

integration. A software design concept that allows users to move easily between application programs or to incorporate data from 1 program into another, such as moving data displayed in a graphics program into a text document.

integrator. A device that responds to an input signal not immediately, but with an output that grows in proportion to the input and the time it is applied.

INTELLECT. One of the first commercially successful natural language interfaces. INTELLECT is sold by Artificial Intelligence, Incorporated, of Waltham, Massachusetts.

intelligence. The degree to which an individual can successfully respond to new situations or problems. It is based on the individual's knowledge level and the ability to appropriately manipulate and reformulate that knowledge (and incoming data) as required by the situation or problem.

intelligent assistant. An artificial intelligence computer program (usually an expert system) that aids a person in the performance of a task.

Intelligent Computer-Assisted Instruction (ICAI). An area of artificial intelligence research with the goal of creating training programs that can analyze a student's learning pattern and modify their teaching techniques accordingly. The components of an ICAI program are problem-solving expertise, student model, and tutoring module.

intelligent system. A system equipped with a knowledge base that can be manipulated in order to make inferences. The distinction between a system that can perform intelligent operations and one that merely manipulates data.

intelligent robot. A robot that can make decisions by itself through its sensing (tactile and visual sensors) and recognizing capabilities. A robot that includes artificial intelligence techniques to allow it to understand its environment and change its actions based on external situations. An intelligent robot is known also as a sensor-controlled robot.

intelligent terminal. One with local processing capability. It does not need to be connected to a larger computer to perform certain functions.

intensity. Brightness or luminescence of a cathode ray tube.

interactive. (1) In interactive processing an image can be modified or edited and the changes seen right away, as contrasted with "batch" processing in which the user must wait for results. (2) Refers to action in more than 1 direction, e.g., when a system accepts information from a terminal, processes that information, and returns results to the terminal.

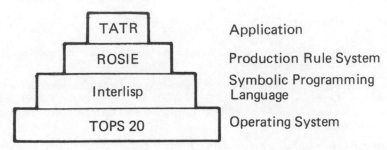

Figure I–7. Interlisp—Example of an AI tool hierarchy. *Reproduced with the permission of AFCEA.*

interactive environment.   A computational system in which the user interacts with the system in real time during the process of developing or running a computer program.

interactive graphics.   The use of a display terminal in a conversational or interactive mode.

interface.   A shared boundary. An interface might be a mechanical or electrical connection between 2 devices; it might be a portion of computer storage accessed by 2 or more programs; or it might be a device for communication to or from a human operator.

interfacing.   The joining of members of a group (such as people, instruments, etc.) in such a way that they are able to function in a compatible and coordinated fashion.

interlacing.   A scanning technique that sends first the even, then the odd, lines of a video display in the refresh cycle. That reduces flickering effect.

INTERLISP.   INTERLISP is a programming language designed for procedure-oriented representation. That dialect of LISP has all the standard LISP features plus an elaborate support environment that includes sophisticated debugging facilities with tracing and conditional breakpoints, a LISP-oriented editor, and a "do what I mean" facility that corrects many kinds of errors on the spot. The environment also allows users to modify normally fixed aspects of the system, such as interrupt characters and garbage collection allocation. INTERLISP operates on a variety of Xerox machines (see INTER-LISP-D). Xerox Corporation developed it as a commercial system. INTERLISP, a general-purpose programming environment that accommodates a broad spectrum of development requirements and programming styles, uses the natural, functional style of LISP. INTERLISP supports a style of programming that has been termed structured growth or incremental development. INTERLISP's data representation methods make it easy to write LISP programs that examine and change other LISP programs. Because its functions are so easy to extend, INTERLISP is especially appropriate when one knows one will need the capability to modify the language. Because user-defined functions may be referenced exactly like INTERLISP primitive functions, the programming process can essentially be viewed as extending the Interlisp language.

INTERLISP-D.   INTERLISP-D is a programming language designed for procedure-oriented representation. This version of INTERLISP operates on Xerox 1100 computer systems. It provides all the standard INTERLISP features plus a sophisticated support environment tied to a graphical monitor. Xerox developed INTERLISP-D as a commercial system.

INTERLISP Programmer's Assistant.   Through the Interlisp Programmer's Assistant, INTERLISP keeps track of all your programming actions during a session. This history mechanism allows one to repeat, modify, and reexecute commands and undo operations, enabling one to back out of certain decisions. If one needs to vary an input format, the Programmer's Assistant executive will instruct INTERLISP to evaluate the new format appropriately.

INTERLISP Structure Editor. Unlike many other members of the LISP family of languages, where the editor environment performs text editing only, INTERLISP's structure editor edits LISP itself. One can save time because one can change the list structure of a function's definitions directly.

INTERLISP VAX. INTERLISP for Digital Equipment Corporation VAX combines the flexible yet structured framework of the LISP programming language with extensive program support facilities designed to make developing and maintaining complex applications as easy as possible. An interactive, fully integrated programming environment based on LISP, INTERLISP for VAX is highly compatible with all versions of INTERLISP. INTERLISP for VAX combines the flexible yet structured framework of the LISP programming of VAX language with extensive program support facilities designed to make developing and maintaining complex applications as easy as possible. An interactive, fully integrated programming environment based on LISP, INTERLISP for VAX is highly compatible with all versions of INTERLISP. The Information Sciences Institute of the University of Southern California developed INTERLISP for VAX specifically for use on VAX computers. INTERLISP's comprehensive programming environment offers you the benefits of a full implementation of INTERLISP and a rich set of programming functions.

internal memory. The part of memory where information that is being worked on is kept. Also called main memory or high-speed memory.

internal sensor. A sensor for measuring displacements, forces, or other variables internal to the robot.

INTERNIST. An expert system that diagnoses diseases. Former name of CADUCEUS diagnosis system for internal medicine.

INTERNIST-I/CADUCEUS. INTERNIST-I/CADUCEUS assists the physician in making multiple and complex diagnoses in general internal medicine, given a patient's history, symptoms, or laboratory test results. The system bases its decisions on a set of disease profiles containing findings that occur in association with each disease. The system is one of the largest medical expert systems developed, containing profiles of more than 500 diseases described by more than 3500 manifestations of disease. Knowledge in the system is represented as a network of findings and diseases and is accessed based on the constraints of the disease taxonomy and causality relations. The system is implemented in LISP. The first version of the system was called INTERNIST-I; the second, CADUCEUS. It was developed at the University of Pittsburgh.

interpolation. The process of using known values to calculate unknown values that lie between them.

interpreter. (1) A language translator that converts individual source statements into multiple machine instructions by translating and executing each statement as it is encountered. Cannot be used to generate object code. (2) In an expert system that part of the inference engine that decides how to apply the domain knowledge. The part of a production system that executes the rules. In a programming system the part of the system that analyzes the code to decide what actions to take next.

interpretation. Establishing a correspondence between the scene and a set of models, or templates. Also, assigning names to an object in a scene.

interpretation-guided segmentation. Using models to help guide image segmentation, by the process of extending partial matches.

interpretive language. Allows a source program to be translated by an interpreter for use in a computer. The interpreter translates the interpretive-language source program into machine code and, instead of producing an object program, lets the program be immediately operated on by the computer. Interpretive language programs are used for solving difficult problems and for running short programs.

interrupt. A break in the normal flow of a system or program occurring in such a way that the flow can be resumed from that point at a later time. Interrupts are initiated by signals of 2 types: signals originating within the computer system to synchronize the operation of the computer system with the outside world; signals originating exterior to the computer systems to synchronize the operation of the computer system with the outside world.

intersection. In set theory, points that are contained in 2 sets make up their intersection.

intonation. The melody of pitch over a word or phrase.

intrinsic characteristics. Properties inherent in an object, such as surface reflectance, orientation, incident illumination and range.

intrinsic images. A set of arrays in registration with the image array. Each array corresponds to a particular intrinsic characteristic. **(See figure p. 141.)**

invoke. To place into action, usually by satisfying a precondition.

IRIS. An expert system that helps physicians to experiment with various consultation systems. IRIS helps physicians diagnose and treat diseases. The system collects information from the physician about the patient's symptoms, giving rise to a set of possible diagnoses. IRIS then chooses a diagnosis and treatment corresponding to the diagnosis. The medical diagnostic expertise is represented using a semantic net that defines the relationships among symptoms, diseases, and treatments. The inference process is controlled by decision tables associated with the nodes of the semantic net. IRIS propagates MYCIN-like certainty factors through the net to help it choose a diagnosis. IRIS was developed at Rutgers University.

IR-NLI. Provides nontechnical users with a natural language interface to the information retrieval services offered by on-line data bases. The system acts as a front end to several available data bases and decides which will be the most appropriate for answering the user's requests. IR-NLI combines the expertise of a professional intermediary for on-line searching with the capability of understanding natural language and carrying out a dialogue with the user. Knowledge is encoded as rules that operate on 2 knowledge bases. One contains domain-specific (DS) knowledge and the other vocabulary (VOC) knowledge. The DS knowledge base uses a semantic net representation technique to define the data base concepts and indicate how they are related. The VOC knowledge base uses frames to define the lexicon of the application domain. IR-NLI is implemented in FRANZ LISP. It was developed at the University of Udine, Udine, Italy.

irradiance. The brightness of a point in the scene.

ISA. ISA schedules customer computer system orders against the current and planned material allocations. ISA takes customer orders, including changes and cancellations, and produces a schedule date for each order. It displays additional information about a problematic order, including the schedule proposed, the problems uncovered, and alternative proposals for scheduling the order. ISA contains significant

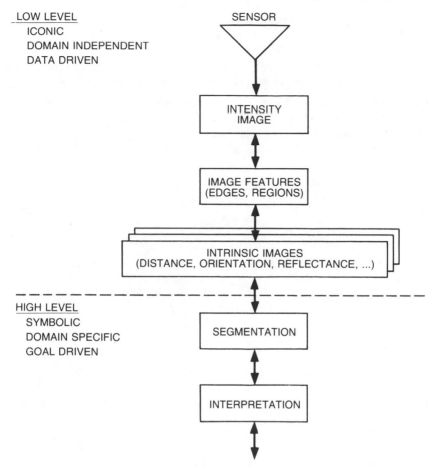

Figure I-8. Intrinsic Images—Organization of a visual system focusing on intrinsic images.

scheduling expertise, such as knowledge about order cancellation probabilities, material availability, and strategies for relaxing scheduling constraints. ISA is a forward-chaining, rule-based system implemented in OPS5. It was developed by Digital Equipment Corporation and is in use at DEC's manufacturing plants.

ISIS. The ISIS project, beginning in 1980, had as its goal to investigate new, artificial intelligence-based approaches to solving problems in the management and control of production in a job-shop environment. The result of the project is an operational prototype. The level of intelligent processing behavior a system may exhibit is limited by the knowledge it has of its task and its environment. To enable ISIS to perform "intelligent" management and production control, an artificial intelligence approach is used to model he production environment. The SRL knowledge representation system is used to model all relevant information. Conceptual primitives have been defined for the modeling of organizations. They include: states (of the organization), object descriptions (e.g., parts, attributes), goals (e.g., shipping orders), causality, and possession.

isolated speech. A method of voice recognition input, referring to a system that only understands single spoken words or utterances, as opposed to phrases.

isolated word recognition. An approach to speech recognition that uses pattern-matching techniques to recognize isolated words.

isolated-word system. A speech-understanding system whose input must consist of words enunciated separately, instead of run together, to make word identification easier for the system.

isomorphic representation. A representation in which there is a 1-to-1 correspondence between the scene and its representation.

J

jaggies. Refers to straight or cuved lines that appear to be jagged or saw-toothed on the cathode ray tube screen.

jitter. Instability of a signal in amplitude or phase or both.

joint. A rotational or translational degree of freedom in a robot manipulator system.

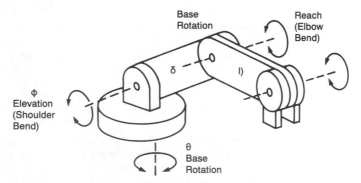

Figure J-1. Joint—Jointed arm used on this robot manipulator.

joint interpolated motion. A method of coordinating the movements of the joints so that all joints arrive at the desired location simultaneously. That method of servo control produces a predictable path regardless of speed and results in the fastest cycle time for a particular move.

joint space. The vector that specifies the angular or translational displacement of each joint of a multi-degree-of-freedom linkage relative to a reference displacement for each such joint.

Josephson Junction. An advanced form of switching technology that may be the basis for the digit circuits of the future. Switching times are as low as 10 picoseconds (trillionths of a second), as much as a hundred times faster than current devices.

jump. Change in sequence of the execution of the program instruction, altering the program counter.

K

KANDOR. A knowledge engineering language for frame-based representation. Its expensive power is purposely limited to provide computational tractability in the form of ease of sue and enhanced performance. The internal structure of KANDOR is intentionally hidden from the user, who is presented instead with a well-defined simple interface to frames, slots, restrictions, and slot fillers. KANDOR is implemented LISP. It was developed at the Fairchild Laboratory for Artificial Intelligence Research.

KAS. KAS is a skeletal knowledge engineering language for rule-based representation. It is basically PROSPECTOR with the knowledge of geology removed. KAS uses inference rules with associated certainty factors together with a partitioned semantic network to encode its knowledge. Inferences are based on forward and backward chaining and the propagation of probabilities through the semantic net. KAS's support environment includes facilities for explanation and knowledge acquisition and provides for synonym recognition, answer revision, summarization, and tracing. The system is implemented in INTERLISP. It was developed by SRI International.

KBS. A knowledge engineering language for object-oriented representation involving simulation models. It also supports frame-based representation methods. KBS's principal characteristic is its use of object-oriented modeling for simulation. The support environment contains interactive model construction and modification tools that are maintained by generic schematics from model libraries of objects and relations. It also contains model consistency and completeness checking facilities. KBS is implemented in SRL, which runs under the VAX FRANZ LISP system. It was developed at the Robotics Institute of Carnegie-Mellon University.

KDS. Knowledge Development System. An expert system shell written in machine code for PCs; developed and marketed by KDS Corporation.

KDS2. KDS Corporation's expert system shell develops expert systems containing 1 or more Knowledge Modules or frames, each containing a maximum of 256,000 facts and 16,000 rules. Rules are induced from up to 4096 examples per frame. The developer may include color graphics produced by readily available "paint" type programs and/or integrated animated designs using built-in graphics primitives and can execute, pass parameters to or from external programs and/or interrupt handlers. Complete applications can be developed requiring no symbolic programming; developer input is in plain English or foreign languages. It is written entirely in assembly language, and the speed approaches 8000 LIPS on IBM-PC. It requires IBM-PC or AT or compatibles. A hard disk is optional. 512K RAM recommended for development, 256K for playback. Color graphics card and monitor necessary only if graphics features are used.

KEE. A knowledge engineering language for frame-based representation. It also supports rule-based, procedure-oriented, and object-oriented representation methods. Its principal characteristics include multiple knowledge bases to facilitate modular system design and forward and backward chaining for its rule interpreter. Its support environment includes a graphics-oriented debugging package and an explanation facility that uses graphic displays to indicate inference chains. KEE is written in INTERLISP and operates on the Xerox 1100 and Symbolics 3600 computer systems. Intellicorp developed it for applications in molecular genetics, but it is now available as a general-purpose commercial system.

kernel. Software routines that create basic displays.

KES. A knowledge engineering language for rule-based and frame-based representation. Its principle characteristics include a backward-chaining control scheme, certainty handling mechanisms, and a statistical pattern classification subsystem based on Bayes' theorem. The support environment contains interface facilities for explaining the system's reasoning and for acquiring new knowledge. KES is implemented in FRANZ LISP and operates on Univac or DEC VAX systems. Software Architecture and Engineering, Inc.

Kestrel Institute. A nonprofit organization providing both scientific research and graduate education in computer science. Its chief research goals include the finalization and incremental automation of software development. Its research is in machine intelligence, very high level languages, program design, transformation and synthesis, software project management, and knowledge-based programming environments.

keystone distortion. The keystone-shaped raster produced by scanning a plane that is not normal to the average direction of the beam.

kinematics. A process for plotting or animating the motion of parts in a machine or a structure under design on the system.

KL-ONE. A knowledge engineering language for frame-based representation. Its principal characteristics include automatic inheritance, support for semantic nets using subsumption and other relations, and an automatic classifier. The support environment contains an interactive graphics-oriented knowledge base editor and display tools. KL-ONE is implemented in INTERLISP-D and operates on Xerox 1100 LISP machines and DEC VAX computer systems. It was developed at Bolt, Beranek, and Newman.

KMS. A knowledge engineering language for frame-based representation, but it also supports rule-based representation methods. It consists of a collection of subsystems, each with its own knowledge representation and inference methods. Its principal characteristics include rule-based deduction, statistical pattern classification using Bayes' theorem, linear discriminant and other scoring functions, and frame-based inference generation. KMS is implemented in LISP and operates on a Univac 1100/40. It was developed at the University of Maryland.

KNEECAP. Aids in the planning of crew activity on board the space shuttle orbiter. As the user plans the entire flight mission, the system checks for inconsistencies in the schedule. KNEECAP uses knowledge about orbiter vehicles, launch and landing sites, astronauts' skill qualifications, current payloads, shuttle activities, and crew roles to make its decisions. That knowledge is encoded as frames using a knowledge representation method similar to the FRL language. KNEECAP is implemented in INTERLISP within a framework taken from the KNOBS expert system. It was developed by the MITRE Corporation.

KNOBS. Helps a controller at a tactical air command and control center perform mission planning. The system uses knowledge about targets, resources, and planned missions to check the consistency of plan components, to rank possible plans, and to help generate new plans. Knowledge in KNOBS is in the form of frames and backward-chaining rules, and it uses a natural language subsystem for data base queries and updates. In the KNOBS literature early articles refer to it as the expert system for mission planning. Later articles use the term KNOBS to mean the KNOBS architecture rather than a specific expert system. The system is implemented in FRL and ZETALISP. It was developed by the MITRE Corporation.

knowledge. The information a computer program must have to behave intelligently. Facts, beliefs, and heuristic rules. An integrated collection of facts and relationships that, when exercised, produces competent performance. The quantity and quality of knowledge possessed by a person or a computer can be judged by the variety of situations in which the person or program can obtain successful results.

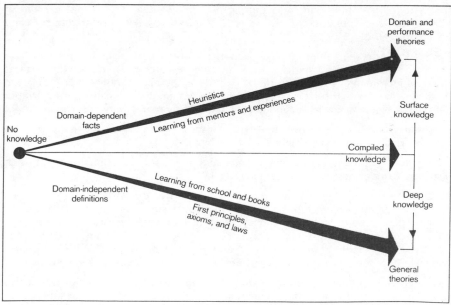

Figure K–1. Knowledge—Varieties of knowledge. *Reprinted with the permission of John Wiley and Sons, from "Expert Systems—Artificial Intelligence in Business" by Paul Harmon and David King.*

knowledge or procedural knowledge. In the form of rules, entries in data memory or another database, or control strategies. Knowledge may be specific to a task domain or general enough to be independent of all domains.

knowledge acquisition. The process of extracting domain knowledge from domain experts. The process of incorporating domain knowledge into an expert system by

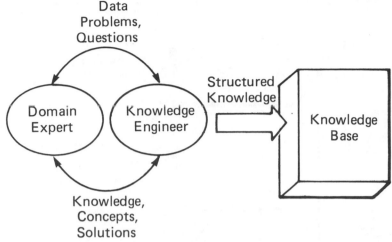

Figure K–2. Knowledge Acquisition—Typical knowledge acquisition process for building an expert system.

extracting it from domain experts and encoding the information into an internal representation, such as rules. An automated process by which a program accepts knowledge from domain experts and incorporates it into an existing expert system. Learning. The process of extracting, structuring, and organizing knowledge from some source, usually human experts, so that it can be used in a program. The person undertaking the knowledge acquisition must convert the acquired knowledge into a form that a computer program can use. The technique by which a knowledge engineer obtains information from experts, textbooks, and other authoritative sources for ultimate translation into a machine language and knowledge base.

knowledge base. A collection of knowledge represented in the form of rules, procedures, schemas, or working memory elements; thus any highly structured and interconnected database. The portion of a knowledge system that consists of the facts and heuristics about a domain. The part of an artificial intelligence system that contains structured, codified knowledge and heuristics used to solve problems. Artificial intelligence systems using such a base are called knowledge-based systems. In an expert system, the knowledge base generally contains a model of the problem, knowledge about the behavior and interactions of objects in the problem domain, and a level of general-purpose knowledge. **(See figure p. 148.)**

knowledge base management system. One of 3 subsystems in an expert system. That subsystem "manages" the knowledge base by automatically organizing, controlling, propagating, and updating stored knowledge. It initiates searches for knowledge relevant to the line of reasoning upon which the inference subsystem is working. The inference subsystem is 1 of the other 2 subsystems in an expert system; the third is the human interface subsystem with which the end-user communicates.

knowledge-based system. A program in which the domain knowledge is explicit and separate from the program's other knowledge. A computer program that applies specialized knowledge to the solution of problems. An expert system is a knowledge-based system that is intended to capture the expertise of human domain experts. **(See figure p. 149.)**

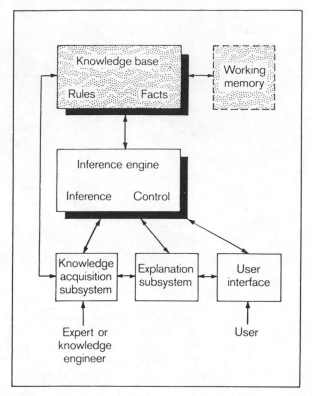

Figure K–3. Knowledge Base—The architecture of a knowledge-based expert system. (*The knowledge base is shaded for emphasis.*) *Reprinted with the permission of John Wiley and Sons, from "Expert Systems—Artificial Intelligence in Business" by Paul Harmon and David King.*

knowledge base management.   Management of a knowledge base in terms of storing, accessing, and reasoning with the knowledge.

KNOWLEDGE-BASED LOGIC SYNTHESIS.   Among the most time-consuming tasks in the design of digital systems is translating register-transfer level primitives into circuit-level primitives. When the translation process is performed with computer assistance, it is termed synthesis. An analogy exists between high-level language compilation into assembly language. Synthesis is a difficult process, since no well-defined mapping exists between the register-transfer level and the circuit level. The synthesis problem is compounded when several possible circuit technologies exist. A knowledge-based tool is currently being developed by the Carnegie Group in OPS5 to aid in the logic synthesis area. The tool will accept a register-transfer level behavioral description of a digital system. A circuit level description, complete with initial transistor size specification, will result. The knowledge-based approach is useful for capturing the many heuristics used by designers in producing a circuit description.

knowledge engineer.   A person who implements an expert system. A knowledge engineer interviews experts to obtain the raw knowledge from which to structure the

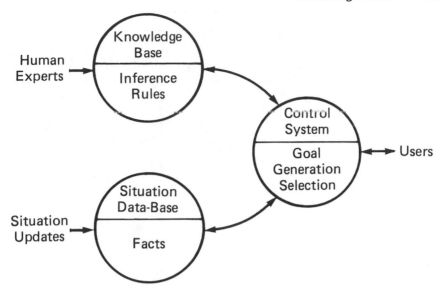

Figure K–4. Knowledge-based System—Knowledge based system (KBS) components.

knowledge base and formulate the rule base and programs raw knowledge into a form that the computer can understand. An individual whose specialty is assessing problems, acquiring knowledge, and building knowledge systems. Ordinarily that implies training in cognitive science, computer science, and artificial intelligence. It also suggests experience in the actual development of one or more expert systems. **(See figure p. 150.)**

Knowledge Information Processing Systems. The new, "fifth" generation of computers that the Japanese propose to build and that will have symbolic inference capabilities, coupled with very large knowledge bases, and superb human interfaces, all combined with high processing speeds, so that the machines will greatly amplify human intellectual capabilities. **(See figure p. 151.)**

Knowledge Craft™. Developed by the Carnegie Group, is an integrated knowledge representation and problem-solving environment for constructing large knowledge-based systems. It functions as a high-performance productivity tool for knowledge engineers and AI system developers. Knowledge Craft dramatically reduces the effort to build knowledge bases and to customize problem-solving strategies for specific domain applications. The Knowledge Craft open-architecture combines a feature-rich knowledge representation language with a variety of powerful problem-solving techniques and facilities. Sophisticated window, text, and graphics management modules are fully integrated with a command system interpreter, providing an interface building tool of significant power. The Carnegie Representation Language, CRL™, is an enhancement of the frame/schema representation language, SRL, developed at Carnegie-Mellon University. It has been used extensively to solve large production problems in a broad range of industrial environments. Knowledge Craft is written in Common LISP, the recognized industry standard. It is portable to standard workstations and a variety of LISP machines. The tools provided by Version 3.0 facilitate a

Inputs

Management
• Identifies problems
  to be solved

Expert
• Describes task
• Explains reasoning
• Identifies successful
  performance

User
• Knows some facts
  and relationships
• Needs advice

KNOWLEDGE ENGINEER

• Knows the strengths
  and weaknesses of tools
• Learns about the task
  from management, experts,
  and users

Outputs

• Choosing a good domain and task
• Analyzing representational needs
  and control strategies
• Building a prototype system
• Expanding the prototype
• Fielding the system
• Maintaining the system

Figure K–5. Knowledge Engineer—The roles of the knowledge engineer. *Reprinted with the permission of John Wiley and Sons, from "Expert Systems—Artificial Intelligence in Business" by Paul Harmon and David King.*

Announced in 1981

| 1982 | 1983 | 1984 | 1985 | 1986 | 1987 | 1988 | 1989 | 1990 | 1991 | 1992 |

Phase I: 3 years
EXPLORATORY RESEARCH

Phase II: 4 years
PROTOTYPE DEVELOPMENT

Phase III: 3 years
COMMERCIALIZATION

Goal:
High-performance
personal PROLOG
machine

$50 million budgeted
for 1982–1984
$450 million budgeted
for 1985–1991

Goals:
VLSI design
Automatic Programming

Responses as of 1985
United States: Microelectronics & Computer Technology Corp (MCC)
Common Market: ESPRIT (5-year program budgeted at $1.3 billion)
Great Britain: Alvey Programme

Figure K–6. Knowledge Information Processing System—Japan's Fifth-Generation computer project. *Reprinted with the permission of John Wiley and Sons, from "Expert Systems—Artificial Intelligence in Business" by Paul Harmon and David King.*

flexible approach to expert system design and encourage rapid prototyping of domain-specific solutions. Version 3.0 enhancements include OPS and Prolog Workbenches, a new compilation process that speeds knowledge representation, extended interface capabilities, and significant improvements to the window and command systems. Runs on Symbolics, TI Explorer, VAX, and MicroVAX processors. Minimum memory requirements: 2 meg.

knowledge representation.   The method used to encode and store facts and relationships in a knowledge base. Semantic networks, object-attribute-value triplets, production rules, frames, and logical expressions are all ways to represent knowledge. A structure in which knowledge can be stored in a way that allows the system to understand the relationships among pieces of knowledge and to manipulate those relationships. The primary methods used to represent knowledge in expert systems are as follows: (1) procedural representation, which combines a number of items to form a solution. From all possible combinations of system options, for example, XCON, Digital's configuration system for VAX and PDP-11 systems, selects and combines the appropriate components to meet a customer's system confirmation requirements. (2) Rule-based representation, a two-part representation that specifies both a pattern and an action to be taken when real-world data matches that pattern. Complex patterns may be structured by linking clauses together with connectives such as AND and OR. For example: a typical rule might be, "IF the patient's temperature is greater than 100 degrees AND the patient has a runny nose, THEN conclude that the patient has a cold." (3) Frame or schema representation, in which objects are represented by "frames" that define the object in terms of its relationship to other objects. For example: the standard properties of a mouse might include its biological parts, color, and habitat. A mouse can also be defined in terms of its relationship to other objects: perhaps as natural prey to a cat.

knowledge source.   A collection of rules, procedures, and/or data that is used to solve problems of a very specific type. A knowledge source is larger than a rule but smaller than an expert system. In blackboard architectures each process that has access to the shared memory is considered a knowledge source. Generally, a body of domain knowledge relevant to a specific problem. In particular, a codification made applicable for an expert system.

knowledge system. A computer program that uses knowledge and inference procedures to solve difficult problems. The knowledge necessary to perform at such a level plus the inference procedures used can be thought of as a model of the expertise of skilled practitioners. In contrast to expert systems, knowledge systems are often designed to solve small, difficult problems rather than large problems requiring true human expertise. In many cases, small knowledge systems derive their utility from their user-friendly nature rather than from their ability to capture knowledge that would be difficult to represent in a conventional program.

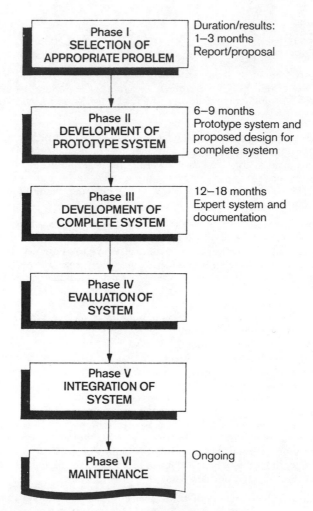

Figure K–7. Knowledge System—Development of a knowledge system. *Reprinted with the permission of John Wiley and Sons, from "Expert Systems—Artificial Intelligence in Business" by Paul Harmon and David King.*

KRL. A knowledge engineering language for frame-based representation that also supports procedural representation methods. Its principal characteristics include procedural attachment, such as associating procedures with the slots in a frame, inheritance of procedural as well as declarative properties of an object, and multiple perspectives such as permitting descriptors corresponding to different viewpoints to be attached to a single object. The KRL system is implemented in INTERLISP. It was developed by the Xerox Palo Alto Research Center.

KRT. A system-building aid that helps members of a large engineering development effort record, communicate, and integrate their designs with other members of the team. With the KRT system, team members can describe what a particular engineering system (e.g., guidance analysis, navigation) does, how it functions, how it is organized, and how its parts are related. That includes a data flow diagram to provide a system overview, process specifications to show how input data are transformed into output data, and a data dictionary that provides a hierarchical description of data. The KRT system is implemented in ZETALISP and FLAVORS for the Symbolics 3600. It was developed by McDonnell Douglas.

KRYPTON. A knowledge engineering language for frame-based representation that also supports logic-based representation methods. Its principal characteristics include a terminological component that helps define frames and networks of frames and an assertional component that uses a nonclausal connection graph resolution theorem prover for maintaining data base of logical assertions about items defined using frames. KRYPTON is implemented in INTERLISP-D. It was developed at Fairchild Laboratory for Artificial Intelligence Research.

L

label. One or more characters that serve to define an item of data or the location of an instruction or subroutine. A character is one symbol of a set of elementary symbols, such as those corresponding to typewriter keys.

labeling. The process of assigning different numbers of the picture elements of different blobs in a binary image.

ladder diagram. A wiring diagram of an electrical system in which all the devices are drawn between vertical lines that represent power sources.

lambert. A unit of luminance equal to the uniform luminance of a perfectly diffusing surface emitting or reflecting light at the rate of 1 lumen per square centimeter.

language. A set of terms or symbols used according to very precise rules to write instructions, or programs, for computers. There are several common languages such as: (1) machine language, one consisting solely or 1s and 0s. It is the only language computers understand. (2) Assembly language: one that replaces each command written in 0s and 1s with a command consisting of 1 or more English letters. (3) High-level language: a code that is easier for humans to use than strings of 0s and 1s or assembly language. FORTRAN, COBOL, and C are all high-level languages.

Language. Language Craft™ created by the Carnegie Group, is an integrated Craft open-architecture environment for constructing natural language interfaces to databases, operating systems, expert systems, and conventional software applications. Language Craft combines a grammar building development environment with a domain-independent natural language interpreter and run-time module. Language Craft can be adapted to a wide variety of applications. Users can develop their own domain-specific natural language interfaces without specialized artificial intelligence of linguistic expertise. Language Craft is based upon the successful DYPAR technology developed at Carnegie-Mellon University. It has been used to develop natural language interfaces to expert systems, databases, and operating systems.

language processor. A computer program that performs such functions as translating, interpreting, and other tasks required for processing a specified programming language.

language-tool spectrum. A continuum along which various software products can be placed. At 1 extreme are narrowly defined tools that are optimized to perform specific

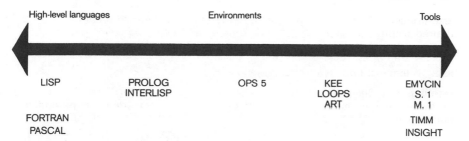

Figure L-1. Language-tool Spectrum—The language-tool spectrum. *Reprinted with the permission of John Wiley and Sons, from "Expert Systems—Artificial Intelligence in Business" by Paul Harmon and David King.*

tasks. At the other extreme are general-purpose languages that can be used for many different applications.

Laplacian operator. The sum of the second derivatives of the image intensity in the x and y directions is called the Laplacian. The Laplacian operator is used to find edge elements by finding points where the Laplacian is zero.

large-grain processing. Parallel processing performed with large microprocessors, usually linked together in small bundles such as 4, 8, 16, 32, etc. The largest of these currently consists of 128 processors.

large hybrid system building tools. A class of knowledge engineering tools that emphasizes flexibility. The systems are designed for building large knowledge bases. They usually include a hybrid collection of different inference and control strategies. Most commercial hybrid tools incorporate frames and facilitate object-oriented programming.

large narrow system building tools. A class of knowledge engineering tools that sacrifices flexibility to facilitate the efficient development of more narrowly defined expert systems. At the moment most large, narrow tools emphasize production rules.

latch. A simple logic storage element. A feedback loop used in a symmetrical digital circuit, such as a flip-flop, to retain a state.

latchable. Function switch setting that allows an operator to toggle between 2 programmed states.

layering. A method of logically organizing data in a data base. Functionally different classes of data are segregated on separate layers, each of which can be displayed individually or in any desired combination.

LDS. Assists legal experts in settling product liability cases. Given a description of a product liability case, it calculates defendant liability, case worth, and equitable settlement amount. Its expertise is based on both formal legal doctrine and informal principles and strategies of attorneys and claims adjustors. The system calculates the value of the case by analyzing the effect of loss: the special and general damages resulting from the injury; liability: the probability of establishing the defendant's liability; responsibility: the proportion of blame assigned to the plaintiff for the injury; characteristics: subjective considerations such as attorney's skill and litigants' appearance; and context: considerations based on strategy, timing, and type of claim. LDS is a rule-based system implemented in ROSIE and was developed by the Rand Corporation.

lead through. Programming or teaching by physically guiding the robot through the desired actions. The speed of the robot is increased when programming is complete.

leading edge. The transition of a pulse that occurs first.

leaf. A terminal node in a tree representation.

learning. Any change in a system that alters its long-term performance. Learning the production systems may be effected by the automatic addition, deletion, or modification of rules.

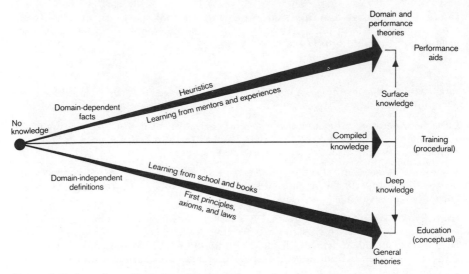

Figure L–2. Learning—Varieties of knowledge and their relationships to instructional strategies. *Reprinted with the permission of John Wiley and Sons, from "Expert Systems—Artificial Intelligence in Business" by Paul Harmon and David King.*

least commitment. A technique for coordinating decision making with the availability of information, so that problem-solving decisions are not made arbitrarily or prematurely but are postponed until there is enough information.

left-hand side. One of the 2 parts of a rule, the other being the right-hand side. The left-hand side specifies the antecedents that must be satisfied if the rule is to be applied. In rules of grammar the left-hand side specifies a string of symbols that can be replaced by another string of symbols. In production systems that use a back-chaining strategy, the left-hand side specifies the subgoals of the goal that is specified on the right-hand side. In forward-chaining production systems, the left-hand side is a set of condition elements that are to be matched against the contents of data memory.

left justified. A field of numbers (decimal, binary, etc.) that exists in a memory cell, location or register, possessing no 0s to its left.

left memory. A data structure in the Rete match algorithm network that is associated with a node. It contains the combinations of working memory elements and variable bindings that constitute a consistent match for the condition element being tested at the node and all preceding condition elements.

legal analysis system. Helps lawyers perform simple legal analyses about the intentional torts of assault and battery. The lawyer presents the system with a set of facts, which the system attempts to relate to relevant legal doctrine. The system then presents its conclusions, including the logic behind them. It provides support for the conclusions by referencing judicial decisions and secondary legal authority. Legal expertise, doctrine, and case facts are represented in semantic net form. Legal Analysis System is implemented in PSL (preliminary study language). It was developed at M.I.T.

Douglas A. Lenat. Attended the University of Pennsylvania, where he received B.A. degrees in math and physics and the M.S. in applied math. His graduate training was in computer science at Sanford University, where he received his Ph.D. in 1976. Dr. Lenat then held the position of assistant professor of computer science at Carnegie-Mellon University and the same position at Stanford University. He began an inquiry into the fundamental nature of heuristic reasoning and in 1982 presented an American Association of Artificial Intelligence award-winning paper on a new synthesis, the new field of Computational Heuretics. He was co-editor of *Building Expert Systems*, Addison-Wesley, 1984, and a co-author with Randall Davis of *Knowledge-Based Systems in AI*. He currently is principal scientist, Artificial Intelligence, at Microelectronics and Computer Technology Corporation (MCC), the U.S.A.'s research consortium in artificial intelligence and microelectronics.

LES. A knowledge engineering language for rule-based representation, but it also supports frame-based representation. Rules are supported through the use of a case grammar frame format. LES's principal characteristics include forward- and backward-chaining control schemes, an agenda of relevant goals and subgoals manipulated by demons, and natural language and explanation facilities. LES is implemented in PL/1. It was developed by the Lockheed Palo Alto Research Laboratory.

level triggered. The state of the clock input, being either logic 0 or logic 1, carries out a transfer of information or completes an action.

levels of software. A continuum that begins at the lowest level with machine language and extends up through low-level languages, high-level languages, tools, and then finally to systems that users can use to actually solve problems.

lexical element. A lexical element is an indentifier, a literal, a delimiter, or a comment.

library. A collection of functions that are stored on discs in the computer and retrieved by programs as needed.

library programs. A software collection of standard routines and subroutines by which problems and parts of problems may be solved on a given computer.

lightguide. An extremely clear, thin glass fiber that is to light what copper wire is to electricity. Synonymous with optical fiber.

lightwave. Particles of light known as photons travel in waves. The length of the waves determines the light's color, speed, and behavior in a lightguide.

limited-degree-of-freedom robot. A robot able to position and orient its end effector in fewer than 6 degrees of freedom.

line. A thin, connected set of points contrasting with neighbors on both sides. Line representations are extracted from edges.

line detectors. Oriented operators for finding lines in an image.

line followers. Techniques for extending lines currently being tracked.

line smoothing. An automated mapping capability for the interpolation and insertion of additional points along a linear entity yielding a series of shorter linear segments to generate a smooth, curved appearance to the original linear component. The additional points or segments are created only for display purposes and are interpolated from a relatively small set of stored representative points. Thus, data storage space is minimized.

linear-array camera. A solid state television camera that has only 1 row of photosensitive elements.

linear interpolation. A function automatically performed in the control that defines the continuum of points in a straight line based on only 2 taught coordinate positions. All calculated points are automatically inserted between the taught coordinate positions upon playback.

linearity. If a change of the input function to a device or system is reproduced in exact proportion at the output, the device or system is said to be linear.

linear protective coding. A parameter-encoding technique that models the human vocal tract with a digital filter whose controlling parameters change with time. Changes are based on previous speech samples.

linear test and merge. An algorithm that employs a directed acrylic graph, performing sequences of tests along chains of directed arcs and merging results of tests at nodes where 2 or more chains intersect.

linkage. A means of communicating information from one routine to another.

LIPS. Logical Inferences Per Second. Measurement of processing speed for symbolic computing, currently measured in thousands. The Japanese hope to have LIPS measured in billions by 1990. Each logical inference requires from 100 to 300 instructions per second.

LISP. A programming language designed specifically to manipulate symbols rather than numeric data. A LISP data element is a list of symbols that may represent any object, including its own list processing functions. A LISP program essen-

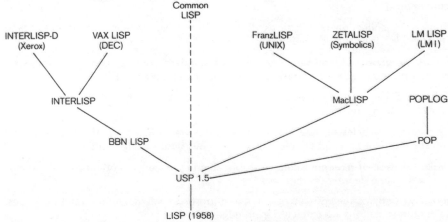

Figure L–3. LISP—The LISP family tree. *Reprinted with the permission of John Wiley and Sons, from "Expert Systems—Artificial Intelligence in Business" by Paul Harmon and David King.*

tially consists of collections of independent procedures called functions. LISP was the first language to concentrate on working with symbols instead of numbers. Although it was introduced by John McCarthy in the early 1960s, continuous development has enabled LISP to remain dominant in artificial intelligence. Lately LISP has proved to be an outstanding language for systems programming as well. Favored by U.S. programmers for its ease of programmability and the amount of control that can be wielded over it. Primary competitor is PROLOG. LISP is a programming language for procedure-oriented representation. Its very flexible language provides a small set of primitive functions from which the user can construct higher-level functions tailored to the needs of the application. LISP has mechanisms for manipulating symbols in the form of list structures; such structures are useful building blocks for representing complex concepts. LISP provides automatic memory management and the uniform treatment of code and data, which allows a LISP program to modify its own code. Many dialects of LISP are available, e.g., INTERLISP, MACLISP, FRANZ LISP, COMMON LISP, and ZETALISP, just to mention a few. LISP was developed at M.I.T. in the late 1950s and has become the most widely used programming language for AI applications. It is the principal programming language of AI, which provides an elegant, recursive, untyped, and applicative framework for symbolic computing; actually a family of variants.

LISP interpreter. A part of many LISP-based software tools that allows specific list-processing operations such as match, join, and substitute, to execute on a general-purpose computer rather than a special-purpose LISP machine.

LISP machine. A single-user workstation with an architecture dedicated to the efficient writing and execution of applications using the LISP programming language.

LISP/VM. A high-level programming language appropriate for many applications, including artificial intelligence applications in expert systems, language processing, robotics, and other advanced technologies. It includes a user-friendly development environment with tools for the creation and maintenance of LISP/VM programs and data sets. The development environment includes both a LISP/VM interpreter and a semantically equivalent LISP/VM compiler. LISP/VM runs under VM/SP on IBM System/370 architecture machines, providing multi-user access across a broad spectrum of computing power. LISP/VM is the result of more than a decade of development activity at the IBM Thomas J. Watson Research Center, where it has been used for development of experimental systems. LISP (LISt Processing) language was first described by John McCarthy in 1959. For many years LISP has been extensively used in artificial intelligence applications such as expert systems, natural language processing, robotics, symbolic algebra, and even human vision simulation. The characteristics of the LISP language that make it particularly suitable for these applications include:

- The ability to handle large quantities of symbolic data, as well as traditional numeric data types.
- The ability within a LISP program, to create, modify, and execute other LISP programs. (That facilitates creation of very flexible applications modeling specific environments.)
- The ability to use (in LISP programs themselves) components of the LISP system such as the parser or interpreter.

Today LISP is being used more than ever before as increasingly complex problems are addressed by computers. The demands of these complex applications outstrip the capabilities of more limited programming languages. LISP is particularly well-suited for capturing the technical knowledge of an expert and making that knowledge available to others. Examples of recent application areas for such expert systems include: medical diagnosis, oil and mineral exploration, design and debugging of electronic systems, natural language interfaces to data base systems, and interactive language translation. Many versions of LISP have been used by educators both to illustrate fundamentals in programming languages and to teach the concepts of artificial intelligence and its applications. LISP/VM is a full-function LISP implementation that includes and augments the generally recognized LISP functions. It retains and enhances the particular strengths of traditional LISP and, in addition, includes current software technology concepts such as adoption of an integrated programming environment and generation of optimized compiled code. LISP/VM builds on the capabilities of VM to provide support of multiple LISP users. In many cases, LISP/VM will provide the most cost-effective solution for multiple LISP users while allowing sharing of data and system resources.

list. In a list processing software language, an ordered sequence of elements, usually found within a pair of matching parentheses: for example: (A B C) is a list composed of the elements A, B, and C. In the LISP programming language, the first element in the list is commonly a program function, and the others are arguments to be acted upon by that function. A sequence of recursively defined objects. In LISP a sequence of 0 or more atoms and lists surrounded by 1 set of matching parentheses.

list structure. A collection of items enclosed by parentheses, where each item can be either a symbol or another list.

listing. An assembler output containing a listing of program mnemonics, the machine code produced, and diagnostics, if any.

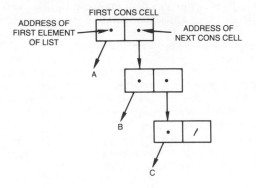

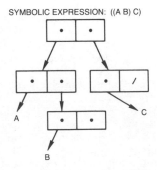

Figure L–4. List Structure—Representation of bit structure in memory.

literal. A literal is either a numeric literal an enumeration literal, a character literal, or a string literal. A literal represents a value literally, that is, by means of letters and other characters.

litho. Assists geologists in interpreting data from oil-well logs. Those data include curves reflecting measurements of rock density, resistivity, sound transmission, and radioactivity. The system uses the log data plus knowledge of the region's geological environment (e.g., geography, paleontology) to characterize the rock encountered in a well. That characterization includes porosity, permeability, composition, texture, and type of layering. It uses a separate pattern recognition program to extract features directly from the log data. Knowledge is represented as rules and accessed through backward chaining. It is implemented in EMYCIN. The system was developed by Schlumberger and reached the stage of a research prototype.

load capacity. The weight a robot can manipulate with a fully extended arm. It should be noted that most robots can handle heavier loads when full arm extension is not required.

load deflection. The difference in position of some point on a body between a nonloaded and an externally loaded condition. The difference in position of a manipulator hand or tool, usually with the arm extended, between a nonloaded condition (other than gravity) and an externally loaded condition. Either or both static and dynamic (inertial) loads may be considered.

loader. A program that operates on input devices to transfer information from off-line memory to on-line memory.

local intelligence. Processing power and memory capacity built in to the terminal so it does not need to be connected to a host computer to perform certain tasks. A "dumb terminal" has no local intelligence.

local network. One of several short-distance data communications schemes typified by common use of a transmission medium by many devices and high data speeds. Also called a local area network, or LAN.

local operation. Machine vision transformers of the gray scale value of the picture elements, according to the gray scale values of the element itself and its neighbors in a given neighborhood. Examples are gradient, sharpening, smoothing or noise filtering, edge extraction, etc.

location. A storage position in memory uniquely specified by an address.

LOES. Monitors the loading of liquid oxygen (LOX) for the space shuttle orbiter at Kennedy Space Center. The input to LOES is a sequence of time-tagged measurements from the launch processing system, a real-time process controller that controls liquid oxygen loading. LOES monitors measurements, such as temperature, pressure, flow rate, and valve position, and determines whether or not the valid sensor data are being revised. When LOES detects an anomaly, it notifies monitoring personnel and activates troubleshooting algorithms. If LOES cannot identify the problem, it offers a list of suspect components and instructions for performing tests to isolate the faulty component. LOES is implemented in ZETALISP within a framework taken from the KNOBS expert system. It was developed by the Mitre Corporation in cooperation with Kennedy Space Center.

logic. A system that prescribes rules for manipulating symbols. Common systems of logic powerful enough to deal with knowledge structures include propositional calculus and predicate calculus.

logical commands. Those issued by the host using logical addressing based on data block size.

logical decision. The ability of a computer to make a choice between 2 alternatives; basically, the ability to answer yes or no to certain fundamental questions concerning equality and relative magnitude.

logical design. The synthesizing of a network of logical elements to perform a specified function. In digital electronics, those logical elements are digital electronic devices, such as gates, flip-flops, decoders, counters, etc.

logical device. One of a number of available peripheral devices allocated and assigned a function in a specific application.

logical element. In a computer or data-processing system, the smallest building blocks that operators can represent in an appropriate system of symbolic logic. Typical logical elements are the AND gate and the flip-flop.

logical inferences per second. A means of measuring the speed of computers used for artificial intelligence applications.

logical interface. Defines the repertoire of operation commands and operation responses.

logical operation. Execution of a single computer instruction.

logical representation. Knowledge representation by a collection of logical formulas, usually in first-order predicate logic, that provide a partial description of the world.

logic-based methods. Programming methods that use predicate calculus to structure the program and guide execution.

LOGIC THEORIST. Solves problems, precursor to GPS, one of the first programs to use heuristics in problem-solving.

long-term memory. A portion of human memory that is exceedingly large and contains all of the information that is not currently being processed.

long-term repeatability. Closeness of agreement of position movements, repeated under the same conditions during a long time interval, to the same location.

look-up table. Table of pixel intensity or color information that increases the range of values that can be displayed. Since the values are stored in the look-up table, they do not have to be computed each time they are called up, and execution time is reduced.

loop. The repeated execution of a series of instructions for a fixed number of times.

LOOPS. A knowledge engineering language for object-oriented representation. It also supports rule-based, access-oriented, and procedure-oriented representation methods. Its principal characteristic is the integration of its 4 programming schemes to allow the paradigms to be used together in system building. For example, rules and rule sets are considered LOOPS objects, and procedures can be LISP functions or rule sets. The support system contains display-oriented debugging tools, such as break packages and editors. LOOPS is implemented in INTERLISP-D and operates on Xerox 1100 series workstations. It was developed at the Xerox Palo Alto Research Center. **(See figure p. 163.)**

low address byte. The 8 least significant bits in the 16-bit memory address word. Abbreviated L or LO.

low-level features. Pixel-based features such as texture, regions, edges, lines, corners, etc.

low-level language. A programming language in which statements translate on a 1-for-1 basis.

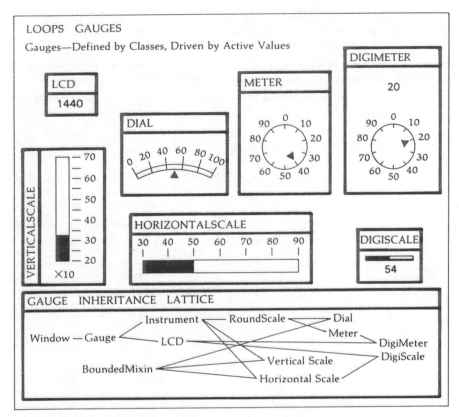

Figure L-5. Loops—LOOPS gauges. *Reprinted with the permission of Addison-Wesley Publishing Company from "A Guide to Expert Systems" by Donald A. Waterman.*

LRS. Helps lawyers retrieve information about court decisions and legislation in the domain of negotiable instruments of law, an area of commercial law that deals with checks and promissory notes. LRS contains subject descriptors that link each data item to the subject area concepts the item is about. A semantic net containing more than 200 legal concepts, built up from 6 primitive concepts (party, legal instrument, liability, legal action, account, and amount of money), forms the basis for that knowledge. The knowledge in LRS provides it with the ability to make inferences about the meanings of queries and to extend user queries to include terms that are implied but not mentioned by the user. LRS was developed at the University of Michigan.

Dr. Fred L. Luconi. President and chief executive officer and co-founder of Applied Expert Systems, Inc. (APEX). Before formation of APEX, Dr. Luconi was a cofounder of Index Systems, Inc., where he was executive vice president and chief financial officer with full responsibility for the company's financial affairs as well as operational responsibility. Previously, Dr. Luconi was a consultant to Arthur D. Little, Raytheon, and Hughes Aircraft. Before cofounding Index Systems, Dr. Luconi was an assistant professor in computer sciences at M.I.T. He was responsible for graduate courses on computer systems as well as lecturing and developing core curriculum in computer sciences. His research activities at that time included modular computer systems design, large data base systems design, and development of next generation computer systems architecture.

lumen. The unit of luminous flux or rate of luminous energy flow. It is equal to the flux radiating through a unit solid angle from a uniform point source of 1 candela.

luminance. Luminous intensity reflected or emitted by a surface in a given direction per unit of apparent area.

M

M (megabyte). Unit of memory, equal to about 1 million characters of text.

machine code. A binary code that a computer decodes to execute a specific function.

machine cycle. A subdivision of an instruction cycle during which time a related group of actions occurs within the microprocessor chip. In the 8080 microprocessor, there exist 9 different machine cycles. All instructions are combinations of 1 or more of these machine cycles.

machine language. A language written in a series of bits that are understandable by, and therefore instruct, a computer. The "first level" computer language, as compared with a "second level" assembly language or a "third level" compiler language.

machine learning. A research effort that seeks to create computer programs that can learn from experience. Such programs, when they become available, will remove a major barrier to the development of very large expert systems.

machine readable. Encoded in digital format.

machine translation. An area of AI research that is attempting to use computers to translate text from 1 language to another. The programs often use a combination of natural language understanding and generation.

MacLISP. A variation of the original LISP developed at MIT, it evolved into LISP MACHINE LISP, which is the basis for most LISP languages utilized today. ZetaLISP is a popular extension of MacLISP for commercial symbolic processing hardware.

macro. Programming with instructions, equivalent to a specified sequence of machine instructions, in a source language. A source language instruction from which many machine-language instructions can be generated.

macro assembler. An assembler routine capable of assembling programs that contain and reference macro instructions.

macro instruction. A symbolic instruction in a source language that produces a number of machine language instructions. It is made available for use by the programmer through an automatic programming system. A macro instruction is a method of describing in a 1-line statement a function, or functions, to be performed by the object program.

macrobend loss. The leakage of light when a lightguide is bent. The remedy is a little common sense in planning lightwave systems.

macro function. A LISP function that serves as a template for translating a LISP form language structure. When a macro is called, a new form is substituted for it and evaluated in place of the macro call.

macro instruction. A symbol that is used to represent a specified sequence of source instructions.

MACSYMA. Performs symbolic manipulation of algebraic expressions and handles problems involving limit calculations, symbolic integration, solution of equations, canonical simplification, and pattern matching. The system uses mathematical expertise organized an individual knowledge sources and chosen for a particular problem by sophisticated pattern-matching routines. MACSYMA achieves very high quality and efficient performance on the mathematical problems within its scope. The system was implemented in LISP and developed under Project MAC at MIT. MACSYMA has reached the stage of a commercial system and is used regularly by engineers and scientists throughout the United States.

magnetic bubble. A device in which information is stored in magnetic film as a pattern of oppositely directed magnetic fields. Magnetic bubble devices hold their pattern even if power is lost.

magnetic disk. A flat, circular plate with a magnetic surface on which data can be stored by selective magnetization of portions of the flat surface.

magnetic tape. A storage system based on the use of magnetic spots (bits) on metal or coated-plastic tape. The spots are arranged so that the desired code is read out as the tape travels past the read-write head.

magnetic tape storage. A storage system that uses magnetic spots, representing bits, on coated plastic tape.

mainframe. Very large computer, generally used by many users at one time in large data-processing operations.

maintenance of an expert system. Unlike conventional computer software that is only infrequently updated, expert systems by their nature are very easy to modify. Most expert systems that are currently in use are constantly being improved by the addition of new rules. In most applications the user organization will want to establish a regular routine to capture and incorporate new knowledge into the system. It's a good idea to make 1 person responsible for entering new rules whenever data or procedures change or whenever questions arise that the current system can not answer.

major motion axes. These axes may be described as the number of independent directions the arm can move the attached wrist and end effector relative to a point of origin of the manipulator such as the base. The number of robot arm axes required to reach world coordinate points is dependent on the design of robot arm configuration.

manipulation. The process of controlling and monitoring data table bits or words by means of the user's program in order to vary application functions. The movement of reorientation of objects, such as parts or tools.

manipulator. A mechanism, usually consisting of a series of segments, jointed or sliding relative to one another, for the purpose of grasping and moving objects usually in several degrees of freedom. It may be remotely controlled by a computer or by a human.

manipulator-oriented language. Programming language for describing exactly where a robot's arm and gripper should go and when. To be contrasted with task-oriented languages for describing what the effect of robot action should be.

manual control. A device containing controls that manipulate the robot arm and allow for the recording of locations and program motion instructions.

mapping. Transforming an image from 1 coordinate system to another.

MARGIE. Early experimental language-understanding and paraphrase-generating system developed by Roger Schank and his students. A principal purpose was to show that language can be understood without attention to details of syntax.

MARS. A knowledge engineering language for rule-based representation of hierarchical, discrete, event-driven simulators. Its principal characteristics include hierarchical specification of the structure and behavior of a design, forward- and backward-chaining control schemes, and symbolic simulation. The support environment contains a compiler that compiles general, rule-based specifications into special procedures for simulation. It also contains a mixed-mode simulator that allows different parts of a design to be simulated at different abstraction levels. An explanation capability is also provided. MARS is implemented in MRS. It was developed at Stanford University.

mask design. The final phase of integrated circuit design by which the circuit design is realized through multiple masks corresponding to multiple layers on the integrated circuit. The mask layout must observe all process-related constraints and minimize the area the circuit will occupy.

masking. A process that uses a bit pattern to select bits from a data byte for use in a subsequent operation.

mass memory. That part of a computer's memory where information is kept that is not currently needed. Also called external memory or slow-speed memory.

master/slave manipulator. A type of teleoperated robot arm that is positioned by a human, who controls it with a remotely located joy stick.

match. In a production system the match process compares a set of patterns from the left-hand sides of rules against the data in data memory to find all possible ways in which the rules can be satisfied with consistent bindings (i.e., instantiations).

match cycle. The stage of processing that occurs in the Rete match algorithm whenever there is a change to working memory. It results in an updating of the Rete network and the conflict set.

MATHLAB 68. Assists mathematicians, scientists, and engineers with the symbolic algebraic manipulation encountered in analysis problems. The system performs differentiation, polynomial factorization, indefinite integration, and direct and inverse Laplace transforms, and solves linear differential equations with constant symbolic coefficients. It contains mathematical expertise in individual modules each with a particular functional specialty. Users' data are classified into 3 categories: expressions, equations, and functions. Rules for the algebraic manipulation of the data vary with the categories. The system is implemented in LISP and formed the cornerstone for the development of MACSYMA. MATHLAB 68 was developed at M.I.T.

matrix. In graphics programming, the array of x, y, and z coefficients for calculating a geometric transformation. In computers a logic network in the form of an array of input leads and output leads with logic elements connected at some of their intersections.

Maxwell triangle. A color diagram in the form of an equilateral triangle, with the primaries represented at the vertices.

MCC. Microelectronics and Computer Technology Corporation. Located in Austin, Texas, this private company has 20 participating corporations, including Honeywell, Sperry, RCA, Eastman Kodak, and a host of others. The intent in setting up the MCC was to develop advanced technology that all the participants could ultimately utilize and market. The MCC is considered the only operation in the U.S. that rivals the Japanese Fifth Generation Project, although no government funds are involved.

John McDermott. Ph.D., principal scientist and associate head of the Computer Science Department at Carnegie-Mellon University. He has pioneered research and development on expert systems ranging from process diagnosis to production management. His first success was R1/XCON, an operational expert system that configures VAX and PDP/11 computer systems for Digital Equipment Corporation.

Dr. David McDonald. Professor of computer and information science at the University of Massachusetts. He is well known for his work on language generation. His primary research areas are natural language processing, knowledge representation, planning, high-performance programming environments, machine tutoring, description and explanation, presentations by intelligent interfaces, and data-directed control and planning. When he received his Ph.D. in 1980, he was a member of M.I.T.'s Artificial Intelligence Laboratory. He edited and contributed to The Brattle Reports.

means-ends analysis. A problem-solving approach (used by General Problem Solver) in which problem-solving operators are chosen in an iterative fashion to reduce the difference between the current problem-solving state and the goal state.

measured value. The actual quantity attained at the output of the system, whether it be angular displacement, velocity, torque, liquid level, pressure, etc.

MEDICO. Gives ophthalmologists advice about the management of chorioretinal diseases. The system contains general clinical knowledge and a large data base of facts about previous patients and events. MEDICO is a forward chaining, rule-based system that handles certainty by associating likelihood estimates provided by domain experts with the rules. Interactive rule acquisition from domain experts is supported by a knowledge acquisition and maintenance module (KAMM). Another module, RAIN (Relational Algebraic INterpreter), supports the examination, update, and reorganization of the rules in the knowledge base. MEDICO is implemented in the programming language C. It was developed at the University of Illinois.

MDX. Diagnoses the existence and cause of the liver syndrome known as cholestasis. The system bases its diagnosis on patient history, signs, symptoms, and clinical data. MDX functions as a community of cooperating expert diagnosticians, each with different specialities. The experts call upon each other to resolve problems requiring special knowledge and expertise. Communication is via a blackboard mechanism. MDX's expertise consists of a diagnostic heuristics and a hierarchical, deep model of the conceptual structure of cholestasis. That knowledge is represented as rules and frames organized around the cholestasis model. PATREC and RADEX are members of the community of expert systems called upon by MDX. MDX is implemented in LISP. It was developed at Ohio State University.

medium-speed data. A data transmission rate of between 300 and 2400 bits per second.

megassembly systems. Multistation, multiproduct assembly systems containing at least 10 robots.

MELD. A knowledge engineering language for rule-based representation, but it also supports frame-based representation methods. Its principal characteristic is the separation of object-level and metalevel heuristic and causal rules. The metalevel rules contain all the knowledge required to select and apply the object-level (task-specific) rules. MELD supports forward and backward chaining, demons, certainty handling, and complex control schemes, and it uses the OPS5 conflict resolution strategy to select metalevel rules. MELD is implemented in OPS5. It was developed by the Westinghouse Research and Development Center.

memory. A feature in the architecture of a computer system for storing information so that it can be read, written, executed, or some combination of the above. In production system architectures there may be conceptually distinct memories for factual, problem-solving, and control knowledge. A device or media used to store information in a form that can be understood by the computer hardware.

memory address. The memory address specifies data location in memory. The memory address takes the form of a code number. In a program memory addresses are referred to rather than the memory word itself.

memory cell. Basic storage unit in a memory chip, which normally comprises many thousands of memory cells.

memory cycle time. The minimum time between 2 successive data accesses from a memory.

memory dump. To copy the contents of all or part of a storage, usually from an internal storage into an external storage.

mental models. The symbolic networks and patterns of relationships that experts use when they are trying to understand a problem. Mental models often take the form of simplified analogies or metaphors that experts use when first examining a problem. Mental models can sometimes be converted into production rules, but in many cases they still defy artificial intelligence techniques and are the object of considerable research in cognitive psychology.

menu. A display on a terminal device that lists options a user may choose.

MES. Helps aircraft technicians diagnose aircraft problems. It is designed to overcome the shortage of technically qualified maintenance personnel by allowing less-qualified technicians to accurately assess problems with aircraft. MES contains knowledge taken from aircraft maintenance manuals, such as component weight and dimensions, ground operations, and troubleshooting and repair procedures. This knowledge is augmented by experiential knowledge from expert technicians. MES is a forward-chaining, rule-based system. It is implemented in LISP on an Apple II+ microcomputer. It was developed at the Air Force Institute of Technology.

message. A group of words, variable in length, transporting an item of information.

message trace analyzer. Helps debug real-time systems such as large telecommunication switching machines containing hundreds of processors. The system examines interprocess message traces, identifying illegal message sequences to localize the fault to within a process. The system considers the sender process ID, the receiver process ID, the message type, and the time stamp fields of messages in the trace. General debugging heuristics and facts about the specific system being debugged are represented as rules and applied using both forward and backward chaining. The system contains a limited explanation facility that allows it to answer questions about its reasoning. It is written in PROLOG. It was developed at the University of Waterloo.

meta-. A prefix indicating that a term is being used to refer to itself. Thus, a meta-rule is a rule about other rules.

metacognition. The capability to think about one's own thought processes.

META-DENDRAL. Helps chemists determine the dependence of mass spectrometric fragmentation on substructural features. It does so by discovering fragmentation rules for given classes of molecules. The system derives those rules from training instances consisting of sets of molecules with known 3-dimensional structures and mass spectra. META-DENDRAL first generates a set of highly specific rules which account for a single fragmentation process in a particular molecule. Then it uses the training examples to generalize those rules. Finally, the system reexamines the rules to remove redundant or incorrect rules. META-DENDRAL is implemented in INTERLISP. It was developed at Stanford University.

metafile. Device-independent file for storing a display and moving it to another system.

metaknowledge. Knowledge about knowledge. Knowledge that tells a system something about what it knows, how its knowledge can be utilized, and what the limits of its knowledge are. Knowledge in an expert system about how the system operates or reasons, such as knowledge about the use and control of domain knowledge. More generally, knowledge about knowledge. Another term for metalevel knowledge. The self-knowledge a system has about the extent and reliability of its knowledge about the domain and when and how to best use its domain knowledge.

metamer. Color that is perceived to be the same as another color, even though they have different spectral energy distributions. Metamers may look the same under 1 lighting condition and show their difference under another condition.

metarule. A rule that embodies metalevel knowledge. Metarules may be used to specify conflict-resolution strategies or to filter and order domain rules. A rule that describes how other rules should be used or modified. A popular subset of the logic rules in an inference engine. Essentially, metarules are specific heuristics used to select proper object rules in running a particular expert system program. Metarules aid in facilitating run time of certain programs by circumventing unnecessary steps.

MFLOPS. Millions of Floating Operations Per Second. The Japanese hope to introduce gigaflop (GFLOPS) machines by 1990.

MI. The Myocardial Infarction system helps physicians diagnose myocardial infarction through analysis of enzyme activity. The system reaches its diagnosis of heart damage by checking for elevated levels of certain enzymes in the blood over a period of several days. MI's expertise includes knowledge about how to deal with the time-dependent nature of the medical findings, including techniques for automatically updating, revising, and interpreting a patient's record. MI is a forward-chaining, rule-based system. It is implemented in a version of EXPERT modified to represent and manipulate time-dependent rules and data. MI was developed at Rutgers University.

Donald Michie. Donald Michie is a Fellow of the British Computer Society and of the Royal Society of Edinburgh, and holds the degrees of M.A., D.Phil. and D.Sc. from Oxford University for studies in the biological sciences. His interest in the possibility of programming human knowledge and intelligence into machines was simulated during the war when he joined the Bletchley code-breaking establishment at Bletchley Park. After pursuing a postwar career in experimental genetics and immunology he returned to machine intelligence in the early 1960s. In 1967 he was elected to a Personal Chair of Machine Intelligence in the University of Edinburgh.

He is editor-in-chief of the Machine Intelligence series and is the author of books and papers on that subject.

micro array computer. A special-purpose multiprocessor system designed for high-speed calculations with arrays of data.

microbend loss. The leakage of light caused by very tiny, sharp curves in a lightguide that may result from imperfections where the glass fiber meets the sheathing that covers it.

microcode. A computer program at the basic machine level.

microcomputer. A small computer containing a microprocessor, input and display devices, and memory all in 1 box. It may or may not interface to a host computer and/or peripheral devices. Sometimes referred to as a desktop computer, or a personal computer.

microprocessor. A basic element of a central processing unit constructed as a single integrated circuit. A microprocessor typically has a limited instruction set that may be expanded by microprogramming. A microprocessor may require additional circuits to become a central processing unit.

microsecond. One-millionth of a second.

microsequencer. A primitive control unit that is not as general as a computer. Today most computers are implemented with microsequencers.

MicroVAX™. A family of 16- and 32-bit super microcomputers based on a single-chip implementation of the Digital Equipment Corporation VAX architecture.

mid-run explanation. The ability of a computer program to stop upon request and explain where it currently is, what it is doing, and what it will seek to accomplish next. Expert systems tend to have features that facilitate mid-run explanation while conventional programs do not.

millisecond. One-thousandth of a second.

MIMD. Multiple instruction, multiple data. This term refers to flow of data in parallel processing. Information is transmitted down a number of paths (not a single one that is ultimately branched) and then synchronized during processing.

minicomputer. A class of computer in which the basic element of the central processing unit is constructed of a number of discrete components and integrated circuits rather than being composed of a single integrated circuit, as in the micro-processor.

MIPS. Millions of Instructions Per Second. Measurement of supercomputer speed during processing.

MITI. Ministry of International Trade and Industry. Japan's organization that has initiated the Fifth Generation Project in order to be a world leader in new artificial intelligence technologies.

MIXER. Helps programmers write microprograms for the Texas Instruments' T1990 VLSI chip. Given a microprogram description, the system generates optimized horizontal microcodes for the T1990. MIXER contains knowledge about T1990 microprogramming taken from manuals and from an analysis of the microcode in the T1990 control ROM. This includes knowledge about how to map written descriptions into sets of intermediate operations, how to allocate appropriate registers to variables, and how to expand intermediate operations into sets of microoperations. MIXER uses this knowledge to determine which microoperations are best for implementing the microprogram. The system represents knowledge as rules and data, with inferencing controlled unification and dynamic backtracking. MIXER is implemented in PROLOG. It was developed at Tokyo University.

mneumonic. Assisting, or designed to assist, memory. A term used to describe the assignment of numbers and letters, in a combination that is mnemonic or memory aiding to the eye or to the ear. Mnemonic symbols are used extensively for coding whenever it is deemed an advantage to be able to memorize code designations.

mneumonic symbol. An easily remembered symbol that assists the programmer in communicating with the system.

mobile robot. A robot mounted on a movable platform.

mode. The path a light ray follows through a fiber.

model. An appropriate representation of a process or system that tries to relate a part or all of the variables in the system so that a better understanding of the system is attained.

Model-Based System. A type of expert system that is based on a model of the structure and behavior of the device it is designed to understand.

model-based vision system. A system that utilizes a priori models to drive a desired description of the original scene from an image. **(See figure p. 173.)**

model directed. Another term for backward chaining. Used in contrast to data directed.

model driven. A top-down approach to problem solving in which the inferences to be verified are based on the domain model used by the problem solver.

model number. A model number is an exactly representable value of a real type. Operations of the real type are defined in terms of operations on the model numbers of the type. The properties of the model numbers and of their operations are the minimal properties preserved by all implementations of the real type.

modeling system. A high-level system for defining objects in world coordinates.

modeling transformation. Transformation that changes a model coordinate system to a user-specified coordinate system.

modular. Made up of subunits that can be combined in various ways. In robots a robot constructed from a number of interchangeable subunits each of which can be 1 of a range of sizes or have 1 of several possible motion styles (prismatic, cylindrical, etc.) and number of axes.

modulation. The use of one signal to control some aspect of another, such as the frequency or amplitude.

module. The module of a counter is the number of distinct states the counter goes through before repeating. A 4-bit binary counter has a module of 16; a decade counter has a module of 10; and a divide-by-7 counter has a module of 7. In a variable module counter, n can be any value within a range of values.

Modus Ponens. A mathematical form of argument in deductive logic. It has the form

> If A is true, then B is true.
> A is true.
> Therefore, B is true.

The formula is (A) (B) $((A) \rightarrow B) \& A) \rightarrow B$

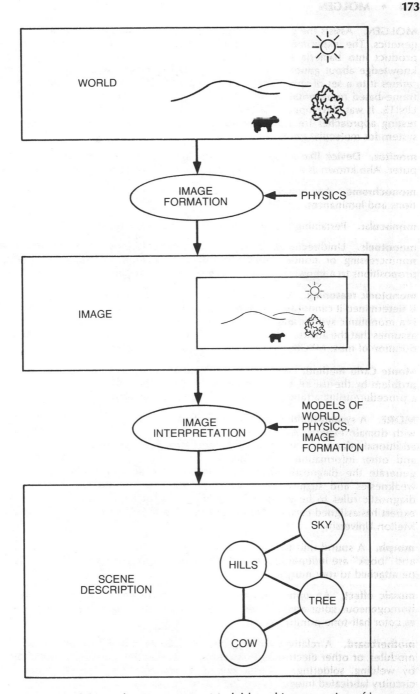

Figure M–1. Model-Based vision system—Model-based interpretation of images.

MOLGEN. Assists the geneticist in planning gene-cloning experiments in molecular genetics. The experiments involve splicing a gene coding for a desired protein product into bacteria so that the bacteria will manufacture it. The system uses knowledge about genetics and the user's goal to create an abstract plan and then refines it to a set of specific laboratory steps. MOLGEN uses an object-oriented and frame-based representation and control scheme, and it is implemented in LISP and UNITS. It was developed at Stanford University. MOLGEN is primarily a vehicle for testing approaches for reasoning about design, rather than an operational expert system for molecular genetics.

monitor. Device like a television screen that displays information from the computer. Also known as a video display terminal (VDT) or cathode ray terminal (crt).

monochrome. Any combination of colors of the same hue, but of different staurations and luminances.

monocular. Pertaining to an image taken from a single viewpoint.

monotonic. Unidirectional. In analysis a monotonic function is one that is either nonincreasing or nondecreasing. In inference a monotonic logic can only add propositions to a knowledge base; it can never remove them.

monotonic reasoning. A reasoning system based on the assumption that once a fact is determined it cannot be altered during the course of the reasoning process. MYCIN is a monotonic system; and, thus, once the user has answered a question, the system assumes that the answer will remain the same throughout the session. Given the brief duration of most MYCIN sessions, this is a reasonable assumption.

Monte Carlo method. Method of obtaining an appropriate solution to a numerical problem by the use of random numbers, for example, the random walk method or a procedure using a random number sequence to calculate an integral.

MORE. A system-building aid that generates diagnostic rules through its interviews with domain experts. As the expert enters symptoms and findings, MORE asks for additional information that could provide a stronger diagnostic assessment. From this and other information, MORE develops a model of the domain and uses it to generate the diagnostic rules. As the rules are accumulated, MORE looks for weaknesses and suggests types of knowledge that would allow more powerful diagnostic rules to be generated. It also checks for inconsistencies in the way the expert has assigned certainty factors to the rules. MORE was developed at Carnegie-Mellon University.

morph. A sound unit that has an associated meaning. Root morphs such as "dog" and "book" are independent morphs; bound morphs (such as "ing" and "ly") must be attached to root morphs.

mosaic effect. An optical fusion of small areas of color that are perceived as a homogeneous color area different from the color of its constituents. Same principle as color half-tone printing.

motherboard. A relatively large piece of insulating material on which components, modules, or other electronic subassemblies are mounted and interconnections made by welding, soldering, or other means, using point-to-point or matrix wire, or circuitry fabricated integrally with the board.

mouse. A palm-sized positioning device containing a ball (except for the optical mouse, which has no moving parts) that rolls across a flat surface; its movements control the cursor's position on the video display screen.

MRS. A knowledge engineering language for rule-based and logic-based representation. Its principal characteristics include a flexible control scheme utilizing forward chaining, backward chaining and resolution theorem proving, and the ability to represent metalevel knowledge, knowledge about the MRS system itself. The MRS programmer can write statements about MRS subroutines just as easily as statements about geology or medicine. The support environment contains interactive graphics-oriented debugging tools. MRS is implemented in INTERLISP. It was developed at Stanford University.

M.1. A knowledge engineering language for rule-based representation. Its principal characteristics include a backward-chaining control scheme and an Englishlike language syntax. The support environment contains graphics-oriented interactive debugging tools for tracing system operation, facilities for explaining the system's reasoning process, and mechanisms for automatically querying the user when the data base lacks the required information. M.1 is implemented in PROLOG and operates on the IBM Personal Computer by running the PC DOS 2.0 operating system. It was developed by Teknowledge.

MUD. Helps engineers maintain optimal drilling fluid properties. It does so by diagnosing the causes of problems with drilling fluids and suggesting treatments. Possible causes include contaminants, high temperatures or pressures, and inadequate use of chemical additives. MUD contains knowledge extracted from domain experts about drilling fluids and the diagnosis of drilling problems. It is a forward chaining, rule-based system and uses MYCIN-like certainty factors to represent the subjective determinations of experts. In addition, it can provide explanations about its recommended treatment plans. MUD is implemented in OPS5. It was developed at Carnegie-Mellon University in cooperation with NL Baroid.

multi-mode fiber. The relatively large core of this lightguide allows light pulses to zig-zag along many different paths. It is ideal for light sources larger than lasers, such as LEDs.

multiple-access network. A flexible system by which every station can have access to the network at all times; provisions are made for times when 2 computers decide to transmit at the same time.

multiple inheritance. The ability of object-oriented programming languages to allow objects to inherit qualities, characteristics, and properties from other unrelated objects. This allows objects to "inherit" qualities without those qualities having to be rewritten specifically for a particular object.

multiple lines of reasoning. A problem-solving technique in which a limited number of possibly independent approaches to solving the problem are developed in parallel.

multiplex. The transmission of multiple data bits through a single transmission line by means of a "sharing" technique.

multiplexer. A digital device that can select 1 of a number of inputs and pass the logic level of that input on to the output. Information for input-channel selection usually is presented to the device in binary weighted form and decoded internally. The device acts as a single-pole multiposition switch that passes digital information in one direction only.

multiprocessor. A computer that can execute 1 or more computer programs employing 2 or more processing units under integrated control of programs or devices.

multiprocessor control. A control scheme that employs more than 1 central processing unit in simultaneous parallel computation.

multiprogramming. A technique for handling numerous routines or programs seemingly simultaneously by overlapping or interleaving their execution, that is, by permitting more than 1 program to time-share machine components.

multivalued attribute. An attribute that can have more than 1 value. If, for example, a system seeks values for the attribute restaurant, and if the restaurant is multivalued, then 2 or more restaurants may be identified.

MUMPS. A procedure-oriented programming language. Like LISP, MUMPS is an interpreted, typeless language that supports atomic and composite variables. It differs from LISP principally in its support for multidimensional arrays as multiway trees with descendents ordered by the values of the array indexes. The implicit ordering of data inserted into the tree structures provides automatic sorting by insertion key. MUMPS supports recursion and provides a set of functions for tree traversal. It has no provision for parameterized procedures or local environments; thus all variables are global in scope. MUMPS was originally developed for use in medical computing. It is available for a wide variety of computer systems, and an ANSI standard definition of the language exists.

Munsell system. A perceptual color system devised by Albert H. Munsell that identifies color in terms of hue, value, and chroma, arranged in orderly scales of equal visual steps. A notation assigning a numerical equivalent to each attribute on its scale yields a unique designation for any given color. Standardized color chips sampling the Munsell color space and labeled by Munsell notation are used internationally to express the perceived color of an object, to match colors, etc.

MVS. Multiple Virtual Storage. One of the most popular IBM host environments, it is a 1973 offshoot of the OS/VS (Operating System/Virtual Storage) environment.

MYCIN. Assists physicians in the selection of appropriate antimicrobial therapy for hospital patients with bacteremia, meningitis, and cystitis infections. The system diagnoses the cause of the infection (e.g., the identity of the infecting organism is pseudomonas) using knowledge relating infecting organisms with patient history, symptoms, and laboratory test results. The system recommends drug treatment (type

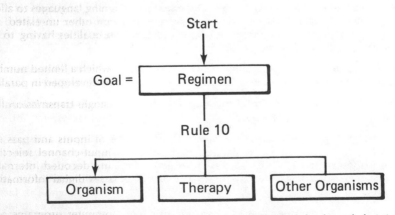

Figure M–2. MYCIN—Beginning of the MYCIN consultation's backward chaining process. Attributes are shown in boxes.

and dosage) according to procedures followed by physicians experienced in infectious disease therapy. MYCIN is a rule-based system employing a backward-chaining control scheme. It includes mechanisms for performing certainty calculations and providing explanations of the system's reasoning process. MYCIN is implemented in LISP. It was developed at Stanford University.

MYCROFT. An expert system that assesses and corrects drawings done by computers programmed to draw by children.

N

name. A construct that stands for an entity: it is said that the name denotes the entity, and that the entity is the meaning of the name.

named association. A named association specifies the association of an item with 1 or more positions in a list, by naming the positions.

NAND. A logic operator having the property that if P is a statement, Q is a statement, R is a statement—then the NAND of P, Q, R is true if at least 1 statement is false, false if all statements are true.

natural deduction. Informal reasoning.

natural frequency. The frequency at which a system would oscillate with no damping applied if a disturbance were injected.

natural language. A person's native tongue. Natural language systems attempt to make computers capable of processing language the way people normally speak it instead of in specialized programming languages, thereby making it easier and more efficient for both inexperienced and sophisticated users to work with computers. Natural language systems are particularly well suited for environments that include many nontechnical users or users who do not spend much time working with computers; for database inquiry systems; and for computer-assisted instruction systems. Today most natural language systems are implemented in English. A segment of AI devoted to using commands in the normal language of the operator. Queries and responses are delivered in conversational style (as opposed to computer commands or jargon), and a machine truly capable of natural language will be able to understand and resolve grammatic idiosyncrasies and ambiguities. The implementation of that process is known as a natural language interface. At the moment, systems can be built that will accept typed input in narrowly constrained domains (e.g., data base inquiries). Several expert systems incorporate some primitive form of natural language in their user interface to facilitate rapid development of new knowledge bases.

natural language. The part of natural language processing research that is attempting to have computers present information in English. Natural language generation programs must decide when to say something, what to say, and how to say it.

natural language interface. A system for communicating with a computer by using a natural language.

natural language processing. Processing of natural language (e.g., English) by a computer to facilitate communication with the computer or for other purposes, such as language translation.

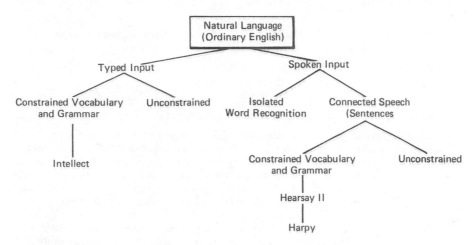

Figure N-1. Natural Language Processing—Types of natural language problems.

Natural Language Processing Toolkit. Rowman & Littlefield developed the Natural Language Processing Toolkit as a collection of Franz Lisp programs for computer systems running under the UNIX Operating System. It provides a starting point for the engineering of an interface to an application system.

natural language understanding. Response by a computer based on the meaning of a natural language input.

NAVEX. Monitors radar station data that estimate the velocity and position of the space shuttle, looks for errors, and warns the mission control center console operators when errors are detected or predicted. When it detects errors, the system recommends actions to take, such as excluding data from a particular radar station or restarting the analysis of the current data. NAVEX is rule-based and frame-oriented and runs in real time, making recommendations based on actual radar data. It is implemented in ART. NAVEX was developed by Inference Corporation in cooperation with NASA at the Johnson Space Center.

NDS. Locates multiple faults in a nationwide communications network called COM-NET by applying expert diagnostic strategies based on knowledge about the network's topology and composition. The system suggests diagnostic tests to perform, and the outcome of each test provides evidence for or against a fault existing in some set of components. The components under consideration include telecommunication processors, modems, telephone circuits, and computer terminals. NDS is a rule-based system implemented in ARBY. The system was developed by Smart Systems Technology in cooperation with Shell Development Company.

negate. To change a proposition into its opposite.

negative edge. The transition from logic 1 to logic 0 in a clock pulse.

negative-edge triggered. Transfer of information occurs on the negative edge of the clock pulse.

negative image. A monochrome display signal with a polarity opposite to the normal polarity (i.e., white and black areas are reversed).

negative logic. A form of logic in which the more positive voltage level represents logic 0 and the more negative level represents logic 1.

negative modulation. A form of modulation in which an increase in transmitted power corresponds to a decrease in display luminance.

NEOMYCIN. Helps physicians diagnose and treat patients with meningitis and similar diseases. The system incorporates expertise derived from MYCIN, represented in a way that facilitates explanation and teaching. The system's knowledge is in the form of rules organized that constitute the diagnostic procedure. The key difference between MYCIN and NEOMYCIN is the explicit separation of the diagnostic procedure from the disease knowledge. NEOMYCIN provides explanations of diagnostic strategy as well as those relating to a causal model of the domain. GUIDON2 uses the NEOMYCIN knowledge base and diagnostic metarules as its source of teaching materials. NEOMYCIN is implemented in INTERLISP-D. It was developed at Stanford University.

nest. To enclose a subroutine inside a larger routine, but not necessarily make it part of the outer routine. A series of looping instructions can be nested within each other.

net. A set of logically related connection points comprising a particular signal in an electrical or electronic design. Also called a logical net.

NETL. A knowledge engineering language for frame-based representation of semantic networks. Its principal characteristic is the ability to create and manipulate virtual copies of arbitrarily large and complex portions of the semantic network. Those copies inherit the entire structure of the descriptions that are copied, including all parts, subparts, and internal relationships. NETL is implemented in MACLISP. It was developed at M.I.T.

net load capacity. The additional weight or mass of a material that can be handled by a machine or process without failure over and above that required for a container, pallet, or other device that necessarily accompanies the material.

network. Computers and communication links that allow computers to communicate with each other and to share programs, facilities, and data and knowledge bases. A network can be local (1 room, 1 office, 1 institution), national, or even international.

NEUREX. Helps physicians diagnose patients with diseases of the nervous system. The system uses the results of a neurological examination of unconscious patients to locate the nervous system damage and classify the patients according to the damage locale (e.g., subtentorial lesion, nonfocal). NEUREX is a rule-based system employing both forward and backward chaining and a MYCIN-like certainty factor mechanism. Rules containing neurological localization expertise are organized into an inference hierarchy in which successively higher levels in the hierarchy represent greater levels of abstraction of the information about the patient. NEUREX is implemented in Wisconsin LISP. It was developed at the University of Maryland.

NEUROLOGIST-I. Helps physicians diagnose neurological disorders by localizing lesions occurring within the central nervous system (CNS). The system analyzes patient data, including neurologic complaints and physical examination results, and then produces a summary of malfunctioning tracts by mapping symptoms to tract status. The system uses physiological knowledge encoded as an analogic/geometric model of the CNS in which nervous tract cross sections are approximated by polygons represented as sets of vertices. NEUROLOGIST-I is implemented in FRANZ LISP. It was developed at the State University of New York at Buffalo.

new frame action. The elimination of all temporary information from a display and the rewriting of all visible retained information. On a hardcopy device, the recording medium is advanced to an unrecorded area.

nibble. A sequence of 4 adjacent bits, or half a byte, is a nibble. A hexadecimal or BCD digit can be represented in a nibble.

NLVMS. Allows a user of the VMS operating system for the DEC VAX to issue commands in the English language. NLVMS does so by transforming an English command or query into the formal DCL command language normally required by VMS. For instance, if the user types "are there any fortran files in smith's directory," NLVMS would translate that into the DCL command "DIRECTORY [SMITH]*.FOR." NLVMS was built using Carnegie Group's PLUME product. PLUME is a software tool for building natural language interfaces to a variety of application systems. NLVMS allows a VMS user to access the capabilities of the operating system without having to learn the complexities of the DCL command language. As such, NLVMS is quite helpful to infrequent or inexperienced users of VMS.

NOAH. An expert system that solves various system repair diagnostic problems.

node. A point in a graph connected to other points in the graph by arcs. Intersection of 2 or more interconnections.

noise. An extraneous signal in an electrical circuit capable of interfering with the desired signal. Loosely, any disturbance tending to interfere with the normal operation of a device or system.

nonalgorithmic. A problem-solving approach that does not follow a step-by-step procedure.

nonhierarchical plan. One category of artificial intelligence techniques used for planning. A nonhierarchical plan represents a plan on 1 level only.

nonmonotonic. Bidirectional. A nonmonotonic function is one that increases over part of its domain and decreases over another part of its domain. In inference a nonmonotonic logic can both add propositions to a knowledge base and remove them.

nonmonotonic logic. A logic in which results are subject to revision as more information is gathered.

nonmonotonic reasoning. Reasoning that can be revised if some value changes during a session. Nonmonotonic reasoning can deal with problems that involve rapid changes in values in short periods of time. A reasoning technique that supports multiple lines of reasoning (multiple ways to reach the same conclusion) and the retraction of facts or conclusions, given new information. It is useful for processing unreliable knowledge and data.

nonoverlapping 2-phase clock. A 2-phase clock in which the clock pulses of the individual phases do not overlap.

nonvolatile memory. A semiconductor memory device in which the stored digital data are not lost when the power is removed (i.e., core memory, EPRAM memory).

NPPC. Helps nuclear power plant operators determine the cause of some abnormal event (e.g., greater than normal containment temperature) by applying rules in conjunction with a model of plant operation. The system uses a model of the primary coolant system, including pumps, reactor, steam generator, and emergency core cooling system to diagnose the cause of an abnormality or accident and then suggests procedures for correcting the problem. The model consists of a common-sense algorithm network that accesses appropriate diagnostic rules. The system was developed at the Georgia Institute of Technology.

null. Empty. Having no memory. Not usable.

null character. A control character that is used to accomplish media-fill, or time-fill, and that may be inserted into or removed from a sequence of characters without affecting the meaning of the sequences; however, the control of equipment of the format may be affected by this character.

object. An entity in a programming system that is used to represent declarative knowledge and possibly procedural knowledge about a physical object, a concept, or a problem-solving strategy. The physical or conceptual entities that have many attributes. When a collection of attributes or rules is divided into groups, each of the groups is organized around an object. In MYCIN, following medical practice, the basic groups of attributes or parameters were clustered into contexts, but more recent systems have preferred the term "object." When a knowledge base is divided into objects, it is often represented by an object tree that shows how the different objects relate to each other. When one uses object-oriented programming, each object is called a frame or unit and the attributes and values associated with it are stored in slots. An object is said to be static if it simply describes the generic relationship of a collection of attributes and possible values. It is said to be dynamic when an expert system consultation is being run and particular values have been associated with a specific example of the object.

Object-Attribute-Value Triplets. One method of representing factual knowledge. It is the more general and common set of terms used to describe the relationships referred to as Context-Parameter-Value Triplets in EMYCIN. An object is an actual or conceptual entity in the domain of the consultant. Attributes are properties associated with objects such as location, depth, productivity. Each attribute can take different values.

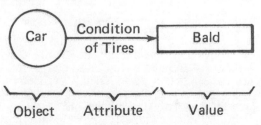

Figure O–1. Object-attribute-valve triplets.

object code. Output from a compiler or assembler that is itself executable machine code or can be processed to produce executable machine code.

object language. The output of an automatic coding routine. Object language and machine language are usually the same; however, a series of steps in an automatic coding system may involve the object language of 1 step acting as a source language for the next step and so on.

object-oriented language. In robotics a synonym for task-oriented language. In general use a programming language in which procedures for doing things are accessed through descriptions of the things to be worked on.

object-oriented methods. Programming methods based on the use of items called objects that communicate with each another via messages in the form of global broadcasts.

object-oriented programming. Programming that focuses on individual program unit objects consisting of instructions and data, rather than on procedures. An object is considered to be a package of information and descriptions of procedures that can manipulate that information.

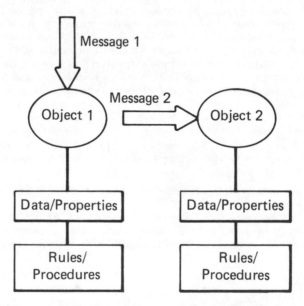

Figure O–2. Object-oriented programming—Message passing in object-oriented programs.

object program. A program in machine language; generally, one that has been converted from a program written in symbolic language.

OCEAN SURVEILLANCE. Helps naval personnel aboard a surveillance ship determine a remotely sensed vessel's destination and mission. The system uses information about the vessel's correlated tracks, history, location, and status to determine its likely destination, arrival time, and probable mission. The knowledge contained in the system includes: deployment histories of particular vessel types, ongoing U.S./Allied naval activities in the area of interest, and the surveillance ship's own activities and movement. The system uses a rule-based knowledge representation scheme employing forward-chaining and certainty factors, and it provides a simple explanation facility. OCEAN SURVEILLANCE is implemented in OPS5 and FRANZLISP. The system was developed at Science Applications International Inc.

OCSS. Assists chemists in synthesizing complex organic molecules. The system analyzes target molecules devised by the chemist by recognizing functional groups, chains, rings and redundancy, or symmetry in the molecular skeleton, applying chemical transformations to them, and evaluating the resulting structure for correctness, uniqueness, and simplicity. The system was implemented on a DEC PDP-1 computer at Harvard University.

octal. A number system based upon the radix 8, in which the decimal numbers 0 through 7 represent the eight distinct states.

OCULAR HERPES MODEL. Assists a physician in diagnosing and treating patients with ocular herpes complex. The system associates patient clinical history and laboratory findings with disease categories and uses that knowledge to diagnose the disease (e.g., patient has a corneal epithelial lesion) and recommend treatment (e.g., administer vidarabine ointment 5 times daily). The system selects therapy based on drug effectiveness and the patient's drug resistance and allergic reaction. The system is a forward chaining, rule-based system implemented in EXPERT. It was developed at Rutgers University.

off-line programming. Programming in which the commands are stored for execution at a later time. Computer program development on a system separate from the computer on board a robot.

offset. The count value output from an analog to digital converter resulting from a zero input analog voltage. Used to correct subsequent nonzero measurements.

Ronald B. Ohlander. Recently retired from the U.S. Navy and DARPA, is currently the division director for Intelligent Systems at the Information Sciences Institute of U.S.C. He received his Ph.D. in Computer Science and Artificial Intelligence from CMU in 1975. After several years at NAVELEX, he transferred to DARPA, where he managed the Intelligent Systems Program and became director for Computer Science Research. He managed the DARPA Artificial Intelligence program and played a major role in structuring the Strategic Computing Program.

ONCOCIN. Assists physicians in treating and managing cancer patients undergoing chemotherapy experiments called protocols. The system selects therapy by relating information about the patient's diagnosis, previous treatments, and laboratory tests to knowledge about protocols—past experiments aimed at measuring the therapeutic benefits and toxic side effects of alternative cancer treatments. The system contains knowledge about 34 Hodgkin's disease and lymphoma protocols. ONCOCIN is a rule-based system employing both forward and backward chaining. It is implemented in INTERLISP. The system was developed at Stanford University.

one-byte instruction. An instruction that consists of 8 contiguous bits occupying 1 successive location.

one-input node. The node in the Rete match algorithm network that is associated with a test of a single attribute of a condition element. It passes a token if and only if the attribute test is satisfied.

ONIX. Automatic program synthesizer, developed by Schlumberger, specialized in helping oil experts working with rock models and bore-hole log data. ONIX generates rock-constituent-computing FORTRAN programs from equations representing hypothesized geology.

on-line. Pertaining to devices under direct control of the central processing unit. Operation where input data are fed directly from the measuring devices into the central processing unit, or where data from the central processing unit are transmitted directly to where they are used. Such operation is in real time.

on-off control. The output from the system or device is either fully on or completely off.

open loop. A control system in which data flow unidirectionally, that is, only from the control to the mechanism but not from the mechanism back to the control. A system in which there is no automatic error correcting, owing to the absence of a feedback signal.

open-loop control. Control achieved by driving control actuators with a sequence of preprogrammed signals without measuring actual system response and closing the feedback loop.

open-loop robot. A robot that incorporates no feedback, i.e., no means of comparing actual output with commanded input of position or rate.

operand. Data that are, or will be, operated upon by an arithmetic/logic instruction; usually identified by the address portion of an instruction, explicitly or implicitly. Value or parameter altered by a programmed process.

operating system. The computer software system that does the "housekeeping" and communication chores for the more specialized systems. Instructions that tell the computer how to use the programs, how to handle input and output, and how to use peripheral devices. Most conventional computers have standard operating systems that software is designed to utilize. Thus, for example, the IBM personal computer uses a version of MS-DOS. Artificial intelligence languages are often used to write operating systems so that the expert system and the operating system are written in the same language. LISP workstations, like the Xerox 1100 series and the Symbolics machines, are computers that use a LISP operating system to improve their efficiency and flexibility when they are running expert systems written in LISP.

operation. An operation in an elementary action associated with 1 or more types. It is either implicitly declared by the declaration of the type, or it is a subprogram that has a parameter or result of the type. Moving or manipulating data in the CPU or between the CPU and peripherals.

operation command. A command issued by the host to initiate some specific unit operation outside the physical interface and associated with a logical interface function.

operating system. A program that manages a computer's hardware and software components. It determines when to run programs and controls peripheral equipment, such as printers.

operations support systems. Software programs and associated hardware designed to help manage specific business functions. They keep records and update usage and equipment needs. Many are interlinked.

operator. Procedures or generalized actions that can be used for changing situations. An operator is an operation with 1 or 2 operands. A unary operator is written before an operand; a binary operator is written between 2 operands. That notation is a special kind of function call. An operator can be declared as a function. Many operators are implicitly declared by the declaration of a type.

OPS. A programming language used in development of expert systems. Developed by Dr. Charles Forgy of Carnegie-Mellon University, it is most famous for being used in developing Digital Equipment's R1 (XCON). The language has a number of variations, such as OPS4, OPS5, and OPS83. The latest version is OPS83, which is written in C.

OPS5. A knowledge engineering language for rule-based representation. Its principal characteristics include a design that supports generality in both data representation and control structures, a powerful pattern-matching capability, and an efficient forward-chaining interpreter for matching rules against the data. The support environment contains editing and debugging packages, including a mechanism to help determine why a rule did not fire when the programmer thought it should. OPS5 has been implemented in BLISS, MACLISP, and FRANZLISP. It is one of the most widely used knowledge engineering languages. OPS5 was developed at Carnegie-Mellon University as part of the OPS family of languages for AI and cognitive psychology applications.

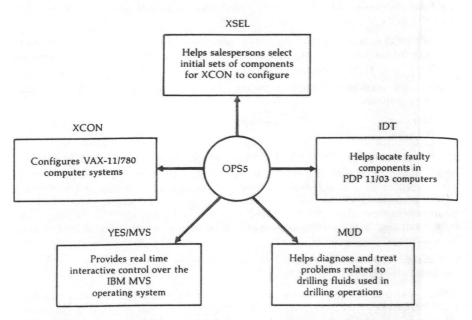

Figure O–3. OPS5—Applications of OPS5. *Reprinted with the permission of Addison-Wesley Publishing Company from "A Guide to Expert Systems" by Donald A. Waterman.*

OPS83. A knowledge engineering language for rule-based and procedure-oriented representation. Its principal characteristic is the integration of the forward chaining, rule-based programming paradigm and the procedural programming paradigm. OPS 83 is essentially a PASCAL-like language augmented with the OPS5 constructs of working memory elements and rules. OPS83 also provides facilities for user-defined data types and permits the user to define conflict resolution procedures, control regimes, and tracing routines. OPS83 operates on DEC VAX 11/750 and 11/780 computer systems. It was developed at Carnegie-Mellon University.

optic sensor. A device or system that converts light into an electrical signal.

optical cavity. The part of a laser where light is amplified by bouncing it between mirrors.

optical character recognition. Machine recognition of printed characters through use of light-sensitive devices.

optical filter. A device that selectively blocks or passes certain wavelengths of light.

optical flow. The distribution of velocities of apparent movement in an image caused by smoothly changing brightness patterns.

ordered dither. Setting the intensity level for pixel display in dithered representation of tonal values.

ordering. A conflict-resolution strategy in which the dominance of 1 instantiation over another is determined by a static ordering that is imposed on the rules.

orthicon. A camera tube in which a low-velocity electron beam scans a photoactive mosaic that has an electrical storage capability.

Ostwald color system. A color-definition system based on color charts. The theoretical variables are hue, full color content, white content, and black content. Hues are indicated by an arbitrary set of hue numbers.

output. Information transferred from the internal storage of a computer to output devices or external storage.

output primitive. Grapics entity or basic display component: point, line segment, character, marker or text string.

overlay. Plane of a graphics display that can be superimposed on another display.

overloading. An identifier can have several alternative meanings at a given point in the program text; that property is called overloading. For example, an overloaded enumeration literal can be an identifier that appears in the definitions of 2 or more enumeration types. The effective meaning of an overloaded identifier is determined by the context. Subprograms, aggregates, allocators, and string literals can also be overloaded.

overshoot. The degree to which a system response, such as change in reference input, goes beyond the desired value.

OWL. A knowledge engineering language for frame-based representation. Its principal characteristics include a semantic net framework that supports a conceptual taxonomy with concept specialization and a flexible inheritance mechanism. All knowledge is maintained in a single, large, unified knowledge base augmented by a small set of embedded LISP and machine language programs and their associated data structures. OWL is implemented in LISP. It was developed at M.I.T.

P

package. A package specifies a group of logically related entities, such as types, objects of those types, and subprograms and parameters of those types. It is written as a package declaration and a package body. The package declaration has a visible part, containing the declarations of all entities that can be explicitly used outside the package. It may also have a a private part containing structural details that complete the specification of the visible entities but are irrelevant to the user of the package. The package body contains implementations of subprograms that have been specified in the package declaration. A package is 1 of the kinds of program unit.

page. A page consists of all the locations that can be addressed by 8 bits (a total of 256 locations) starting at 0 and going through 255. The address within a page is determined by the lower 8 bits of the address, and the page number (0 through 255) is determined by the higher 8 bits of a 16-bit address.

paging. Organizing a display into sets of images that can be recalled individually from the host computer memory.

painting. Raster design technique based on illuminating specified red, green, and blue phosphors.

pairing. A faulty interlace scan during which alternate raster lines overlap each other, reducing the effective vertical resolution of the display.

Palladian Software, Inc. An applications software developer producing expert systems for both decision making and problem solving. In a field where an employee's exposure to artificial intelligence is a few years, Palladian boasts more than 100 years of combined experience from its small staff of approximately 22 persons. Their areas of expertise range from finance to manufacturing and logistics. Palladian Software has developed the Capital Investment Expert System using a wide range of sophisticated financial techniques. That helps managers make the correct financial decisions. The system helps in new product proposal evaluations, capacity expansion plans, cost reduction proposals, decisions on making, leasing, or buying, and assessing major acquisitions and investments. The expert system is completely user friendly and provides not only alternatives and analysis but also its methods at arriving at each decision. Palladian Software has also developed the Manufacturing and Logistics Expert System, which deals with complex time sensitive operational problems. It can evaluate and recommend improvements in processes and procedures for production, distribution, and warehousing, assist in designing new processes and facilities, identify operational bottlenecks, evaluate work in process inventory, estimate lead time and smooth production flow, and plan future capacity needs. The system provides full explanations of its conclusions and requires no knowledge of computers to use it.

palette. Range of selectable colors on a color terminal.

Palladian Financial Advisor. Palladian Software, Inc., application program for expert systems for business executives, managers, and analysts, who must develop and evaluate capital intensive projects and proposals such as new products, expand production facilities, examine business lines, or install cost saving measures. Requires Symbolics 3600, Texas Instruments Explorer, Sperry Explorer. Minimum memory requirement is 4 megabytes.

PALLADIO. Assists circuit designers in the design and testing of new VLSI circuits. PALLADIO is a circuit design environment that includes interactive graphics editors that manipulate high-level electronic components, a rule editor that helps modify the behavioral specifications of circuit components, a simulator that uses the structural and behavioral specification of a circuit to stimulate it, and mechanisms for refining and creating design specifications at different levels of abstraction. PALLADIO has been used to design a variety of nMOS circuits. The system is implemented in LOOPS, which provides object-oriented, rule-based, and logic-oriented representation mechanisms. PALLADIO was developed at Stanford University.

pan. Translation across x and y grid.

PAN. Uses for a novel type of adaptive network system are being explored. That information-processing mechanism is called a "parallel associative network," or "PAN." Several applications have been studied, including the ANEX expert system developed at PASC, logic-gate implementations, and vision-processing networks. IBM is engaged in a joint effort to apply parallel associative networks in a robotic vision system. **(See figure p. 191.)**

paradigm. Consultation paradigms describe generic types of problem-solving scenarios. Particular system building tools are typically good for 1 or a few consultation paradigms and not for others. Most commercial tools are designed to facilitate rapid development of expert systems that can deal with the diagnostic/prescriptive paradigm.

parallax. Apparent image translation from initial location to point indicated by a light pen.

parallel circuit. A circuit in which 2 or more of the connected components or symbolic elements are connected to the same pair of terminals so that current flow divides between the parts, as contrasted with a series connection, where the parts are connected end to end so that the same current flows through all.

parallel communications. A digital communication method that transmits the bits of a message several at a time (usually 8 to 17 bits at a time); usually used only over distances of a few feet with electrical cables as the transmission medium.

parallel operation. Operates on all bits of a word simultaneously.

parallel processing. A new architecture for computers that would allow a computer to run several programs simultaneously. It would mean that a computer would have several central processors simultaneously processing information as opposed to the sequential processing in a conventional (von Numann) type of computer architecture. Operation of a computer in which 2 or more programs are executed concurrently, as compared with serial processing. Parallel processing is going to figure heavily in

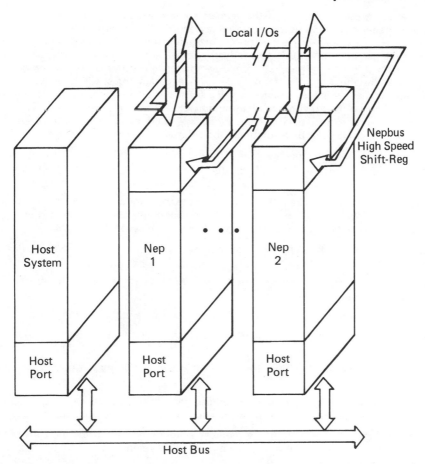

Figure P-1. PAN—Parallel Associative Networks (PAN) structure developed by IBM. *Reprinted with the permission of IBM Palo Alto Scientific Center.*

artificial intelligence applications where cross-referencing, indexing, and list process-ing are required, because of time and memory economies. Most processing today is done 1 routine at a time, serially and sequentially.

parallel projection.   An isometric graphics display of a 3-dimensional object without size reduction for distance or depth.

parallel transmission.   Parallel transmission of data occurs when all bits of the infor-mation are transmitted simultaneously, usually over multiple wires.

parallelism.   Performing more than 1 operation in a single unit of time. Parallel computer hardware executes more than 1 machine instruction during a single machine cycle. Parallel production systems fire more than 1 instantiation on each recognize-act cycle. Parallelism always can be simulated, although slowly, on serial machines.

parameter. A parameter is 1 of the named entities associated with a subprogram, entry, or generic unit and used to communicate with the corresponding subprogram body, accept statement, or generic body. A formal parameter is an identifier used to denote the named entity within the body. An actual parameter is the particular entity associated with the corresponding formal parameter by a subprogram call, entry call, or generic instantiation. The mode of a formal parameter specifies whether the associated actual parameter supplies a value for the formal parameter, or the formal supplies a value for the actual parameter, or both. The association of actual parameters with formal parameters can be specified by named associations, by positional associations, or by a combination of those.

parent type. A parent type is a type whose operations and values are replicas of those of an existing type. The existing type is called the derived type off the parent type.

parity. A method of checking the accuracy of binary numbers. If even parity is used, the sum of all the 1s in a number and its corresponding parity bit is always even. If odd parity is used, the sum of all the 1s and the parity bit is always odd.

parity bit. A binary digit appended to an array of bits of make the sum of all the bits always odd or always even.

parity check. A check that tests whether the number of 1s (or 0s) in an array of binary digits is odd or even.

PARRY. An expert system that models behavior of a paranoid human being.

parsing. Identifying the components of language statements as various parts of speech.

part classification. The identification of differing parts, by a robot, usually by means of vision.

partial animation. A crude form of animation that employs as few as 2 or 3 frames per second as opposed to the 24 frames per second required for full animation.

partial bindings. The set of working memory elements and bindings that constitutes a consistent binding for a prefix sequence of condition elements of a rule.

partial match. A set of associations between condition elements and working memory elements that partially satisfy the left-hand side of the rule. Not all condition elements need be matched; sometimes a threshold specifies the minimum number that must be matched.

partitioning. The process of assigning specified portions of a system responsibility for performing specified functions.

part orientation. The angular displacement of a product being manufactured relative to a coordinate system referenced to a production machine, e.g., a drilling or milling axis. Reorientation is often required as the product proceeds from 1 processing step to another.

part programming language. A group of symbols, codes, format, and syntax definitions that describe machining operations understandable to computers or controls.

PASCAL. Popular general-purpose, high-level programming language, descendant from ALGOL.

passive accommodation. Compliant behavior of a robot's end point in response to forces exerted on it. No sensors, controls, or actuators are involved. The remote center compliance provides that in a coordinate system acting at the tip of a gripped part.

passive mode. In computer graphics a mode of operation of a display device that does not allow an on-line user to alter or interact with a display image.

passive sensor. A sensor that simply accepts incoming signals is passive. An ultrasonic system is active because it actively transmits a signal that is reflected off the participant's body and then sensed.

password. A unique string of characters that a program, computer operator, or user must supply to meet security requirements before gaining access to a system.

patch. A section of coding inserted in a program in order to rectify an error in the original coding or to change the sequence of operation.

path. A particular track through a state graph.

PATHFINDER. Helps pathologists interpret findings occurring from the microscopic examination of lymph node tissue. The system poses questions to the pathologist in a manner designed to reduce the uncertainty in the differential diagnosis, and it can provide a justification for the most recent question posed. The system bases its decisions on a set of disease profiles containing findings that are normally associated with each disease. That expertise in the diagnosis of lymph node pathology comes from expert hematopathologists. PATHFINDERS's knowledge is encoded using frames. The system was developed at Stanford University.

PATREC. Manages a data base of patient records, providing diagnostic physicians and the MDX expert system with sophisticated access to the records. It handles patient data in the context of diagnosing for the syndrome called cholestasis. PATREC accepts data from the user, stores them appropriately, provides a query language for question answering, prepares summary reports, and makes suggestions helpful in diagnosis. Knowledge in PATREC includes a conceptual model of medical data (e.g., the significance of a particular lab test and its expected values) and a patient model (e.g., individual patient histories and clinical episodes). Knowledge is represented as frames with attached rules to perform bookkeeping functions, data input, and automatic temporal inferencing. PATREC is implemented in LISP. It was developed at Ohio State University.

pattern. The description of something for which a system should search, either in a knowledge base or a rule base.

pattern directed. Driven by configurations of data. Production systems are a special case of pattern-directed systems.

pattern directed invocation. The activation of procedures by matching their antecedent parts to patterns present in the global data base.

pattern matching. A process performed by an expert system during a search through its knowledge base. The objective of the search is to match real world data—such as questions, problem statements, etc., against knowledge stored in the knowledge base.

pattern recognition. Identification of visual images by classification into categories. Pattern recognition is usually considered a part of artificial intelligence. A technique that classifies images into predetermined categories, usually using statistical methods and template comparisons.

payload. The maximum weight or mass of a material that can be handled satisfactorily by a machine or process in normal and continuous operation.

PC Scheme. Texas Instruments Inc. developed programming language. PC Scheme is an implementation of the Lisp programming language that allows artificial intelligence applications to be developed on personal computers. A key feature is PC Scheme's incremental, optimizing compiler; the compiler produces code that can execute 3 to

10 times faster than interpretive Lisp programs (depending on the application). Since code is compiled in stages, the compiler also preserves the interactive nature of Lisp. Runs on TI- and IBM-compatible computers. Minimum memory requirement is 320K. Requires MS-DOS 2.1 or greater or PC-DOS 2.0 or greater.

PDS.   Diagnoses malfunctions in machine processes by interpreting information from sensors attached to the process. The system uses diagnosis methods that relate sensor readings to component malfunctions. PDS uses a forward chaining, rule-based representation scheme implemented in SRL, a frame-based knowledge engineering language. The result is an inference net representation paradigm similar to that found in PROSPECTOR. The system was developed at Carnegie-Mellon University in cooperation with Westinghouse Electric Corporation. PDS is actually closer to an architecture or tool for building expert sensor-based diagnosis systems than an expert system.

PEC.   Helps primary health workers diagnose and treat common and potentially blinding eye disorders. Its initial set of yes/no questions (such as, "Is the eye red?") leads to further sets of questions about the patient. When enough information has been gathered, the system outputs a summary of the case, followed by its diagnostic conclusions and management recommendations. PEC's knowledge comes from the World Health Organization guide to primary eye care, and it is represented as rules using a forward chaining inference scheme. The system was initially implemented in EXPERT and was then translated automatically into BASIC for use on microcomputers. PEC was developed at Rutgers University.

PECOS.   An expert system that transforms program descriptions to aid automatic program generation.

pen plotter.   A device that draws lines on paper or other media to create drawings from a computer.

perception.   A robot's ability to sense by sight, touch, or some other means its environment and to understand it in terms of a task, for example, the ability to recognize an obstruction or find a designated object in an arbitrary location.

peripheral.   A device or subsystem external to the central processing unit that provides additional system capabilities. Devices, such as disk drives, tape machines, printers and plotters, that are attached to a computer.

permutation.   An ordered arrangement of a given number of different elements selected from a set.

persistence.   The length of time an image produced on a display device by activated phosphors remains clear, bright, and sharp.

personal AI computer.   New, small, interactive, stand-alone computers for use by researchers in developing artificial intelligence programs. Usually specifically designed to run an artificial intelligence language, such as LISP.

PERSONAL CONSULTANT.   A knowledge engineering language for rule-based representation, but it also supports frame-based representation methods. Its principal characteristics include backward- and forward-chaining control schemes, certainty handling mechanisms, class hierarchies with inheritance, and the ability to access user-defined LISP functions. The user interface includes a window-oriented device that utilizes a color display and an explanation facility. The support environment contains a knowledge base editor, a trace facility, and a regression testing facility. PERSONAL CONSULTANT is written in IQLISP (a dialect of LISP) and operates on the TI Professional computer, the TI Explorer computer, and other MS-DOS compatible microcomputers. Texas Instruments Inc.

perspective projection. Graphics displays simulating depth and distance by representing parallel lines merging at a vanishing point.

phonemes. Set of abstract units that can be used for writing a language in a systematic and unambiguous way. English has roughly 40 phonemes, 16 vowel phonemes and 24 consonant phonemes.

phosphor. A substance on the interior of a display screen capable of luminescence when it is excited by an energy source (e.g., electromagnetic waves, accelerated electrons, an electrical field), thus creating an image.

phosphor persistence. Measure of the time for a phosphor's brightness to drop to one-tenth of its initial value; the tendency of a phosphor to continue to emit light when it is no longer excited by an electron beam.

phosphorescent. A material that, when exposed to light absorbs it and then continues to emit it after the source is removed, is said to be phosphorescent.

photocell. An electrical device for detecting light.

photoelectric effect. The emission of electrons by a material when it is exposed to light. Albert Einstein, who never got a Nobel Prize for his famous theories of relativity, received one for explaining the phenomenon.

photo-isolator. A solid state device that allows complete electrical isolation between the field wiring and the controller.

photometric stereo. An approach in which the light source illuminating the scene is moved to different known locations, and the orientation of the surfaces deduced from the resulting intensity variations.

photon. The fundamental unit of light and other forms of electromagnetic energy. Photons are to optical fibers what electrons are to copper wires; like electrons, they have a wave motion.

photopic vision. The eye-brain response to luminance levels sufficient to permit the full discrimination of colors. Also called daylight vision, as contrasted with twilight or scoptopic vision.

physical block. The physical representation of data on the media. It is used to prevent confusion between the industry usage of terms such as sector or record on disk, and block or record on tape. If physical commands are issued, it is the responsibility of the host to ensure that the correct physical block address is used.

pick. Event triggered by an electronic device that reports identifying data for the detected display item and the segment containing it.

pick-and-place robot. A simple robot, often with only 2 or 3 degrees of freedom, that transfers items from place to place by means of point-to-point moves. Little or no trajectory control is available. Often referred to as a bang-bang robot.

PICON. A system-building aid for developing process control expert systems [developed by Lisp Machines Inc.]. It supports object-oriented, frame-based, and rule-based representation methods and combines both forward and backward chaining control schemes. Knowledge acquisition from a domain expert is accomplished through a graphics-oriented interface, which helps transfer structural information, process descriptions, and heuristics into the knowledge base. PICON also provides an explanation facility and the ability to dynamically update the expertise contained in the system. PICON is implemented in ZETALISP and the C programming language and operates on LMI's Lambda/Plus workstations.

PIE. A system-building aid that extends the capabilities of SMALLTALK-76 by facilitating the representation and manipulation of designs. SMALLTALK-76 is an object-oriented programming language. PIE's principal characteristic is the use of multiple perspectives. The mechanism provides a way to specify independent specialized behaviors for an object. The support environment consists of all of the features and support facilities of SMALLTALK. The Xerox Palo Alto Research Center developed PIE.

pin-cushion distortion. A distortion that makes a displayed image appear to bulge inward on all 4 sides.

PIP. Assists physicians by taking the history of the present illness of a patient with edema. The system interweaves the processes of information gathering and diagnosis, alternating between asking questions to gain new information and integrating that new information into a developing picture of the patient. Knowledge contained in PIP includes prototypical findings, such as signs, symptoms, laboratory data, the time course of the given illness, and rules for judging how closely a given patient matches a hypothesized disease or state. PIP's questions are controlled by a set of diagnostic hypotheses suggested by the patient's complaints. The ability of the hypotheses to account for the findings of the case is averaged with the "measure of fit" to arrive at a final certainty measure for ranking hypotheses. Knowledge in PIP is represented using frames. PIP is implemented in CONNIVER and was developed at M.I.T.

pipelining. The practice of creating an assembly line of processing elements. The output of 1 processor becomes the input of the next, and so on. All processors are continually in operation.

pitch. The angular rotation of a moving body about an axis perpendicular to its direction of motion and in the same plane as its top side. A frequency of vibration of the vocal cords. The psychological correlate to the fundamental frequency of a voice sound.

pixel. The smallest unit of resolution on a raster-scan display; on a computer system, a pixel is the smallest portion of the screen that can have its light characteristics converted to computer-readable expressions of electric current.

plan. A sequence of actions to transform an initial situation into a situation satisfying the goal conditions.

PLANNER. Extinct experimental programming language similar in many respects to modern PROLOG.

planning and decision support. An area of AI research that is applying AI techniques to the planning and decision-making process to help managers who have decision-making responsibilities.

PlanPower. An expert software system for personal financial planning that uses artificial intelligence technologies. PlanPower serves as an expert assistant to the planner, offering second opinions, performing sophisticated analysis, and producing a complete financial plan in a few hours. PlanPower is offered as a fully configured personal workstation, with the XEROX 1186 AI workstation and the Hewlett-Packard laser jet printer. PlanPower is marketed through 2 distribution channels. It is sold to independent financial planners through such distributors as First Financial Planner Services, Inc., a subsidiary of the Travelers Insurance Company. APEX sells PlanPower to large institutions, such as brokerage houses, banks, accounting firms, and insurance companies through its own direct sales force. PlanPower is an integrated personal workstation (including an English-language interface, word processing, spreadsheet analysis, exhibit production and high-resolution graphics), which gives financial planners a unique means of collecting and analyzing data and producing comprehensive, personalized financial plans. Under development for 3 years, PlanPower includes a built-in feature called the Expert Planner, which automates the planning process. It contains an AI-developed knowledge base that incorporates a depth of financial expertise not possible with traditional computer technology. As an expert assistant and consultant to the professional financial planner, PlanPower significantly reduces the amount of time required for plan analysis and preparation and substantially increases the planner's knowledge and professional capability. For instance, with PlanPower, a planner can analyze more than 125 financial products, from securities, fixed income assets and insurance to real estate, tax incentive partnerships, closely held business interests, and tangible investments. Besides providing sophisticated analysis, PlanPower addresses individual needs and strategies for capital management, income tax planning, cash management, risk management, and estate conservation. The result is a comprehensive, individualized plan that integrates specific recommendations for a client's financial situation over a 5-year period.

PLANT/cd. Predicts the damage to corn caused by the black cutworm. The system uses knowledge about the particular field being studied, such as moth trap counts, field weediness, larval age spectrum, soil condition, and corn variety to predict the degree of damage the cutworm will cause. The system uses a combination of rules and a set of black cutworm simulation programs to produce the predictions. Knowledge is represented as rules accessed by a backward-chaining control mechanism. The system is implemented in ADVISE. It was developed at the University of Illinois.

PLANT/ds. Provides consultation on the diagnosis of soybean diseases using knowledge about disease symptoms and plant environment. The system uses such information as the month of occurrence, the temperature, plant height, and condition of leaves, stems, and seeds to decide which of 15 or so diseases is most likely. Knowledge is in the form of 2 types of rules: (1) rules representing the system's diagnostic expertise, and (2) rules obtained from an automated inductive inference program called AQ11. PLANT/ds is implemented in ADVISE. It was developed at the University of Illinois.

plasma panel. A type of cathode ray tube utilizing an array of neon bulbs, each individually addressable. The image is created by turning on points in a matrix comprising the display surface. The image is steady, long-lasting, bright, flicker-free, and selective erasing is possible.

playback accuracy. Difference between a position command recorded in an automatic control system and that actually produced at a later time when the recorded position is used to execute control. Difference between actual position response of an automatic control system during a programming or teaching run and that corresponding response in a subsequent run.

plotter. A graphic hard copy output device that can use any of a number of technologies to "plot" an image. Pen plotters, electrostatic plotters, photo-plotters, ink-jet plotters, and laser plotters are some examples.

PLUME. A system-building aid for developing natural language interfaces to expert systems. It is based on the DYPAR-II natural language interpreter developed at Carnegie-Mellon University. Adapting PLUME to a new application domain involves extending the lexicon and writing case frames and grammatical rules for the words and phrases commonly used within the domain application. PLUME can handle ellipsis, ambiguous input, and pronoun resolution. The support environment includes grammar rule and case frame editing tools and trace and debugging facilities. PLUME is implemented in COMMON LISP and operates on the Carnegie Group workstations, the DEC VAX/VMS systems, and the Symbolics 3600 series workstations. The Carnegie Group Inc. developed it as a commercial system.

point operation. Transformation of the gray scale value of the picture elements according to a given function. Examples are thresholding and contrast enhancement.

point-to-point control. A control scheme whereby the inputs or commands specify only a limited number of points along a desired path of motion. The control system determines the intervening path segments.

polar coordinate system. A mathematical coordinate system used to define positions on a plane using 1 linear and 1 circular axis. In this system a position is defined by the number of degrees of rotation from the zero position and the distance from the center of rotation.

polarity. The potential of a portion of the display signal representing a dark area relative to the potential representing a light area. Polarity is stated as "black negative" or "black positive."

POLITICS. Experimental narrative-understanding natural language system developed by Roger Schank and his students. Successor to MARGIE, predecessor to BORIS.

polling. Periodic interrogation of each of the devices that share a communications line to determine whether it requires servicing. The multiplexer or control station sends a poll that has the effect of asking the selected device, "Do you have anything to transmit?"

polygon fill. Coloring or cross-hatching of a closed, multi-sided, program-defined surface.

POMME. Helps farmers manage apple orchards by providing advice on how to improve the apple crop. The system contains expertise obtained from plant pathologists and entomologists on pest control and weather-damage recovery. That includes knowledge about fungicides, insecticides, and freeze, frost, and drought damage. POMME uses a combination of rule-based and frame-based representation methods. It is implemented in PROLOG and runs on a VAX 11/780 computer. The system was developed at Virginia Polytechnic Institute and State University.

pop. Retrieving data from a stack.

POPLOG. An integrated logic programming language consisting of characteristics of PROLOG, LISP, and POP-11. Developed by Systems Designers Software (UK) to run on DEC VAX machines.

port. A device or network through which data may be transferred or where device or network variables may be observed or measured.

portable programs. Software that is both host-computer and display-device independent.

portability. The ease with which a computer program developed in 1 programming environment can be transferred to another.

position error. A servomechanism that operates a manipulator joint, the difference between the actual position of that joint and the commanded position.

positional association. A positional association specifies the association of an item with a position in a list, by using the same position in the text to specify the item.

positioning accuracy and repeatability. Accuracy is a measure of the robot's ability to move to a programmed position. Repeatability is its ability to do that time after time. With the pick-and-place robot, accuracy and repeatability are interchangeable. With a programmable robot repeatability can be improved by fine-tuning the controls.

postcondition. A proposition that is true following the execution of a piece of code. If a precondition is satisfied preceding the execution of the code and if the code executes correctly, the postcondition will be true following execution.

position sensor. A device, such as a potentiometer, that measures displacement and converts the information into a signal that can be used by a control system.

positive edge. The transition from logic 0 to 1 in a clock pulse.

positive-edge triggered. Transfer of information occurs on the positive edge of the clock pulse.

positive logic. A form of logic in which the more positive voltage level represents logic 1 and the more negative level represents logic 0.

postprocessor. A computer program that transforms cutter path coordinate data into a form that a specific control system can interpret correctly.

Post Production System. A mathematical model of computation devised by Emil Post and considered to be the original of all other production systems.

power tool. Any powerful programming device that dramatically increases programmer productivity.

pragma. A pragma conveys information to the compiler.

precondition. A proposition that must be satisfied preceding the execution of a piece of code. If the precondition is satisfied and the code executes correctly, a postcondition will be true following execution of the code.

predicate. A predicate is a function that returns a truth value. Predicates are used to select among conditional alternatives.

predicate calculus. An extension of propositional calculus. Each elementary unit in predicate calculus is called an object. Statements about objects are called predicates.

predicate logic. A modification of propositional logic to allow the use of variables and functions of variables. A form of logic that can be utilized in knowledge-based programs. The basis of the AI language Prolog.

prefix notation. A list representation (used in LISP programming) in which the connective, function, symbol, and predicate are given before the arguments.

premise. A first proposition on which subsequent reasoning rests.

preprocessor. A computer program that takes a specific set of instructions and converts them into the form required to be run by the processor program.

presence sensing device. A device designed, constructed, and installed to create a sensing field or area around a robot that will detect an intrusion into such field or area by a person, robot, etc.

presentation graphics. High-quality graphics intended to visually reinforce points made in the presentation of proposals, plans, and budgets to top management.

pretty-printing. The style of printing implemented by a specific LISP function that arranges LISP forms on indented lines to make them easier to read.

prefix. A prefix is used as the first part of certain kinds of a name. A prefix is either a function call or a name.

primal sketch. A primitive description of the intensity changes in an image. It can be represented by a set of short line segments separating regions of different brightnesses.

primitive. A program subroutine that automatically creates familiar and frequently used shapes, such as circles.

primitive attribute. A general characteristic of a display primitive, such as color, intensity, linestyle, or linewidth.

primitive element. A graphic element such as a point or line segment that can be readily called up or extrapolated or combined with other primitive elements to form more complex objects or images in 2 or 3 dimensions.

Primitive Interface Utility. A primitive interface utility is an external program written in any language that runs under Unix, such as Fortran, Pascal, or C, which provides for communications with an external information source. Those sources can be large data bases or a computational algorithm that depends on parameters passed to it. Real time inputs or varying inputs, such as instruments, can also provide information for use in providing a diagnosis, a control strategy, or advice.

priority. A preferential rating. Pertains to operations that are given preference over other system operations.

PRISM. Many areas within IBM are considering expert systems technology as a way to solve application problems. There is a need, therefore, for a way to easily build expert systems that can be used in a variety of problem areas, and that can run efficiently on IBM hardware. Motivation for the Expert Systems project has come from the observed difficulty with which expert systems are built (each is often 1 of a kind). It also stems from the belief that the control flow of a dialog must be declared as a part of the problem expertise (instead of being fixed in the expert system program) if the expert system is to be effective. A Prototype Interface System, PRISM, may be used to construct a variety of expert system applications. It provides general capabilities to create and manage knowledge structures, process those knowledge structures, and conduct dialog sessions. The particular knowledge structures supported by PRISM include rules, (a popular and well-understood representation) for representing domain knowledge and a control structure for representing problem decomposition and dialog flow. PRISM's contributions to the state of the art in expert system technology lie principally in its support of mixed representations and the ability to explicitly define the inference logic (control flow) of the system. For descriptive knowledge, parameters define basic data, and inferential knowledge is supported through "IF . . . antecedent . . . THEN . . . consequent action . . ." production rules. Those rules associate antecedent conditions with consequent actions and are used by the system to assert the consequent whenever the antecedent is true. The PRISM system includes a set of basic inferencing processing functions. Examples include backward chaining and forward chaining. The control language and its control structures, called focus control blocks, allow a user to partition a knowledge base and through the PRISM control language orchestrate the processing of PRISM. Control in expert systems built with PRISM is dictated by the specific focus control blocks used with the control language. Those blocks are essentially the program decomposition to be followed by the expert system. They can be highly specific to the problem domain (e.g., a Personal Computer configurator) or very general with respect to problem domains (e.g., a MYCIN-like system). A knowledge engineer using PRISM would employ general functional subsystems, such as rule chaining, and would provide problem specific control only when required by the particular domain; that is the principal way in which PRISM will achieve its objective of rapid system development. PRISM is being used by system designers and implementers who would otherwise be required to build their expert system in a base programming language, such as PROLOG, LISP, PASCAL, etc.

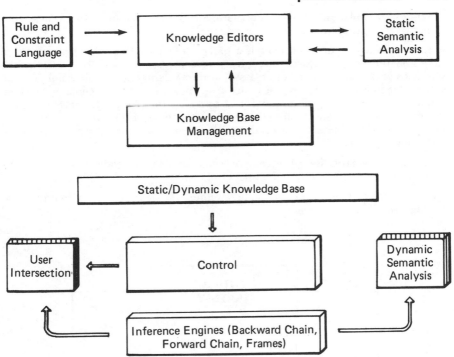

Figure P–2. PRISM—PRISM System Structure. *Reprinted with the permission of IBM Palo Alto Scientific Center.*

private type.   A private type is a type whose structure and set of values are clearly defined, but not directly available to the user of the type. A private type is known only by its discriminants and by the set of operations defined for it. A private type and its applicable operations are defined in the visible part of a package or in a generic formal part. Assignment, equality, and inequality are also defined for private types, unless the private type is limited.

probability propagation.   The adjusting of probabilities at the nodes in an inference net to account for the effect of new information about the probability at a particular node.

probability.   Various approaches to statistical inference that can be used to determine the likelihood of a particular relationship. Expert systems have generally avoided probability and used confidence factors instead. Some systems, however, use a modified version of Bayesian probability theory to calculate the likelihood of various outcomes.

problem-oriented language.   A computer language designed for a particular class of problems, e.g., FORTRAN, designed for efficiently performing algebraic computations, and COBOL, with features for business record keeping.

problem reduction.   A problem-solving approach in which operators are used to change a single problem into several subproblems.

problem reformulation. Converting a problem stated in some arbitrary way to a form that lends itself to a fast, efficient solution.

problem solving. Problem solving is a process in which one starts from an initial state and proceeds to search through a problem space in order to identify the sequence of operations or actions that will lead to a desired goal. Successful problem solving depends upon knowing the initial state, knowing what an acceptable outcome would be, and knowing the elements and operators that define the problem space. If the elements or operators are very large in number or if they are poorly defined, one is faced with a huge or unbounded problem space and an exhaustive search can become impossible.

Problem-Solving Expertise. The component of an ICAI program that contains the information being presented to the student.

problem-solving method. A procedure, either an algorithm or a heuristic, for finding a solution to a problem.

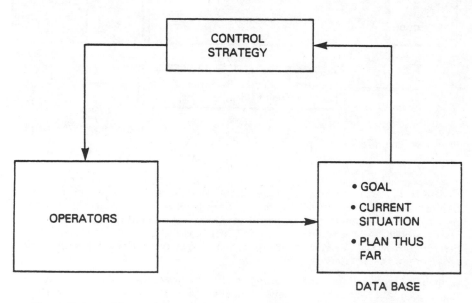

Figure P–3. Problem-solving method—Automatic problem solving relationship.

problem-solving methods, weak and strong. Heuristic for control. Weak methods are domain independent, while strong methods exploit domain knowledge to achieve greater performance.

problem space. A graph in which the nodes represent all possible states of partial or complete solution of a problem and arcs represent operators that transform 1 state to another. Finding a solution to the problem under consideration is represented by the isomorphic problem of finding a path from the node representing initial state to a node representing a goal state.

problem state. The condition of the problem at a particular instant.

procedural knowledge representation. A representation of knowledge about the world by a set of procedures—small programs that know how to do specific things.

procedural versus declarative. Two complementary views of a computer program. Procedures tell a system what to do (e.g., multiply A times B and then add C). Declarations tell a system what to know (e.g., V = IR).

procedural knowledge. Knowledge that can be immediately executed using declarative knowledge as data but that may not be examined.

procedural language. A computer language (e.g., ALGOL, PASCAL, FORTRAN) in which language-level instructions mirror Von Neumann machine instructions and the state of an execution is defined by a program counter.

procedure. A set of instructions for performing a task. A program that embodies an algorithm or a heuristic. A syntactic unit of a program in a procedural language that can be parameterized so that the same segment of code can be invoked from different places in the program with different data. Any representation for procedural knowledge.

procedure-oriented methods. Programming methods using nested subroutines to organize and control program execution.

processor. As an item of electronic hardware, equipment that performs a systematic sequence of operations under the control of software programs.

production. An IF-THEN statement or rule used to represent knowledge in a human's long-term memory.

production memory. The set of all rules in a production system. The other components of a production system are data memory and the inference engine.

production node. A special node in the Rete match algorithm network that associates a rule with the set of nodes that test whether the rule's conditions are satisfied.

production rule. A procedural response triggered by a pattern. Rules are commonly structured in an if . . . then . . . format (IF the pattern is matched, THEN schedule a procedure for execution). When the condition is met, the rule causes the system to add an assertion (the patient has a fever) to its knowledge base. In practice, a rule that has been activated by a pattern match may be in competition with other activated rules. The system's inference engine decides which of the activated rules should be executed and in what order. Production rules simplify the generation of prompts (rules can easily be turned into questions) and the return of explanations to a user (rules can be modified to produce answers to questions).

production section. The section of an OPS5 program that contains the definitions of rules. The section must follow the declaration section.

production system. A computer program consisting entirely of if-then statements called productions. Production systems maintain 2 databases called working memory and production memory. Working memory contains a model of the current state of the problem, and production memory stores the productions. Productions are so structured that if a set of conditions about working memory are true simultaneously, some specified set of actions should be executed. Production system languages are nonprocedural—that is, the order of the rules in the program does not affect its operation. Because the programmer never needs to know the order of execution, the rules in a production system can be located for ease of maintenance. OPS5 is an expert system building tool that is normally referred to as a production system; it was initially developed in an effort to model supposed human mental operations.

production system language.   A computer language that employs as a prominent component an architecture that is a production system.

production-system model.   A style of problem-solving and programming characterized by a production-system architecture. Other models include procedural programming (e.g., PASCAL), applicative programming (e.g., LISP), logic programming (e.g., PROLOG), and object-oriented programming (e.g., SMALLTALK).

production-system program.   An application program that is written in a production-system language and in which a major part of the problem is accomplished by the firing of rules.

program.   A plan for the solution of a problem. A complete program includes plans for the transcription of data, coding for the computer, and plans for the absorption of the results into the system. The list of coded instructions is called a routine. To plan a computation or process from the asking of a question to the delivery of the results, including the integration of the operation into an existing system. Thus programming consists of planning and coding, including numerical analysis, systems analysis, specification of printing formats, and any other functions necessary to the integration of a computer in a system.

program counter.   A register containing the address of the next instruction to be executed. It is automatically incremented each time program instructions are executed.

program label.   A symbol that is used to represent a memory address.

Programmer's Apprentice.   M.I.T., under the direction of Professors Patrick Winston and Drs. Charles Rich and Rich Waters, is developing an expert system whose knowledge base will consist of program fragments called "clichés." The programmer would make use of these clichés through a dialog as if the expert system were a programmer's apprentice. The goal of this study is to implement a feasibility demonstration, integrating an analysis module, a synthesis module, a reasoning module, and a knowledge-based editor. Thus far, the data structures have been defined and initial analysis, and synthesis modules have been coded and tested. In addition, the synthesis module has been integrated with a LISP editor to provide an excellent human factor interface for carrying out the work of the remainder of the project. Recent improvements include improved performance and a module that comments the program from the derived programming code.

programmable.   Capable of being instructed to operate in a specified manner or of accepting set points or other commands from a remote source.

programmable controller.   A solid state control system that has a user programmable memory for storage of instructions to implement specific functions such as: input/output control logic, timing, counting, arithmetic, and data manipulation. A programmable controller consists of a central processor, input/output interface, memory, and programming device that typically uses relay-equivalent symbols. The programmable controller is purposely designed as an industrial control system that can perform functions equivalent to a relay panel or a wired solid state logic control system.

programmable manipulator.   A device that is capable of manipulating objects by executing a stored program resident in its memory.

programmable read-only memory.   A read-only memory that can be modified by special electronic procedures.

Programmer's Apprentice. An expert system that helps programmers program by keeping track of decisions, recalling program skeletons, automatically testing revised programs, supporting natural language interaction, and translating to and from various program representations.

programming environment. The total programming setup, including the interface, the languages, the editors, and other programming tools. A programming environment is about halfway between a language and a tool. A language allows the user complete flexibility. A tool constrains the user in many ways. A programming environment, like INTERLISP, provides a number of established routines that can facilitate the quick development of certain types of programs.

program unit. A program unit is any one of a generic unit, package, subprogram, or task unit.

PROJCON. Helps a software development project manager diagnose the project's problems and their causes. The system consults with the project manager and builds a model of the specific project and its problems (e.g., schedule slippage). When possible causes of the problem have been determined, PROJCON displays its diagnosis and explains its reasoning processes. Its expertise comes from project management experts. That knowledge is encoded as rules applied by a goal-directed, backward-chaining inference mechanism. PROJCON is implemented in EMYCIN. It was developed at Georgia Institute of Technology.

PROLOG. A programming language for logic-based representation. Programs in PROLOG consist of rules (inference relations) for proving relations among objects. The PROLOG interpreter attempts to find proofs of the truth of specified relations through backward chaining, using unification and backtracking as needed. Many versions and implementations of PROLOG exist, a number of which embed PROLOG within a LISP environment for additional flexibility. PROLOG is available commercially from various vendors to run on a large number of computer systems. For example, Quintus Computer Systems is marketing a version of PROLOG that operates on DEC 10 and DEC 20 computers. A symbolic or artificial intelligence programming language based on predicate calculus. PROgramming in LOGic. The language choice of Japan's Fifth Generation mandate. Developed in France in the early 1960s, it is ideal for performing query/assumption functions. There is, however, little programmer control after the PROLOG application is set in place. PROLOG is a powerful programming language that consists of logical relationships expressed in logic-based statements. Unlike many conventional programming languages, which require that programmers tell the computer how to solve problems, PROLOG allows programmers to supply a series of facts and a set of rules about how those facts are related to each other. When you supply the facts, PROLOG makes inferences from 1 fact to another. The straightforward nature of logic programming allows programmers to concentrate on the application—on formatting rules of expert judgment and developing natural language interfaces that make it easy for less experienced users to work with the system—rather than on creating techniques for manipulating data inside the computer. Logic-based programs are also easier to write, modify, and maintain than programs requiring complex procedures. PROLOG differs from LISP, another symbolic processing language, mainly in approach: PROLOG programs use assertions about objects and relationships to handle queries about them. The program answers inquiries by consulting its knowledge base of relations. PROLOG is well suited as a base for relational database and natural language systems and for applications that require simultaneous execution of different parts of the program.

proof tree. A tree data structure in which the root node represents a theorem to be proved, and the children of each node represent theorems that, when proved, suffice to prove the theorem represented by their parent. A proof tree may be an and/or tree.

prompt. A message or menu on the display surface calling for operator action.

propagation delay. A measure of the time required for a logic signal to travel through a logic device or a series of logic devices. It occurs as the result of 4 types of circuit delays—storage, rise, fall, and turn-on-delay—and is the time between when the input signal crosses the threshold-voltage point and when the responding voltage at the output crosses the same voltage point.

property. A characteristic of an object. Properties that have values are called attributes. The components of frames and schemas, which may be of arbitrary complexity, are sometimes called properties.

property list. A knowledge representation technique by which the state of the world is described by objects in the world via lists of their pertinent properties and their associated attributes and values. A construct in LISP that associates with an object is called an atom, a set of 1 or more pairs, each composed of a "property" and the "value" of that property for that object.

proportional control. A control system in which the correcting signal is directly proportional to the deviation error.

proportional-integral-derivative control. Control scheme whereby the signal that drives the actuator equals a weighted sum of the difference, time integral of the difference, and time derivative of the difference between the input and the measured actual output.

proposition. A logic statement that can be true or false.

Propositional Calculus. A system of formal logic that provides a step-by-step inference system for determining whether a given proposition is true or false.

propositional logic. An elementary logic that uses argument forms to deduce the truth or falsehood of a new proposition from known propositions.

proprioceptors. In robotics the term means sensing the posture of a mechanical manipulator, legs, or other jointed mechanism.

PROSPECTOR. Acts as a consultant to aid exploration geologists in their search for ore deposits. Given field data about a geological region, it estimates the likelihood of finding particular types of mineral deposits there. The system can assess the potential for finding a variety of deposits, including massive sulfide, carbonate lead/zinc, porphyry, copper, nickel sulfide, sandstone uranium, and porphyry molybdenum deposits. Its expertise is based on (1) geological rules that form models of ore deposits, and (2) a taxonomy of rocks and minerals. PROSPECTOR uses a combination of rule-based and semantic net formalism to encode its knowledge and bases its inferences on the use of certainty factors and the propagation of probabilities associated with the data. The system was implemented in INTERLISP and developed by SRI International. PROSPECTOR reached the stage of a production prototype. One of the first commercially successful expert system programs, developed by SRI International. It was used to find a molybdenum deposit in Washington State after other attempts had failed. Experimental expert system intended to help geologists interpret mineral data and predict the location of mineral deposits. **(See figure p. 207.)**

prosthetic robot. A robotic device that substitutes for lost manipulative or mobility functions of the human limbs.

protocol. The rules under which computers exchange information, including the organization of the units of data to be transferred.

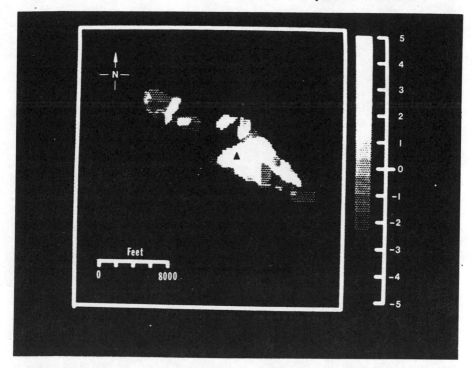

Figure P-4. Prospector—Photograph of a printout made by PROSPECTOR that indi-cates the site of porphyry molybdenum mineralization that is found in 1978 at Mt. Tolman. *Reprinted with the permission of John Wiley and Sons, from "Expert Sys-tems—Artificial Intelligence in Business" by Paul Harmon and David King.*

prototype. In expert systems development, a prototype is an initial version of an expert system, usually a system with from 25 to 200 rules, that is developed to test effectiveness of the overall knowledge representation and inference strategies being employed to solve a particular problem. **(See figure p. 208.)**

proximal. Close to the base, away from the end effector of the robot arm.

proximity sensor. A device that senses that an object is only a short distance (e.g., a few inches or feet) away, and measures how far away it is. Proximity sensors work on the principles of triangulation of reflected light, lapsed time for reflected sound, or intensity induced eddy currents, magnetic fields, back pressure from air jets, and others.

pruning. In expert systems, it refers to the process whereby 1 or more branches of a decision tree are "cut off" or ignored. In effect, when an expert system consultation is under way, heuristic rules reduce the search space by determining that certain branches, or subsets of rules, can be ignored.

pseudo-colors. Also called false colors. Colors arbitrarily assigned to an image to represent data values, rather than natural likeness.

pseudo instruction. A symbolic representation of information to a compiler or interpreter. A group of characters having the same general form as a computer

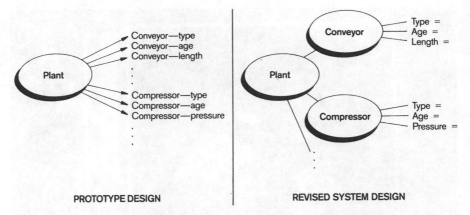

PROTOTYPE DESIGN | REVISED SYSTEM DESIGN

Figure P-5. Prototype—Prototype testing often reveals needed changes in the overall representation of objects and the hierarchical relationships among objects. *Reprinted with the permission of John Wiley and Sons, from "Expert Systems—Artificial Intelligence in Business" by Paul Harmon and David King.*

instruction but never executed by the computer as an actual instruction. A mnemonic that modifies the assembler operation but does not produce an object code.

pseudoreduction. An approach to solving the difficult problem case where multiple goals must be satisfied simultaneously. Plans are found to achieve each goal independently and then integrated using knowledge of how plan segments can be intertwined without destroying their important effects.

PSL. A procedure-oriented programming language. This portable dialect of LISP is designed to run on a wide variety of computer systems, providing all of the features of Standard LISP and additional language and interface extensions. The support environment includes an integrated compiler, a debugging facility, and a multiwindow, full-screen editor that permits the execution of expressions and display of output in windows. The PSL interpreter is written entirely in PSL itself and operates on a number of computer systems, including the DECSystem-20, DEC VAXs, and Apollo workstations. PSL was developed by the University of Utah.

PTRANS. Helps control the manufacture and distribution of Digital Equipment Corporation's computer systems. It uses customer order descriptions and information about plant activity to develop a plan for assembling and testing the ordered computer system, including when to build the system. PTRANS monitors the progress of the technicians implementing the plan, diagnoses problems, suggests solutions, and predicts possible impending shortages or surpluses of materials. It is designed to work with XSEL, a salesperson's assistant, so that once an order is made, the delivery date can be confirmed. PTRANS is a forward chaining, rule-based system implemented in OPS5. It was developed jointly by Digital Equipment Corporation and Carnegie-Mellon University.

PUFF. Diagnoses the presence and severity of lung disease in a patient by interpreting measurements from respiratory tests administered in a pulmonary (lung) function laboratory. The data being interpreted include test results (e.g., total lung capacity, residual volume) and patient history. The system bases its decisions on knowledge about the kinds of tests results produced by different pulmonary disorders. PUFF is

```
PRESBYTERIAN HOSPITAL OF PMC
  CLAY AND BUCHANAN, BOX 7999
  SAN FRANCISCO, CA. 94120
  PULMONARY FUNCTION LAB

WT 40.8 KG,  HT 161 CM,  AGE 69   SEX F
REFERRAL DX-
********************************************************TEST DATE 05/13/80
                            PREDICTED                    POST DILATION
                            (+/-SD)     OBSER(%PRED)      OBSER(%PRED)
INSPIR VITAL CAP (IVC)  L    2.7         2.3  ( 86)       2.4  ( 90)
RESIDUAL VOL     (RV)   L    2.0         3.8  (188)       3.0  (148)
TOTAL LUNG CAP   (TLC)  L    4.7         6.1  (130)       5.4  (115)
RV/TLC                  %    43.         62.              56.

FORCED EXPIR VOL (FEV1) L    2.2         1.5  ( 68)       1.6  ( 73)
FORCED VITAL CAP (FVC)  L    2.7         2.3  ( 86)       2.4  ( 90)
FEV1/FVC                %    73.         65.              67.
PEAK EXPIR FLOW  (PEF)  L/S  7.1         1.8  ( 25)       1.9  ( 26)
FORCED EXP FLOW 25-75% L/S   1.8         0.7  ( 39)       0.7  ( 39)
AIRWAY RESIST(RAW) (TLC= 6.1) 0.0(0.0)   1.5             2.2

DF CAP-HGB=14.5      (TLC= 4.8)  24.     17.4  ( 72)   ( 74%IF TLC = 4.7)
************************************************************************
```

INTERPRETATION: ELEVATED LUNG VOLUMES INDICATE OVERINFLATION. IN ADDITION, THE
RV/TLC RATIO IS INCREASED, SUGGESTING A MODERATELY SEVERE DEGREE OF AIR TRAPPING.
THE FORCED VITAL CAPACITY IS NORMAL. THE FEV1/FVC RATIO AND MID-EXPIRATORY FLOW
ARE REDUCED AND THE AIRWAY RESISTANCE IS INCREASED, SUGGESTING MODERATELY SEVERE
AIRWAY OBSTRUCTION. FOLLOWING BRONCHODILATION, THE EXPIRED FLOWS SHOW MODERATE
IMPROVEMENT. HOWEVER, THE RESISTANCE DID NOT IMPROVE. THE LOW DIFFUSING
CAPACITY INDICATES A LOSS OF ALVEOLAR CAPILLARY SURFACE, WHICH IS MILD.

CONCLUSIONS: THE LOW DIFFUSING CAPACITY, IN COMBINATION WITH OBSTRUCTION AND A
HIGH TOTAL LUNG CAPACITY IS CONSISTENT WITH A DIAGNOSIS OF EMPHYSEMA. ALTHOUGH
BRONCHODILATORS WERE ONLY SLIGHTLY USEFUL IN THIS ONE CASE, PROLONGED USE MAY
PROVE TO BE BENEFICIAL TO THE PATIENT.

PULMONARY FUNCTION DIAGNOSIS:
1. MODERATELY SEVERE OBSTRUCTIVE AIRWAYS DISEASE.
    EMPHYSEMATOUS TYPE.

Figure P-6. PUFF—Screen of PUFF analysis of a patient. Note the conclusions on the bottom. *Reprinted with the permission of John Wiley and Sons, from "Expert Systems—Artificial Intelligence in Business" by Paul Harmon and David King.*

a backward chaining, rule-based system implemented in EMYCIN. It was developed at Stanford University and tested at the Pacific Medical Center in San Francisco. PUFF reached the stage of a production prototype. A direct descendant of MYCIN, this expert system diagnoses lung disorders (acronym for Pulmonary Function).

purity. An objective term that denotes a measurement that can be visualized on a chromaticity chart as a position between the equal energy mixture of all colors (white) to the dominant wavelength of the color.

push. Putting data into a stack.

pyramid. A hierarchical data structure that represents an image at several levels of resolution simultaneously.

quadtree. A representation obtained by recursively splitting an image into quadrants until all pixels in a quadrant are uniform with respect to some feature, such as gray level.

qualified expression. A qualified expression is an expression preceded by an indication of its type or subtype. Such qualification is used when, in its absence, the expression might be ambiguous.

query. In data communication the process by which a master station asks a slave station to identify itself and to give its status.

QUEST. An intelligent tutoring system for teaching qualitative reasoning about electrical circuits in general and troubleshooting of automotive electrical systems in particular. The system is designed to provide a simulation environment within which students can solve circuit problems. It also serves a tutorial function and can be called upon to solve problems, demonstrate troubleshooting procedures, and explain the functioning of circuits with verbal explanations and diagrams. Knowledge about electrical circuits is represented in QUEST as a causal model that includes information about the structure of the circuit, the functioning of the devices within the circuit, and electrical principles for evaluating circuits. (e.g., knowledge of the flow of current in parallel and serial circuits). Associated with each device are rules for determining the state of the device (e.g., a capacitor can be charging, charged, discharging, or discharged), the internal conductivity of the device (e.g., devices can be conductive or nonconductive, resistive or nonresistive), and whether or not the device is a voltage source (e.g., a capacitor in the state of discharging is a source of voltage). The model is actually a program that can be run to simulate the behavior of the circuit when faults are introduced into the system or when troubleshooting tests are administered. It is sensitive to changes in the states of any of the devices and to processes that occur over time (e.g., field building of a coil). The simulation incorporates topological search processes that are used to determine whether or not devices such as batteries and capacitors have paths through which to discharge and whether a device has an electrical potential across it. It can generate a graphic representation of the path through which current will flow and depict openings and shorts in the circuit. QUEST also has knowledge about a troubleshooting strategy that is used by experts in the field. The goal of the strategy is to divide the circuit into 2 parts and then to infer which portion of the circuit contains the fault. The troubleshooting logic is then recursively applied to the faulty segment until the fault has been localized. That strategy has the advantage of minimizing the demands on memory and being easy to follow. Troubleshooting tests that the student is allowed to make include introducing a test light into the circuit and detaching parts of the circuit. Instruction is organized in terms of a series of carefully selected problems of increasing difficulty. By working through the problems, and requesting help when needed, the student gradually acquires a sequence of increasingly sophisticated cognitive models that correspond to deeper levels of understanding of electrical circuit concepts.

queue. A priority-ranked collection of tasks waiting to be performed in line on the system.

queued. Describes a unit's ability to accept multiple operation commands from the host and execute them in a sequence, according to unit-defined or host-defined algorithms.

Quirtus Prolog. Designed to make building software for intelligent systems smooth and cost-effective. It offers a high-performance development environment that provides foundation for artificial intelligence and other symbolic processing applications. Quintus Prolog was developed at Quintus Computer Systems by several of the founding fathers who created the original version of Prolog, which runs on the DEC 10/20™ systems. Quintus Prolog is now available from Digital for use on the VAX computer.

QUIP. Experimental work station, under development by Schlumberger, for geologists oriented toward enabling rapid testing of geological and rock models.

R

R1/XCON. An artificial intelligence system that configures DEC's VAX 11/750 and 11/780 computers. Given a customer's purchase order, it determines what, if any, substitutions and additions have to be made to the order to make it consistent and complete and produces a number of diagrams showing the spatial and logical relationships among the 90 or so components that typically constitute a system. The system uses a rule-based approach, implemented in the OPS5 programming language, to solve the configuration problem. Under that approach a set of rules is established that specify actions to be taken if a particular set of conditions is met. Those rules are stored in a rule memory. There is also a working memory that describes the current state of the situation, which in this case would be a partial configuration. An interpreter searches the list of rules to find one whose conditions match the contents of working memory and applies the rule's actions to working memory, thus altering the situation. It then searches the rules again to find one whose conditions match the new state of working memory. The process continues until a solution is found. The working and rule memories were augmented with a third database, which contained a description of each of the computer components. As R1/XCON begins to configure an order, it retrieves the relevant component descriptions. A multistage process was used to obtain the information needed to create the rules of the system. To come up with an initial set of rules, the investigators reviewed the configuration manuals and interviewed DEC personnel. That initial set of rules was incorporated in a prototype. The prototype's output was reviewed by experts who suggested many additional rules to improve the system's performance. The full system was then validated by DEC and put into operation, performing actual configurations. DEC has taken over the maintenance of the system and plans to extend it to its PDP-11 series.

RABBIT. An expert system that helps users to formulate queries to a database. The intelligent database assistant guides the formulation of queries for users who have only a vague idea of what they want or who have limited knowledge of the given database. The system's retrieval expertise involves "retrieval by reformulation," where the user makes a query by incrementally constructing a partial description of the desired database items. RABBIT is implemented in SMALLTALK and operates on a set of databases represented in KL-ONE. The system was developed at Xerox Palo Alto Research Center.

radial. Refers to the bit-significant address of units or devices.

Radian Corporation. Radian Corporation has grown, since its beginnings in 1969, from a 1-base operation dealing with environmental technology to a broad-based organization providing service and products in the fields of environment, health, and safety. Radian also works with environmental impact assessments and toxic and hazardous waste disposal including acid rain. The staff now operates from several locations including McLean, Virginia; Research Triangle Park, North Carolina; Sacramento, California; Salt Lake City, Utah; Houston, Texas; and its corporate headquarters in Austin, Texas. The corporation's primary expert system product is called "Rulemaster," a software tool for building expert systems. It features automatic generation of rules from examples, portability between computers using "C" compilers, interface with other existing programs, and complete explanations. The applications of Rulemaster include both situation refining diagnosis and control including diagnosis for classifying from a set of observables, fault finding, monitoring, and forecasting. The control functions provide advice on regulation of a product. Another software package recently introduced is called CPS/PC, an advanced system for gridding, contour mapping, and analysis. Its applications include: mineral exploration for petroleum geology, scenic exploration, mining and mine planning, civil engineering, weather mapping, cartography, and oceanography.

radiant energy. Energy transferred by an electromagnetic wave; in color it refers to the visible part of the electromagnetic spectrum.

RADEX. Helps physicians and the MDX expert system diagnose the liver syndrome cholestasis. The radiology consultant takes summary descriptions of a patient's medical images and uses them as a basis for answering questions about the patient's anatomical or physiological abnormalities. The system's expertise consists of a conceptual model of relevant organs and organ abnormalities that can appear on various images. Knowledge is represented as frames containing the descriptions, default values, relationships, and attached procedures for 4 kinds of entities: the imaging procedures, such as liver scan and ultrasonogram; major organs, such as liver and gallbladder; parts of organs, such as lumen and lobe; and abnormalities and deformities in the organs, such as tumor and stricture. RADEX is implemented in LISP. It was developed at Ohio State University.

radix. The fundamental number in a number system, for example, 10 in the decimal system, 8 in the octal system, and 2 in the binary system. Synonymous with base. In a radix-numeration system, the positive integer by which the weight of the digit place is multiplied to obtain the weight of the next higher digit place—for example, in the decimal-numeration system, the radix of each digit place is 10; in a binary code, the radix of each position is 2.

RADIAL. A knowledge engineering language for rule-based and procedural representation. It is the underlying environment used by the RULEMASTER system-building aid and has its formal basis in finite automata theory. A RADIAL program consists of a set of modules, each containing a transition network of states, where each state contains a single rule in the form of a decision tree. RADIAL is a block-structured language with scoped variables, argument passing between modules, recursive module invocation, and conditional branching. It can explain its reasoning and has certainty handling mechanisms for dealing with fuzzy logic. RADIAL is implemented in the C programming language and operates on minicomputers and microcomputers, such as VAXs and Sun workstations, under the Unix operating system. It was developed by the Radian Corporation.

RAIL. Modern programming language for robot programming. A product of Automatix, Incorporated, of Billerica, Massachusetts.

random-access memory. A data storage device wherein the time required for obtaining data from or placing data into storage is independent of the location of the data most recently obtained or placed into storage. A memory whose information media are organized into discrete locations, sectors, etc., each uniquely identified by an address. Data may be obtained from such memory by specifying the data address(es) to the memory, e.g., core, drum, disk, cards.

random-access storage. A storage device such as magnetic core, magnetic disk, and magnetic drum in which each record has a specific predetermined address that may be reached directly; access time in that type of storage is effectively independent of the location of the data.

range. A range is a contiguous set of values of a scalar type. A range is specified by giving the lower and upper bounds for the values. A value in the range is said to belong to the range.

range constraint. A range constraint of a type specifies a range and thereby determines the subset of the values of the type that belong to the range.

raster. The horizontal scanning pattern of the electron gun in computer monitors that use cathode-ray tube display. A raster display device stores and displays data as horizontal rows of uniform grid or picture cells (pixels).

raster plotter. Plotter that reproduces displays in dot matrix patterns.

raster unit. The distance between 2 adjacent addressable points located horizontally or vertically on a cathode ray tube display.

rate control. Control system in which the input is the desired velocity of the control object.

rated load capacity. A specified weight or mass of a material that can be handled by a robot that allows for some margin of safety relative to the point of expected failure.

rational number. A real number that is the quotient of an integer divided by an integer other than zero.

RBMS. Uses a flight manifest to schedule the use of Johnson Space Center FCRs (flight control rooms) over a period of months. The system replaces the STAP computer program that uses a statistical approach to the problem. The input to RBMS is the flight manifest containing flight numbers, launch dates, type of flight, duration, whether it is a space laboratory mission, and other data. RBMS produces as output a schedule indicating the daily FCR usage (activities scheduled, number of hours required) and the average hours per day used by each FCR per month. The system is written in LISP and OPS5 and runs on the DEC VAX computers. RBMS was developed by Ford Aerospace for NASA.

reach. Defines the robot's arm movement or work envelope.

REACTOR. Assists reactor operators in the diagnosis and treatment of nuclear reactor accidents by monitoring instrument readings, such as feed-water flow and containment radiation level, looking for deviations from normal operating conditions. When the system detects a deviation, it evaluates the situation and recommends appropriate action, using knowledge about the reactor configuration and the functional relations of its components together with knowledge about the expected behavior of the reactor under known accident conditions. REACTOR is implemented in LISP as a rule-based system that uses both forward and backward chaining. It was developed by EG&G Idaho.

read. To copy, usually from 1 form of storage to another, particularly from external or secondary storage to internal storage. To sense the meaning of arrangements of hardware. To sense the presence of information in a recording medium.

reader. A device capable of sensing information stored in an off-line memory media and generating equivalent information in an on-line memory device.

read-only memory. A more permanent memory technique than random access memory since it is nonvolatile and remains active if power is lost. The ultimate version of this is EPROM, an erasable programmable read-only memory that can be erased with ultraviolet light and reprogrammed. Generally read-only memory carries the basic instructions to control a robot.

real-time. Taking place during the actual occurrence of an event. Real-time refers to computer systems or programs that perform a computation during the actual time that a related physical process transpires, in order that the results of the computation can be recorded or used to guide the physical process.

real time image generation. Performance of the computations necessary to update the image is completed within the refresh rate, so the sequence appears correct to the viewer. An example is flight simulation, in which thousands of computations must be performed to present an animated image, all within the 30-to-60-cycles-per-second rate at which the frames change.

real type. A type whose values represent approximations to the real numbers. There are 2 kinds of real type: fixed point types are specified by absolute error bound; floating point types are specified by a relative error bound expressed as a number of significant decimal digits.

real-world problem. A complex, practical problem that has a solution useful in some cost-effective way.

reasoning. The process of drawing inferences or conclusions.

reason maintenance. The process of keeping track of the dependencies between assertions in a knowledge base to assist in making and withdrawing deductions as new information becomes available.

recency. A conflict-resolution strategy that favors instantiations whose working memory elements were most recently created or modified. That strategy lends sensitivity to a production system, since subgoals can be spawned as soon as new data arrive.

recognition. A match between a description derived from an image and a description obtained from a memory-stored model or template.

recognize-act cycle. The cycle of events in a production or forward-chaining system. During the recognize phase rules are examined to see if their clauses are based on information currently stored in memory. During the act phase, 1 of the rules is selected and executed and its conclusion is stored in memory. An iterative loop, each cycle of which consists of 3 successive phases: match, conflict resolution, and the firing of rules.

record. A collection of fields. The information relating to 1 area of activity in a data processing activity, i.e., all information on 1 inventory item. Sometimes called item.

recording density. The closeness with which data are stored on magnetic tape. The most common densities are 200, 556, 800, and 1600 characters per inch.

record-playback robot. A manipulator for which the critical points along desired trajectories are stored in sequence by recording the actual values of the joint position encoders of the robot as it is moved under operator control. To perform the task, those points are played back to the robot servo system.

record type. A value of a record type consists of components that are usually of different types or subtypes. For each component of a record value or record object, the definition of the record type specifies an identifier that uniquely determines the component within the record.

rectangular coordinates. Spatial coordinates defined by 3 distances. Some robots are programmed in rectangular coordinates.

recursion. Defining an item in terms of itself.

recursive operations. Operations defined in terms of themselves.

Raj Reddy. Ph.D., professor of computer science and director of the Robotics Institute at Carnegie-Mellon University and chief scientist at the Paris-based Centre Mondial for computing. He led the most successful DARPA speech project culminating in HEARSAY II, a novel cooperative problem-solving environment, and HARPY, the first 1000-word 95% accuracy continuous speech recognizer that introduced the use of beam search.

REDESIGN. Assists engineers in the redesign of digital circuits to meet altered functional specifications. Given the redesign goal, the system generates plausible local changes to make within the circuit, ranks the changes based on implementation difficulty and goal satisfaction, and checks for undesirable side effects associated with the changes. The system provides design assistance by combining causal reasoning, analyzing the cause-effect relations of circuit operation with functional reasoning, and analyzing the purposes or roles of the circuit components. Circuit knowledge in REDESIGN is represented as a network of modules and data paths. The system was developed at Rutgers University.

redundancy. A fabrication method for memory chips that builds in extra rows of memory cells or other elements to be used as "spares" if required.

reflectance. The ratio of total reflected to total incident illumination at each point.

reflectance model. Function that describes light on a surface by making assumptions concerning light sources, angles, surface texture, etc. Also called illumination model.

refractive index. The ratio of the speed of light in a vacuum to its speed in a given material such as glass. The larger the ratio, the more the light entering the material is bent.

refraction. A conflict-resolution strategy that prevents an instantiation from firing if it has fired on a previous occasion. Refraction derives its name from a property of neurons: During the refractory period, a short interval following the firing of a neuron, that neuron will not fire when stimulated.

refresh. The process by which dynamic random access memory cells recharge the capacitive node to maintain the stored information. The charged nodes discharge because of leakage currents, and without refresh the stored data would be lost. The process must recur every so many microseconds. During refresh the Random Access Memory cannot be accessed.

refresh logic. The logic required to generate all the refresh signals and timing.

region. A set of connected pixels that show a common property, such as average gray level, color or texture, in an image.

region growing. Process of initially partitioning an image into elementary regions with a common property and then successively merging adjacent regions having sufficiently small differences in the selected property until only regions with large differences between them remain.

register. A memory device capable of containing 1 or more computer bits or words. A register has zero memory latency time and negligible memory access time.

registration. Processing images to correct geometrical and intensity distortions, relative translational and rotational shifts, and magnification differences between 1 image and another or between an image and a reference map. When the image is registered, there is a 1-to-1 correspondence between a set of points in the image and in the reference.

relational graph. An image representation in which nodes represent regions and arcs between nodes represent properties of and relations between these regions.

relative address. A relative address is a memory address formed by adding the immediate data included with the instruction to the contents of the program counter or some other register.

relative coordinate system. A coordinate system whose origin moves relative to world or fixed coordinates.

relaxation approach. An iterative problem-solving approach in which initial conditions are propagated utilizing constraints until all goal conditions are adequately satisfied.

relevant backtracking. Backtracking, during a search, not to the most recent choice point, but to the most relevant choice point.

remote center compliance. A compliant device used to interface a robot or other mechanical workhead to its tool or working medium. The remote center compliance allows a gripped part to rotate about its tip or to translate without rotating when pushed literally at its tip. The remote center compliance thus provides general lateral and rotational float and greatly eases robot or other mechanical assembly in the presence of errors in parts, jigs, pallets, and robots. It is especially useful in performing very close clearance or interference insertions.

remote terminal. Computer terminal that is cabled to a larger computer. A remote terminal may or may not have local processing capability.

REMUS. The financial model reviewing expert for the ROME system. Given a financial model and a set of constraints entered by users that represent plan reviewer expectations and corporate goals, REMUS scans the model to detect constraint violations, which are then reported to the user. When a constraint violation is detected, REMUS attempts to determine the underlying circumstances that account for it by examining the formulas, input, and intermediate variables that are involved in its computation. By that process, REMUS can localize the source of a constraint violation to the input variable(s) that seem to be responsible. An integrated version of ROME is currently undergoing testing and development. The capabilities of the system are being expanded in 3 areas: the causal diagnosis of constraint violations, the dependency-based revision of financial models in the face of inconsistency or change, and the support of user exploration of hypothetical plans.

renaming declaration. A renaming declaration declares another name for an entity.

rendezvous. A rendezvous is the interaction that occurs between 2 parallel tasks when 1 task has called an entry of the other task, and a corresponding accept statement is being executed by the other task on behalf of the calling task.

repaint. Refresh a display surface with an updated display.

repeatability. As opposed to accuracy, a measurement of the deviation between a taught robot location point and the played-back location. Under identical conditions of load and velocity, the deviation will be finer than accuracy tolerance. The closeness of agreement among the number of consecutive movements made by the robot arm to a specific point.

replicate. To generate an exact copy of a design element and locate it on the cathode ray tube at any point(s), and in any size or scale desired.

representation. A symbolic description or model of objects in the image or scene domain. Formalization and structuring of knowledge in a computer so that it can be manipulated by the knowledge base management system. The way in which a system stores knowledge about a domain. Knowledge consists of facts and the relationships between facts.

representation clause. A representation clause directs the compiler in the selection of the mapping of a type, an object, or a task onto features of the underlying machine that executes a program. In some cases representation clauses completely specify the mapping; in other cases they provide criteria for choosing a mapping.

reset. A computer system input that initializes and sets up certain registers in the central processing unit and throughout the computer system. One of the initializations is to load a specific address into the program counter. The 2 bytes of information in that and the succeeding address are the starting address for the system program.

resolution. The inference strategy used in logical systems to determine the truth of an assertion. The complex, but highly effective, method establishes the truth of an assertion by determining that a contradiction is encountered when one attempts to resolve clauses, 1 of which is a negation of the thesis one seeks to assert. Resolution theorem proving is a particular use of deductive logic for proving theorems in the first-order predicate calculus. The method makes use of the following resolution principle: (A v B) and ($-$A v C) implies (B v C).

resolved motion rate. A control scheme whereby the velocity vector of the end point of a robot manipulator arm is commanded and the computer determines the joint angular velocities to achieve the desired result. Coordination of a robot's axes so that the velocity vector of the end point is under direct control. Motion in the coordinate system of the end point along specified directions or trajectories is possible. Used in manual control of manipulators and as a computational method for achieving programmed coordinate axis control in robots.

resolver. A rotary or linear feedback device that converts mechanical motion to analog electric signals that represent motion or position.

response time. The time span between the end of a request for information or action and the beginning of receipt of a reply.

result element. A temporary structure used in OPS5 to build a description of a working memory element for the purpose of modifying working memory. The modify and call actions are implemented using result elements.

Rete match algorithm. An algorithm for efficiently determining which rules can be satisfied by the contents of working memory on each recognize-act cycle by computing bindings between patterns and data. This algorithm, devised by Charles L. Forgy, exploits redundancy in production systems by saving partial results of the match computation so that they need not be recomputed at a later time. The name comes from an English word meaning "network."

return. A special type of jump in which the central processor resumes execution of the main program at the contents of the program counter at the time that the jump occurred.

right-hand side. One of the 2 parts of a rule, the other being the left-hand side. In production systems with backward-chaining architecture, the right-hand side specifies a goal to be solved, the subgoals of which are given on the left-hand side of the rule. In forward-chaining production systems, the right-hand side consists of a series of actions to be performed in the specified sequence when an instantiation of the rule is fired, using values that were bound to variables on the left-hand side.

right justified. A field of numbers (decimal, binary, etc.) that exists in a memory cell, location, or register possessing no significant zeros to its right is considered to be right justified. Thus, 0001200000 is considered to be a seven-digit field, right justified, and 000001200 is a 2-digit field, not right justified.

right memory. A data structure in the Rete match algorithm network that is associated with a condition element. It contains a list of working memory elements that match the condition.

ring network. A system in which all stations are linked to form a continuous loop or cycle.

ripple counter. A binary counting system in which flip-flops are connected in series.

rise time. The time required for an output voltage of a digital circuit to change from a logic 0 to a logic 1 state.

RITA. A knowledge engineering language for rule-based representation. Its principal characteristics include forward- and backward-chaining control schemes and support for developing user agents, which are front ends to remote computing systems and networks. The support environment consists of tracing, debugging, and explanation facilities, a front end for the interactive creation and development of rule sets, and a mechanism for accessing the UNIX operating system support environment. RITA is implemented in the C programming language and operations under UNIX on PDP-11/45 and PDP-11/70 computer systems. It was developed by the Rand Corporation.

RLL. A knowledge engineering language for frame-based representation. Its flexibility allows the user to specify a domain-specific representation language by expressing a particular set of representations, inheritance strategies, and control schemes. RLL also allows procedural attachment and general LISP structures to be incorporated as slots of frames. The support environment includes a sophisticated editor capable of checking both syntax and semantics. RLL is implemented in INTERLISP. It was developed at Stanford University.

robomation. A contraction of the words "robot" and "automation" meaning the use of robots to control and operate equipment or machines automatically.

robot. A robot is a reprogrammable multifunctional manipulator designed to move material, parts, tools, or specialized devices, through variable programmed motions for the performance of a variety of tasks. **(See figure p. 220.)**

robot programming language. A computer language especially designed for writing programs for controlling robots.

robot systems. A "robot system" includes the robot hardware and software, consisting of the manipulator, power supply, and controller; the end effector(s); any equipment, devices, and sensors the robot is directly interfacing with; any equipment, devices, and sensors required for the robot to perform its task; and any communications interface that is operating and monitoring the robot, equipment, and sensors.

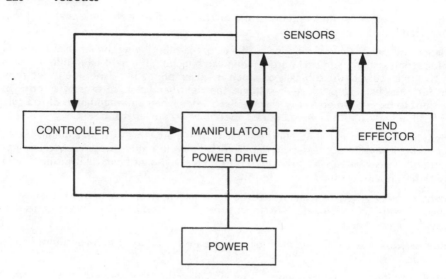

Figure R–1. Robot—Block diagram of Robot System.

robotics. The branch of artificial intelligence research that is concerned with enabling computers to "see" and "manipulate" objects in their surrounding environment. Artificial intelligence is concerned with developing the techniques necessary for developing robots that can use heuristics to function in a highly flexible manner while interacting with a constantly changing environment.

robustness. That quality of a problem solver that permits a gradual degradation in performance when it is pushed to the limits of its scope of expertise or is given errorful, inconsistent, or incomplete data or rules.

ROGET. A system-building aid that helps a domain expert design a knowledge base for a diagnosis-type expert system. It interacts with the expert, asking pertinent questions that identify types of subproblems the expert system must solve, the results or solutions the system must produce, the evidence or data required to solve the problem, and the relationships between the data or facts of a case and its solution (e.g., what factors support the determination of the solution or indicate other factors). The system has been tested in the medical domain. ROGET is implemented in an extended version of EMYCIN that permits forward chaining rules and calls to subroutines called task blocks. It was developed at Stanford University as an experimental system. (It is named for Peter Mark Roget (1779–1869) of *Roget's Thesaurus* fame.)

roll. The angular displacement around the principal axis of a body, especially its line of motion.

rolloff. A gradual decrease in a signal level.

ROME. Many business decisions are based on information produced by computerized financial planning models. While the models themselves may be quite sophisticated, their computer implementations generally do little more than calculate and display the results. Not much attention is given to screening the input data for anomalies, verifying that the data satisfy the assumptions of the model, or checking to make sure that the outputs seem reasonable for the situation at hand. Nor are there facilities for explaining what the outputs represent, showing their derivation, or justifying the results to users who are not familiar with what a particular program does. Traditionally, these tasks have been left to human analysts who could intelligently apply a programmed model to answer managerial questions. The ROME project is an effort to develop a knowledge-based system that could itself perform many of the above tasks and hence more effectively support decision making in the area of long-range financial planning. The approach is based on the idea that current programs are limited by a lack of knowledge, i.e., they simply do not know what the variables in the models they manipulate mean. For example, they have no knowledge of how the variables are defined in terms of real-world entities, and so they cannot explain for what the variables stand. They fail to keep track of the relationships used to derive variables and hence cannot explain how they got their values. They have no knowledge of "normal" versus "abnormal" circumstances and so cannot detect peculiar values, whether they are for input, intermediate, or output variables. Finally, they have no sense of the consequences implied by the variables, and hence cannot tell "good" values from "bad" ones with respect to the goals of the organization. In contrast, the overall goal for ROME is to make the meaning of the variables available to and usable by the system itself. Hence, an expressive representation for financial models using the SRL knowledge representation language was developed. That representation allows ROME to keep track of the logical support for model variables, such as their external source, method of calculation, and assumptions that must hold for the variables' values to be valid. Tracing back through the dependencies associated with a variable's computation can be used to explain why a value should be believed. Similarly ROME can challenge the values of a particular variable by comparing them against relevant expectations, organizational goals, and independently derived values. Prototype implementation of 2 ROME subsystems, called ROMULUS and REMUS, has been completed.

ROMULUS.   User interface for the ROME system. Instead of the rigid and stylized input language used with most computerized support systems, ROMULUS was designed to accept natural language queries about the model expressed in English sentence form. The query types currently understood are those that relate to definitions and calculations such as "What is the definition of production spending?" and "How was line 46 calculated?" ROMULUS also supports the interactive construction and editing of financial models in natural language by allowing the addition of new variables, formulas, and constraints on variables. Examples of acceptable user assertions are "Define year end people to be direct labor + indirect labor," and "Expect direct labor to go up." A major goal for ROMULUS has been to make the system as cooperative as possible by including ways to recover from user mistakes (e.g., by spelling correction) and to tolerate user ignorance (e.g., by accepting synonyms and variations in syntactic form).

root node.   The initial (apex) node in a tree representation.

ROSIE.   A knowledge engineering language for rule-based representation, but it also supports procedure-oriented representation methods. Its principal characteristics include an Englishlike syntax, a procedure-oriented structure that permits nested and recursive subroutines, powerful pattern-matching facilities, and an interface to the local operating system that gives ROSIE control over remote jobs. The support environment includes editing and debugging tools. ROSIE is implemented in INTER-LISP and is being converted to run in the C programming language. ROSIE was developed at the Rand Corporation. **(See figure p. 222.)**

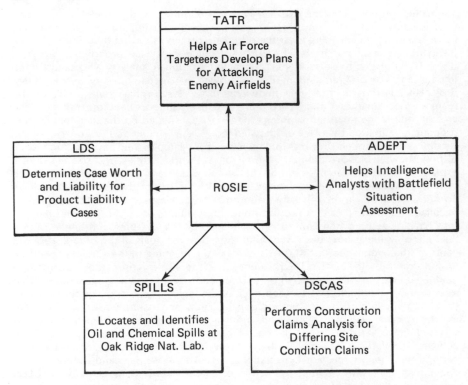

Figure R-2. ROSIE—Applications of ROSIE. *Reprinted with the permission of Addison-Wesley Publishing Company from "A Guide to Expert Systems" by Donald A. Waterman.*

ROSS   A programming language for object-oriented representation and simulation. It supports inheritance of attributes and behaviors from multiple parents and permits the free mixing of ROSS commands and LISP function calls. The support environment consists of a display editor for objects and an abbreviation package to facilitate program readability. ROSS is implemented in FRANZ LISP and operates on DEC VAX systems under UNIX. It was developed by the Rand Corporation.

rotation.   Movement of a body around an axis, i.e., so that at least 1 point remains fixed.

routine.   Set of instructions to the computer to perform a certain function. For example, an inking routine translates the graphic input from a light pen into visible continuous lines, giving the user the impression of sketching with the stylus.

RPMS.   Assists the user with general planning and scheduling tasks, such as defining a schedule and minimizing resources like time, manpower, and materials. The schedule is represented graphically as a network containing tasks with bars indicating their durations and arrows pointing to successor and predecessor tasks. The user can define formal constraints between tasks, such as Task A must occur before Task B by moving tasks (nodes) in the network. The system also contains rules that allow it to reconfigure the network itself, attempting to level out the use of resources. The system is implemented in ZETALISP and OPS5 and makes heavy use of the FLAVORS object-oriented features of ZETALISP. RPMS was developed by Ford Aerospace and is being applied to the space shuttle reconfiguration process for the Johnson Space Center. It is closer to a tool for expert system design than an expert system.

RTC. Classifies ships by interpreting radar images. The system extracts features from the images and matches them against the high-level models of the possible ship classes stored in the system's knowledge base. RTC stores only 1 3-dimensional model for each ship, matching image features to the model by mapping the 3-dimensional model into the 2-dimensional view appropriate for the given features. RTC is a rule-based system implemented in FRANZ LISP. It was developed by Advanced Information and Decision Systems.

rubber banding. A capability that allows a component to be tracked (dragged) across the cathode ray tube screen, by means of an electronic pen, to a desired location, while simultaneously stretching all related interconnections to maintain signal continuity.

RUBRIC. Helps a user to access unformatted textual data bases. The system performs conceptual retrieval; e.g., when the user names a single topic, RUBRIC automatically retrieves all documents containing text related to that topic. In RUBRIC the relationships between topics, subtopics, and low-level word phrases are defined in rule form. The rules also define alternative terms, phrases, and spellings for the same topic or concept. The user can formulate a query in the form of a rule that specifies retrieval criteria, e.g., a heuristic weight that specifies how strongly the rule's pattern indicates the presence of the rule's topic. During retrieval, RUBRIC presents the user with documents that lie in a cluster containing at least 1 document with a weight above a user-provided threshold. That prevents an arbitrary threshold from splitting closely ranked documents. RUBRIC is implemented in FRANZ LISP. It was developed at Advanced Information and Decision Systems.

rule. A formal way of specifying a recommendation, directive, or strategy, expressed as IF premise THEN conclusion or IF condition THEN action. A conditional statement of 2 parts. The first part, consisting of 1 or more if clauses, establishes conditions that must apply if a second part, consisting of 1 or more then clauses, is to be acted upon. The clauses of rules are usually A-V pairs or O-A-V triplets. Rules are ordered pairs that consist of a left-hand side and a right-hand side. In a formal grammar rules specify the way in which sentences can be derived and parsed. In production systems rules are the units of production memory and are used to encode procedural knowledge. A rule is also called a production. **(See figure p. 224.)**

rule-based methods. Programming methods using IF-THEN rules to perform forward or backward chaining.

rule-based program. A computer program that explicitly incorporates rules or ruleset components. A program similar in spirit to a production-system program in that the knowledge is represented explicitly by means of rules rather than through procedures. But a rule-based program is not necessarily implemented in a general-purpose production-system language and need not make exclusive use of the production-system architecture.

rule-based system. System in which knowledge is stored in the form of simple if-then or condition-action rules.

rule cluster. A set of rules that work together to achieve a goal or the set of rules related to a context element.

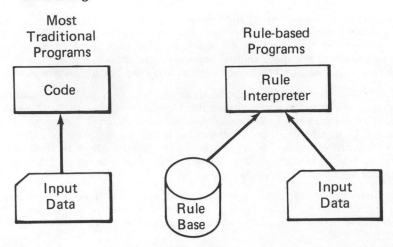

Figure R–3. Rule—Contrast between traditional programs and rule-based programs. A rule-based program is divided into a general-reasoning program, called the rule interpreter, and a file of judgmental rules obtained from an expert, called the rule base or knowledge base. The rule interpreter loads the rule base into an internal representation and uses the rule base to guide an interactive consultation with the user. *Courtesy: AFCEA.*

rule filtering. Restricting for the sake of efficiency the portion of production memory that participates in the match process to a subset.

rule induction. The creation of a rule from a set of examples. The information embodied in the examples is generalized to cover many cases that are not specified by that example set. Induction is important because experts are able to express their knowledge in the form of declarative examples rather than procedural rules. Usually the induced rule is a very compact representation of information that takes more space when expressed as examples.

rule interpreter. The control structure for a production rule system. In production systems another term for interpreter.

RuleMaster. A system of programs that allows the user to construct rule-based advisory or diagnostic aids for many different applications. The technology behind the approach is based on the methods developed by Professor Donald Michie at Edinburgh University, currently executive director of the Turing Institute. After developing the expert system building packages known as Expert-Ease and EX-TRAN, his organization in a teaming arrangement with Radian developed the expert system building package, RuleMaster. The technical paper, "A Second Generation Knowledge Engineering Facility," by Donald Michie et al., was presented at the AAAI/IEEE joint conference in Denver on December 7, 1984. This public presentation announced the official entry of Radian's RuleMaster system to the industrial and government marketplace. Many features have been incorporated into RuleMaster to make it a unique expert system building package. The features of RuleMaster give it the power to produce industrial-scale, cost-effective solutions to today's cognitive or rule-based problems. One important feature is the automatic generation of rules from examples. That feature facilitates expert system development because it is easier for the expert to provide examples rather than specific rules or procedures. In other words, declarative (examples) information may be used in building RuleMaster systems instead of, or in addition to, procedural (rules) information. Another important feature is the versatility of RuleMaster to run on most computers that utilize the C language. To have portability from machine to machine, even including some personal computers, is a major advancement in expert systems. Full-scale, industrial-size expert systems can be constructed on small computers (with appropriate memory) running under the UNIX or XENIX operating system. The expensive LISP-type computers are not required by RuleMaster for development and execution of real-world, cost-effective expert systems. RuleMaster has the capability of interfacing with other existing programs written in various languages. That means existing models, database systems, parametric evaluation programs, and other statistical results can be accessed by a RuleMaster system concurrent with execution of a specific problem domain. Associated with that feature is the ability to interface real-time information sources to RuleMaster expert systems that allow control, prediction, or diagnostic systems to be implemented. The ability of an expert system to explain the rationale behind certain decisions makes the system more usable. RuleMaster develops in English languagelike fashion complete explanations that work back through the decision tree for every rule that has been exercised. It is even possible to ask "Why?" when the system asks the user a question, to determine the reason for that question. Without an extensive description, other features of RuleMaster cannot be discussed in a brief overview. However, 1 unique structural component of RuleMaster is the ability to hierarchically order modules and have a multi-state system. That is a feature of great importance for timely construction, enhancement, and modification of a system. That attribute is not available in most production systems with inference engine approaches. Most important, RuleMaster provides the complete framework to build useful and cost-effective expert systems.

rule memory. Another term for production memory.

ruleset. A collection of rules that constitutes a module of heuristic knowledge.

RULE WRITER. A system-building aid that helps knowledge engineers formulate rules in the EXPERT language. RULE WRITER uses knowledge about training cases, a taxonomy of plausible associations in the domain, and causal mechanisms to produce a model that correctly classifies the training cases on the basis of their stored findings. Its associational and causal knowledge guides a rule induction process performed on the example training cases. The classification rules learned from training cases are expressed directly in EXPERT. RULE WRITER is implemented in LISP. It was developed at Rutgers University.

run-length encoding. A data-compression technique for reducing the amount of information in a digitized binary image. It removes the redundancy that arises from the fact that such images contain large regions of adjacent pixels that are either all white or all black.

runtime version or system. Knowledge system building tools allow the user to create and run various knowledge bases. Using a single tool, a user might create a dozen knowledge bases. Depending on the problem the user was facing, he or she would load an appropriate knowledge base and undertake a consultation. With such a tool the user can easily modify a knowledge base. Some companies will want to develop a specific knowledge base and then produce copies of the tool and that specific knowledge base. Under those circumstances the organization will not want the user to have to "load" the knowledge base, nor will it want the user to be able to modify the knowledge base. When an expert system building tool is modified to incorporate a specific knowledge base and to deactivate certain programming features, the resulting system is called a runtime system or a runtime version.

RX. Helps users perform studies on large nonrandomized, time-oriented, clinical data bases by automating the process of hypothesis generation and exploratory analysis. RX has been applied to the problem of finding causal relationships within the American Rheumatism Association Medical Information System (ARAMIS) data base. The system uses nonparametric correlations to generate lists of hypothesized relationships. The hypotheses are tested using appropriate statistical methods, and positive results are incorporated into the data base. RX contains a tree-structured knowledge base representing a taxonomy of relevant aspects of medicine and statistics. The medical expertise includes knowledge about systemic lupus erythematosus and limited areas of general internal medicine. RX is implemented in INTERLISP. It was developed at Stanford University.

S

SACON. Helps engineers determine analysis strategies for particular structural analysis problems. The engineers can then implement that strategy with MARC, a program that uses finite-element analysis methods to stimulate the mechanical behavior of objects. SACON identifies the analysis class of the problem and recommends specific features of the MARC program to activate when performing the analysis. SACON uses knowledge about stresses and deflections of a structure under different loading conditions to determine the appropriate strategy. Structures that can be analyzed include aircraft wings, reactor pressure vessels, rocket motor casings, and bridges. SACON is a backward chaining, rule-based system implemented in EMYCIN. It was developed at Stanford University.

SADD. Assists engineers in the design of digital circuits. From the engineer the system accepts a functional description of the proposed circuit in English and uses that to build an internal model of the circuit. The system uses knowledge about the model, component characteristics, and circuit behavior to design a plausible circuit, which it tests for correctness by simulating its operation. SADD uses a frame-based representation of knowledge about circuit components. The system is implemented in LISP. It was developed at the University of Maryland.

SAFE. SAFE generates a program from a prepared English specification.

SAIL. A programming language for procedure-oriented representation. It is a derivative of the block-structured programming language ALGOL 60, augmented with an associative memory capability and a large set of low-level input-output and data manipulation functions. Additional extensions include flexible linking to hand-coded assembly language procedures, a primitive multiprocessing facility, a compile-time macro system, and record, set, and list data types. The support environment consists of a high-level debugger and user-modifiable error handling, backtracking, and interrupt facilities. SAIL was originally designed to operate on PDP-10 computers under the TOPS-10 and TENEX operating systems. It was developed by Stanford University.

SAL. Helps attorneys and claims adjustors evaluate claims related to asbestos exposure. The system currently handles one class of disease, asbestosis, and 1 class of plaintiffs, insulators. SAL provides estimates of how much money should be paid to plaintiffs in active cases, helping to promote rapid settlement. The system uses knowledge about damages, defendant liability, plaintiff responsibility, and case characteristics, such as the type of litigants and skill of the opposing attorneys. SAL is a forward-chaining, rule-based system implemented in ROSIE. The system is being developed at the Rand Corporation.

sample. Query a graphic device for coordinate data or operating status.

sampling rate. Frequency at which points are recorded in digitizing an image. Sampling errors can cause aliasing effects.

San Marco LISP Explorer. An on-line tutorial that has been used successfully to train programmers in artificial intelligence techniques. Written by Patrick H. Winston, head of M.I.T.'s artificial intelligence laboratory and prominent educator in the field of artificial intelligence technology, and San Marco Associates, this 1000-frame tutorial teaches concepts and strategies of LISP programming and artificial intelligence techniques. It features numerous tested programming examples and introduces programmers to advanced artificial intelligence programming methodologies, such as pattern matching, optimal search procedures, and natural language analysis.

satisfice. A process during which one seeks a solution that will satisfy a set of constraints. In contrast to optimization, which seeks the best possible solution, when one satisfies, one simply seeks a solution that will work. A problem-solving strategy that terminates with success when a potential solution satisfies specified minimal criteria of acceptability. The solution is not necessarily optimal. In many problems finding the optimal solution is unnecessary and prohibitively time-consuming.

saturation. A subjective term that usually refers to the difference of a hue from a gray of the same value. Colors can be desaturated by adding white, adding black, adding gray, or adding the complementary color. In a subtractive system, adding the complement will make the color darker. In an additive system, adding the complement will make the color lighter. That creates confusion since value as well as saturation is changed.

SAVOIR. A knowledge engineering language for rule-based representation. Its principal characteristics include backward- and forward-chaining control schemes, a knowledge base compiler, support for fuzzy logic, built-in certainty factor handling mechanisms, and demon control structures. The support environment contains an on-line help facility, a menu interface, and an explanation facility. SAVOIR operates on a wide range of computers and operating systems including DEC VAX systems and IBM PCs. It was developed by a British company called ISI.

scalar. In programming languages, 1 of the primitive data types; typically an integer, floating-point number, character, logical value, or symbolic atom, but not a list, array or record.

scalar type. An object or value of a scalar type does not have components. A scalar type is either a discrete type or a real type. The values of a scalar type are ordered.

scaling problem. The difficulty associated with trying to apply problem-solving techniques developed for a simplified version of a problem to the actual problem itself. **(See figure p. 229.)**

scan. To examine signals or data point by point in logical sequence.

scan conversion. Process of putting data into grid format for display on a raster device.

scanner. A device that examines a spatial pattern 1 part after another and generates analog or digital signals corresponding to the pattern. Scanners are often used in mark sensing, pattern recognition, or character recognition.

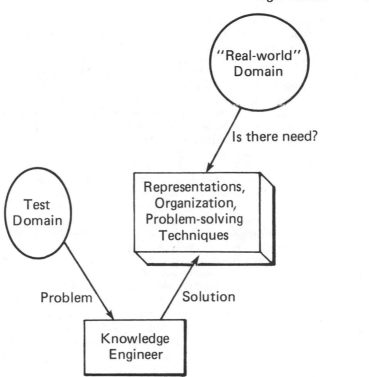

Figure S–1. Scaling Problem—The scaling problem in AI.

scanning lines. The total number of lines scanned in 1 direction during a frame interval, including those which are blanked during the vertical retrace. Calculated by dividing the line frequency by the frame frequency.

SCENARIO-AGENT. Assists war gamers by providing a model of nonsuperpower behavior in strategic conflict situations. SCENARIO-AGENT provides the user and the war gaming system with information on whether the nonsuperpowers will grant access rights to the superpowers (including the use of military bases) and whether they will contribute forces to the main conflict. The knowledge is encoded as rules describing the behavior of the nonsuperpowers in various conflict situations. The system uses a forward-chaining, rule-based, and procedure-oriented inference mechanism. SCENARIO-AGENT is implemented in ROSIE. It was developed at the Rand Corporation.

scene. A 3-dimensional environment from which an image is generated.

scene analysis. The process of seeking information about a 3-dimensional scene from information derived from a 2-dimensional image. It usually involves the transformation of simple features into abstract descriptions.

Roger Schank. Dr. Roger Schank has been professor of computer science and psychology at Yale University since 1976 and is also the director of the Artificial Intelligence Lab at Yale. Dr. Schank, recognized worldwide as an expert in the field of natural-language processing, received tenure at Yale University at the age of 30. He is the author of seven books, including *The Cognitive Computer*, with Peter Childers (Addison-Wesley, 1984), a discussion of AI issues for the general public, *Dynamic Memory* (Cambridge University Press, 1983), a theoretical discussion of the organization of human memory, *Inside Computer Understanding*, with Christopher Riesbeck (Lawrence Erlbaum Associates, 1981), a discussion of 5 natural-language understanding programs from the Yale AI Lab, *Reading and Understanding* (Lawrence Erlbaum Associates, 1982), a discussion of some of the principles of AI and human cognition as they apply to the educational process, and *Scripts, Plans, Goals and Understanding*, with Robert Abelson (Lawrence Erlbaum Associates, 1977), a landmark work in the natural-language processing literature. He has also authored or coauthored 16 journal articles, 21 articles in books, and 35 technical reports. Dr. Schank is noted for his early work in analyzing the role of semantics in human language cognition. The AI Lab at Yale, under his direction, built the first robust story-understanding programs that successfully processed real-world text. His later work in analyzing complex human cognitive processes, such as the organization of human memory, has established Dr. Schank as one of the leading AI researchers in the world. He is a founder of the Cognitive Science Society, a member of the editorial board of many major AI journals, and past program chairman of IJCAI (International Joint Conference on Artificial Intelligence). Dr. Schank lectures at universities, conferences, and colloquiums throughout the world and has been interviewed extensively by the popular media, including *The McNeil-Lehrer Report, Nova, The Today Show, Business Week, Fortune* magazine, *Psychology Today, The New York Times,* and *The Wall Street Journal.* Dr. Schank holds an M.A. and a Ph.D. in linguistics from the University of Texas at Austin and a B.S. in mathematics from the Carnegie Institute of Technology.

scheduler.   The part of the inference engine that decides when and in what order to apply different pieces of domain knowledge.

scheduling.   Determining the order of activities for execution, usually based on control heuristics. Developing a time sequence of things to be done.

schema.   Any formalism for representing information about a single concept in terms of properties related to it. The properties are usually represented by a slot and can consist of attached procedures for computing properties that are not immediately available. A framelike representation formalism in a knowledge engineering language (e.g., SRL).

SCHOLAR.   The first intelligent tutoring system. It was developed at Bolt, Beranek, and Newman to simulate the behavior of an experienced tutor. It engaged the user in a dialogue concerning the geography of the countries of South America. The dialogue was mixed-initiative, in that students could interrupt the questioning by the system to ask questions of their own. Knowledge of geography was represented in the system as a semantic net containing attributes (e.g., geographical features, cities, climate) and values of the attributes (e.g., Andes Mountains, Santiago, temperate). Each entry in the knowledge base had a fixed importance tag ranging from 0 (most important) to 6 (least important). Each high level topic in the net was allowed a set of nested subtopics. Information could be represented at multiple points in the net, providing extensive cross-referencing. The system also had knowledge of generic terms, such as city and capital, that could be used to explain incorrect answers and answer user-initiated questions. SCHOLAR could make plausible inferences from its semantic net about information that was not specifically stored. The organization of the knowledge base in terms of nested topics permitted both breadth and depth of coverage. The tutor could cover all topics at the highest levels only, or, alternatively, it could trace a single topic through all of its nested subtopics. Tutorial strategy could be manipulated by varying the parameters of time allocation and importance threshold. In its tutorial mode, SCHOLAR adopted what is called a web strategy, covering all important topics on the first pass through the material and then pursuing topics in increasingly more detail on subsequent passes. As an expert system, SCHOLAR incorporated many of the features of a good tutor observed in human tutorial dialogues. They included the abilities to communicate with the student in natural language (though not perfectly), set priorities for depth versus breadth, pose questions, evaluate and keep track of responses, explain incorrect answers, present new information, review old material, and answer questions. The system was unique in incorporating 4 important features of human tutorial interaction:

(1) The selection of topics. In SCHOLAR, the particular topics that were discussed depended upon their overall importance as well as on the user's responses. For example, if the tutor asked about rivers and the student mentioned the Amazon, then the tutor would proceed with questions about the Amazon.
(2) The interweaving of questioning and presentation. SCHOLAR took the user through the domain by asking questions until an error was encountered. SCHOLAR then presented the student with 2 or 3 new pieces of information and continued the questioning along the next path.
(3) Reviewing. SCHOLAR took the student on at least 2 separate passes through the domain. Review was provided by repeating any question that the student missed on the preceding pass, while skipping any questions the student answered correctly.
(4) Error correction. SCHOLAR compared the student's response with the correct response and explained the most important differences. It also pointed out when an answer was nearly correct.

SCI. Strategic Computer Initiative. Program set up under DARPA to develop advanced architecture and software for military applications.

scissoring. The automatic erasing of all portions of a design on the cathode ray tube that lie outside user specified boundaries.

scoptopic vision. The eye-brain response to luminance levels below that required for the full discrimination of colors. Also called twilight or night vision, as contrasted with photopic or daylight vision.

scratch pad. The term applies to memory that is used temporarily by the central processing unit to store intermediate results.

scratch pad memory. A high-speed memory used to temporarily store small amounts of information that can be fetched when needed. A knowledge representation form based on stereotyped situations. When activities fit into stereotypes, a system equipped with a script can predict other likely events by analogy, "assuming" that the script will continue to hold true.

scripts. Framelike structures for representing sequences of events.

scrolling. Translating text strings or graphics vertically.

sculptured surface. A mathematically described surface consisting of a composite of interconnected, bounded, parametric surface patches, each patch representing an image of a unit square in parametric space.

search. The process of trying different actions in a system until a sequence of actions is discovered that will achieve an acceptable solution or a goal state.

search function. A robot system can adjust the position of data points within an existing cycle based on changes in external equipment and workpieces. One use of the search function is in stacking operations, especially when the stacked items are fragile or have irregular thicknesses. The time delay inherent in deceleration from the input signal activation will permit some movement beyond the robot's receipt of the signal; so, if the signal originates through a limit switch that is closed upon contact with the stack, some compliancy must be built into the robot gripper. A fragile workpiece would also require a slow velocity during the search segment.

search space. The implicit graph representing all the possible states of the system may have to be searched to find a solution. In many cases the search space is infinite. The term is also used for non-state-space representations.

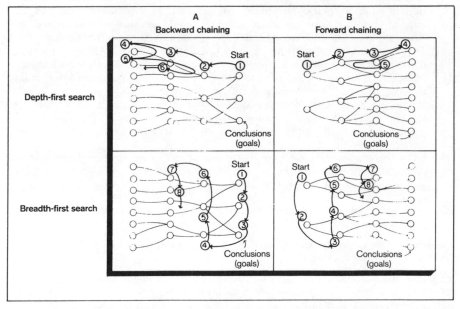

Figure S–2. Search Space—Major categories of search strategies used by inference engines. *Reprinted with the permission of John Wiley and Sons, from "Expert Systems—Artificial Intelligence in Business" by Paul Harmon and David King.*

SECS. Assists chemists in synthesizing complex organic molecules. The chemist presents the structure of a target molecule, and the system generates a plan to create the target molecule from basic building block molecules. The plan is basically a series of chemical reactions applied to functional groups of atoms. The system, with the help of the chemist, systematically works backward from the target toward simpler molecules until a synthesis route is found from the target to the building blocks. SECS is implemented in FORTRAN. It was developed at the University of California, Santa Cruz.

SEEK. A system-building aid that gives advice about rule refinement during the development of a diagnostic-type expert system. It helps refine rules represented in the EXPERT language but expressed in a tabular format. SEEK suggests possible ways to generalize or specialize rules by looking for regularities in the rules' performance on a body of stored cases with known conclusions. The system is interactive; it suggests the type of change (generalization or specialization) and what components to change, but it lets the user decide exactly how to generalize or specialize those components. This refinement method works best when the expert's knowledge is fairly accurate, and small changes in the knowledge base may lead to significant improvement in the performance of the expert system. SEEK is implemented in FORTRAN and was originally designed to operate on a DEC-20 system. It was developed at Rutgers University.

segmentation. The process of breaking up an image into regions (each with uniform attributes) usually corresponding to surfaces of objects or entities in the scene.

segment attribute. A general characteristic of a retained segment, such as visibility, highlighting, detectability, and image transformation.

segmented program. A program that has been divided into parts in such a manner that each segment is self-contained. Interchange of information between segments is by means of data tables in known memory locations. Each segment contains instructions to cause the transfer to the next segment.

segment variable. A variable in a pattern that can match a subpart of a list.

selected component. A selected component is a name consisting of a prefix and of an identifier called the selector. Selected components are used to denote record components, entries, and objects designated by access values; they are also used as expanded names.

selective erase. Deletion of specified portions of a display without affecting other portions.

semantic. Refers to the meaning of an expression. It is often contrasted with syntactic, which refers to the formal pattern of the expression. Computers are good at establishing that the correct syntax is being used; they have a great deal of trouble establishing the semantic content of an expression. For example, look at the sentence "Mary had a little lamb." It is a grammatically correct sentence; its syntax is in order. But its semantic content—its meaning—is very ambiguous. As we alter the context in which the sentence occurs, the meaning will change.

semantic interpretation. Producing an application-dependent scene description from a feature set derived from the image.

semantic network. A type of knowledge representation that formalizes objects and values as nodes and connects the nodes with arcs or links that indicate the relationships between the various nodes. A data structure for representing declarative knowledge. The structure is a graph in which the nodes represent concepts, and the arcs (which may be labeled) represent relationships among concepts. **(See figure p. 234.)**

semantic primitives. Basic conceptual units in which concepts, ideas, or events can be represented.

sensitivity. The responsivity of a system to the dynamically changing demands of its environment. The sensitivity of a production system is influenced by its conflict-resolution strategy.

sensor. A transducer or other device whose input is a physical phenomenon and whose output is a quantitative measure of that physical phenomenon.

sensory control. Control of robot based on sensor readings. Several types can be employed: sensors used in threshold tests to terminate robot activity or branch to other activity; sensors used in a continuous way to guide or direct changes in robot

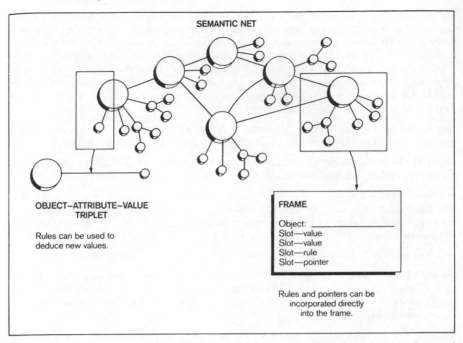

SEMANTIC NET

OBJECT–ATTRIBUTE–VALUE
TRIPLET

Rules can be used to
deduce new values.

FRAME

Object: _____
Slot—value
Slot—value
Slot—rule
Slot—pointer

Rules and pointers can be
incorporated directly
into the frame.

Figure S–3. Semantic Network—Semantic nets, object—attrribute—value triplets and frames. *Reprinted with the permission of John Wiley and Sons, from "Expert Systems—Artificial Intelligence in Business" by Paul Harmon and David King.*

motions; sensors used to monitor robot progress and to check for task completion or unsafe conditions; and sensors used to retrospectively update robot motion plans prior to the next cycle.

sensory-controlled robot.   A robot whose program sequence can be modified as a function of information sensed from its environment. Robot can be servoed or non-servoed.

sensory deprivation.   The total denial of sensation.

sensory hierarchy.   A relationship of sensory processing elements whereby the results of lower level elements are utilized as inputs by higher level elements.

sensory intelligence.   The ability to understand the input signals related to the working area.

SEQ.   Helps molecular biologists perform several types of nucleotide sequence analysis. The system can store, retrieve, and analyze nucleic acid sequences, and it can provide a statistical analysis of structural homologies and symmetries. SEQ's searching routines can be customized by manipulating a set of default parameters; for example, the biologist may vary the weights for penalties and size of gap results during a Needleman-Wunch alignment. SEQ is implemented in LISP. It was developed as part of the MOLGEN project at Stanford University and then further developed by Intellicorp.

sequence robot. A robot whose motion trajectory follows a preset sequence of positional changes.

sequential-access memory. An auxiliary memory device that lacks any addressable data areas. A specific piece of data can be found only by means of a sequential search through the file.

sequential processing. The computer technique of performing actions 1 at a time in sequence.

serial. The handling of data in a sequential fashion to transfer or store data in a digit-by-digit time sequence or to process a sequence of instructions 1 at a time.

serial interface. A method of data transmission that permits transmitting a single bit at a time through a single line. Used where high speed input is not necessary. Requires only 1 wire.

serial operation. A type of information transfer performed by a digital computer in which all bits of a word are handled sequentially.

Serial Processing. See von Neumann Processing.

serial transmission. Moving data in sequence 1 character at a time, as opposed to parallel transmission.

seven-segment display. An electronic display that contains 7 lines or segments spatially arranged in such a manner that the digits 0 through 9 can be represented through the selective lighting of certain segments to form the digit.

servo controlled. Controlled by a signal that is determined by the difference between a present position and a desired position. A feedback control system.

servo-controlled robot. A robot driven by servomechanisms, i.e., motors whose driving signal is a function of the difference between commanded position and/or rate and measured actual position and/or rate. Such a robot is capable of stopping at or moving through a practically unlimited number of points in executing a programmed trajectory.

servomechanism. An automatic control that incorporates feedback controlling the physical position of an element by changing either the values of the coordinates or the values of their time derivatives.

setpoint. The required or ideal value of a controlled variable, usually preset in the computer or system controller by an operator.

S-expression. A symbolic expression. In LISP, a sequence of zero or more atoms or S-expressions enclosed in parentheses.

shades of gray. A division of the gray scale from black to white into a series of discrete luminance shades with a square-root-of-2 difference between successive shades.

shading. An unintentional large-area brightness gradient in a display. Also used to describe graphics software algorithms that establish the appearance of solid-object surfaces.

shake. Vibration of a robot's "arm" and "hand" during or at the end of a movement. Lack of shake is one of the hallmarks of a quality robot.

shield. Defines an opaque viewport or window for menu, title, or message display.

shift. To move information serially right or left in a register of a computer. Information shifted out of a register may be lost, or it may be reentered at the other end of the register.

short relative vector. Vector of a limited length with endpoint identified in terms of x, y, and z distances from the current beam position.

short-term memory. That portion of human memory that is actively used when one thinks about a problem. By analogy to a computer, short-term memory is like random access memory; it contains all the data that are instantly available to the system. The content of human short-term memory is usually conceptualized in terms of chunks. Most cognitive theories hold that human short-term memory can contain and manipulate about 4 chunks at 1 time.

shoulder. The robot manipulator arm linkage joint that is attached to the base.

shrinking. On machine vision, an operation that causes a large block to shrink into a smaller blob.

SIAP. Detects and identifies various types of ocean vessels using digitized acoustic data from hydrophone arrays. Those data take the form of sonogram displays, which are analog histories of the spectrum of received sound energy. The system uses knowledge about the sound signature traits of different ship classes to perform the interpretation. SIAP attempts to identify the vessels and to organize them into higher-level units, such as fleets. It provides real-time analysis and situation updating for continuously arriving data. Knowledge is represented as rules within a blackboard architecture using a hierarchically organized control scheme. HASP (also known as SU/X) was an initial investigation phase and formed the foundation for SIAP. The system is implemented in INTERLISP and was developed through a joint effort by Stanford University and Systems Control Technology.

sign. The symbol or bit that distinguishes positive from negative numbers.

signal processing. Complex analysis of wave forms to extract information.

significant digit. A digit that contributes to the precision of a numeral. The number of significant digits is counted beginning with the digit contributing the most value, called the "most significant digit," and ending with the 1 contributing the least value, called the "least significant digit."

silicon. A dark gray, hard, crystalline solid. Next to oxygen, the second most abundant element in the earth's surface. It is the basic material for most integrated circuits and semiconductor devices.

SIMULA. One of the first object-oriented programming languages. Originally intended for simulation work.

SIMD. Single Instruction, Multiple Data. The easiest form of parallel processing to implement because it resembles von Neumann processing. Information flows in a single (serial) stream and is separated out of this 1 stream, allowing greater control over processing instructions.

simulation. An AI technique that uses a model of intelligent human behavior to determine if the computer will exhibit the same intelligent behavior as a human.

simulator. A program in which a mathematical model represents an external system or process. For example, an engineer can simulate the forces that act on a building during an earthquake to find out how much damage is likely to be incurred.

simultaneous contrast. Changes in the appearance of a color relative to its background or adjacent colors.

situation. A state of data memory corresponding to some set of properties in the domain being modeled by the production system. Rules are sometimes called situation-action pairs.

skeletal knowledge engineering language. A computer language designed for building expert systems and derived by removing all domain-specific knowledge from an existing expert system.

skeleton representation. A representation of a 2-dimensional region by the medial line and the perpendicular distance to the boundary at each point along it.

sketch map. A rough line drawing of a scene.

skill. The efficient and effective application of knowledge to produce solutions in some problem domain.

slew rate. The maximum velocity at which a robot manipulator joint can move; a rate imposed by saturation somewhere in the servo loop controlling that joint. The maximum speed at which the tool tip can move in an inertial Cartesian frame.

slot. An element in a frame representation to be filled with designated information about the particular situation. Slots may correspond to intrinsic features such as name, definition, or creator, or they may represent derived attributes such as value, significance, or analogous objects. An attribute associated with a node in a frame system. The node may stand for an object, a concept, or an event; e.g., a node representing the object employee might have a slot for the attribute name and one for the attribute address. Those slots would then be filled with the employee's actual name and address.

Small-Grain Processing. Utilization of thousands (ultimately millions) of low-power processors to achieve parallel processing. Best utilized for problems that have many facets but require little memory. Artificial intelligence applications fit into this category in that they do not require intensive number crunching.

small knowledge system building tools. Tools that can run on personal computers.

small knowledge systems. In general, small knowledge systems contain under 500 rules. They are designed to help individuals solve difficult analysis and decision-making tasks without aspiring to being the equivalent of any human expert.

SMALLTALK. A programming language for object-oriented representation. Objects are organized hierarchically into classes with each subclass inheriting the instance storage requirements and message protocols of its superclass. Subclasses may also add new information of their own and may override inherited behaviors. The SMALLTALK environment consists of a graphical, highly interactive user interface that makes use of a high-resolution graphics display screen and a mouse or other pointing device. SMALLTALK was developed by the Xerox Palo Alto Research Center throughout the 1970s and early 1980s as a research system and operates on Xerox 1100 workstations. Tektronix offers the latest version of the language, SMALLTALK-80, as a commercial system that operates on the TEK 4404 workstation.

Small-X. RK-Software-developed expert system tool. Small-X is a programming language for developing expert systems on personal computers. Features include manipulation of integer, real string, and list data types; forward- and backward-chaining inference engines; sophisticated string and list pattern matching; list operations similar to those in LISP; ability to execute DOS commands and run DOS programs from within the Small-X interpreter and Small-X rule programs; ability to read and write external DOS files; ability to run scripts giving the capability of running rule programs of unlimited size. Run-time system capability. IBM PC or compatible running MS DOS 2.0 or later.

smart sensor. A sensing device whose output signal is contingent upon mathematical or logical operations and inputs other than from the sensor itself.

Smart Systems Technology. Smart Systems Technology Corporation (SST) provides training in applying AI techniques. Its expertise is divided between 3 business areas:

- Consulting and Expert Systems Implementation
- Software Tools Development,
- Education and Training

smoothing. Fitting together curves and surfaces so that a smooth, continuous geometry results.

soak. A means of uncovering problems in software and hardware by running them under operating conditions while their developers closely supervise them.

SOAR. A general problem-solving architecture for rule-based representation of heuristic search-oriented problem solving. The system provides a means for viewing a problem as a search through a problem space, a set of states representing solutions and a set of operators that transform 1 state into another. The principal characteristics of SOAR include the automatic creation of a hierarchy of subgoals and problem spaces and a parallel rule interpreter. Although SOAR is designed for generality, it has been applied to a knowledge-intensive expert system task (see R1-SOAR). SOAR was originally implemented in XAPS2 (a parallel production system architecture) and was reimplemented in a modified version of OPS5 with extensions for parallel execution. SOAR was developed at Carnegie-Mellon University.

Sobel Operator. A popular convolution operator for detecting edges. Similar to other difference operators such as the Prewitt Operator.

soft copy. Information stored in the computer that can be used to generate a display on the computer screen. This information can also be used to print a hard copy on paper.

software. Programs, languages, procedures, rules, and associated documentation used in the operation of a data processing system.

Software Architecture and Engineering, Inc. Software Architecture and Engineering, Inc., has developed a product called Knowledge Engineering System (KES), a family of software tools for developing and supporting expert systems. The software allows users to develop spread sheets on expert systems without special computer experience and at a relatively low cost.

software engineer. An individual who designs computer software. This individual serves a role similar to a knowledge engineer in the development of a conventional software program.

software engineering. A broadly defined discipline that integrates the many aspects of programming, from writing code to meeting budgets, in order to produce affordable software that works.

software maintenance. The continual improvements and changes required to keep programs up to date and working properly.

solid modeling. A type of 3-dimensional modeling in which the solid characteristics of an object under design are built into the data base so that complex internal structures and external shapes can be realistically represented.

solid-state camera. A television camera with a solid-state integrated circuit to convert light images into electronic signals.

solution path. A successful path through a search space.

SOPHIE. Teaches students how to troubleshoot electrical circuits. The system demonstrates how to locate a circuit fault by allowing the student to select a fault in a simulated circuit and then proceed through the steps necessary to find the fault. At each step the system asks the student to predict the qualitative behavior of the test instrument. (For example, will the measured voltage be too high, too low, or about right?) When the student makes an error, the system shows the measurement and explains it. The system provides a printed history of the diagnosis session for the student's review. The circuit simulator in SOPHIE contains a mechanism for modeling and portraying causal fault propagation, i.e., how the failure of 1 component can causes others to fail. SOPHIE is implemented in INTERLISP and FORTRAN, the latter being used for the circuit simulation package. The system was developed at Bolt, Beranek, and Newman and has evolved through 3 versions.

source. Register, memory location, or I/O device that can be used to supply data for use by an instruction.

source language. A symbolic language comprising statements and formulas used in computer processing. It is translated into object language by an assembler or compiler for execution by a computer.

source program. In a language, a program that is an input to a given translation process.

SPAM. Interprets high resolution airport scenes where the image segmentation has been performed in advance. The system labels individual regions in the image (e..g, runways and hangars) and interprets the collection of those regions as major functional areas of an airport model. SPAM has 3 major system components: (1) an image/map data base (called MAPS) that stores facts about feature existence and location, (2) a set of image processing tools that include an interactive segmentation system and a linear feature extraction and 3-dimensional junction analysis program, and (3) a rule-based inference system that guides scene interpretation by providing the image-processing system with the best next task to perform. Knowledge of spatial constraints comes from a body of literature on airport planning. SPAM is implemented in OPS5. It was developed at Carnegie-Mellon University.

spatial data. Locational data. Usually refer to distribution of a variable or the relationships between variables in a geographic region. Demographic features, marketing distributions, energy resource data, and topographic data are examples of information readily represented spatially, i.e., on a map.

SPE. Distinguishes between various causes of inflammatory conditions in a patient (e.g., cirrhosis of the liver, myeloma—a form of cancer) by interpreting waveforms (serum protein electrophoresis patterns) from a device called a scanning densitometer. The system makes interpretations by applying knowledge about how the instrument readings and patient data relate to disease categories. SPE is a forward-chaining, rule-based system, first implemented in EXPERT and then translated into the assembly language for the Motorola 6809 microprocessor. The system was developed at Rutgers University and has been incorporated into CliniScan, a scanning densitometer marketed by Helena Laboratories.

speaker dependent. A voice recognition system that understands only the utterances of a preprogrammed user.

speaker-dependent recognition. An approach to speech recognition that recognizes the speed of a particular person.

speaker independent. A voice recognition system that is capable of understanding any user at any given time.

speaker-independent recognition. An approach to speech recognition that recognizes the speech of any speaker.

SPEAR. An expert system that analyses computer error logs, used in field engineering.

specialist. An expert in a narrow problem domain, especially 1 of the several expert subsystems that cooperate in a HEARSAY-II architecture.

specificity. A conflict-resolution strategy that prefers instantiations of more specific rules, typically measured in terms of numbers of variables and constants or numbers of left-hand side tests. This principle embodies the heuristic that rules with more detailed antecedents are more discriminating than those with fewer and are likely to produce a better result.

spectral analysis. Interpreting image points in terms of their response to various light frequencies or colors.

spectral color. Color of a single wavelength on the visible portion of the electromagnetic spectrum.

spectrogram. Machine-made graphic representation of sounds in terms of their component frequencies.

spectrum. Refraction or diffraction of white light into spectral hues in the order of their wavelengths, beginning with violet with the shortest wavelength, through blue, green, yellow, orange, and ending with red at the longest wavelength. The spectrum does not include black, white, or colors that are mixtures of wavelengths, such as purple (a mixture of red and violet light).

speech construction. Joining synthetic sound units to form words, phrases, or sentences.

speech-generation system. A system that translates text into audible speech with correct pronunciation.

speech recognition. Recognition by a computer (primarily by pattern matching) of spoken words or sentences.

speech synthesis. Developing spoken speech from text or other representations.

speech understanding. The use of artificial intelligence methods to process and interpret audio signals representing human speech.

speech understanding system. A system that converts the digitized signals of audible speech into printed text.

speed. The maximum speed at which the robot can move. Usually, the maximum tool tip speed in an inertial reference frame.

speed-payload tradeoff. The relationship between corresponding values of maximum speed and payload with which an operation can be accomplished to some criterion of satisfaction and with all other factors remaining the same.

SPERIL-I. Performs structural damage assessment of existing structures that are subjected to earthquakes. Given accelerometer and visual inspection data, the system determines the damage state of the structures. SPERIL-I's expertise consists of knowledge collected from experienced civil engineers and includes relations between such factors as structural damping, stiffness, creep, and buckling. That knowledge is represented as rules accessed through a forward chaining inference procedure. The system uses certainty factors combined with fuzzy logic to calculate the damage class of a structure. SPERIL-I is written in the programming language C. It was developed at Purdue University's school of civil engineering.

SPERIL-II. Evaluates the general safety and damageability of an existing structure. The system analyzes inspection data and instrument records of structural responses during an earthquake, such as acceleration and displacement at certain locations in the structure. It then evaluates relevant safety characteristics (e.g., interstory drift, stiffness, and damping) and the damageability of the structure's elements. The system's knowledge comes from case studies and is represented as rules of predicate logic. SPERIL-II uses several reasoning methods, including both forward and backward chaining. It also uses certainty factors that are combined using the Dempster-Shafer algorithm. The system is implemented in a dialect of PROLOG. SPERIL-II was developed at Purdue University.

SPEX. Assists scientists in planning complex laboratory experiments. The scientist describes the objects to be manipulated (i.e., the physical environment of the experiment and the structure of the experimental objects), and the system assists in developing a skeletal plan for achieving the experimental goal. The system then refines each abstract step in the plan, making them more specific by linking them to techniques and objects stored in the system's knowledge base. Although the system has been tested exclusively in the domain of molecular biology, it contains no built-in molecular biology mechanisms; thus it could be applied to other problem areas. SPEX is implemented in UNITS, a frame-based language for representation. The system was developed at Stanford.

S.1. A knowledge engineering language for rule-based representation that also supports frame-based and procedure-oriented representation methods. Its principal characteristics include a backward-chaining control scheme, built-in certainty handling mechanisms, and control blocks that support procedure-oriented representation and programming methods. The support environment contains an explanation facility and graphics-oriented debugging tools for tracing and breaking during consultations. S.1 is written in INTERLISP and operates on Xerox 1100 and 1108 workstations. It was developed by Teknowledge.

spherical coordinate robot. A robot whose manipulator arm degrees of freedom are defined primarily by spherical coordinates.

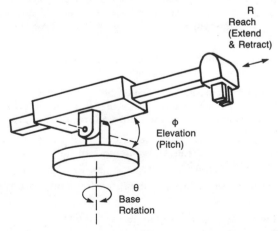

Figure S–4. Spherical Coordinate Robot—Spherical coordinate robot manipulator.

SPILLS. An artificial intelligence program designed for assisting in the location, assessment, and cleanup of hazardous spills and for the training of spills personnel who must deal with those matters.

split data bus. Two data buses, 1 for incoming communications and 1 for outgoing communications. An 8-bit data bus in split data bus system takes 16 lines.

spot size. Diameter of spot produced by beam on cathode ray tube surface, expressed in mils or thousandths of an inch; gives stroke display line width.

spreading activation. In an activation network, spreading activation is a method of changing the pattern of activation or attention in the network so that activation flows outward from active nodes, activating nodes that are connected directly or indirectly. Propagation occurs on 1 or more successive activation cycles, during which activation spreads to the next set of nodes not yet reactivated.

springback. The deflection of a body when external load is removed. Usually refers to deflection of the end effector of a robot manipulator arm.

square wave. A periodic binary waveform that is always either 0 or 1.

SRL. A knowledge engineering language for frame-based representation. Its principal characteristics include automatic and user-definable inheritance relationships and multiple contexts. SRL provides a set of primitives for defining relations and their inheritance semantics, including search specification parameters to modify the inheritance search procedure. Each frame or schema in SRL may have metalevel knowledge associated with it, that is, knowledge about how SRL uses its domain knowledge. Multiple contexts are provided to support revision management of models and for reasoning in alternative worlds. A dialect of SRL called SRL/1.5 is implemented in native worlds. A dialect of SRL called SRL/1.5 is implemented in FRANZ LISP and operates on a DEC VAX running UNIX. It was developed at the Robotics Institute of Carnegie-Mellon University.

SRL+. A knowledge engineering language for frame-based representation. It also supports logic-based, rule-based, and object-oriented representation methods. Its principal characteristics include user-definable inheritance relations, procedural attachment, an agenda mechanism, a discrete simulation language, and a user-definable error handling facility. The support environment includes an embedded data base management system, support for producing 2-dimensional and business graphics, and an interface based on the PLUME natural language parser. SRL+ is implemented in COMMON LISP and FRANZ LISP and operates on Carnegie Group workstations, DEC VAXs under VMS, and Symbolics 3600 workstations. It was developed by the Carnegie Group Inc.

stability. The continuity of behavior of a system. The stability of a production system is influenced by its conflict-resolution strategy.

stack. A specified section of sequential memory locations used as a LIFO (last in, first out) file. The last element entered is the first one available for output. A stack is used to store program data, subroutine return addresses, and processor status.

stack pointer. A register that contains the address of the system read/write memory used as a stack. It is automatically incremented or decremented as instructions perform operations with the stack.

staircasing. The visual effect created when a step function is used to approximate a continuous waveform.

stairstepping. Jagged raster representation of diagonals or curves; corrected by anti-aliasing.

star network. A system in which all stations radiate from a common controller.

star bit. A bit or group of bits that identifies the beginning of a data word.

state. Defines the immediate condition of the interface, excluding transitions, as indicated by the control signals.

state graph. A graph in which the nodes represent the system state and the connecting arcs represent the operators, which can be used to transform the state from which the arcs emanate to the state at which they arrive.

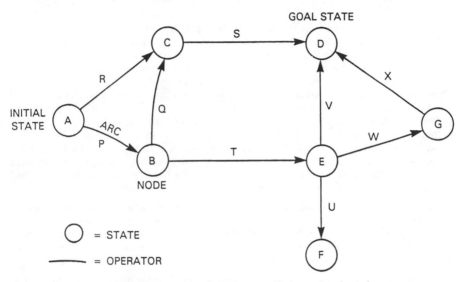

Figure S–5. State Graph—State graph for a simple task.

statement. An instruction in source language. A statement specifies 1 or more actions to be performed during the execution of a program.

state vector An ordered list that fully describes the state of a system. The vector consists of a fixed number of items, each of which is a parameter of the current state.

static RAM. A random access memory that uses a flip-flop for storing a binary data bit. Does not require refresh.

STEAMER. The first intelligent tutoring system that combined the techniques of quantitative simulation and qualitative explanation. It was developed at Bolt, Beranek, and Newman in collaboration with the Navy Personnel Research and Development Center to facilitate training in the operation and maintenance of a ship's steam propulsion plant. Steam plants are complex systems with thousands of components, and the procedures necessary to operate even a small plant fill several volumes. STEAMER reduced that complexity by providing the student with a conceptual framework for understanding the various devices and mechanisms that go into the design of a plant and the actions required to operate them. STEAMER accomplished its goal in several ways. First, it gave students the means to experiment with the system. For example, they could open and shut valves or turn components on and off and observe the ensuing results. Use of the simulated environment had 2 advantages over practice in the real plant. First, it allowed students to observe effects that would ordinarily be invisible. For example, in a real plant, the main engine lube oil system is constructed from opaque material distributed across several spaces. Therefore it is difficult to visualize what is happening. STEAMER made the important parameters of that and other subsystems available for inspection by use of its interactive animated color graphics display. Many different diagrams were used to show overall system operation, isolated subsystems, and individual components. The diagrams contained varying amounts of detail in order to emphasize important features of the systems they depicted. In addition to providing a laboratory for experimentation, STEAMER served as a tutor. The tutor's knowledge was organized in terms of abstract device models. They consisted of a set of parameters and statements of qualitative relationships. For example, for a tank with an input and an output, the device model specified that if the level began to decrease, then either the flow into the tank was decreasing or the flow out was increasing. The device models could be embedded within each other. For example, the underlying device model in the heat exchanger was made up of fragments that appeared in the device models of many other components. The abstract device models therefore enabled students to reason qualitatively about large numbers of components. The tutor also had knowledge, associated with the device models, of abstract procedures and rationales (e.g., before you admit steam into a closed chamber, you should first open its drain. If you do not open the drains, water can mix with the steam and subsequently will be forced through the pipes at very high speeds, causing damage to equipment downstream). The tutor therefore was able to provide the student with feedback and advice about the procedures to follow in solving particular problems.

stepwise refinement. A programming methodology in which a program is first specified at a very high level of abstraction and then, in successive steps, abstractly specified parts of the program are replaced by slightly more concrete instantiations of the abstract description. The term is attributed to Niklaus Wirth and is almost synonymous with top-down programming.

steroscopic approach. Use of triangulation between 2 or more views, obtained from different positions, to determine range or depth.

stereotyped situation. A generic, recurrent situation, such as "eating at a restaurant" or "driving to work."

stipple. Pattern of pixel illumination chosen to produce variations in raster color or intensity.

stop. A mechanical constraint or limit on some robotic motion that can be set to stop the motion at a desired point.

stop bit. A bit or group of bits that identifies the end of a data word and defines the space between data words.

stored program computer. A computer controlled by internally stored instructions that can synthesize, store, and sometimes alter instructions as if they were data and that can then execute those instructions.

streaking. A display condition in which objects appear to extend horizontally beyond their normal boundaries.

string. A series of values.

STRIPS. STRIPS solves a wide range of operational problems, used in the SHAKEY mobile robot designed at Stanford Research Institute.

STROBE. A programming language for object-oriented representation within INTER-LISP. It augments the INTERLISP environment, giving it the ability to support structured objects (much as FLAVORS provides object-oriented support for ZETALISP). Its principal characteristics include multiple resident knowledge bases, support for generalization hierarchies, a flexible property inheritance mechanism, procedural attachment, and indirect procedure invocation. STROBE also allows nonobject nodes in its knowledge base, such as S-expressions, LISP functions, bit maps, and arrays. STROBE is implemented in INTERLISP. It was developed by Schlumberger-Doll Research.

stroke character generator.   Electronic processor that forms alphanumeric characters from line segments.

structured light.   Sheets of light and other projective light configurations used to directly determine shape or range or both from the observed configuration that the projected line, circle, grid, etc., makes as it intersects the object.

structured programming.   The practice of organizing a program into modules that can be designed, prepared, and maintained independently of each other. Makes programs easier to write, check, read, and modify.

structural similarity.   The syntactic commonalities among rules in a production system. Rules that have identical values for attributes, identical condition elements, or sequences of identical condition elements are structurally similar. The Rete match algorithm exploits structural similarity by sharing chains of 1-input nodes in its network for rules with identical sequences of conditions.

structured light.   Illumination that is projected in a particular geometrical pattern.

STUDENT.   An expert system that solves algebra problems.

Student Model.   The component of an ICAI program that analyzes the student's performance to determine why the student is having difficulty.

subgoal.   One of a set of goals that, when achieved, suffices to assure that another goal is also achieved. In backward-chaining systems the unachieved goals are decomposed into simpler subgoals in the hope that the latter can be solved more readily. In goal trees the relationship of a goal to its subgoals is represented as the parent-child relationship.

subgoals.   Goals that must be obtained to achieve the original goal.

subplan.   A plan to solve a portion of the problem.

subproblem.   Another term for subgoal.

subprogram.   A subprogram is either a procedure or a function. A procedure specifies a sequence of actions and is invoked by a procedure call statement. A function specifies a sequence of actions and also returns a value called the result, and so a function call is an expression. A subprogram is written as a subprogram declaration, which specifies its name, formal parameters, and its result; and a subprogram body, which specifies the sequence of actions. The subprogram call specifies the actual parameters that are to be associated with the formal parameters. A subprogram is one of the kinds of program units.

subroutine.   A series of computer instructions to perform a specific task for many other routines. It is distinguishable from a main routine in that it requires as 1 of its parameters a location specifying where to return to the main program after its function has been accomplished.

subtractive color mixture.   Mixture in which light interacts with a colorant (pigments, dyes, filters, etc.), which filters out or subtracts some of the colors from it by absorption. All colors (or the subtractive primaries) added equally together make black. Yellow absorbs blue light, magenta absorbs green light, and cyan absorbs red light. A white color results from all colors being reflected. Complementary pairs combine equally to form neutral grays.

subtype. A subtype of a type characterizes a subset of the values of the type. The subset is determined by a constraint on the type. Each value in the set of values of a subtype belongs to the subtype and satisfies the constraint determining the subtype.

supervisory control. A control scheme whereby a person or computer monitors and intermittently reprograms, sets subgoals, or adjusts control parameters of a lower level automatic controller, while the lower level controller performs the control task continuously in real time.

supervisory-controlled robot. A robot incorporating a hierarchical control scheme, whereby a device having sensors, actuators, and a computer, which is capable of autonomous decision making and control over short periods and restricted conditions, is remotely monitored and intermittently operated directly or reprogrammed by a person.

support environment. Facilities associated with an expert-system-building tool that help the user interact with the expert system. They may include sophisticated debugging aids, friendly editing programs, and advanced graphic devices.

surface knowledge. Knowledge that is acquired from experience and is used to solve practical problems. Surface knowledge usually involves specific facts and theories about a particular domain or task and a large number of rules-of-thumb.

surface of revolution. Surface produced when a line is rotated about an axis.

SWIRL. Aids military strategists by providing interactive simulations of air battles and an environment in which to develop and to debug military strategies and tactics. The system embodies an air penetration simulation of offensive forces attacking a defensive area. Here penetrators enter an airspace with a preplanned route and bombing mission, and the defensive forces must eliminate them before they reach their targets. As SWIRL executes, it displays animated simulations on a color graphics output device. SWIRL's expertise consists of simulation analysis abilities and offensive and defensive battle strategies and tactics. The system uses an object-oriented knowledge representation scheme, where objects, such as offensive penetrators, defensive radars, and SAMs, communicate via the transmission of messages. SWIRL is implemented in ROSS. It was developed at the Rand Corporation.

syllable. A unit of speech consisting of a vowel and the surrounding consonants that are pronounced together.

syllogism. A deductive argument in logic whose conclusion is supported by 2 premises.

symbol. Any character string used to represent a label, mnemonic, or data constant. A string of characters that stands for some real-world concept. A LISP data object used to name a variable, a functional definition, or a LISP object with properties.

symbolic. Relating to the substitution of abstract symbol representations for concrete objects.

symbolic address. Also called floating address. In digital computer programming, a label chosen in a routine to identify a particular word, function, or other information that is independent of the location of the information within the routine.

symbolic atom. A data type that permits only the primitive operations of assignment and testing for equality. Two symbolic atoms are considered to be equal if they have the same print name, which is a sequence of alphabetic and special characters used to specify the identity of the atom.

symbolic code. A code by which programs are expressed in source language; that is, storage locations and machine operations are referred to by symbolic names and addresses that do not depend upon their hardware-determined names and addresses.

symbolic coding. Broadly, any coding system in which symbols other than actual machine operations and addresses are used. In digital computer programming any coding system using symbolic rather than actual computer addresses.

symbolic computing. Involves the processing of information in symbols instead of digits and characters. It allows for memory flexibility when it is adding new properties or values with a minimum of restructuring.

symbolic control. Pertaining to control by communication of discrete alpha-numeric or pictorial symbols that are not physically isomorphic with the variables being controlled, usually by a human operator. A device for effecting such control.

symbolic description. Noniconic scene descriptions, such as graphic representations.

symbolic inference. The process by which lines of reasoning are formed; for example, syllogisms and other common ways of reasoning step by step from premises. In the real world, knowledge and data—premises—are often inexact. Thus, some inference procedures can use degrees of uncertainty in their inference making. In an expert system the inference subsystem works with the knowledge in the knowledge base. The inference subsystem in an expert system is 1 of 3 subsystems necessary for achieving expert performance; the other 2 subsystems are the knowledge base management subsystem and the human interface subsystem.

symbolic language. "Human-oriented" programming language. Any programming language prepared in coding other than the specific machine language that thus must be "translated" by compiling, assembly, etc.

Symbolic Layout Tool. The Symbolic Layout Tool currently under development by the Carnegie Group is a knowledge-based design tool implemented in OPS5, which aids the IC chip designer in developing an optimal chip layout at the symbolic level. The designer will enter a circuit topology through an interactive graphics system. Circuit components, such as transistors and contacts, will be represented symbolically. Using the input topology as a guide, the Symbolic Layout Tool converts the symbolic layout into actual geometric primitives and compacts the layout to obtain a final design. The process of compacting removes unused space from the layout, thus maximizing the chip density and allowing for more components per unit chip area.

symbolic processing. A type of processing that primarily uses symbols rather than numeric representations of data. Artificial intelligence systems are used to simulate intelligent human behavior and reasoning. Since people do not think in numbers but symbolically, symbolic processing capabilities more readily meet the needs of these systems. Although all computers process symbols, the symbols of traditional software programs primarily represent numbers and numeric functions. In expert systems symbols are not restricted to a numeric context but may represent objects, concepts, processes, etc. Expert systems reason by processing these symbols.

symbolic reasoning. Problem solving based on the application of strategies and heuristics to manipulate symbols representing problem concepts.

symbol table. A table of labels and their corresponding numeric values.

symbolic versus numeric programming. A contrast between the 2 primary uses of computers. Data reduction, database management, and word processing are examples of conventional or numerical programming. Knowledge systems depend on symbolic programming to manipulate strings of symbols with logical rather than numerical operators.

symbol-manipulation language. A computer language designed expressly for representing and manipulating complex concepts, e.g., LISP and PROLOG.

SYN. Assists engineers in synthesizing electrical circuits. The engineer inputs partially specified circuit diagrams and constraints on particular circuit components, and the system combines that information with knowledge about constraints inherent in the circuit structure to specify the circuit completely (e.g., fill in the impedance of resistors and voltages of power sources). The system combines constraints by using symbolic algebraic manipulation of the formulas describing the circuit components. The system was developed at M.I.T.

synaesthesia. The combination of stimuli and sensation so that the normal boundaries of perception are broken down.

SYNCHEM. Synthesizes complex organic molecules without requiring user interaction. The system uses knowledge about chemical reactions to create a plan for developing the target molecule from a set of given starting molecules. The system works backward, beginning with the target molecule, and tries to determine which reactions could produce it and what materials (molecules) would be required. That continues until a synthesis route is found from the target to the starting materials. The system is implemented in PL/1. It is the predecessor of SYNCHEM2 and was developed at the State University of New York at Stony Brook.

SYNCHEM2. Synthesizes complex organic molecules without assistance or guidance from a chemist. It tries to discover a plausible sequence of organic synthetic reactions that will turn a set of available starting materials into the desired target molecule. SYNCHEM2 uses knowledge about chemical reactions to generate a plan for creating the target molecule from basic building block molecules. The system attempts to find an optimal synthesis route from the starting materials to the target compound by applying heuristics that limit the search to pathways satisfying the problem constraints. Those constraints may include information about toxic reaction conditions and the quality and yield of the desired product. The system is implemented in PL/1. It is the successor to SYNCHEM and was developed at the State University of New York at Stony Brook.

synchronous. Operation of a switching network by a clock pulse generator. All circuits in the network switch simultaneously, and all actions take place synchronously with the clock.

syntactic. Pertaining to the form or structure of a symbolic expression, as opposed to its meaning or significance.

syntactic analysis. Recognizing images by a "parsing" process as being built up of primitive elements.

syntax. The rules of grammar in any language, including computer language. A set of rules describing the structure of statements allowed in a computer language. To make grammatical sense, commands and routines must be written in conformity to those rules. The structure of a computer command language.

syntax error. An occurrence in the source program of a label, expression, or condition that does not meet the format requirements of the assembler program.

Syntelligence. Syntelligence develops and markets expert system application software for the financial services industry. Initial applications under development are for property/casualty insurance underwriting and commercial bank lending. The company was founded in 1983 and has received private financing of $8 million from venture capital organizations among which are Capital Management, Hambrecht & Quist, Arthur Rock & Co., Asset Management, John Hancock Venture Capital, Arthur D. Little, and others. The founders of the company are individuals with experience in commercial software development, software marketing, and management of high growth companies and include recognized leaders in the field of expert system development. Systems are under development that run on IBM computers, the first of which will be delivered in 1986. One system is an Underwriting Advisor™ System designed to assist property-casualty insurance underwriters in evaluating, structuring, and pricing risks for property, general liability, worker's compensation, and other lines of commercial insurance. For the banking community, a system is under development that acts as a Lending Advisor™ System to assist credit officers in making commercial loan decisions. Both those systems capture and codify the critical experience and judgment of the most senior professionals in certain specialties within financial institutions. Once codified, that expertise is distributed through workstations so the entire field organization can do almost as good a job as the best experts. The Underwriting Advisor and Lending Advisor Systems offer many benefits to insurance companies and banks, including significant decreases in insurance losses and bad loans, increases in the productivity of professionals, and a dramatic shortening of training time. With those systems, financial institutions will have the ability to implement management policy changes and instantly inform all underwriters or credit officers in an organization. The systems ensure consistent judgment and improved management awareness of the detailed profit-and-loss decisions made in large financial institutions. Syntelligence systems are being developed in collaboration with several leading insurance companies and banks in order to guarantee that sufficient working knowledge and user requirements are incorporated in the software.

synthetic speech. Artifically reproduced acoustic signals that are recognizable as human speech.

system. A collection of parts or devices that form and operate as an organized whole through some form of regulated interaction.

SYSTEM D. Helps physicians diagnose the probable cause of dizziness in a patient. The system prompts the physician to enter findings (e.g., current medications) and manifestations (e.g., sensation of impending faint) and produces a diagnosis, including a ranking of competing alternatives. SYSTEM D handles situations where multiple causes of dizziness may be present simultaneously. The knowledge contained in SYSTEM D includes both case-specific information and expertise concerning diagnosis of causes of dizziness. The diagnostic knowledge is distributed across multiple medical specialties corresponding to the numerous potential causes of dizziness. The system uses a frame-based knowledge representation scheme and a sequential generate-and-test inference mechanism. SYSTEM D is implemented in KMS. It was developed at the University of Maryland.

T

table. A collection of data, each item being uniquely identified either by some label or by its relative position. A data structure used to contain sequences of instructions, addresses, or data constants.

table lookup. A procedure for obtaining the function value corresponding to an argument from a table of function values.

tablet. In computer graphics, an input device with a writing surface having direct correspondence between positions on the tablet and addressable points on the display surface of a display device. An input device that digitizes coordinate data designed by stylus position.

tactile. Perceived by the touch or having the sense of touch.

tactile sensor. A transducer that is sensitive to touch. A sensor that makes physical contact with an object in order to sense it; includes touch sensors, tactile arrays, force sensors, and torque sensors. Tactile sensors are usually constructed from micro-switches, strain gauges, or pressure-sensitive conductive elastomers.

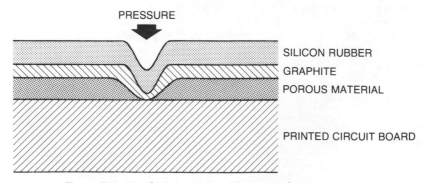

Figure T–1. Tactile Sensor—Tactile corpuscle sensor array.

task. A task unit is 1 of the kinds of program unit. A task type is a type that permits the subsequent declaration of any number of similar tasks of the type. A value of a task type is said to designate a task. Another name for context or, in backward-chaining systems, for a goal.

task domain. In expert systems this is another term for domain.

task-oriented language. Programming language for describing what the effect of robot action should be. To be contrasted with manipulator-oriented languages for describing exactly where a robot's arm and gripper should go and when.

TATR. Helps an air force tactical air targeteer develop a plan for attacking enemy airfields. The system, under the interactive guidance of the targeteer, produces a preferential ordering of enemy airfields, determines the target elements to attack on those airfields, and identifies the weapons systems that would be most effective against those target elements. The system projects the effects of implementing the plan over a period of days so the targeteer can revise the plan if it fails to meet the attack objectives. TATR is a forward chaining, rule-based system implemented in ROSIE. It was developed at the Rand Corporation.

TAXADVISOR. Assists an attorney with tax and estate planning for clients with large estates (greater than $175,000). The system collects client data and infers actions the clients need to take to settle their financial profile, including insurance purchases, retirement actions, transfer of wealth, and modifications to fit and will provisions. TAXADVISOR uses knowledge about estate planning based on attorney's experiences and strategies as well as more generally accepted knowledge from textbooks. The system uses a rule-based knowledge representation scheme controlled by backward chaining. TAXADVISOR is implemented in EMYCIN. It was developed at the University of Illinois, Champaign-Urbana, as a Ph.D. dissertation.

TAXMAN. Assists in the investigation of legal reasoning and legal argumentation using the domain of corporate tax law. The system provides a framework for representing legal concepts and a transformation methodology for recognizing the relationships among those concepts. Transformation from the case under scrutiny to related cases create a basis for analyzing the legal reasoning and argumentation. The knowledge contained in TAXMAN is represented using frames and includes corporate tax cases, tax law, and transformation principles. TAXMAN I originally used a framelike, logical template representational formalism. Later versions employ a prototype-plus-deformation model, describing concepts in terms of their differences from certain prototypical legal concepts. TAXMAN is implemented in AIMDS. It was developed at Rutgers University.

teach. To program a manipulator arm by guiding it through a series of points or in a motion pattern that is recorded for subsequent automatic action by the manipulator.

teach box. A hand-held control with which a robot can be programmed.

tearing. A display condition in which groups of horizontal lines are displayed in an irregular manner.

technology transfer. In the context of expert systems, this is the process by which knowledge engineers turn over an expert system to a user group. Since expert systems need to be continually updated, the knowledge engineers need to train the users to maintain a system before it arrives in the user environment. In effect, some users must learn how to do some knowledge engineering.

TEIRESIAS. A system-building aid that facilitates the interactive transfer of knowledge from a domain expert to a knowledge base. The system interacts with the user in a restricted subset of English to acquire new rules about the problem domain.

TEIRESIAS also assists with knowledge base debugging, using mechanisms for explanation and simple consistency checking. TEIRESIAS is implemented in INTERLISP. It was developed at Stanford University as a research system. (Named for the blind seer Teiresias in the Greek tragedy *Oedipus the King*.) Randall Davis developed the experimental system for helping human experts formulate rules for rule-based expert systems.

TEKNOWLEDGE. Teknowledge is one of the leading public AI/ES firms in the United States. Teknowledge provides both software products and consulting design and training services.

telecommunication. A means of communication in which computers use telephone lines to transmit and receive information.

teleoperator. A device having sensors and actuators for mobility or manipulation or both, remotely controlled by a human operator. A teleoperator allows an operator to extend his or her sensory-motor function to remote or hazardous environments.

template. A prototype iconic model that can be used directly to match image characteristics for object recognition or inspection and speech recognition.

template matching. Correlating an object template with an observed image field—usually performed at the pixel level.

temporal redundancy. The tendency of production systems to make relatively few changes to data memory, and hence to the conflict set, from 1 recognize-act cycle to the next. The Rete match algorithm exploits temporal redundancy to avoid recomputing all matches unnecessarily.

Dr. Harry Tennant. Currently developing a new symbolic processing research group for Texas Instruments. He received his Ph.D. in computer science from the University of Illinois in 1981. His research has centered on natural language understanding, and he invented the concept of menu-based natural language understanding systems. He is the author of *Natural Language Processing: An introduction to an Emerging Technology*, Petrocelli, 1981. He was recently selected as one of the 100 outstanding scientists under age 40 by *Science Digest* magazine.

terminal node. The final leaf node emanating from a branch in a tree or graph representation.

TESS. Project currently under development by the Carnegie Group and based on Common LISP having as its goal the development of a system capable of analyzing extended pieces of natural language text up to several pages in length. The result of the analysis is a classification of the text into user-defined categories plus extraction of critical information appropriate to each of the categories. For instance, if the texts are telexes to an international bank, TESS might classify them into various kinds of transfer and debit categories, based on what kind of currencies, amounts, banks, etc., are involved; the critical information to be extracted would include transaction amounts, accounts involved, etc. Other possible domains of application include news wire analysis for stories on a certain topic or classification of legal case histories. TESS uses the same kind of natural language processing technology as Carnegie Group's PLUME product.

text editor. A program that makes it possible to alter written material that is stored in a computer.

text string. Series of alphanumeric characters.

texture. A local variation in pixel values that repeats in a regular or random way across a portion of an image or object.

theorem. A proposition, or statement, to be proved based on a given set of premises.

theorem proving. A problem-solving approach in which a hypothesized conclusion (theorem) is validated using deductive logic.

three-byte instruction. An instruction that consists of 24 contiguous bits occupying 3 successive memory locations.

thresholding. The process of quantizing pixel brightness to a small number of different levels. A threshold is a level of brightness at which the quantized image brightness changes.

throughput. Transmission and processing from the instant data is put into a computer until it becomes output.

THYROID MODEL. Helps physicians diagnose disorders of the thyroid, such as hypothyroidism. The system accepts an initial set of patient findings (e.g., demographic information, symptoms, laboratory test results) and prompts for the additional data needed for a diagnosis. The system's expertise consists of diagnostic reasoning rules and a taxonomic structure of thyroid function and thyroid pathology. THYROID MODEL is a forward chaining, rule-based system. It explains why hypotheses are confirmed by showing the decision rules applied and the associated certainty factors. THYROID MODEL is implemented in EXPERT. It was developed at Rutgers University.

time sharing. An approach to using computers that allows many people to share the resources of a computer at the same time.

time tag. A number attached to a working memory element that varies monotonically with time and is used for indexing the recency of the element.

TIMM. A number of major United States corporations, government agencies, and educational institutions are using TIMM, General Research Corporation's Expert System Builder. They are developing expert systems in areas as diverse as production and quality control, insurance underwriting, computer performance monitoring, and personnel management. TIMM's users repeatedly identify the system's unusual flexibility, ease-of-use and practicality as key factors in helping them rapidly capture and disseminate expertise within their organizations without specialized hardware, software or personnel resources. Written in FORTRAN, TIMM requires no special-purpose hardware, software or personnel. It is currently implemented on IBM, Amdahl, VAX, Prime, IBM-PC XT and AT and Zenith 100 computers.

- No knowledge engineers or programmers are required.
- Multiple experts can train a single system
- Multiple expert systems can be linked in complex networks
- Expert systems developed with TIMM can be embedded in and called from other software systems and can be exercised using data from external systems and data bases
- TIMM always makes a decision and provides for uncertainty

TIMM's primary functions are BUILD, TRAIN, and EXERCISE. Using the BUILD function, an expert defines the choices that the expert system will make and the factors that influence that choice. Then, after defining the values associated with each factor, the system is TRAINED using rules generated by both the expert and the system. Once the system is trained, it is available for EXERCISE by nonexperts who can now use the system built with TIMM to make decisions in a wide variety of application areas.

TIMM-Tuner. A product of artificial intelligence technology, is General Research Corporation's (GRC) system for helping tune the VMS operating system more rapidly and effectively. TIMM-Tuner was developed using TIMM (The Intelligent Machine Model), an expert system builder that is also a GRC product. Tuning the VMS operating system is a complex and dynamic process. More than 150 parameters must be set by the system manager, and considerable adjustment and modification are required in response to changes in system configuration and loading. Additional terminals, disks, compilers, memory and programs as well as changes in user profiles, all affect VAX performance and require system parameter changes. TIMM-Tuner makes that a much more efficient process. Using TIMM-Tuner involves three steps:

- Data Collection and Reduction
- Use of the Expert System
- Evaluation of Effectiveness

token. An instance of a type. A unique atom that can be used as a label. A symbol used in the Rete match algorithm to represent a working memory element.

token-sharing network. A system by which all stations are attached to a common bus and an access token is passed from station to station.

tolerance. A term used in connection with the generation of a robot nonlinear tool path consisting of discrete points. The tolerance controls the number of these points. In general, the term denotes the allowed variance from a given standard, i.e., the acceptable range of data.

T-1. A system-building aid in the form of a tutorial package that provides an introduction to knowledge engineering for technical professionals and managers. It includes videotape lectures, laboratory exercises, demonstration software systems, and reading materials. The software systems used to demonstrate basic knowledge engineering concepts used a modified version of Teknowledge's M.1 language and operate on the IBM PC running the PC DOS 2.0 operating system. T.1 was developed by Teknowledge.

tool. A shorthand notation for expert-system-building tool. A term used loosely to define something mounted on the end of the robot arm; for example, a hand, a simple gripper, or an arc welding torch.

tool builder. The person who designs and builds the expert-system-building tool.

tools. Tools are computer software packages that simplify the effort involved in building an expert system. Most tools contain an inference engine and various user interface and knowledge acquisition aids and lack a knowledge base. Expert system building tools tend to incorporate restrictions that make them easy to use for certain purposes and hard to impossible to use for other purposes. In acquiring a tool, you must be careful to select a tool that is appropriate for the type of expert system you wish to build. More broadly, a tool is a shell that allows the user to rapidly develop a system that contains specific data. In this sense, an electronic spreadsheet program is a tool. When the user enters financial data, he or she creates a system that will do specific financial projections just as the knowledge engineer uses a tool to create an expert system that will offer advice about a specific type of problem.

tools for knowledge engineering. Programming systems that simplify the work of building expert systems, especially generic task packages, such as EMYCIN, and very high-level languages for heuristic programming, such as ROSIE.

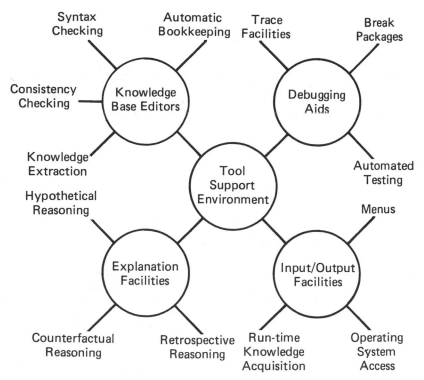

Figure T–2. Tools for Knowledge Engineering—Components of a support environment for expert system tools.

top down. A strategy of proceeding from the complex and abstract to the simple and concrete. As applied to a problem-solving strategy, it refers to the method of starting with a complex problem and decomposing it into subproblems that are easier to solve. Backward-chaining systems often engage in top-down problem solving. As applied to a programming methodology, the term refers to a style in which the abstract program organization is determined in stages of increasing concreteness culminating with the writing of primitive components that can be directly executed. The opposite strategy is bottom up.

top down approach. An approach in which the interpretation stage is guided in its analysis by trial or test descriptions of a scene. Sometimes referred to as "Hypothesize and Test." An approach to problem solving that is goal-directed or expectation-guided based on models or other knowledge. **(See figure p. 256.)**

top-down logic. A problem-solving approach used in production systems, where production rules are employed to find a solution path by chaining backward from the goal.

TOPSI 3.0. Dynamic Master Systems, Inc. expert system shell. Earlier versions of TOPSI provided the essential capability to execute OPS5 on the IBM PC and its clones.

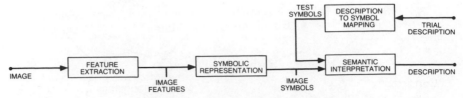

Figure T–3. Top Down Approach—A hierarchical top-down approach for Expert Systems.

Version 3.0 adds windows, pull-down menus, and a built-in "smart" editor to improve the software development environment. Unlike the earlier versions, 3.0 needs 100% PC compatibility (access to video memory) and 512K bytes of memory.

touch sensitive display. Display surface that receives data through physical contact.

toy problem. An artificial problem, such as a game, or an unrealistic adaptation of a complex problem.

TQMSTUNE. Fine-tunes a triple quadrupole mass spectrometer (TQMS) by inter-preting signal data from the TQMS, such as spectral peak ratios, widths, and shapes. The system uses knowledge about how varying the TQM's instrument control settings affects sensitivity and spectral configurations. Knowledge is represented using the frame-based features of KEE, the implementation language for TQMSTUNE. The system was developed by Intellicorp.

trace. Scanning path of the beam in a raster display.

trace interval. The time during which a visible raster line is scanned.

tracing facility. A mechanism in a programming or knowledge engineering language that can display the rules or subroutines executed, including the values of variables used.

tracking. Processing sequences of images in real time to derive a description of the motion of one or more objects in a scene.

trailing edge. The transition of a pulse that occurs last, such as the high-to-low transition of a positive clock pulse.

transducer. A device that converts 1 form of energy into another.

transfer machine. An apparatus or device for grasping a workpiece and moving it automatically through states of a manufacturing process.

transfer vector. A transfer table used to communicate between 2 or more pro-grams. The table is fixed in relationship with the program for which it is the transfer vector. The transfer vector provides communication linkage between that program and any remaining sub-programs.

transformation. Performance of mathematical calculations such as matrix algebra to rotate, scale, or otherwise manipulate a graphic image whose coordinates are stored in the computer.

transient response. The behavior of the output of a system when the input signal undergoes a sudden change.

transistor. A small block of semiconducting material through which a flow of current can be modulated to provide either amplification or switching.

TRANSISTOR SIZING SYSTEM.   Helps circuit designers with the design of integratred circuits by performing part of the refinement from a schematic circuit diagram to an nMOS layout. The system determines the physical size of the transistors in the circuit by considering designer goals of speed and power consumption combined with knowledge of the relationship between speed and power for nMOS circuits. TRAN-SISTOR SIZING SYSTEM analyzes the circuit to determine critical paths with respect to delay and produces a trade-off curve based on simple delay models. The designer then selects a goal point on the curve, and the system resizes the transistors in accordance with that goal. TRANSISTOR SIZING SYSTEM uses a frame-base and object-oriented knowledge representation scheme. It is implemented in LOOPS and embedded in the PALLADIO environment. The system was developed at Stanford University.

transition.   The instance of changing from one state to a second state.

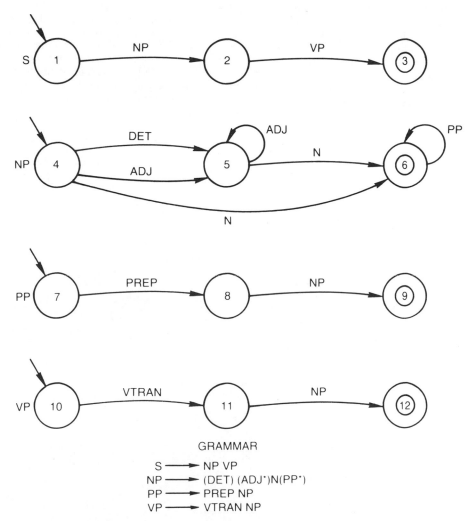

Figure T-4. Transition—Parsing transition network.

TransLisp. Solution Systems developed LISP Interpreter, TransLisp is a Common LISP system for learning LISP on microcomputers. More than 250 Common LISP functions are provided, along with numerous extensions. TransLisp includes comprehensive documents (written for the new LISP programmer), on-line help, a full-screen editor, and other tools, as well as a number of sample LISP programs. MS-DOS 2.0 or above, at least 256K of RAM, 1 disk drive. TransLisp is not copy-protected. IBM PC or compatible required for graphics functions, Microsoft Mouse for mouse functions.

transparent. Describes a computer operation that does not require user intervention.

trap. An unprogrammed conditional jump to a known location, automatically activated by hardware, with the location from which the jump occurred.

tree. A graph in which there is exactly one path between any two distinct nodes.

tree structure. A way of organizing information as a connected graph where each node can branch into other nodes deeper in the structure. A graph in which 1 node, the root, has no predecessor node, and all other nodes have exactly 1 predecessor. For a state-space representation, the tree starts with a root node (representing the initial problem situation). Each of the new states that can be produced from that initial state by application of a single operator is represented by a successor node of the root node. Each successor node branches in a similar way until no further states can be generated or a solution is reached. Operators are represented by the directed arcs from the nodes to their successor nodes.

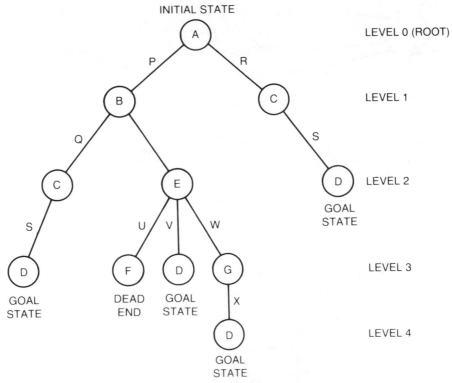

Figure T–5. Tree Structure—Tree representation of paths through the state graph.

truth maintenance. A method of keeping track of beliefs and their justifications, developed during problem solving, so that if contradictions occur, the incorrect beliefs or lines of reasoning and all conclusions resulting from them can be retracted. The task of preserving consistent beliefs in a reasoning system whose beliefs change over time.

truth table. A tabulation that shows the relation of all output logic levels of a digital circuit to all possible combinations of input logic levels in such a way as to characterize the circuit functions completely.

truth value. One of the 2 possible values—true or false—associated with a proposition in logic.

Turing test. Test devised by Alan Turing, a British logician, during the 1950s. In that test an operator sits at a keyboard and queries an unknown source, which can be either man or machine. If the machine provides answers to the operator's queries that are incomprehensible to the operator then that machine qualifies as having humanlike abilities and reasoning.

turnkey system. Pertaining to a computer system in which a supplier is totally responsible for building, installing, and testing the system, including hardware and software.

Tutoring Module. The component of an ICAI program that selects the strategies for presenting tutorial information to a student.

TWIRL. Aids military tacticians by providing interaction simulations of ground combat engagements between 2 opposing military forces and an environment in which to develop and debug military tactics. The system uses a hasty river-crossing simulation as a test for exploring issues in command, control, communications countermeasures, electronic warfare, and electronic combat. Its expertise includes simulation control and offensive and defensive battle tactics. TWIRL uses an object-oriented knowledge representation scheme with rules defining the behaviors of objects. The system includes a color graphics facility that produces an animated display of the simulation. TWIRL is implemented in ROSS. It was developed at the Rand Corporation and reached the stage of a research prototype. (Tactical Warfare In the ROSS Language).

twist. Robot rotational displacement around a reference line; same as roll.

two-byte instruction. An instruction that consists of 16 contiguous bits occupying 2 successive memory locations.

two-input node. Nodes in the Rete match algorithm network that merge the matches for a condition element with the matches for all preceding condition elements.

two-phase clock. A 2-output timing device that provides 2 continuous series of timing pulses from the second series always following a single clock pulse from the first series. Depending on the type of 2-phase clock, the pulses in the first and second series may or may not overlap each other. Usually identified as phase 1 and phase 2.

type. A type characterizes both a set of values and a set of operations applicable to those values. A type definition is a language construct that defines a type. A particular type is either an access type, an array type, a private type, a record type, a scalar type, or a task type.

U

ultrasonic. Refers to sounds that are at higher frequencies than the human ear can hear.

uncertainty. In the context of expert systems, uncertainty refers to a value that cannot be determined during a consultation. Most expert systems can accommodate uncertainty. That is, they allow the user to indicate if he or she does not know the answer. In that case the system either uses its other rules to try to establish the value by other means or relies on default values.

unconditional. Not subject to conditions external to the specific computer instruction.

unconditional jump. A computer instruction that interrupts the normal process of obtaining the instructions in an ordered sequence and specifies the address from which the next instruction must be taken.

unification. The name for the procedure for carrying out instantiations. In unification the attempt is to find substitutions for variables that will make 2 atoms identical.

unit package. A knowledge engineering language for frame-based representation. Its principal characteristic is the organization of frames into a partitioned semantic network. A built-in generalization relationship supports hierarchical structures with several modes of property inheritance. UNIT PACKAGE also provides pattern matchers and an attached procedure mechanism. UNIT PACKAGE is implemented in INTERLISP and operates under the TENEX and TOPS20 operating systems. It was developed at Stanford University.

units. A framelike representation formalism employing slots with values and procedures attached to them.

UNITS. An expert system for knowledge representation system used in building MOLGEN and AGE.

UNIX. A versatile operating system developed at AT&T Bell Laboratories in 1969 by Ken Thompson. May be used on micro, mini and maxicomputers for a wide range of tasks from word processing to local networking. It can handle multiple users and programs simultaneously and can be applied to many different kinds of computers.

upper arm. That portion of a jointed robot arm that is connected to the shoulder.

user interface. The component of an expert system that allows bidirectional communication between the expert system and its user. Most user interfaces utilize natural language processing techniques.

user. A person who uses an expert system, such as an end-user, a domain expert, a knowledge engineer, a tool builder, or a clerical staff member.

use clause. A use clause achieves direct visibility of declarations that appear in the visible parts of named packages.

user-defined. Program units that extend an implementation language. Many programming languages permit the definition of complex program structures that can be referenced as a unit. Languages such as PASCAL, C, and OPS5 allow the programmer to define, name, and access nonprimitive data types. In almost all languages program segments can be defined, named, and invoked with a syntax identical to that used for built-in functions. The nonprimitive units are called user-defined types and user-defined functions.

utility program. Standard programs prepared and generally used to assist in the operation of data-processing systems.

V

valuator device. Graphic input device, such as a control dial, that inputs graduated values within a user-defined range.

value. Comparison of a chromatic color to an achromatic color, situating it along a gray scale from white to black. Other words used synonymously are brightness, brilliance, intensity, lightness, luminosity, and luminance. Sometimes a distinction is made that value is the perceived nonblackness of a color, whereas brightness is the measurable amount of energy in a color. The brightness definition is used when colors must be chosen to remain distinguishable on a black and white monitor, whereas value can be used when fully saturated or pure hues are given equal weight. Lightness, the amount of energy present in a color, refers to nonself-luminous objects, while brightness refers to self-luminous objects. Luminosity is a subjective term for the amount of light emitted, transmitted, or reflected. Luminance is an objective term for the amount of radiant energy per unit area.

variable. A term in a data or processing structure that can assume any value from a set of values. The values become the domain of the variable, which can be determined by syntactic or semantic properties.

variant part. A variant part of a record specifies alternative record components, depending on a discriminant of the record. Each value of the discriminant establishes a particular alternative of the variant part.

VAX LISP. An implementation of Common LISP, a dialect of LISP that runs on the VAX family of computers using the VMS/VMS Operating System. With the exception of complex numbers and the INSPECT function, VAX LISP is a complete, interactive Common LISP environment.

Common LISP is the work of a committee of individuals and institutions involved with Artificial Intelligence research and LISP programming with the goal of standardizing and stabilizing the language and maintaining maximum compatibility with major existing LISP implementations in MacLISP dialects and derivatives. *Common LISP: The Language,* written by Guy Steele and published by Digital Press in 1984, is the standard reference for the language specifications. LISP was invented by Professor John McCarthy at M.I.T. in the late 1950s for applications in Artificial Intelligence and software development where the symbolic processing of relationships between data is as important as numerical computations. Recursion is particularly easy and powerful in LISP.

VAX LISP/VMS. Digital Equipment Corporation programming language VAX LISP/VMS provides integration with the VMS and Micro VMS operating systems. VAX LISP/VMS supports an interpreter, a compiler, a debugger, a pretty printer, and a LISP-sensitive text editor. On the AI VAXstation and the VAXstation II, VAX LISP/VMS supports multiwindowing, graphics, and a mouse. VAX LISP/VMS is compatible with VAX LISP/ULTRIX and allows programs written on 1 operating system to run on the other. Runs on any valid VAX configuration under VMS or MicroVMS Version 4.2 or later operating systems with the exception of VAX-11/725, the MicroVAX I, and VAXstation I. Licensed from $4,800 for the MicroVAX II to $24,000 for the VAX 8800.

VAX LISP/ULTRIX. Digital Equipment Corporation programming language VAX LISP/ULTRIX incudes a lexically scoped, interactive Common LISP interpreter and compiler, a debugger, a pretty printer, an alien structures mechanism, a full array of data types, and a call-out facility that allows the calling of routines written in other languages. VAX LISP/ULTRIX is compatible with VAX LISP/VMX and allows programs written on 1 operating system to run on the other. Runs on any valid VAX configuration under ULTRIX-32 or ULTRIX-32m Version 1.2 or later operating system with the exception of VAX-11/725, the MicroVAX I, and VAXstation I. Licensed from $4,800 for the MicroVAX II to $24,000 for the VAX 8800.

VAX OPS5. Digital Equipment Corporation software tool VAX OPS5 is a VAX/VMS layered product for developing and delivering expert systems. The VAX OPS5 native-mode compiler is written in BLISS-32. Programs written in VAX OPS5 can call and be called by routines written in any language supporting the VAX Calling Standard. Software requirements: VMS or Micro VMS Version 4.0 or later. Application Development Hardware: The VAX OPS5 compiler executed on any valid MicroVAX II or VAX configuration, except the dual-RL01 VAX-11/730. VAX OPS5 applications will run on any valid VAX or MicroVAX II configuration. Licensed from $3,000.

vector attribute. In OPS5 an attribute that can assume a sequence of atomic values.

vector-graphics display. A display system in which the electron beam "paints" the desired image on the display screen; unlike raster-scan displays, vector-graphics displays do not scan horizontal lines to create images.

velocity feedback. In a speed-controlled servomechanism, a signal proportional to the velocity of the output shaft is used as feedback and improves the speed regulation during system disturbances. In a position-control system the velocity feedback is used for damping the system's response.

vertical resolution. In raster-scan graphics systems, the number of visible raster lines displayed by a monitor, or the number of display-memory addresses representing pixels along the vertical axis of the display.

Very Large Scale Integration (VLSI). The process of combining several hundred thousand electronic components on a single chip of semiconductor material.

video display. Television type display, which uses an analog signal. A data-to-analog converter transforms the digital information to a video signal that is used for display.

vidicon. An electron tube device used in a video camera to convert an optical image into an electrical signal through the scanning of an electron beam over a photosensitive window. **(See figure p. 264.)**

view site. Coordinate point on an object through which the view vector passes; used to determine position of object in relation to hypothetical viewer.

view surface. 2-dimensional display surface mapped to represent 3-dimensional normalized device coordinate space.

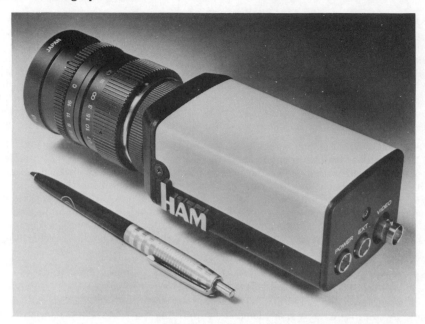

Figure V–1. Vidicon—Ham Vidicon machine vision camera.

viewing operation. An operation that maps positions in world coordinates to positions in normalized device coordinates. It also specifies the portion of the world coordinate space that is to be displayed.

viewpoint. Specified window on display surface that marks limits of a display.

virtual device interface. A proposal to standardize the way computer graphics software relates to graphics devices. The VDI consists of a set of commands for an abstract device; the commands are translated by the driver for each device used.

virtual device metafile. Stored device-independent display that can be moved from 1 system to another.

virtual memory. A programming method that allows the operating system to provide essentially unlimited program address space. In a VAX-11 computer, the virtual memory design means that a VAX-11 program can address more than 4 gigabytes (4 billion bytes) of address space.

virtual storage. Addressable space that appears to the user to be real storage, from which instructions and data are mapped into real storage locations. Virtual-storage size is limited by the addressing scheme of the computing system and by the amount of available auxiliary storage, rather than by the actual number of real storage locations.

visibility. At a given point in a program text, the declaration of an entity with a certain identifier is said to be visible if the entity is an acceptable meaning for an occurrence at that point of the identifier. The declaration is visible by selection at the place of the selector in a selected component or at the place of the name in a named association. Otherwise, the declaration is directly visible, that is, if the identifier alone has that meaning.

vision. The process of understanding the environment based on image data.

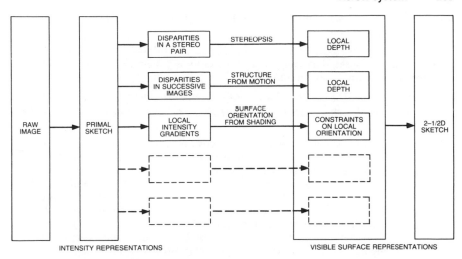

Figure V-2. Vision—Framework for theory of visual information processing.

vision addressability. The number of positions (pixels) in the X axis and in the Y axis that can be displayed on the crt. A measure of picture display quality or resolution.

VISIONS. An expert system that provides artificial vision.

vision system. A device that collects data and forms image that can be interpreted by a robot computer to determine the position of to "see" an object. A system that interprets digitized input about the shape, location, and sometimes the color of

Figure V-3. Vision System—Control Automation, Inc. CAV-1000 Machine Vision System can be used as intelligent sensor input.

objects, in order to determine what the input represents and what the significant features of the object are.

visual acuity.   The capacity of the eyes to resolve small details in the discrimination of form. The threshold separation of 2 small spots is 1 measure of acuity. Nominal value for visual acuity is one minute of arc.

visual recognition.   The ability of a computer system (which includes a camera or sensor, digitizer, and interpretive computer) to "see," describe, and define a particular object.

VM.   Provides diagnostic and therapeutic suggestions about postsurgical patients in an intensive care unit. The system identifies possible alarm conditions, recognizes spurious data, characterizes the patient state, and suggests useful therapies. The system interprets quantitative measurements from an ICU monitoring system, such as heart rate, blood pressure, and data regarding a mechanical ventilator that provides the patient with breathing assistance by applying knowledge about patient history and expectations about the range of monitored measurements. VM is a rule-based system implemented in INTERLISP. It was developed at Stanford University and tested at the Pacific Medical Center and the Stanford University Medical Center.

voice recognition.   The ability of a computer system to recognize, as opposed to understand, a spoken command, and react accordingly. Voice recognition is achieved by the computer sampling specific voice patterns hundreds of times per second in order to digitize the attack, decay, sustain and release of an utterance. This process is extremely memory intensive, which accounts for the limited amount of vocabulary in currently available systems.

volatile memory.   A memory system in a computer or control system which requires a continual source of electric current to maintain the data it is storing intact. Removal of power from a volatile memory system results in the loss of the data being stored.

Von-Neumann Architecture.   The current standard computer architecture that uses sequential processing.

Von Neumann Machine.   Named for mathematician John von Neumann. Von Neumann's architecture forms the basis for present-day computers in that they meet this criteria: contains memory, has input/output devices, has a central processor, and has a unit to perform arithmetic functions and calculations.

Von Neumann Processing.   Serial processing that forms the basis of modern computer architecture. It involves the transmitting of computer data in a single line of information, where all data are processed in the order received.

VS.   Virtual Storage. Storage space that is peripheral or auxiliary memory space addressable by the user. Because of that addressability, VS is perceived to be main storage space.

W

walk through. Programming by giving the robot instructions one by one, with the robot executing each before receiving the next. The speed of the robot is increased when programming is satisfactory. A teach box is usually used.

warm colors. The yellow, orange, red portion of the spectrum.

Donald A. Waterman. A senior computer scientist at The Rand Corporation in Santa Monica. He received his B.S. in electrical engineering from Iowa State University, his M.S. in electrical engineering from the University of California at Berkeley, and his M.S. and Ph.D. in computer science from Stanford University. Dr. Waterman's research and writing has encompassed both artificial intelligence and cognitive psychology. His current research interests focus on applications of expert systems in government and industry. This includes the design and development of tools for building expert systems and the development of legal decision systems.

WASTE. The WASTE project is an investigation into the use of causal models for the purpose of process diagnosis and design. The domain is the treatment of chemical wastewater. During operation of the treatment system, pipes and valves clog, pumps break down and sensors fail. While shallow fault models of the system might tie symptoms of these failures to the fault, they cannot operate robustly. When the problems are unusual or complex the shallow models are of little use. The project also shares models between multiple applications. Models are difficult and expensive to both build and maintain. If a single model can be constructed which can be used for multiple functions, efficiencies have been achieved. Thus, a simulation model constructed to aid in the design of a process which can be used later to also diagnose process faults if of great value. Complex, quantitative simulation models of this kind used for process design and analysis are taken as a starting point for the diagnosis system. These are represented as SRL models and augmented by representations of the physical structure of the process' environment. Diagnosis is then performed based

WAVE. Early experimental robot programming language on which VAL was based in part.

waveform. The shape a signal has when its amplitude is plotted with respect to time.

waveform encoding. Synthesis technique that reproduces speech by reconstructing the original speech waveform.

on these deep models. The complexity of these models, however, requires that a variety of tools be brought into play to make diagnosis possible. First, the simulation models typically consist of real world functions. There are literally an infinite number of different configurations of these models' parameters that could be explored to find one which explains the process' faults. To abstract away some of the information, a qualitative interpretation of the simulation models is taken. The actual real-valued functions are transformed into equations which reflect only how the direction of change of one parameter affects the direction of change of other parameters. Belief knowledge is used to help focus the search for correct diagnosis. Components that have a history of failure are noted as such and faults involving these components are explored more quickly than those which are usually functioning. As the more common faults are exhausted, less and less likely faults are explored.

WAVES. An expert system that advises engineers on the use of seismic data analysis procedures for oil industry.

Webber's Law. The approximate luminance-difference threshold is a constant fraction of the luminance value over a wide range.

weighted value. The numerical value assigned to any single bit as a function of its position in the code world.

WEST. An expert system which teaches students who are enabled to learn by interacting with a coach.

WHY. An intelligent tutoring system that was developed at Bolt, Beranek, & Newman as an outgrowth of the SCHOLAR project. Like SCHOLAR, it engaged students in a tutorial discussion based upon the Socratic method. WHY went beyond previous work in attempting to teach about a complex process, specifically, the causes of rainfall. To acquire an understanding of the factors that influence rainfall, the student had to learn to make predictions, distinguish between necessary and sufficient conditions, and evaluate hypotheses, in addition to mastering new facts. Knowledge of rainfall was represented in terms of scripts. The main script consisted of a set of four major events, in chronological order: absorption of moisture by warm air mass, movement of air mass, cooling, and precipitation. These steps were linked by temporal (e.g., "precedes") or causal (e.g., "enables") relationships. The scripts were hierarchically organized, with subscripts under each of the major events that expanded on those events. For example, a subscript on evaporation expanded on the first major event, the absorption of moisture. Each script had a set of roles associated with it (e.g., AIR MASS, BODY OF WATER) that could be instantiated for different cases (e.g., Oregon, Ireland). The WHY tutor conversed with the student in simple English and asked questions designed to uncover errors and omissions in the student's understanding. The dialogue was conducted by applying production rules derived from observation of human tutors. These rules, which took the form of if-then statements, specified when the tutor was to ask for predictions (e.g., Does the Amazon jungle have heavy rainfall? . . . How does that affect the rainfall? . . . What happens after that?), suggest factors (e.g., Do you think the Andes mountain range has any effect on the rainfall in the Amazon jungle?), ask questions about necessary and sufficient factors (e.g., Do you think that any place with mountains has heavy rainfall?), and present counterexamples (Southern California has mountains. Why doesn't Southern California have heavy rainfall?). These rules enabled the tutor to apply techniques, such as the selection of judicious cases and the presentation of counterexamples, that are hallmarks of Socratic teaching.

WHEEZE. Diagnoses the presence and severity of lung disease by interpreting measurements of pulmonary function tests. The system bases its diagnosis on clinical laboratory test results (e.g., age, history of smoking). WHEEZE's expertise consists of a translation of the rules used by PUFF into a frame-based representation. The frames contain two types of certainty factors, one indicating the likelihood of an assertion when its manifestations are believed, and the other indicating the degree to which the assertion is believed to be true during a particular consultation. WHEEZE's control mechanism provides a kind of backward and forward chaining, implemented by using an agenda, with each suggested assertion placed on the agenda according to a specified priority. WHEEZE is implemented on RLL. It was developed at Stanford University.

WHISPER. An expert system which reasons by means of analogical representation.

WHY. An expert system that teaches students about rainfall, an extension of SCHOLAR.

WILLARD. Helps meteorologists forecast the likelihood of severe thunderstorms occurring in the central United States. The system queries a meteorologist about pertinent weather conditions for the forecast area and then produces a complete forecast with supporting justifications. The user may specify a particular geographical area for WILLARD to consider. The system characterizes the certainty of severe thunderstorm occurrence as "none," "approaching," "slight," "moderate," or "high," and each is given a numerical probability range. WILLARD's expertise is represented as rules generated automatically from examples of expert forecasting. WILLARD was implemented using RULEMASTER, an inductive rule generator. It was developed at Radian Corporation.

Winchester disk. A hermetically sealed electromechanical device for file storage that employs a rotating magnetic disk.

window. An application software design concept that allows several programs to be run and displayed on the screen simultaneously, and supports integration of data between application programs. Use of multiple windows in a development environment permits system developers to monitor multiple processes or system states without the need to exit from one module to observe another.

windowing. A means of dividing the computer screen into several areas so that a variety of information can be displayed simultaneously.

Patrick H. Winston. Director of M.I.T.'s Artificial Intelligence Laboratory. He is a professor of electrical engineering and computer science. Professor Winston joined the M.I.T. faculty in 1970 and became director of the laboratory in 1973. He received the B.S. degree, the M.S., and the Ph.D. all from M.I.T. Professor Winston's research interests concentrate in artificial intelligence and allied fields. He is particularly involved in the study of learning by analogy, common-sense problem solving, expert systems, and robotics. In addition to the many books he has authored, he is an editor of *Artificial Intelligence* and coeditor of the M.I.T. Press Series on artificial intelligence. Professor Winston is also a member of the board of directors of Artificial Intelligence Corporation, a company specializing in English access to database packages.

Wireframe Model. A three-dimensional (3-D) computerized model, similar to a wireframe, in which an object is determined in terms of edges and vertices.

A. William Woods. Chief scientist at Applied Expert Systems and an internationally recognized leader in the research of artificial intelligence, natural communication between man and machine, and understanding human intellectual processes. Dr. Woods is noted for development of the augmented transition network model of grammar and for his work in parsing and semantic interpretation of natural English questions. As chief scientist, he is responsible for development of APEX's ongoing technologies. Before joining APEX, he was a principal scientist at Bolt, Beranek and Newman Inc., where he was manager of the artificial intelligence department. While at BBN he developed, on behalf of NASA, the Lunar Sciences Natural Language Information System, which enabled geologists to extract information using natural English from data collected in NASA's Lunar Project. In addition to being chief scientist at APEX, Dr. Woods holds an appointment as Gordon McKay Professor of the Practice of Computer Science at Harvard University, where he teaches courses in knowledge representation and language understanding.

word. The maximum number of binary digits that can be stored in a single addressable memory location of a given computer system.

word length. The number of bits in a word.

work cell. A manufacturing unit consisting of 1 or more workstations.

work coordinates. The coordinate system referenced to the work piece, jig, or fixture.

working envelope. The set of points representing the maximum extent or reach of the robot hand or working tool in all directions. The work envelope can be reduced or restricted by limiting devices which establish limits that will not be exceeded in the event of any foreseeable failure of the robot or its controls. The maximum distance which the robot can travel after the limit device is actuated will be considered the basis for defining the restricted (or reduced) work envelope.

working memory. In expert systems, working memory consists of all of the attribute-value relationships that are established while the consultation is in progress. Since the system is constantly checking rules and seeking values, all values that are established must be kept immediately available until all the rules have been examined. The dynamic portion of a production system's memory. Working memory contains the database of the system, which changes as rules are executed. Another name for data memory (e.g., in OPS5).

working memory element. The unit of working memory. In OPS5, working memory elements are attribute-value elements.

working range. All positions within the working envelope. The range of any variable within which the system normally operates.

working space or volume. The physical space bounded by the working envelope in physical space. **(See figure p. 271.)**

workstation. Configuration of computer equipment designed to be used by one person at a time. A workstation may have a terminal connected to a larger computer, or may be a "stand alone" with local processing capability. It generally consists of an input device, a display device, memory, and an output device such as a printer or plotter.

world coordinate system. A device-independent three-dimensional Cartesian coordinate system in which 2- and 3-dimensional objects are described to a viewing system.

world knowledge. Knowledge about the world (or domain of interest).

world model. A representation of the current situation. **(See figure p. 271.)**

wraparound. Effect of positioning a display item so it extends beyond the device space boundary and a portion appears on the opposite side of the display surface.

WRIGHT. An intelligent design completion system is a knowledge-based CAD system that provides a design environment and assists the designer in analyzing and synthesizing designs. For example, the designer may generate a partial design and

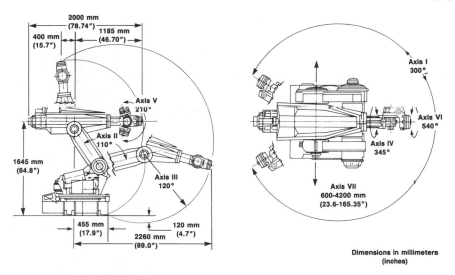

Figure W-1. Working Space or Volume—Working space or volume for General Electric Robot.

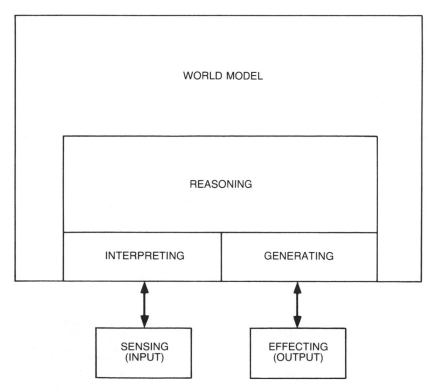

Figure W-2. World Model—Basic diagram showing elements of world model.

have the system carry out a diagnostic evaluation or complete the design. Such a system would be composed of 2 major components: a knowledge base and a drafting system. The WRIGHT system is an interactive CAD system, which the designer can use in representing, analyzing, and generating kitchen designs. The goals in building such a system are to understand the architecture and components of a design-completion system and to understand the types of knowledge required for analyzing and synthesizing designs. The application domain chosen for the WRIGHT system is kitchen design. It was chosen because kitchen design has been extensively researched and knowledge has been generated. However, it is still an ill-structured task, and in this way it is representative of design tasks. WRIGHT has 2 components. WRIGHT-DRAFT is a drafting system. It has its own user interface for graphical input, a name with one or more drawing primitives, based on semantics. The primitives are: point, line and arc. WRIGHT-SRL is the knowledge base. The concepts of design such as states, acts, design levels, design units, constraints, and geometric relations are represented by schemata using SRL. Design analysis and completion is organized into levels. Design completion is carried out using constraint directed search, where the solution at a higher level guides search at the next level. The designer can intervene at any level to fix certain elements in the design. Design rules for generating and testing are represented in PSRL.

wrist. A set of rotary joints between the robot arm and hand that allows the hand to be oriented to the workpiece.

write. Process of inserting data into memory. This is a destructive process, in that any data already in a particular memory location is destroyed when new data is written into that location.

WUMPUS. An expert system which teaches logic, probability theory, decision theory and geometry.

X

XCON. Configures VAX 11/780 computer systems. From a customer's order it decides what components must be added to produce a complete operational system and determines the spatial relationships among all of the components. XYCON outputs a set of diagrams indicating these spatial relationships to technicians who then assemble the VAX system. XYCON handles the configuration task by applying knowledge of the constraints on component relationships to standard procedures for configuring computers. The system is in noninteractive, is rule-based, and uses a forward chaining control scheme. XCON is implemented in OPS5 and was developed through a collaboration between researchers at Carnegie-Mellon University and Digital Equipment Corporation (DEC) in Hudson, Massachusetts. This commercial expert system configures VAX computers on a daily basis for DEC and is the largest and most mature rule-based expert system in operation. **(See figure p. 274.)**

XENIX. A spinoff of UNIX created by Microsoft in 1980. Xenix is designed for 16-bit computers and is an operating system heavily favored by IBM.

XSEL. Helps a salesperson select components for a VAX 11/750 and VAX 11/780 computer system and assists in designing a floor layout for them. XSEL selects a central processing unit, primary memory, software, and peripheral devices, such as terminals and disk drives, and then passes it to XCON to be expanded and configured. XSEL contains domain knowledge about the relations between components and the various applications a customer might have and knowledge about how to lead a user through a selection process. The system is interactive, is rule-based, and uses a forward chaining control scheme. XSEL is implemented in OPS5. To prepare an order, XSEL must determine what components are needed and the exact subtype and version of the component that should be included in the order. It obtains those data by prompting the customer for information on how the system will be used. In some cases it must also perform calculations based on the information to determine usage statistics. In addition to preparing the customer order, XSEL has an extensive facility for explaining its reasoning to the user. Thus the user can find out why XSEL chose a particular component. By helping the user understand how the order was prepared, the system increases the likelihood of acceptance of its results. **(See figure p. 275.)**

XSYS-II. California Intelligence's expert system shell XSYS is a LISP-based expert system that displays advanced knowledge representation and manipulation features:

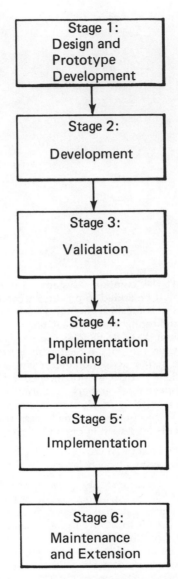

Figure X–1. XCON—Overview of the development of DEC's XCON (R1). *Reprinted with the permission of John Wiley and Sons, from "Expert Systems—Artificial Intelligence in Business" by Paul Harmon and David King.*

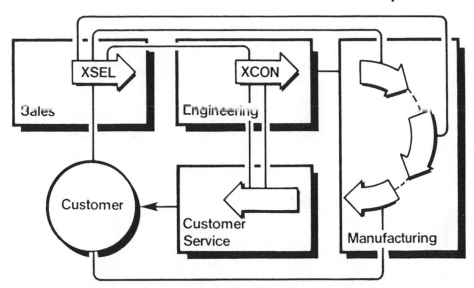

Figure X-2. XSEL—Knowledge Network. *Reprinted with the permission of Digital Equipment Corporation.*

bidirectional search strategy; knowledge base hierarchies; variables in IF and THEN parts; operators in IF and THEN parts ("methods") system- or user-defined; export/ import of session results; explanation facilities (internal or external files); external file and table search capabilities. The XSYS includes a 70-page users' manual with examples. Requires IBM PC/XT/AT with 640K IQLISP.

XYZ space. A three-dimensional coordinate system based on the CIE chromaticity diagram which plots x, y, and z as the tristimulus values of a color.

Y

Y signal. The component of a color-encoded display signal representing luminance information. The signal produces a black-and-white image on a standard monochrome monitor.

yaw. The angular displacement of a moving body around an axis that is perpendicular to the line of motion and the top side of the body. In robotics the rotation, especially of the "hand," in a horizontal place when the "arm" is extended horizontally.

YES/MVS. Helps computer operators monitor and control the MVS (multiple virtual storage) operating system, the most widely used operating system in large mainframe IBM computers. YES/MVS addresses 6 major categories of tasks: maintaining adequate JES (job entry system) queue space, handling network communications between computers on the same site, scheduling large batch jobs off prime shift, responding to hardware errors, monitoring subsoftware systems, and monitoring overall system performance. YES/MVS runs in real time, directly interpreting MVS messages and sending either commands to the operating system or recommendations to the console operator. YES/MVS is a rule-based expert system with a forward-chaining control scheme. It is implemented in an extended version of OPS5 by an expert systems group at the IBM T.J. Watson Research Center in Yorktown Heights, New York.

Z

zero-page. The lowest 256 address locations in memory. Where the highest 8 bits of address are always 0s and the lower 8 bits identify any location from 0 to 255. Therefore, only a single byte is needed to address a location in zero-page.

zero-page addressing. The second byte of the instruction contains a zero-page address.

zero-page indexed addressing. The second byte of the instruction is added to the index register to form a zero-page effective address. The carry is dropped.

zero point. The origin of a coordinate system.

zero suppression. The elimination of nonsignificant zeros in a numeral.

ZETALISP. A programming language for procedure-oriented representation. This dialect of LISP is based on M.I.T.'s MACLISP, but it is substantially extended and improved. It provides all of the standard LISP features, a large number of extensions (e.g., FLAVORS), and a sophisticated support environment. The support environment includes a high-resolution, bit-map graphics display, a window system, an integrated program/text editor, and a display-oriented debugger. ZETALISP operates on Symbolics' LM-2 and 3600 computer systems and on LMI's Lambda and Lambda/Plus machines. It was developed at M.I.T.

zoom. In computer graphics, continuously scaling the display elements of display image to more clearly perceive and manipulate details not readily perceived in the previous view.

Points of Contact

Artificial Intelligence/Expert Systems

Abacus Programming Corporation
14545 Victory Boulevard, #300
Van Nuys, CA 91411
(818) 785-8000
Dr. Ron Citrenbaum, Chairman

Adage
531 Pylon Drive
Raleigh, NC 27606
(919) 833-5401
Herman Towles, Section Manager

Advanced Computer Tutoring
701 Amberson Ave.
Pittsburgh, PA 15232
(412) 578-2815

Advanced Decision Systems
201 San Antonio Circle, #286
Mountain View, CA 94040
(415) 941-3912
Clifford Reid, Program Development
  Manager

Aegis Medical Systems
3000 Lincoln Drive East
Marlton, NJ 08053
(609) 983-0110

AI Decision Systems
8624 Via del Sereno
Scottsdale, AZ 85258
(602) 991-0599
Ralph Lunt, President

AI Mentor
1000 Elwell Court, Suite 205
Palo Alto, CA 94301
(415) 969-4500

Aion Corporation
101 University Avenue, 4th Floor
Palo Alto, CA 94301
(415) 328-9595
Joel Voelz, Director, Marketing

Airus
11830 SW Kerr Pkwy
Lake Oswego, OR 97034
(503) 246-1105

Aldo Ventures
169 Waverly St.
Palo Alto, CA 94301
(415) 322-2233

Alloy Comp. Products
100 Pennsylvania Ave.
Framingham, MA 01701
(617) 875-6100

American Business Consultants
  Corporation
6250 Westpark
Houston, TX 77057
(713) 784-9686
John Lee Hudson, Chairman

Analog Devices
Route One Industrial Park
Norwood, MA 02090
(617) 329-4700
Marcel Singleton, Sales Engineer

Anorad
110 Oser Avenue
Hauppauge, NY 11788
(516) 231-1990/1995
Tom Derenzo, Director, Marketing

Apollo Computer Inc.
330 Billerica Road, Dept. A1
Chelmsford, MA 01824
(617) 256-6600
Paul Armstrong, Vice President

Applicon (Schlumberger)
32 Second Ave.
Concord, MA 01803
(617) 272-7070

Applied Expert Systems Inc. (APEX)
5 Cambridge Center
Cambridge, MA 02142
(617) 492-7322
Fred Luconi, President

Applied Intelligent Systems
110 Parkland Plaza
Ann Arbor, MI 48103
(313) 995-2035
Kayla Tomsic, Sales Administrator

Arity
358 Baker Avenue
Concord, MA 01742
(617) 371-2422
Carolyn Bender, Sales Representative

Artelligence Inc.
14902 Preston Road, Suite 212-252
Dallas, TX 75240
(214) 437-0361
Paul Robertson, Chairman

Arthur D. Little
25 Acorn Park
Cambridge, MA 02140
(617) 864-5770
Karl Wiig, Director, AI Programs

Artificial Intelligence Corporation
200 Fifth Avenue
Waltham, MA 02254
(617) 890-8400
Dr. Larry Harris, President

Artificial Intelligence Inc.
P.O. Box 81045
Seattle, WA 98108
(206) 271-8633
James Svoboda, Director, Marketing

Artificial Intelligence Research Group
921 N. La Jolla Avenue
Los Angeles, CA 90046
(213) 656-7368
Steve Grumette, Proprietor

AT&T/Bell Laboratories
Whippany Road
Whippany, NJ 07981
(201) 386-6929
Gregory Vesonder, Supervisor

Audo Pilot
516 Walt Whitman Rd.
Huntington, NY 11746
(516) 351-4862
Phil McLaughlin, Director of Marketing

Autech
7060 Huntley Road
Columbus, OH 43229
(614) 888-9924
Stan Grimm

Automated Language Processing
   Systems (ALPS)
190 West 800 North
Provo, UT 84604
(801) 375-0090
Fred Zirkel, Executive Vice President

Automated Reasoning Corporation
290 W. 12th Street, Suite 1-D
New York, NY 10014
(212) 206-6331
Richard Cantone, Project Director

Automation Engineering
3621 Marine Drive
Toledo, OH 43609
(419) 385-2521
John Kolpenstein, Vice President,
   Marketing

Automation Intelligence Inc.
1200 West Colonial Drive
Orlando, FL 32804
(305) 843-7030
Theodore Fluchradt, President

Battelle Columbus Laboratories
505 King Avenue
Columbus, OH 43201
(614) 424-7728
Dr. James R. Brink, Manager, AI Program

BDM Corporation
7915 Jones Branch Drive
McLean, VA 22102
(703) 821-5000
Dr. Michael D. Kelly, Senior Prin.
   Staff Member

Ben Franklin Industries
Route One
Casey Creek, KY 42723
(606) 787-5002
Dr. Jay Lubkin, President

Boeing Computer Services
P.O. Box 24346/MS 7A-03
Seattle, WA 98124
(206) 763-5268
George Roberts, GM, Advanced
  Technology

Bolt Beranek and Newman Inc.
10 Moulton Street
Cambridge, MA 02238
(617) 491-1850
Robert Harvey, Vice President,
  Development

Brattle Research Corporation
55 Wheeler Street
Cambridge, MA 02138
(617) 492-1982
Ken Jeffers, Director, Marketing

Breit International
1790 30th St., Suite 320
Boulder, CO 80301
(303) 444-3535

Brodie Associates
636 Beacon Street—Suite 203
Boston, MA 02215
(617) 720-2133
William Brodie, President

Businessoft
703 Giddings Avenue
Annapolis, MD 21401
(301) 263-1962

California Intelligence
912 Powell Street, Suite 8
San Francisco, CA 94108
(415) 391-4846
Ray Weinstock, President

Carnegie Group, Inc.
Commerce Court at Station Square
Pittsburgh, PA 15219
(412) 642-6900
Michael Chambers, Vice President

Centigram
1883 Ringwood Avenue
San Jose, CA 95131
(408) 291-8200
Harry Schwedock, Vice President,
  Marketing

Cericor
716 East 4500 South
Salt Lake City, Utah 84107
(801) 357-1700
Karen Gailey, Marketing Assistant

Clairvoyant Systems
1921 Rock Street, Suite 17
Mountain View, CA 94043
(415) 364-6380
Pierre Bierre, President

Clarity Software
P.O. Box 839
Chesterland, OH 44026
(216) 729-1132

Cognitive Systems Inc.
234 Church Street
New Haven, CT 06510
(203) 773-0726
Kenneth Wirt, Vice President, Marketing

Colorado Video Inc.
Post Office Box 928
Boulder, CO 80306
(303) 444-3972
Cynthia Keen, Marketing Manager

Composition Systems, Inc.
570 Taxter Road
Elmsford, NY 10523
(914) 592-3600
Marvin Berlin, Executive Vice President

Computer*Thought Corporation
1721 W. Plano Parkway, Suite 125
Plano, TX 75075
(214) 424-3511
Mark Miller, Chairman, CEO

COMTAL/3M
505 W. Woodbury Road
Altadena, CA 91001
(818) 441-1900
Patty Svetich, Administration

Control Automation, Inc.
Post Office Box 2304
Princeton, NJ 08540
(609) 799-6026
Scott Jones, Vice President, Marketing

Control Data Corporation
Post Office Box 0
Minneapolis, MN 55440
(612) 853-6137
Joanne Henry, Marketing Manager

Convex Computer Corporation
1819 Firman Drive
Richardson, TX 75081
(214) 669-3700
Denis Burrows, Marketing

Covox, Inc.
675-D Conger Street
Eugene, OR 97402
(503) 342-1271
Brad Stewart, Vice President

Cray Research
608 Second Avenue
S. Minneapolis, MN 55402
(612) 333-5889
John Rollwagen, Chairman

Customized Research
16 Plymouth Drive
Freehold, NJ 07728
(201) 462-8418

Data General Corporation
77 Technology Way
Westboro, MA 01580
(617) 366-8911
Chuck Piper, Project Manager

Decision Support Software
1300 Vincent Plain
McLean, VA 22101
(703) 442-7900
Mary Ann Selly, President

Decisionware
4030 Gulf of Mexico Drive
Longboat Key, FL 33548
(813) 383-9557
Robert W. DePree, President

Denelcor
17000 E. Ohio Place
Aurora, OH 80017
(303) 337-7900 No longer in service
David Miller, CEO

Diffracto Limited
6360 Hawthorne Drive
Windsor, Ontario, Canada CN N8T 1J9
(519) 945-6373
Walt Pastorius, Vice President, Marketing

Digital Equipment Corporation
145 Main Street
Maynard, MA 01754
(617) 897-5111
Neil Pundit, Senior Engineer Manager

Dragon Systems Inc.
55 Chapel Street
Newton, MA 02158
(617) 527-0372
Janet Baker, President

Dynamic Master Systems
P.O. Box 566456
Atlanta, GA 30356
(404) 565-0771
David Smith, President

Eikonix
23 Crosby Drive
Bedford, MA 01730
(617) 275-5070
Robert Patnaude, Sales Manager

EIS (Experience in Software)
239 Shattuck Avenue, Suite 401
Berkeley, CA 94704
(415) 644-0694

Electro-Optical Industries
Post Office Box 3770
Santa Barbara, CA 93130
(805) 964-6701
Lloyd Sims, Sales Liaison

Elxsi
2334 Lundy Place
San Jose, CA 95131
(408) 942-1111
Jacob F. Vigil, President

Emerson and Stern Associates
10150 Sorrento Valley Road, Suite 210
San Diego, CA 92121
(619) 481-3242
Jan Zimmerman, Marketing Director

Enhansys, Inc.
20111 Stevens Creek Boulevard
Cupertino, CA 95014
(408) 255-2920
Bert Moyer, President

EOIS (Electro-Optical Information
   Systems)
710 Wilshire Boulevard, Suite 501
Santa Monica, CA 90401
(213) 451-8566
Nancy Meyers, Operations Manager

ESL, Inc.
495 Java Drive
Sunnyvale, CA 94088-3510
(408) 738-2888
George Hodder, Marketing Director

ETA Systems
1450 Energy Park Drive
St. Paul, MN 55108
(612) 642-3400
Bob Robertson, Vice President,
Marketing

Everett/Charles Automation Systems, Inc.
2887 N. Towne Avenue
Pomona, CA 91767
(714) 621-9511
Jay Malloy, Marketing Manager

Expert Knowledge Systems
6313 Old Chesterbrook Road
McLean, VA 22101
(703) 734-6966
Dr. James Naughton

Expert Systems International
1150 First Avenue
King of Prussia, PA 19406
(215) 337-2300
Angelos Kolokouris, President

Expert Systems, Inc.
868 West End Avenue, Suite 3A
New York, NY 10025
(212) 662-7206
Jeffrey Millman, President

Expert Technologies, Inc.
2600 Liberty Avenue
Pittsburgh, PA 15230
(412) 355-0900
Kelly Hickel, President

ExperTelligence, Inc.
559 San Ysidro Road
Santa Barbara, CA 93108
(805) 969-7874
Denison Bollay, President

Exsys, Inc.
P.O. Box 75158, Con. Station 14
Alburquerque, NM 87194
(505) 836-6676
Dustin Huntington, President

Foster-Miller
350 Second Avenue
Waltham, MA 02254
(617) 890-3200
Lee Bystock, Marketing Specialist

Foundation Technologies
266 Western Avenue
Cambridge, MA 02139
(617) 868-8215
Tod Loofbourow, Partner & Erik
Vrynjolfsson, Partner

Fountain Hills Software, Inc.
6900 E. Camelback Road, Suite 1000
Scottsdale, AZ 85251
(602) 945-0261
Loretta Mahoney, Vice President

Franz Inc.
2920 Domingo Avenue
Berkeley, CA 94703
(415) 540-1224
Fritz Kunze, President

Frey Associates, Inc.
Chestnut Hill Road
Amherst, NH 03031
(603) 472-2800
Sandra Newcombe, Vice President

General Electric (Robotics & Vision
Systems)
P.O. Box 17500
Orlando, FL 32860-7500
(305) 889-1200
Ted Chace, Manager Marketing Comm.

General Intelligence Corporation
3008 Hillegass
Berkeley, CA 94705
(415) 548-8873

General Optimization
2251 North Geneva Terrace
Chicago, IL 60614
(312) 248-0465

General Research Corporation
7655 Old Springhouse Road
McLean, VA 22102
(703) 893-5915
Wanda Rappaport, Ph.D., Marketing
Director

General Scanning
500 Arsenal Street
Watertown, MA 02172
(617) 924-1010
Mark McPike, Application Engineer

Gerber Systems Technology
40 Gerber Road
South Windsor, CT 06074
(203) 644-2581

GMIS
250 W. Lancaster Avenue, Suite 340
Paoli, PA 19301
(215) 296-3838
Mike Nightgaile, President

Gold Hill Computers, Inc.
163 Harvard Street
Cambridge, MA 02139
(617) 492-2071
Eugene Wang, Vice President, Marketing

Hamamatsu Systems, Inc.
40 Bear Hill Road
Waltham, MA 02254
(617) 890-3440
Karen Yomas, Marketing Director

Hewlett Packard Labs
1501 Page Mill Road
Palo Alto, CA 94304
(415) 857-5356
Ira Goldstein, AI Director

Hughes Optical Products
2000 S. Wolf Road
Des Plaines, IL 60018
(312) 699-7700
Ted Nackland, General Manager

Human Edge Software
2445 Faber Place
Palo Alto, CA 94303
(415) 493-1593
James Johnson, President

IBM Corporation
P.O. Box 218
Yorktown Heights, NY 10598
(914) 945-3036
Fred Jelinek, Technology Director

Iconics
8502 E. Via de Ventura
Scottsdale, AZ 85258
(602) 948-2600
Roger Philips, President

Inference Corporation
5300 W. Century Boulevard
Los Angeles, CA 90045
(213) 417-7997
Dr. Alex Jacobson, President

Infographics
17961 Cowan Drive
Irvine, CA 92714
(714) 474-1530
Roger Kershaw, Director

Information Access Systems (IAS)
1823 Folsom, Suite 101
Boulder, CO 80302
(303) 442-6224
Dr. Earline Busch, President

Institute for Artificial Intelligence
1888 Century Park East, #1207
Los Angeles, CA 90067
(213) 201-0106

Integral Quality, Inc.
P.O. Box 31970
Seattle, WA 98103
(206) 527-2918
Bob Rorschach, President

Integrated Automation
1301 Harbor Bay Parkway
Alamede, CA 94501
(415) 769-5400
David Fain, President

Intelledex
33840 Eastgate Circle
Corvallis, OR 97333
(503) 758-4700
David Schendler, Product Manager

Intellicorp
33840 Eastgate Circle
Mountain View, CA 94040
(415) 323-8300
Thomas Kehler, Executive Vice President

Intelligent Business Systems
246 Church Street, Suite 201
New Haven, CT 06510
(203) 785-0813
Mary Mayer, Marketing Manager

Intelligent Environments
500 Howard Street
San Francisco, CA 91405
(860) 443-0100

Intelliware
4676 Admiralty Way, Suite 401
Marina del Rey, CA 90291
(213) 305-9391

Intgermetrics, Inc.
733 Concord Avenue
Cambridge, MA 02138
(617) 661-1840
William Zimmerman, Marketing Director

International Imaging Systems
1500 Buckeye Drive
Milpitas, CA 95035
(408) 262-4444
Keith Burton, Senior App Engineer

International Robomation/Intelligence
2281 Las Palmas Drive
Carlsbad, CA 92008
(619) 438-4424
Lawrence Goshorn, President

Interstate Voice Products
1849 W. Sequoia Avenue
Orange, CA 92668
(714) 937-9010
Sam Viglione, President

Ion Technology Services, Inc.
81 Prospect Street
Gloucester, MA 01930
(617) 281-5720
H. Dale Briscoe, President

Itek Optical
10 Maguire Road
Lexington, MA 02173
(617) 276-2000
Peter Howes, Manager

Itran Corporation
P.O. Box 670
Manchester, NH 03105
(603) 669-6332
Stan Lapidus, President

Jeffrey Perrone and Associates Inc.
3685 17th Street
San Francisco, CA 94114
(415) 431-9562
Thea J. Landsberg, Marketing Manager

JS&A Products
1 JS&A Plaza
Northbrook, IL 60062
(312) 564-7000

KDS Corporation
934 Hunter Road
Wilmette, IL 60091
(312) 251-2621
Bill Wallace and Mike Zolno, Marketing

Key Image Systems Inc.
20100 Plummer Street
Chatsworth, CA 91311
(818) 993-1911
Gerald Rovder, Regional Sales Manager

KJ Software
3420 E. Shea Boulevard, Suite 161
Phoenix, AZ 85028
(602) 953-1544
Ken Jacuzzi, President

Knowledge Systems
1103 Dulles Avenue, Suite 401
Stafford, TX 77477
(713) 261-2233

Kurzweil Applied Intelligence
411 Waverly Oaks Road
Waltham, MA 02154
(617) 893-5151
Michael Tomasic, President

LDS Hospital
8th Avenue & C Street
Salt Lake City, UT 84143
(801) 321-1100
Dr. Homer Warner, Chairman,
   Biophysics

Level Five Research
4980 South A1A
Melbourne Beach, FL 32951
(305) 729-9046
Henry Seiler, President

Levien Instrument Company
P.O. Box 31
McDowell, VA 24458
(703) 396-3345
Jack Levien, President

Lightyear, Inc.
1333 Lawrence Expressway, #210
Santa Clara, CA 95051
(408) 985-8811
Henry A. Kaplan, Vice President, Finance

Lincom
18100 Upper Bay Road, Suite 100
Houston, TX 77058
(713) 333-1625
Dan Bochsler, Technical Director of AI
   Applications

LISP Machine Inc.
6 Tech Drive
Andover, MA 01810
(617) 689-3554

Logica Database Products
666 Third Avenue
New York, NY 10017
(212) 682-9344
Lud Worsham, Vice President

Logical Business Machines
264 Santa Ana Court
Sunnyvale, CA 94086
(408) 737-1911
Howard Cotterman, President

Logicware Inc.
1000 Finch Avenue, West, Suite 600
Downsview, Ontario, Canada,
   CN M3J 2V5
(416) 665-0022
Ian MacLachlan, Vice President

Logos Corporation
100 Fifth Avenue
Waltham, MA 02154
(617) 890-0160
Glen Ransier, Product Marketing
  Manager

Lokersystems
5050 Powdermill Road
Beltsville, MD 20705
(301) 595-5855
Reuel Launey, Vice President

Lucid
707 Laurel Street
Menlo Park, CA 94025
(415) 329-8400
David Shlager, Vice President, Sales

Machine Vision International
  Corporation
325 E. Eisenhower Parkway
Ann Arbor, MI 48104
(313) 996-8033
Dr. Stanley Sternberg, President

MAD Intelligent Systems
2950 Zanker Road
San Jose, CA 95134
(408) 943-1711

Martin Marietta Data Systems
Post Office Box 2392
Princeton, NJ 08540
(609) 799-2600
Glenn Frantz, Marketing Director

Matchware Computer Services
6435 Castleway Drive
Indianapolis, IN 46250
(317) 841-8100

McDonnell Douglas—Knowledge
  Engineering
20705 Valley Green Drive, VG2-BO1
Cupertino, CA 95014
(408) 446-6553
Ron Engdahl, Marketing Contact

MDBS (Micro Database Systems)
P.O. Box 248
Lafayette, IN 47902
(317) 463-2581
Ron Grimsley, Marketing Representitive

Medical Graphics
350 Oak Grove Pkwy
St. Paul, MN 55110
(612) 484-4874

Medicomp
9524C Lee Highway
Fairfax, VA 22031
(703) 591-0914
Peter Goltra, President

MEDX Systems
Springdale Court, P.O. Box 2000
Dover, MA 02030
(617) 785-2527

Merit Technology
17770 Preston Road
Dallas, TX 75252
(214) 248-2502
Mel Barney, Vice President, Business
  Development

Metatronics
101 W. 78th St.
New York, NY 10024
(212) 580-8513

Microelectronics & Computer
  Technology Corporation (MCC)
9430 Research Boulevard
Austin, TX 78759
(512) 343-0860
Douglas Lenat, Project Leader

Microphonics Technology Corporation
234 SW 43rd Street, Suite B
Renton, WA 98055
(206) 251-9009
Ralph Jarvis, President

Microrim
3380 146th Place SE
Bellevue, WA 98008
(206) 641-6619
Wayne Erickson, CEO

Microsoft Corporation
10700 Northup Way, Box 97200
Bellevue, WA 98009
(206) 828-8080
Bill Gates, Chairman

Migent Software, Inc.
8300 North Hayden, Suite 203
Scottsdale, AZ 85258
(602) 483-1515
Richard Hykes, President

Miller Microcomputer Services
61 Lakeshore Road
Natick, MA 01760
(617) 653-6136
Dick Miller, President

Mitchell Associates
Post Office Box 6189
San Rafael, CA 94903
(415) 924-4696
Mitch Modeleski, President

Mitre Corporation
Burlington Road
Bedford, MA 01730
(617) 271-2000
Richard Brown, Group Leader, AI

Molecular Design Limited
2132 Farellon Drive
San Leandro, CA 94577
(415) 895-1313
Ken Moilanen, Sales Manager

Mountain View Press
P.O. Box 4656
Mountain View, CA 94040
(415) 961-4103
Roy Martins, President

MPSI Americas Inc.
8282 South Memorial Drive
Tulsa, OK 74133
(918) 250-9611
Jacque LaFrance, Manager

Soft Warehouse, Inc.
3615 Harding Avenue, Suite 505
Honolulu, HI 96816
(808) 734-5801
Albert Rich, President

NEC America Inc.
Eight Old Sod Farm Road
Melville, NY 11747
(516) 753-7000
Steve Lynch, Manager

Neuron Data
444 High Street
Palo Alto, CA 94301
(415) 321-4488

Object Recognition Systems, Inc.
440 Wall Street
Princeton, NJ 08540
(609) 924-1667
Len Gustafsson, President

Opcon Inc.
720 8th Street SW
Everett, WA 98203
(206) 353-0900
Mary Crumb, President

Optron Corporation
30 Hazel Terrace
Woodbridge, CT 06525
(203) 389-5384
Dan Hemperly, Application Engineer

Palladian
41 Munroe Street
Cambridge, MA 02142
(617) 661-7171
Phil Cooper, Chairman

Pangaro
800 Third Street NE
Washington DC 20002
(202) 547-7775

Perceptron, Inc.
23855 Research Drive
Farmington Hills, MI 48024
(313) 478-7710
Gregory Knudson, Director of Marketing

Perceptronics
21111 Erwin Street
Woodland Hills, CA 91367
(818) 884-7572
Azad Madni, Vice President, AI &
   Man-Machine Systems

Perq Systems Corporation
P.O. Box 2600
2600 Liberty Avenue
Pittsburgh, PA 15230
(412) 355-0900
Kelly Hickel, President

Perrone & Associates
3685 17th Street
San Francisco, CA 94114
(415) 431-9562

Persoft, Inc.
600 West Cummings Park
Woburn, MA 01801
(617) 935-0095
Frederik Wiersema, Vice President,
   Marketing

Planning Research Corporation
1500 Planning Research Drive
McLean, VA 22102
(703) 556-1111

PPE, Inc.
P.O. Box 2027
Gaithersburg, MD 20879
(301) 977-1489
Steve Anthony, Programmer

PPT-Pattern Processing
Technologies, Inc.
511 11th Avenue South
Minneapolis, MN 55415
(612) 339-8488
Larry J. Werth, President

Production Systems Technologies
642 Gettysburg Street
Pittsburgh, PA 15206
(412) 362-3117
Dianna Connan, Marketing,
Vice President

Productivity Products International
27 Glen Road
Sandy Hook, CT 06482
(203) 426-1875
Chester J. Wisinski, Director Product
Sales

Programming Logic Systems
31 Crescent Drive
Milford, CT 06460
(203) 877-7988
Anthony Kowalski, President

Project Software & Development, Inc.
20 University Road
Cambridge, MA 02138
(617) 661-1444

Prophecy Development Company
308 Boylston Street
Boston, MA 02116
(617) 266-1825

Public Domain S.W.
3080 Olcott Drive, Suite B130
Santa Clara, CA 95054
(408) 988-0230
Lisa Amereh, Product Manager

Quantex Corporation
252 N. Wolfe Road
Sunnyvale, CA 94086
(408) 733-6730
Mel Packard, Sales Manager

Quintus
2345 Yale Street
Palo Alto, CA 94306
(415) 494-3612
Dr. Doug DeGroot, Vice President,
Research & Development

r/l Group
7623 Leviston Street
El Cerrito, CA 94530
(415) 527-1438
Grant Ricketts, Marketing Director

Racal-Norsk (Norsk Data N.A.)
1000 Quail Street, #220
Newport Beach, CA 92660
(714) 752-5081
John B. Lewis, Marketing Representative

Raden Research Group
P.O. Box 1809, Madison Sq.
New York, NY 10159

Radian Corporation
Post Office Box 9948
Austin, TX 78766
(512) 454-4797
Ben Finkel, Marketing Manager

Reasoning Systems
1801 Page Mill Road
Palo Alto, CA 94303
(415) 494-6201
Joseph Rockmore, Vice President

Recognition Concepts Inc.
924 Incline Way, P.O. Box 8510
Incline Village, NV 89450
(702) 831-0473
John Fowler, Vice President, Marketing

Robotic Vision Systems, Inc.
425 Rabro Drive East
Hauppauge, NY 11788
(516) 273-9700
Thomas Meaney, Senior VP

Rohm & Haas
727 Norristown Road
Spring House, PA 19477
(215) 641-7000

Savvy (Excalibur Technologies
Corporation)
800 Rio Grande Boulevard
Albuquerque, NM 87104
(800) 551-5199
Robert E. Patterson, Executive Vice
President

Schlumberger-Doll Research
Old Quarry Road
Ridgefield, CT 06877
(203) 431-5000
Peter Will, Director

Science Applications International
1200 Prospect Street
La Jolla, CA 92037
(619) 454-3811

Scott Instruments Corporation
1111 Willow Springs Drive
Denton, TX 76205
(817) 387-9514
Brian Scott, Executive Vice President,
  Chief Scientist

Servio Logic Development Corporation
2700 Georgia Pacific Building
Portland, OR 97204
(503) 227-3777
John L. Cundiff, Manager

Silogic
6420 Wilshire Boulevard, Suite #2000
Los Angeles, CA 90048
(213) 65306470
Technical Staff Director

Smart Systems Technology
7700 Leesburg Pike
Falls Church, VA 22043
(703) 448-8562
Craig Cook, President

Softbridge Microsystems Corporation
186 Alewife Brook Parkway
Cambridge, MA 02138
(800) 325-6060
Joanne Carignan, Product Consultant

Software Architecture & Engineering Inc.
1500 Wilson Boulevard, Suite 800
Arlington, VA 22209
(703) 276-7910
Joseph Fox, Chairman

Solution Systems
335 Washington Street
Norwell, MA 02061
(617) 871-5435
John Chappell, Technical Director

Spectron Engineering
800 West 9th Avenue
Denver, CO 80204
(303) 623-8987
Paul Herz, Vice President, Marketing

Speech Systems, Inc.
18356 Oxnard Street
Tarzana, CA 91356
(818) 881-0885
Deana Murchison, Product Marketing

SRI International
333 Ravenswood Avenue
Menlo Park, CA 94025
(415) 326-6200
Stan Rosenschein, Director AI Lab

Sterling Wentworth Corporation
2319 South Foothill Drive, #150
Salt Lake City, UT 84109
(801) 467-7510
Paul Savage, Marketing Director

Stochastic Models, Inc.
11 Broadway Suite 1032
New York, NY 10004
(212) 422-0903

Stocker and Yale
Route 128 and Brimbal Avenue
Beverly, MA 01915
(617) 927-3940
James Bittman, President

Sun Microsystems
2550 Garcia Avenue
Mountain View, CA 94043
(800) 821-4643
Margie Corbin, Product Manager

Symantec
10201 Torre Avenue
Cupertino, CA 95014
(408) 253-9600
Gordon Eubanks, CEO

Symbolics, Inc.
11 Cambridge Center
Cambridge, MA 02142
(617) 577-7500
Russel Noftsker, President

Syn-Optics
1225 Elko Drive
Sunnyvale, CA 94089-2262
(408) 734-8563
John Anderson, Vice President,
  Marketing

Syntelligence
1000 Hamlin Court
Sunnyvale, CA 94088
(408) 745-6666
Steve Weyl, Marketing Director

Synthetic Vision Systems, Inc.
2929 Plymouth Ste. 211
Ann Arbor, MI 48105
(313) 665-1850
Dave Trail, Vice President, Marketing

Systems Control Technology Inc. (SCT)
1801 Page Mill Road, POB 10180
Palo Alto, CA 94303
(415) 494-2233
Greg Gibeons

Systems Designers Software, Inc.
5203 Leesburg Turnpike, #1201
Falls Church, VA 22041
(703) 820-2700
Marlyse Smith, Sales Manager

Systems Research Laboratories
2800 Indian Ripple Road
Dayton, OH 45440
(513) 426-6000

Technology Research Corporation
Springfield Professional Park
8328-A Traford Lane
Springfield, VA 22152
(703) 451-8830
V. Daniel Hunt, President

Teknowledge, Inc.
525 University Avenue
Palo Alto, CA 94301-1982
(415) 327-6600
Mike Dolbec, Corporate Marketing

Tektronix, Inc.
P.O. Box 1700
Beaverton, OR 97075
(800) 547-1512

Tenchstar/Metacomco
201 Hoffman Avenue
Monterey, CA 93940
(408) 375-5012
Alan Hamilton, Marketing Manager

Tetrax
9000 Owensmouth Avenue
Canoga Park, CA 91304
(818) 709-1981
Antonio Leal, President

Texas Instruments
P.O. Box 809063
Dallas, TX 75380-9063
(800) 527-3500

The LISP Company
P.O. Box 487
Redwood Estates, CA 95044
(408) 354-3668
John R. Allen, President

Thinking Machines Corporation
245 First Street
Cambridge, MA 02142
(617) 876-1111
Sheryl Handler, President

Thoughtware
2699 S. Bayshore Drive, Suite 1000A
Coconut Grove, FL 33133
(305) 854-2318
Henry Kaplan, Vice President, Marketing

Transform Logic
8502 E. Via de Ventura
Scottsdale, AZ 85258
(602) 948-2600

Unimation/Westinghouse
5 Shelter Rock Lane
Danbury, CN 06810
(203) 796-1201
Richard J. Casler, AI Manager

Verac, Inc. (Applied Computer
    Science Group)
9605 Scranton Road, Suite 500
San Diego, CA 92121
(619) 457-5550
Dr. Charles Moorefield, President

View Engineering
1650 N. Voyager Avenue
Simi Valley, CA 93063
(805) 522-8439
Richard Ganz, Director of Sales

Vision Systems International
3 Milton Drive
Yardley, PA 19067
(215) 736-0994
Nello Zuech, Proprietor

Voice Control Systems, Inc.
16610 Dallas Parkway
Dallas, TX 75248
(214) 248-8244
Dr. R. Eugene Helms, Director of
    Product Development

Votan
4487 Technology Drive
Fremont, CA 94538
(415) 490-7600
James Ragano, President

Vuebotics
6086 Corte Del Cedro
Carlsbad, CA 92008
(619) 438-7994
D. J. Kelley, President

Weidner Communications Corporation
40 Skokie Boulevard, Suite 300
Northbrook, IL 60062
(312) 564-8122
Ralph Strozza, Marketing Representative

Westchester Distribution Systems
P.O. Box 324
Scarsdale, NY 10583
(914) 723-4352
Martin Scheider, President

Xerox Corporation
250 N. Halstead Street
Pasadena, CA 91109
(818) 351-2351
Gary Moskovitz, AI Manager

ROBOTICS ASSOCIATIONS

Robot Institute of America
One SME Drive
P.O. Box 930
Dearborn, MI 48128
(313) 271-0778

Robotics International of SME
One SME Drive
P.O. Box 930
Dearborn, MI 48128

Japan Industrial Robot Association (JIRA)
Kikai Shinko Kaikan Building
3-5-8 Shiba-koen
Minato-ku
Tokyo 105
JAPAN

British Robot Association
3539 High Street
Kempston
Bedford MK42 7BT
ENGLAND

Swedish Industrial Robot Association
(SWIRA)
Box 5506
Storgatan 19
SWEDEN-14 85 Stockholm

Association Francaise de Robotique
Industrieele (AFRI)
89 Rue Falgueire
75015 Paris,
FRANCE

Societa Italiana Robotica Industriale
(SIRI)
Instituto de Electtrotechnica
ed Elettronics
Politechmico di Milano
Piazza Leonardo da Binci 32
20133 Milano
ITALY

ROBOT VENDORS

Accumatic Machinery Corporation
3537 Hill Avenue
Toledo, Ohio 43607
(419) 535-7997

Acrobe Positioning Systems Inc.
3219 Doolittle Drive
Northlake, Illinois 60062
(312) 273-4302

Advanced Robotics Corporation
Newark Ohio Industrial Park
Building 8, Route 79
Hebron, Ohio 43025
(614) 929-1065

Ameco Corporation
P.O. Box 385
W158 N9335 Nor-X-Way Avenue
Menomonee Falls, Wisconsin 53051
(414) 255-3910

American Robot Corporation
354 Hookstown Road
Clinton, Pennsylvania 15026
(412) 262-2085

Anorad Corporation
110 Oser Avenue
Hauppauge, New York 11788
(516) 231-1990

Armax Robotics Inc.
38700 Grand River Avenue
Farmington Hills, Michigan 48018
(313) 478-9330

Automatic Incorporated
217 Middlesex Turnpike
Burlington, Massachusetts 01803
(617) 273-4340

Automaton Corporation
23996 Freeway Park Drive
Farmington Hills, Michigan 48024
(313) 471-0554

Bendix Robotics
21238 Bridge Street
Southfield, Michigan 48034
(313) 352-7700

Binks Manufacturing Company
9201 W. Belmont Avenue
Franklin Park, Illinois 60131
(312) 671-3000

Cincinnati Milacron
215 S. West Street
South Lebanon, Ohio 45036
(513) 932-4400

Comet Welding Systems
900 Nicholas Boulevard
Elk Grove Village, Illinois 60007
(312) 956-0126

Control Automation Inc.
P.O. Box 2304
Princeton, New Jersey 08540
(609) 799-6026

Copperweld Robotics
1401 East 14 Mile Road
Troy, Michigan 48084
(313) 585-5972

Cybotech Corporation
P.O. Box 88514
Indianapolis, Indiana 46208
(317) 298-5890

Cyclomatic Industries Inc.
7520 Convoy Court
San Diego, California 92111
(714) 292-7440

The DeVilbiss Company
300 Phillips Avenue
P.O. Box 913
Toledo, Ohio 43692
(419) 470-2169

Elicon
273 Viking Avenue
Brea, California
(714) 990-6647

Expert Automation
40675 Mound Road
Sterling Heights, Michigan 40878
(313) 977-0100

Fleximation Systems Corporation
53 Second Avenue
Burlington, Massachusetts 01803
(617) 229-6670

GCA Corporation
Industrial Systems Group
One Energy Center
Naperville, Illinois 60566
(312) 369-2110

General Electric Company
Automation Systems
1285 Boston Avenue
Bridgeport, Connecticut 06602
(203) 382-2876

GMFanuc Robotics Corporation
5600 New King Street
Troy, Michigan 48098
(313) 641-4100

General Numeric Corporation
390 Kent Avenue
Elk Grove Village, Illinois 60007
(312) 640-1595

Graco Robotics Inc.
12898 Westmore Avenue
Livonia, Michigan 48150
(313) 261-3270

Hitachi America Ltd.
59 Route 17-S
Allendale, New Jersey 07401
(201) 825-8000

Hobart Brothers Company
600 W. Main Street
Troy, Ohio 45473
(513) 339-6011

Hodges Robotics
International Corporation
3710 N. Grand River
Lansing, Michigan 48906
(517) 323-7427

IBM
P.O. Box 1328
Boca Raton, Florida 33432
(305) 998-2000

Ikegai America Corporation
770 W. Algonquin Road
Arlington Heights, Illinois 60005
(312) 437-1488

Industrial Automates Inc.
6123 W. Mitchell Street
Milwaukee, Wisconsin 53214
(414) 327-5656

Intelledex
33840 Eastgate Circle
Corvallis, Oregon 97333
(503) 758-4700

International Intelligence/Robomation
6353 El Camino Real
Carlsbad, California 92008
(714) 438-4424

I.S.I. Manufacturing, Inc.
31915 Groesbeck Highway
Fraser, Michigan 48026
(313) 294-9500

Lamson Corporation
P.O. Box 4857
Syracuse, New York 13221
(315) 432-5500

Mack Corporation
3695 East Industrial Drive
Flagstaff, Arizona 86001
(602) 526-1120

Microbot, Inc.
453-H Ravendale Drive
Mountain View, California 94043
(415) 968-8911

Mobot Corporation
980 Buenos Avenue
San Diego, California 92110
(714) 275-4300

Nordson Corporation
555 Jackson Street
Amherst, Ohio
(216) 988-9411

Nova Robotics
262 Prestige Park Road
East Hartford, Connecticut 06108
(203) 528-9861

Pickomatic Systems
37950 Commerce
Sterling Heights, Michigan 48077
(313) 939-9320

Positech Corporation
Rush Lake Road
Laurens, Iowa 50554
(712) 845-4548

Prab Robots, Inc.
5944 E. Kilgore Road
Kalamazoo, Michigan 49003
(616) 349-8761

Reis Machines
1426 Davis Road
Elgin, Illinois 60120
(312) 714-9500

Rob-Con Ltd.
12001 Globe
Livonia, Michigan 48150
(313) 591-0300

Sandu Machine Design Inc.
308 S. State Street
Champaign, Illinois 61820
(217) 352-8485

Schrader Bellows/Scovill Inc.
200 W. Exchange Street
Akron, Ohio 44309
(216) 375-5202

Seiko Instruments, Inc.
2990 W. Lomita Boulevard
Torrance, California 90505
(213) 330-8777

Sigma
6505C Serrano Avenue
Anaheim, California 92807
(714) 974-0166

Sormel/Black & Webster
281 Winter Street
Waltham, Massachusetts 02254
(617) 890-9100

Sterling Detroit Company
261 E. Goldengate Avenue
Detroit, Michigan 48203
(313) 366-3500

Swanson-Erie Corporation
814 E. 8th Street
P.O. Box 1217
Erie, Pennsylvania 16512
(814) 453-5841

TecQuipment Inc.
P.O. Box 1074
Acton, Massachusetts 01720
(617) 263-1767

Thermwood Corporation, Inc.
P.O. Box 436
Dale, Indiana 47523
(812) 937-4476

Unimation, Inc.
Shelter Rock Lane
Danbury, Connecticut 06810
(203) 744-1800

United States Robots
650 Park Avenue
King of Prussia, Pennsylvania 19406
(215) 768-9210

Westinghouse Electric Corporation
Industry Automation Division
400 High Tower Office Building
400 Media Drive
Pittsburgh, Pennsylvania 15205
(412) 778-4349

Yaskawa Electric America, Inc.
305 Era Drive
Northbrook, Illinois 60062
(312) 564-0770

ROBOT VENDORS (EUROPE)

Volkswagenwerk AG
Abt. Industrieverkauf
3180 Wolfsburg
West Germany

KUKA
Schweissanlagen & Roboter GmbH
P.O. Box 431280
Zugspitzstr. 140
D-8900
Augsburg 43
West Germany

Nimak
Werkstrabe
Postfach 86
5248 Wissen/Sieg
West Germany

Jungheinrich Unternelmensverwaltug
Friedrich-Ebert-Dabb 129
2000 Hamburg 70
West Germany

ASEA AB
S-72183 Vasteras
Sweden

R. Kaufeldt AB
P.O. Box 42139
S-126 12 Stockholm
Sweden

Electrolux AB
Industrial Systems
S-105 45 Stockholm
Sweden

Unimation, Inc.
Units A3/A4
Stafford Park 4
Telford, Salop
United Kingdom

Hall Automation Limited
Colonial Way
Watford
Herts, WD2 4FG
United Kingdom

Mouldmation Limited
2 Darwin Close
Burntwood, Walsall
Staffs WS7 9HP
United Kingdom

Pendar
Bridgwater
Somerset
United Kingdom

British Federal Welder & Machine Co.,
Ltd.
Castle Mill Works
Dudley
West Midlands, DY1 4DA
United Kingdom

Regie Nationale des
Usines renault SA
66Av Edouard Vaillaut
Boulogne-Billancourt
France

Sormel
rue Becquerel
25009 Besanicon Cedex
France

A.O.I.P. Kremlin Robotique
6 rue Maryse Bastie
9100 Evry
France

Digital Electronics Automation SpA
Co Torino 70
Moncalieri, Piemonte 10024
Italy

Camel Robot SRL
Palozzolo Milanese
Italy

Olivetti SpA
Controllo Numerico
Fr S Berenardo
V Torino 603
Ivrea, Piemonte
Italy

Fiat Auto SpA
CSO Agnelli 200
Torino, Piemonte
Italy

Trallfa
Paint-Welding Robot systems
P.O. Box 113
4341 Bryne
Norway

ROBOT MANUFACTURERS (JAPAN)

Dainichi Kiko Co., Ltd.
Kosai-cho
Nakakomagun Yeamanshi Pref.
400-04
Japan

Fanuc, Ltd.
3-5-1
Asahigoaka, Hino City
Tokyo
Japan

Hitachi, Ltd.
Shin-Maru Bldg.
1-5-1
Marunouchi, Chiyoda-ku
Tokyo
Japan

Kawasaki Heavy Industries Ltd.
World Trade Center Bldg.
2-4-1
Hamamatsucho, Minato-ku
Tokyo
Japan

Matsushita Industrial Equipment Co. Ltd.
3-1-1 Inazumachi
Toyonaka City Osaka Pref.
Japan

Mitsubishi Heavy Industries Ltd.
2-5-1
Marunouchi, chiyoda-ku
Tokyo
Japan

Sankyo Seiki Mfg. Co., Ltd.
1-17-2
Shunbashi, Minati-ku
Tokyo 105
Japan

Tokico Ltd.
1-6-3
Funta, Kawasaki-ku
Kawasaki City
Kanagaw Pref.
Japan

Yaskawa Electric Mfg. Co. Ltd.
Ohtemachi Bldg.
1-6-1
Ohtemachi, Chiyoda-ku
Tokyo
Japan

ROBOT RENTAL/LEASE FIRMS

Hi-Tec Assembly
8130 N. Knox
Stokie, Illinois 60076
(312) 676-0080

Thermwood Machinery Manufacturing
Co. Inc.
P.O. Box 436
Dale, Indiana 47523
(812) 937-4476

Rob-Con Ltd.
12001 Globe Road
Livonia, Michigan 48150
(313) 591-0300

ROBOT CONSULTING/ APPLICATIONS FIRMS

Automation Systems/American
Technologies
1900 Pollitt Drive
Fair Lawn, New Jersey 07410
(201) 797-8200

Blanarovich Engineering
Box 292
Don Mills, Ontario M3C 2S2
Canada
(416) 438-6313

Franklin Institute Research
Laboratory, Inc.
The Benjamin Franklin Parkway
Philadelphia, Pennsylvania 19103
(215) 448-1000

Productivity Systems Inc.
21999 Farmington Road
Farmington Hills, Michigan 48024
(313) 474-5454

RMT Engineering Ltd.
P.O. Box 2333, Station B
St. Catherines, Ontario L2M 7M7
Canada
(416) 937-1550

Robot Systems, Inc.
50 Technology Parkway
Norcross, Georgia 30092
(404) 448-4133

Technology Research Corporation
Springfield Professional Park
8328-A Traford Lane
Springfield, Virginia 22152
(703) 451-8830
Contact: V. Daniel Hunt

U.S. ROBOTICS RESEARCH ORGANIZATIONS

Carnegie-Mellon University
The Robotics Institute
Schenley Park
Pittsburgh, Pennsylvania 15213
(412) 578-2597

Charles Stark Draper Laboratory, Inc.
555 Technology Square
Cambridge, Massachusetts 02139
(617) 258-1000
Contact: Mr. James Nevins

Environmental Research Institute
of Michigan
Robotics Program
P.O. Box 8618
Ann Arbor, Michigan 48107
(313) 994-1200

George Washington University
725 23rd Street NW
Washington, D.C. 20052
(202) 676-6083

Hughes Research Laboratories
3011 Malibu Canyon Road
Malibu, California 90265

Jet Propulsion Labs
Robotics Group
4800 Oak Grove Drive
Pasadena, California 91103
(213) 354-6101

MIT
Artificial Intelligence Lab
545 Technology Square
Cambridge, Massachusetts 02139
(617) 253-6218

Naval Research Laboratory
Code 7505
Washington, D.C. 20375
(202) 545-6700

North Carolina State University
Raleigh, North Carolina 27650
(919) 737-2336

Purdue University
School of Electrical Engineering
West Lafayette, Indiana 47906
(317) 749-2607

Rensselaer Polytechnic Institute
Room 5304 JEC
Troy, New York 12181
(518) 270-6724

Robotics Institute
Carnegie-Mellon University
Schenley Park
Pittsburgh, Pennsylvania 15213
(412) 578-3611

Stanford University
Artificial Intelligence Lab
Stanford, California 94305
(415) 497-2797
Dr. John McCarthy, Director

SRI International
Artificial Intelligence Center
Menlo Park, California 94025
(415) 859-2311

Texas A&M University
Dept. of Industrial Engineering
College Station, Texas 77840
(713) 845-5531

United States Air Force
AFWAL/MLTC (USAF ICAM)
Wright Patterson AFB
Ohio 45433
(513) 255-2232

University of Central Florida
College of Engineering
P.O. Box 25000
Orlando, Florida 32816
(305) 275-2236

University of Cincinnati
Institute of Applied
Interdisciplinary Research
Loc #72
Cincinnati, Ohio 45221

University of Florida
Institute for Intelligent Machines &
Robotics
Room 300, Mechanical engr.
Gainesville, Florida 32601
(904) 392-0814

University of Michigan
Robotics Program
ECE Department
Ann Arbor, Michigan 48109
(313) 764-7139

University of Rhode Island
College of Engineering
102 Bliss Hall
Kingston, Rhode Island 02881
(401) 792-2187

University of Wisconsin
1513 University Avenue
Madison, Wisconsin 53706
(608) 262-3543

MACHINE VISION SYSTEM MANUFACTURERS

Applied Intelligent Systems, Inc.
1955 Pauline Boulevard
Ann Arbor, Michigan 48103
(313) 995-2035

Automatix Inc.
217 Middlesex Turnpike
Burlington, Massachusetts 01803
(617) 273-4340

Cognex Corporation
1505 Commonwealth Avenue
Boston, Massachusetts 02135
(617) 254-1231

Control Automation, Inc.
Princeton-Windsor Industrial Park
P.O. Box 2304
Princeton, New Jersey 08540
(609) 799-6026

Copperweld Robotics
1401 E. Fourteen Mile Road
Troy, Michigan 48084
(313) 585-5972

Cyberanimation, Inc.
4621 Granger Road
Akron, Ohio 44313
(216) 666-8293

Diffracto Ltd.
P.O. Box 36716
Detroit, Michigan 48236
(313) 965-0410

Everett/Charles
Automation Modules, Inc.
9645 Arrow Route, Suite A
Rancho Cucamonga, California 91730
(714) 980-1525

General Electric Company
Optoelectronic Systems Operation
Bldg. 3, Electronics Park
Syracuse, New York 13221
(315) 456-2832

Ham Industries, Inc.
Inspection Products Division
835 Highland Road
Macedonia, Ohio 44056
(216) 467-4256

Inspection Technology, Inc.
Penn Video, Inc.
929 Sweitzer Avenue
Akron, Ohio 44311
(216) 762-4840

Machine Intelligence Corporation
330 Potrero Avenue
Sunnyvale, California 94086
(408) 737-7960

Object Recognition Systems, Inc.
1101-B State Road
Princeton, New Jersey 08540
(212) 682-3535

Octek, Inc.
7 Corporate Place
South Bedford Street
Burlington, Massachusetts 01803
(617) 273-0851

Perceptron
23920 Freeway Park Drive
Farmington Hills, Michigan 48024
(313) 478-7710

Prothon
Division Video Tek, Inc.
199 Pomeroy Road
Parsippany, New Jersey 07054
(201) 887-8211

Robotic Vision Systems Inc.
536 Broadhollow Road
Melville, New York 11747
(516) 694-8910

Selective Electronic, Inc.
P.O. Box 250
Valdese, North Carolina 28690
(704) 874-2289

Spectron Engineering
800 West 9th Avenue
Denver, Colorado 80204
(303) 623-8987

Syn-Optics
1240 Birchwood Drive
Sunnyvale, California 94086
(408) 734-8563

Unimation Inc.
Shelter Rock Lane
Danbury, Connecticut 06810
(203) 744-1800

View Engineering
9736 Eton Avenue
Chatsworth, California 91311
(213) 998-4230

VISION SYSTEM CONSULTANTS

Automated Vision Systems
1590 La Pradera Drive
Campbell, California 95008
(408) 370-0229

Digital Vision Consultants
International Trades Bldg., Suite 121
400 Brookes Drive
St. Louis, Missouri 63042
(314) 895-1703

L.N.K. Corporation
302 Notley Court
Silver Spring, Maryland 20904
(301) 927-3223

Technology Research Corporation
Springfield Professional Park
8328-A Traford Lane
Springfield, Virginia 22152
(703) 451-8830
Attn: V. Daniel Hunt, President

VISION SYSTEM RESEARCH ORGANIZATIONS

Carnegie-Mellon University
The Robotics Institute
Pittsburgh, Pennsylvania 15213
(412) 578-3826

Environmental Research Institute
 of Michigan
Robotics Program
P.O. Box 8618
Ann Arbor, Michigan 48107
(313) 994-1200

George Washington University
725 23rd Street, N.W.
Washington, D.C. 20052
(202) 676-6919

Jet Propulsion Labs
Robotics Group
4800 Oak Grove Drive
Pasadena, California 91103
(213) 354-6101

Massachusetts Institute of Technology
Artificial Intelligence Lab
545 Technology Square
Cambridge, Massachusetts 02139
(617) 253-6218

Naval Research Lab
Code 2610
Washington, D.C. 20375
(202) 767-3984

North Carolina State University
Department of Electrical Engineering
Raleigh, North Carolina 27650
(919) 737-2376

Purdue University
School of Electrical Engineering
West Lafayette, Indiana 47906
(317) 749-2607

Rensselaer Polytechnic Institute
Center for Manufacturing Productivity
Jonsson Engineering Center
Troy, New York 12181
(518) 270-6724

SRI International
Artificial Intelligence Center
Menlo Park, California 94025
(425) 497-2797

Stanford University
Artificial Intelligence Lab
Stanford, California 94022
(415) 497-2797

U.S. Air Force
AFWAL/MLTC
Wright Patterson AFB, Ohio 45437
(513) 255-6976

University of Central Florida
IEMS Department
Orlando, Florida 32816
(305) 275-2236

University of Cincinnati
Institute of Applied Interdisciplinary
 Research
Location 42
Cincinnati, Ohio 45221
(513) 475-6131

University of Maryland
Computer Vision Laboratory
College Park, Maryland 20742
(301) 454-4526

University of Rhode Island
Department of Electrical Engineering
Kingston, Rhode Island 02881
(401) 792-2187

University of Southern California
School of Engineering
University Park
Los Angeles, California

University of Texas
Austin, Texas 78712
(512) 471-1331

University of Washington
Department of Electrical Engineering
Seattle, Washington 98195
(206) 543-2056

ACRONYMS

ACRONYMS AND ABBREVIATIONS

AAAI	American Association for Artificial Intelligence
ABEL	Acid Base ElectroLyte
ACE	Automated Cable Expertise
ACES	Ai Cartographic Expert System
ACLS	Analog Concept Learning System
ACM	Association for Computing Machinery
AFCEA	Armed Forces Communication and Electronics Association
AGE	Attempt to GEneralize
AI	Artificial Intelligence
AI/ES	Artificial Intelligence/Expert Systems
AI/MM	Artificial Intelligence Mathematical Model
AIRID	AIRcraft IDentifier
ALICE	A Language for Intelligent Combinatorial Exploration
AL/X	Advice Language X
AMUID	Automated Multisensor Unit IDentification
APES	A Prolog Expert system Shell
ARAMIS	American Rheumatism Association Medical Information System
ARS	Antecedent Reasoning System
ART	Advanced Reasoning Tool
ASTA	Assistant for Science and Technology Analysis
ATN	Augmented Transition Network
ATR	Automatic Target Recognizer
BBN	Bolt Beranek and Newman
BDS	Baseboard Distribution System
BEAGLE	Bionic Evolutionary Algorithm Generating Logical Expressions
C-13	Carbon 13
CADHELP	Computer-Aided Design HELP
CARGUIDE	Computer for Automobile Route GUIDancE
CASNET/GLAUCOMA	Causal-Association NETwork/GLAUCOMA
C.M.U.	Carnegie-Mellon University
CODES	COnceptual DESign system
COMPASS	Central Office Maintenance Printout Analysis and Suggestion System
CONCHE	CONsistency CHEcker
CONGEN	CONstrained GENerator
CONPHYDE	CONsultant for PHYsical property DEcisions

COUSIN	COoperative USer INterface
C-P-V	Context-Parameter-Value triplets
CRIB	Computer Retrieval Incidence Bank
CRT	Cathode Ray Tube
CSRL	Conceptual Structures Representation Language
DAA	Design Automation Assistant
DARPA	Defense Advanced Research Projects Agency
DART	Diagnostic Assistance Reference Tool
DEC	Digital Equipment Corporation
DELTA	Diesel-Electric Locomotive Troubleshooting Aid
DENDRAL	DENDRitic ALgorithm
DETEKTR	Development Environment for TEKtronix TRoubleshooters
DFT	Design For Testability system
DSCAS	Differing Site Condition Analysis System
DTA	Dialysis Therapy Advisor
ECESIS	Environmental Control Expert System In Space
EMYCIN	Essential MYCIN
ERS	Embedded Rule-based System
ES	Expert Systems
ETS	Expertise Transfer System
EXPRS	EXpert PRolog System
FRL	Frame Representation Language
GCA	Graduate Course Advisor
GCLISP	Golden Common LISP
GEN-X	GENeric-eXpert system
GKS	Graphics Kernel System
GPS	General Problem Solver
GLIB	General Language for Instrumental Behavior
GPSI	General Purpose System for Inferencing
GUESS	General Purpose Expert System Shell
HCPRVR	Horn Clause theorem PRoVeR
HDDS	Hodgkin's Disease Decision Support system
HPP	Stanford University Heuristic Programming Project
HPRL	Heuristic Programming and Representation Language
HWIM	Hear What I Mean
IA	Intelligent Assistant
ICOT	Japan's Institute for new generation COmputing Technology
IFIPS	International Federation of Information Processing Societies
IN-ATE/KE	INtelligent-Automatic Test Equipment/Knowledge Engineering
IJCA	International Joint Conference on AI
IPL	Information Processing Language
IR-NLI	Information Retrieval-Natural Language Interface
ISA	Intelligent Scheduling Assistant
ISIS	Intelligent Scheduling and Information System
IUP	Image Understanding Project
KAMM	Knowledge Acquisition and Maintenance Module
KAS	Knowledge Acquisition System
KBS	Knowledge-Based Simulation system
KBS	Knowledge-Based System
KE	Knowledge Engineer
KEE	Knowledge Engineering Environment
KES	Knowledge Engineering System

KMS	Knowledge Management System
KNOBS	KNOwledge Based System
KIPS	Knowledge Information Processing System
KRL	Knowledge Representation Language
LES	Lockheed Expert System
LISP	LISt Processing language
LIST	LIST processing
LRS	Legal Research System
LSI	Large Scale Integration
LT	Logic Theorist
MARS	Multiple Abstraction Rule-based System
MCC	Microelectronics and Computer technology Corporation
MECS-AI	MEdical Consultation System-by means of Artificial Intelligence
MELD	MEta-Level Diagnosis
MES	Maintenance Expert System
MI	Myocardial Infarction system
MIPS	Millions of Instructions Per Second
M.I.T.	Massachusetts Institute of Technology
MITI	Ministry of International Trade and Industry
MODIS	Machine-Oriented Diagnostic Interactive System
MRS	Metalevel Representation System
NAPLPS	North American Presentation-Lend Protocol Syntax
NAVEX	NAVigation EXpert
NPPC	Nuclear Power Plant Consultant
OAV	Object-Attribute-Value
PAN	Parallel Associative Network
PATREC	PATient RECords system
PDS	Portable Diagnostic System
PEC	Primary Eye Care system
PICON	Process Intelligent CONtrol system
PIE	Personal Information Environment
PIP	Present Illness Program
POMME	Pest and Orchard ManageMent Expert system
PROJCON	PROJect CONsultant
PSL	Portable Standard LISP
PSYCO	Production SYstem COmpiler
RADEX	RA-Diology EXpert
RAIN	Relational Algebraic INterpreter
RAM	Random Access Memory
RBMS	Rule-Based Modeling System
RITA	Rand Intelligent Terminal Agent
RLL	Representation Language Language
ROSIE	Rule-Oriented System for Implementing Expertise
ROSS	Rule-Oriented System for Simulation
RPMS	Resource Planning and Management System
RTC	Radar Target Classification system
RUBRIC	Rule-Based Retrieval of Information by Computer
SADD	Semi-Automatic Digital Designer
SAL	System for Asbestos Litigation
SECS	Simulation and Evaluation of Chemical Synthesis
SEQ	SEQuence analysis system
SIAP	Surveillance Integration Automation Project

SIGART	ACM Special Interest Group on ARTificial intelligence
SIGCSE	ACM Special Interest Group on Computer Science Education
SIGCUE	ACM Special Interest Group on Computer Uses in Education
SIGGRAPH	ACM Special Interest Group on GRAPHics
SIGPLAN	ACM Special Interest Group on Programming LANguages
SOPHIE	SOPHisticated Instructional Environment
SPAM	System for Photo interpretation of Airports using Maps
SPE	Serum Protein Electrophoresis diagnostic program
SPEX	Skeletal Planner of EXperiments
SRI	Stanford Research Institute
SRL	Schema Representation Language
SRL+	Schema Representation Language + (plus)
SUR	Speech Understanding Research
SWIRL	Simulating Warfare In the Ross Language
SYN	circuit SYNthesis program
SYSTEM D	SYSTEM for Diagnostic problem solving
SZKI	Hungary's institute for computer coordination
TATR	Tactical Air Target Recommender
TI	Texas Instruments
TIMM	The Intelligent Machine Model
TINLAP	workshops on Theoretical Issues in Natural LAnguage Processing
TQMSTUNE	Triple-Quadrupole Mass Spectrometer TUNEr
TRC	Technology Research Corporation
TWIRL	Tactical Warfare In the Ross Language
VDI	Virtual Device Interface
VDM	Virtual Device Metafile
VDT	Video Display Terminal
VM	Ventilator Manager
XCON	eXpert CONfigurere of VAX 11/780 computer systems
YES/MVS	Yorktown Expert System for MVS operators

Bibliography

Abelson, Harold; Sussman, Gerald Jay, and Susman, Julie. "Structure and Interpretation of Computer Programs," The MIT Press, 1985.

Agin, G. J., "Computer Vision Systems for Industrial Inspection and Assembly," *Computer*, May 1980, pp. 11–20.

Agin, G. J., "Real-Time Robot Control with a Mobile Camera," *Robotics Today*, Fall 1979.

Aikins, J. S., Kunz, J. C., Shortliffe, E. H., and Fallat, R. J., "PUFF: An Expert System for Interpretation of Pulmonary Function Data." In *Readings in Medical Artificial Intelligence: The First Decade*, edited by B. C. Clancey and E. H. Shortliffe. Reading, MA: Addison-Wesley Publishing Company, 1984.

Alexander, Tom, "Computers on the Road to Self-Improvement," *Fortune*, June 14, 1982, pp. 148–160.

Alexander, Tom, "Practical Uses for a Useless Science," *Fortune*, May 31, 1982, pp. 138–145.

Alexander, Tom, "Teaching Computers the Art of Reason," *Fortune*, May 17, 1982, pp. 82–92.

Allen, John R., "Anatomy of LISP," McGraw-Hill, Inc., 1978.

Allen, John R., Davis, Ruth E., and Johnson, John F. "Thinking about (TLC) Logo," Holt, Rinehart and Winston, 1984.

Arai, Joji, "Robot Growth in Japan," *Manufacturing Productivity Frontiers*, October 1982.

Arons, A. B., "Computer-based Instructional Dialogues in Science Courses," *Science*, vol. 224, no. 4653, June 8, 1984.

"Artificial Intelligence Is Here," *Business Week*, July 9, 1984, pp. 54–62.

Austin, Howard, "Market Trends in Artificial Intelligence," In *Artificial Intelligence Applications for Business*, edited by Walter Reitman. Norwood, NJ, Ablex Publishing Corp., 1984.

"Autofact III Conference Proceedings," Computer and Automated Systems Association of SME, Detroit, Michigan, November 9–12, 1981.

Ayres, Robert, and Miller, Steve, "The Impacts of Industrial Robots," Carnegie-Mellon University, Pittsburgh, 1981.

Ayres, Robert V., and Miller, Steven M., "Robotics—Applications & Social Implications," Ballinger Publishing Company, 1983.

Bachant, Judith, and McDermott, John, "R1 Revisited: Four Years in the Trenches," AI Magazine, fall 1984, pp. 21–32.

Bachant, J., and McDermott, J., "R1 Revisited: Four Years in the Trenches," AI Magazine 5 (3), 1984.

Bailey, Robert W., "Human Performance Engineering: A Guide for System Designers," Englewood Cliffs, N.J., 1982.

Barr, Avron, and Feigenbaum, Edward A. (eds.), Vols. I and II, Cohen, Paul R., and Feigenbaum, E. A. (eds.), Vol. III, "The Handbook of Artificial Intelligence,"

Heuris Tech Press, Stanford, California, 1981, © by William Kaufman, Inc., Los Altos, California, Vol. I, 1981, and Vols. II and III, 1982.

Barrow, H. G., and Tenenbaum, J. M., "Computational Vision," *Proceedings of the IEEE*, Vol. 69, No. 5, May 1981, pp. 575–579.

Barstow, David, "A Perspective on Automatic Programming," *The AI Magazine*, Spring, 1984.

Berger, Charles, "Selecting Robots for Assembly Operations," *Manufacturing Productivity Frontiers*, September 1982.

Bernhard, Robert, "The Fifth Generation—Awesome Obstacles," *Systems & Software*, January 1985, pp. 132–138.

Binford, Thomas O., "Inferring Surfaces from Images," *Artificial Intelligence*, 17, 1981, pp. 205–244.

Boden, Margaret A., "Artificial Intelligence and Natural Man," Basic Books, Inc., New York, 1977.

Brady, Michael, "Preface—The Changing Shape of Computer Vision," *Artificial Intelligence*, 17, 1981, pp. 1–5.

Brady, Michael, "Seeing Machines: Current Industrial Applications," *Mechanical Engineering*, November 1981, pp. 52–59.

Bramer, Max, and Bramer, Dawn, "The Fifth Generation: An Annotated Bibliography," Addison-Wesley Publishing Company, Inc., 1985.

Brooks, Thurston L., "Visual and Tactile Feedback Handle Tough Assembly Task," *Robotics Today*, October 1982.

Brosilow, Rosalie, "How to Step up to Robotic Arc Welding," *Welding Design and Fabrication*, August 1982, pp. 49–53.

Brown, J. S., "The Low Road, the Middle Road, and the High Road." In *The AI Business: The Commercial Uses of Artificial Intelligence*, edited by P. H. Winston and K. A. Prendergast. The MIT Press, Cambridge, Massachusetts, 1984.

Brownell, James R., et al., "Robotics Research and Research Needs: An Exploratory Study," Kappa Systems, Inc., February 1982.

Brownston, Lee, et al., "Programming in OPS5: An Introduction to Rule-Based Programming," Addison-Wesley Publishing Company, Reading, 1985.

Brownstone, Kant, Farrell and Martin, "Programming Expert Systems in OPS5: An Introduction to Rule-Based Programming," Addison-Wesley Publishing Company, Inc., 1985.

Buchanan, B. G., and Shortliffe, E. H., "Rule-Based Expert Systems: The MYCIN Experiments of the Stanford Heuristic Programming Project," Addison-Wesley Publishing Company, Inc., Reading, Massachusetts, 1984.

Buy, Ugo, Caio, Francesco, Guida, Giovanni, and Somalvico, Marco, "BIS: A Problem-Solving Based Methodology for Program Synthesis," *Conference Proceedings of the Second Annual Meeting on Artificial Intelligence*, Leningrad, U.S.S.R., November 1980.

Campbell, J. A. (ed.), "Implementations of Prolog," (Ellis Horwood Limited, Publishers, Chichester) *Halsted Press*, New York, 1984.

Canon, T. M., and Hunt, B. R., "Image Processing by Computer," *Scientific American*, October 1981, pp. 214–225.

Card, S. K., Moran, T. P., and Newell, A., "The Psychology of Human-Computer Interaction," Lawrence Erlbaum Associates, Inc., Hillsdale, New Jersey, 1981.

Casasent, D., "Pattern Recognition: A Review," *Spectrum*, March 1981, pp. 28–33.

Catalano, Frank, "Robotics, Vision Advances Emerge from Industry, University Co-operation," *Mini-Micro Systems*, February 1983.

Charniak, Eugene, and McDermott, Drew, "Introduction to Artificial Intelligence," Addison-Wesley Publishing Company, Inc., 1985.

Charniak, E., Riesbeck, C. K., and McDermott, D. V., "Artificial Intelligence Programaming," Lawrence Erlbaum Associates, Inc., Hillsdale, New Jersey, 1980.

Chester, Michael, "Robotic Software Reaches Out for Task-Oriented Languages," *Electronic Design*, May 12, 1983, pp. 119–129.

Clancey, B. C., and Shortliffe, E. H. (eds.), "Readings in Medical Artificial Intelligence: The First Decade," Addison-Wesley Publishing Company, Inc., Reading, Massachusetts, 1984.

Clancey, W. J., "The Use of MYCIN's Rules for Tutoring." In *Rule-Based Expert Systems: The MYCIN Experiments of the Stanford Heuristic Programming Project,* edited by B. G. Buchanan and E. H. Shortliffe. Addison-Wesley Publishing Company, Inc., Reading, Massachusetts, 1984.

Clark, Keith L., and McCabe, Frank G., "Micro-PROLOG: Programming in Logic," *Prentice-Hall,* 1984.

Clark, K. L., and Tarnlund, S. A. (eds.), "Logic Programming," Academic Press, New York or London, 1982.

Clocksin, W. G., and Mellish, C. S., "Programming in Prolog," Springer-Verlag, Berlin, West Germany, 1981.

Clocksin, William F., and Mellish, Christopher S., "Programming in Prolog," Springer-Verlag, second edition, 1984.

Clocksin, William F., and Young, Jon D., "Introduction to Prolog, A 'Fifth-Generation' Language," *Computer World,* August 1, 1983, pp. 1–16.

Coates, Vary T., "The Potential Impact of Robotics," *The Futurist,* February 1983.

Cohen, Paul R., and Feigenbaum, Edward A., "The Handbook of Artificial Intelligence," Vol. 3 (of 3 volumes). William Kaufmann, Inc., 1982.

Collins, A., and Quillian, M. R., "Retrieval Time from Semantic Memory," *Journal of Verbal Learning & Verbal Behavior 8* (1969), pp. 240–247.

d'Agapeyeff, Alex, "Report to the Alvey Directorate on a Short Survey of Expert Systems in UK Business," *Alvey News,* Supplement to Issue No. 4, April 1984.

Davis, R., "Amplifying Expertise with Expert Systems." In *The AI Business: The Commercial Uses of Artificial Intelligence,* edited by P. H. Winston and K. A. Pendergast. The MIT Press, Cambridge, Massachusetts, 1984.

Davis, R., "Expert Systems: Where are We? And Where Do We Go from Here?" *AI Magazine 2,* 1982.

Davis, Randall, and Lenat, Douglas B., "Knowledge-Based Systems in Artificial Intelligence," McGraw-Hill, Inc., New York, 1982.

Deering, Michael F., "Hardware and Software Architectures for Efficient AI," *Proceedings of the National Conference on Artificial Intelligence,* 1984, University of Texas at Austin, (C) 1983, The American Association for Artificial Intelligence, distributed by William Kaufman, Inc., Los Altos, California, 1984.

de Kleer, Johan, "Book Review: E. A. Feigenbaum and P. McCorduck, The Fifth Generation," *Artificial Intelligence: An International Journal 22* (1984), pp. 225.

Dickson, Edward M., "Comparing Artificial Intelligence and Genetic Engineering: Commercialization Lessons," *AI Magazine,* winter, 1985, pp. 44–47.

DiMaria, Eugene, "In Europe, France Pushes Robot Research," *American Metal Market/Metalworking News,* November 1, 1982.

Dodd, George G., and Rossol, Lothar, "Computer vision and Sensor-Based Robots," Plenum, New York, 1979.

Duda, Richard O., and Reboh, Rene, "AI and Decision Making: The PROSPECTOR Experience." In *Artificial Intelligence Applications for Business,* edited by Walter Reitman. Ablex Publishing Corp., Norwood, New Jersey, 1984.

Dun & Bradstreet, Inc., "An Analysis of the Robotics Industry," 1983.

Eastwood, Dr. Margaret A., "Introduction to Robot Control," *Tooling & Production,* February 1983, pp. 89–94.

Edson, Dan, "Vision Systems for Bin-Picking Robots Increase Manufacturing Options," *Mini-Micro Systems, July 1984.*

Engleberger, J. F., "Robotics in Practice," *Amacom Division of American Management Associations,* 1980.

Ennals, Richard, "Beginning micro-PROLOG," Harper & Row, Publishers, second edition, 1984.

Evanczuk, Stephen, and Manuel, Tom, "Practical Systems Use Natural Languages and Store Human Expertise," *Electronics,* December 1, 1983, pp. 139–145.

"Expert Systems Interview: Alex d'Agapeyeff," *Expert Systems,* Vol. 1, No. 2, 1984, pp. 129–135.

Fabrizi, Daniele, "Italian Industrial Robots and the Italian Society for Industrial Robots," *Italian Machinery and Equipment,* September 1982.

Fahlman, Scott, "Computing Facilities for AI: A Survey of Present and Near-Future Options," *AI Magazine,* winter, 1980–1981, pp. 16–23.

Feigenbaum, Edward A., "Themes and Case Studies of Knowledge Engineering." In *Expert Systems in the Micro-Electronic Age,* Donald Michie (ed.), Edinburgh University Press, 1979.

Feigenbaum, Edward A. and Barr, Avron (eds.), Vols. I and II, Cohen, Paul R., and Feigenbaum E. A. (eds.), Vol. III, "The Handbook of Artificial Intelligence," Heuris Tech Press, Stanford, California, 1981, © by William Kaufman, Inc., Los Altos, California, Vol. I, 1981, and Vols. II and III, 1982.

Feigenbaum, E. A., and McCorduck, P., "The Fifth Generation," Addison-Wesley Publishing Company, Reading, Massachusetts, 1983.

Ferrai, D., Bolognani, M., and Goguen, J. (eds.), "Theory and Practice of Software Technology," North-Holland Publishing Company, 1983.

Ferreti, Marc, "Assembly et Vision Artificielle," *Le Nouvelle Automatisme,* (in French), June 1982, pp. 49–55.

Fisk, J. D., "Industrial robots in the United States: Issues and Perspectives," Congressional Research Service, The Library of Congress, Report No. 81–78E, March 30, 1981.

Forgy, Charles L., "OPS5 User's Manual," Department of Computer Science, Carnegie-Mellon University, Pittsburgh, 1981.

Forgy, C., and McDermott, J., "OPS: A Domain-Independent Production System Language," *IJCAI-5,* pp. 933–939.

Forsyth, Richard, "Expert Systems," Chapman and Hall, 1984.

Fox, Jeff, "Big Ideas from SMALLTALK," *PC World,* March 1984, pp. 72–75.

Freedman, Roy S., "The Common Sense of Object-Oriented Languages," *Computer Design,* February 1983, pp. 111–118.

Friedman, Daniel P., "The Little Lisper," Science Research Associates, Inc., Chicago, 1974.

Fu, K. S., and Rosenfeld, Azriel, "Pattern Recognition and Computer Vision," *IEEE Computer,* October 1984, pp. 274–282.

Geschke, Clifford, "A Robot Task Using Visual Tracking," *Robotics Today,* Winter, 1981–1982, pp. 39–43.

Gevarter, William B., "An Overview of Artificial Intelligence and Robotics, Volume II," U.S. Department of Commerce, *National Bureau of Standards,* March 1982.

Gevarter, William B., "An Overview of Computer Vision," U.S. Department of Commerce, National Bureau of Standards, September 1982.

Gevarter, William B., "The Languages and Computers of Artificial Intelligence," *Computers in Mechanical Engineering,* November 1983, pp. 33–38.

Gilbert, Thomas F., "Human Competence," McGraw-Hill, New York, 1978.

Gleason, G. J., and Agin, G. J., "A Modular vision System for Sensor-Controlled Manipulation and Inspection," Proceedings of the 9th International symposium on Industrial Robots, Washington, D.C., March 1979.

Glorioso, Robert M., and Osorio, Fernando C. Colon, "Engineering Intelligent Systems: Concepts, Theory, and Applications," 1980.

Goebel, Karl, "A Guide to Coating Robot Applications," *Robotics World*, February 1983.

Goldberg, A., and Robson, D., "Smalltalk-80: The Language and Its Implementation," Addison-Wesley Publishing Company, Reading, Massachusetts, 1983.

Gray, "Logic, Algebra and Databases," *Ellis Horwood Ltd.* (in the UK) and the Halstead Press of John Wiley & Sons, Inc., (in the USA), 1984.

Gupta, Parveen, "Multiprocessing Improves Robotic Accuracy and Control," *Computer Design*, November 1982, pp. 169–176.

Hall, Philip M., "An Inspection Process-Untouched by Human Eyes," *Tooling & Production*, June 1982, pp. 86–89.

Harmon, Paul, "The Design of Instructional Materials: A Top-Down Approach," *Journal of Instructional Development* 6, no. 1, Fall, 1982.

Harmon, Paul and King, David, "Expert Systems," John Wiley & Sons, Inc., 1985.

Hesemer, Tony, "Looking at LISP," Addison-Wesley Publishing Company.

Hayes and Michie (eds.), "Intelligent Systems," Ellis Horwood Ltd. (in the UK) and the *Halstead Press* of John Wiley & Sons, Inc. (in the USA), 1983.

Hayes-Roth, F., "Knowledge-Based Expert Systems: The Technological and Commercial State of the Art," *Computer*, August 1984.

Hayes-Roth, F., Lenat, D. B., and Waterman, D. A., (eds.), "Building Expert Systems," Addison-Wesley Publishing Company, Reading, Massachusetts, 1983.

Heer, Ewald, "Robots and Manipulators," *Mechanical Engineering*, November 1981, pp. 42–49.

Heidorn, G. E., Jensen, K., Miller, L. A., Byrd, R. J., and Chodorow, M. S., "The EPISTLE Text-Critiquing System," *IBM Systems Journal*, Vol. 21, No. 3, 1982.

Hendrix, Gary G. (ed., contributor), "Tutorial No. 3 on Natural Language Processing" AAAI Convention held in Washington, D.C., (Copyright held by Gary G. Hendrix.) 1983.

Highberger, Deb, and Edson, Dan, "Intelligent Computing Era Takes Off," *Computer Design*, September 1984, pp. 79–95.

Hillis, William Daniel, "Active Touch Sensing," *MIT Industrial Liaison Report, AI Memo 629*, April 1981.

Hodges, Andrew, "Turing, The enigma," Simon and Schuster, New York, 1983.

Hofstadter, D. R., "Godel, Escher, Bach: An Eternal Golden Braid," Basic Books, New York, 1979.

Hogger, Christopher John, "Introduction to Logic Programming," Academic Press, Inc., 1984.

Holderby, William, "Approaches to Computerized Vision," *Computer Design*, December 1981, pp. 153–160.

Holland, S. W., Rossol, L., and Ward, M. R., "CONSIGHT-I: A Vision-Controlled Robot System for Transferring Parts from Belt Conveyors," *General Motors Research Publication GMR-2912*, Warren, Michigan, February 1979.

Hollan, James D., Hutchins, Edwin L., and Weitzman, Louis, "Steamer: An Interactive Inspectable Simulation-Based Training System," *The AI Magazine*, Summer, 1984.

Hunt, V. Daniel, "Industrial Robotics Handbook," Industrial Press, Inc., New York, 1983.

Hunt, V. Daniel, "Smart Robots," A Handbook of Intelligent Robotic Systems, Chapman and Hall, Inc., New York, 1985.

Iversen, Wesley R., "Vision Systems Gain Smarts," *Electronics*, April 1982, pp. 89–90.

James, Mike, Artificial Intelligence in BASIC," Butterworth & Co. Ltd., 1984.

Johnson, Jan, "Easy Does It," *Datamation*, June 15, 1984, pp. 48–60.

Jones, Keith, "Knowledge Engineering: AI with a European Flavor," *Electronic Business*, November 1983.

Kawanobe, K., "Present Status of the Fifth Generation Computer Systems Project," *ICOT Symposium—Report,* based on lectures given at the ICOT symposium held June 21, 1984, pp. 13–21.

Keller, Erik L., "Clever Robots Are Set to Enter Industry En Masse," *Electronics,* November 17, 1983, pp. 116–129.

Kinnucan, Paul, "How Smart Robots Are Becoming Smarter," *High Technology,* September–October 1981, pp. 32–40.

Klein, Art, "Vision Systems Boost Robot Productivity," *Appliance Manufacturer,* August 1982, pp. 50–54.

Kolbus, David L, and Mazzetti, Claudia C., "Artificial Intelligence Emerges," *Research Report 673, SRI International,* Menlo Park, California, November 1982.

Korf, Richard E., "Space Robotics," Carnegie-Mellon University, Pittsburgh, 1982.

Kowalski, J. A., "Logic Programming—Past, Present and Future," *New Generation Computing,* Vol. 1, 1983, pp. 107–124.

Kowalski, R., "Logic for Problem Solving," North-Holland, New York, 1979.

Kraft, A., "XCON: An Expert Configuration System at Digital Equipment Corporation." In *The AI Business: The Commercial Uses of Artificial Intelligence,* edited by P. H. Winston and K. A Prendergast. The MIT Press, Cambridge, Massachusetts, 1984.

Kunz, J. C., Kehler, T. P., and Williams, M. D., "Applications Development Using a Hybrid AI Development System," *AI Magazine,* 5(3), 1984.

Lamb, John, "Alvey Is on Its Way," *Datamation,* June 15, 1984, pp. 60, 84.

Lehnert, Wendy, Dyer, Michael G., et al., "BORIS—An Experiment in In-Depth Understanding of Narratives," *Yale University Department of Computer Science Research Report #188,* January 1981.

Lenat, Douglas, B., "Computer Software for Intelligent Systems," *Scientific American,* September 1984, pp. 204–213.

Li, "A PROLOG Database System," *Research Studies Press, Ltd.* (in the UK) and John Wiley & Sons, Inc. (in the USA), 1984.

Lindsay, R. K., Buchanan, B. G., Feigenbaum, E. A., and Lederberg, J., "Applications of Artificial Intelligence for Chemical Inference: The DENDRAL Project," McGraw-Hill, New York, 1980.

Lindsay, Peter H., and Norman, Donald A., "Human Information Processing: An Introduction to Psychology," Academic Press, New York, 1972.

Lundquist, Eric, "Robotic Vision Systems Eye Factory Applications," *Mini-Micro Systems,* November 1982, pp. 201–211.

Manna, Zohar and Waldinger, Richard, "The Logical Basis of Computer Programming, Volume 1: Deductive Reasoning," Addison-Wesley Publishing Company, 1985.

Manuel, Tom, "Lisp and Prolog Machines Are Proliferating," *Electronics,* November 3, 1983, pp. 132–137.

Mayo, William T. Jr., "On-Line Analyzers Help Machines See," *Instruments & Control Systems,* August 1982, pp. 30–34.

McCarthy, J., "History of LISP," *SIGPLAN Notices,* 13:217–223. Reprinted in *The Handbook of Artificial Intelligence,* vol. 2, p. 15.

McCorduck, Pamela, "Machines Who Think," W. H. Freeman and Company, 1979.

McDermott, John, "R1: A Rule-Based Configurer of Computer Systems," *Carnegie-Mellon University Report CS-80-119,* April 1980.

McDermott, John, "R1's Formative Years," *AI Magazine,* Vol. 2, No. 2, Summer, 1981, pp. 21–29.

McGhie, Dennis and Hill, John W., "Vision controlled Subassembly Station," *Report MS78-685, Society of Manufacturing Engineers,* Dearborn, Michigan, 1978.

Merritt, Rich, "Industrial Robots: Getting Smarter All the Time," *Instruments & Control Systems,* July 1982.

Michalski, R. S., Carbonell, J., and Mitchell, T. M. (eds.), "Machine Learning: An Artificial Intelligence Approach," Tioga Press, Palo Alto, California, 1983.

Miller, Steve and Ayres, Robert, "Industrial Robots on the Line," *Technology Review,* May/June 1982.

Mokhoff, Nicolas, "Parallelism Makes Strong Bid for Next Generation Computers," *Computer Design,* September 1984.

Morley, Richard E., "An Overview: Programmable Controllers and Robots in Automated Factories," *Design Engineering,* December 1982, pp. 24–26.

Morris, Henry M., "Adding Sensory Inputs to Robotic Systems Increases Manufacturing Flexibility," *Control Engineering,* March 1983.

Movich, Richard C., "Robotic Drilling and Riveting Using computer vision," *Report MS80-712, Society of Manufacturing Engineers,* Dearborn, Michigan, 1980.

Mumford, Enid, "Designing Human Systems," Manchester Business School, Manchester, England, 1983.

Nagel, Roger N. et al., "Experiments in Part Acquisition using Robot Vision," *Report MS79-784, Society of Manufacturing Engineers,* Dearborn, Michigan, 1979.

National Research Council, "State of the Art for Robots and Artificial Intelligence: A Summary," *National Productivity Review,* Autumn, 1984, pp. 375–381.

Naylor, Chris, "Build Your Own Expert System," Halstead Press, a Division of John Wiley & Sons, 1983.

Negoita, "Expert Systems and Fuzzy Systems," Benjamin/Cummings, 1985.

Newell, A., and Simon, H., "Human Problem Solving," Prentice-Hall, Englewood Cliffs, New Jersey, 1972.

Nilsson, Nils J., "Artificial Intelligence Prepares for 2001," *The AI Magazine,* Winter, 1983, pp. 7–14.

Nilsson, N. J., "Principles of Artificial Intelligence," Tioga Press, Palo Alto, California, 1980.

Niwa, Kiyoshi, et al., "An Experimental Comparison of Knowledge Representation Schemes," *AI Magazine,* Summer, 1984, pp. 29–36.

Nowak, Glen, "The Advent of Machine Vision Systems," *Manufacturing Engineering,* November 1982, pp. 56–60.

Oakey, Steve, "LISP for Micros," Butterworth & Co. Ltd., 1984.

O'Connor, Dennis E., "Using Expert Systems to Manage Change and Complexity in Manufacturing." In *Artificial Intelligence Applications for Business,* edited by Walter Reitman. Ablex Publishing Corp., Norwood, New Jersey, 1984.

O'Shea, Tim and Eisenstadt, Marc, (eds.), "Artificial Intelligence," Harper & Row, Publishers, New York, 1984.

Palmer, Richard, "LISP and Artificial Intelligence," *ICP Interface,* Spring, 1983, pp. 16–22.

Parker, Richard and Mokhoff, Nicolas, "An Expert for Every Office," *Computer Design,* Fall, 1983, pp. 37–46.

Parsons, H. M. and Kearsley, G. P., "Human Factors and Robotics: Current Status and Future Prospects," Human Resources Research Organization, October 1981.

Pearl, Judea, "Heuristics: Intelligent Search Strategies for Computer Problem Solving," Addison-Wesley Publishing Company, 1984.

Polit, Stephen, "R1 and Beyond: Technology Transfer at DEC," *AI Magazine,* Winter, 1985, pp. 76–78.

Polya, G., "How to Solve It: A New Aspect of Mathematical Method," Princeton University Press, 1957.

Pople, Harry E., Jr., "Heuristic Methods for Imposing Structure on Ill-Structured Problems: The Structuring of Medical Diagnostics," (Chapter 5) in *Artificial Intelligence in Medicine (AAAS Selected Symposium 51),* edited by Peter Szolovits. Westview Press, Boulder, Colorado, 1982.

Pugh, John R., "Actors Set the Stage for Software Advances," *Computer Designs,* September 1984, pp. 185–189.

Quinlan, Joe, "Those Big, Brainy Eyes," *Material Handling Engineering*, July 1982, pp. 74–81.

Raibert, Marc H., Brown, H. Benjamin Jr., and Chepponis, Michael, "Experiments in Balance with a 3D One-Legged Hopping Machine," *The International Journal of Robotics Research*, Vol. 3, No. 2, Summer, 1984, pp. 75–89.

Rauch-Hindin, Wendy, "Artificial Intelligence: A Solution Whose Time Has Come," *Systems & Software*, December 1983, pp. 150–177.

Rauch-Hindin, Wendy, "Artificial Intelligence Coming of Age," *Systems & Software*, August 1984, pp. 108–118.

Rauch-Hindin, Wendy, "Natural Language: An Easy Way to Talk to Computers," *Systems & Software*, January 1984, pp. 187–230.

Rauch-Hindin, Wendy, "Speak the Language," *Systems & Software*, December 1983, pp. 174–177.

Reddy, D. R., Erman, L. D., Fennell, R. D., and Neely, R. B., "The HEARSAY Speech Understanding System: An Example of the Recognition Process," *IJCAI-3*, pp. 185–193.

Reitman, Walter, (ed.), "Artificial Intelligence Applications for Business," Ablex Publishing Corp., Norwood, New Jersey, 1984.

Research Resources Information Center, "The Seeds of Artificial Intelligence: SUMEX-AI," Bethesda, Maryland, Division of Research Resources, National Institutes of Health, U.S. Department of Health, Education, and Welfare, Public Health Service, *NIH Publication No. 80-2071*, March 1980.

Rheinhold, A. G. and Venderbrug, G., "Robot Vision for Industry: The Autovision System," *Robotics Age*, Vol. 2, No. 3, Fall, 1980, pp. 22–28.

Rich, Charles and Waters, Richard C., "Abstraction, Inspection and Debugging in Programming," *A.I. Memo No. 634*, Massachusetts Institute of Technology Artificial Intelligence Laboratory, June 1981.

Rich, Elaine, "Artificial Intelligence," McGraw-Hill Book Company, New York, 1983.

Rich, Elaine, "The Gradual Expansion of Artificial Intelligence," *Computer*, May 1984, pp. 4–12.

Rifkin, Susan B., "Industrial Robots: A Survey of Foreign and Domestic U.S. Patients," U.S. Department of Commerce, National Technical Information Service, August 1982.

Robot Institute of America, "Robot Institute of America Worldwide Robotics Survey and Directory," 1982.

Robson, David, "Object-Oriented Software Systems," *Byte*, August 1981, pp. 74–86.

Rosen, C. A., "Machine Vision and Robotics: Industrial Requirements," *TN 174, SRI International*, Menlo Park, California, November 1978.

Rosen, Charles A. and Nitzan, David, "Use of Sensors in Programmable Automation," *Computer*, Vol. 10, No. 12, December 1977, pp. 12–13.

Sagalowicz, Daniel, "Development of an Expert System," *Expert Systems*, Vol. 1, No. 2, 1984, pp. 137–141.

Sanderson, R. J., et al., "Industrial Robots—A Summary and Forecast for Manufacturing Managers," Tech Tran Corporation, January 1982.

Sanderson, Ronald J., "A Survey of the Robotic Vision Industry," *Robotics World*, February 1983.

Santane-Toth, E., "PROLOG Applications in Hungary." In K. L. Clark and S. A. Tarnlund (eds.), *A.P.I.C. Studies in Data Processing, No. 16, Logic Programming.* Academic Press, New York, 1982.

Schank, Roger C., "The Current State of AI: One Man's Opinion," *The AI Magazine*, Winter/Spring, 1983, pp. 3–8.

Schank, Roger C. and Riesbeck, Christopher K., "Inside Computer Understanding," Lawrence Erlbaum Associates, Inc., 1981.

Schank, Roger, Kolodner, Janet, and DeJong, Gerald, "Conceptual Information Retrieval," *Yale University Department of Computer Science Research Report #190*, December 1980.

Schmucker, "Fuzzy Sets, Natural Language Computations and Risk Analysis," Computer Science Press, 1984.

Schon, Donald A., "The Reflective Practitioner: How Professionals Think in Action," Basic Books, New York, 1983.

Sell, Peter S., "Expert Systems—A Practical Introduction," MacMillan Publishers Ltd (in Great Britain) and *Halstead Press*, a Division of John Wiley & Sons, Inc. (in the USA), 1985.

Shannon, Claude E., "Programming a Computer for Playing Chess," *Philosophical Magazine*, Series 7, Vol. 41, 1950, pp. 256–275.

Sheil, B., "Power Tools for Programmers," *Datamation*, February 1983.

Shimoda, H., "Fifth-Generation Computer: From Dream to Reality," *Electronic Business*, November 1, 1984, pp. 68–72.

Shunk, Dan L., et al., "Applying the Systems Approach and Group Technology to a Robotic Cell," *Robotics Today*, October 1982.

Siklossy, Laurent, "Let's Talk LISP," Prentice–Hall, Inc., 1976.

Simon, H. A., "The Sciences of the Artificial," The MIT Press, Cambridge, Massachusetts, 1969.

Simons, "Introducing Artificial Intelligence," *NCC Publications* (in the UK) and the *Halstead Press*, a Division of John Wiley & Sons, Inc. (in North America), 1984.

Simons, G. L., "Toward Fifth-Generation Computers," *NCC Publications*, Manchester, England, 1983.

Sleeman, D. and Brown, J.S., (eds.), "Intelligent Tutoring Systems," Academic Press, New York, 1982.

Smith, Reid G., "On the Development of Commercial Expert Systems," *AI Magazine*, Fall, 1984, pp. 61–73.

Sowa, John F., "Conceptual Structures: Information Processing in Mind and Machine," Addison-Wesley Publishing Company, 1984.

Spacek, "An Introduction to PROLOG," *Ellis Horwood Ltd.* (in the UK) and the Halstead Press of John Wiley & Sons, Inc., (in the USA).

Spitznogle, Frank, "Practical Tools Earn a New Level of Respectability," *Computer Design*, September 1984, pp. 197–200.

Stauffer, Robert N., "IBM Advances Robotic Assembly in Building a Word Processor," *Robotics Today*, October 1982.

Steele, Guy L., Jr., "COMMON LISP: The Language," Digital Press, Maynard, Massachusetts, 1984.

Stefik, M., Bobrow, D. G., Mittal, S., and Conway, L., "Knowledge Programming in LOOPS: Report on an Experimental Course." *AI Magazine*, 4(3), 1983.

Sternberg, R. J., (ed.), "Handbook of Human Intelligence," Cambridge University Press, New York, 1982.

Stevens, "Artificial Intelligence," *Hayden Book Co.*, 1985.

"A Survey of Industrial Robots," First Edition, Productivity International, Inc., 1980.

Susnjara, Ken, "A Manager's Guide to Industrial Robots," Corinthian Press, 1982.

"Symbolics 3600 Technical Summary," Symbolics, Inc., Cambridge, Massachusetts, May 1984.

Tanner, William R., "Industrial Robots," Volumes I and II, Society of Manufacturing Engineers, Dearborn, Michigan, 1981.

"Targeting AI Hardware: How Machines Mix in the Marketplace," *Target; The Artificial Intelligence Business Newsletter*, Vol. 1, Issue 1, March 1985, pp. 1–6.

Tate, Paul, "The Blossoming of European AI," *Datamation*, International Edition, November 1, 1984, pp. 85–88.

Teitelman, W., "INTERLISP Reference Manual," Xerox Palo Alto Research Center, Palo Alto, California, 1978.

Tesar, Dr. Delbert, "The Robotics Race is On," *Robotics World,* January 1983.

Thames, Cindy, "Electronics' Newest Labor Force: The Steel-Collar Worker," *Electronic Business,* June 15, 1984, pp. 102–103.

"The Race to Build a Supercomputer," *Newsweek,* July 4, 1983, pp. 58–64.

Thomas, Rick, "Sensing Devices Extend Applications of Robotic Cells," *IE Magazine,* March 1983, pp. 24–32.

Thornton, Jack, "Robots Bringing Changes to CNC Machines," *American Metal Market/Metalworking News,* October 4, 1982, pp. 10–12.

Thornton, Jack, "Robots: Is the Shakeout Here?" *American Metal Market/Metalworking News,* November 1, 1982.

Toepperwein, L., Blacknow, M. T., et al., "ICAM Robotics Application Guide," *Report AFWAL-TR-80-4042,* Vol. II. Air Force Wright Aeronautical Laboratories, Materials Laboratory, Wright-Patterson Air Force Base, Ohio, 1980.

Torrance, "The Human Interface," Ellis Horwood Ltd. (in the UK) and the Halstead Press of John Wiley & Sons, Inc., (in the USA), 1984.

Tosti, Donald T. and Ball, John R., "A Behavioral Approach to Instructional Design and Media Selection," *AV Communication Review 17,* No. 1, Spring, 1969, pp. 5–25.

Touretzsky, David S., "LISP: A Gentle Introduction to Symbolic Computation," Harper & Row Publishers, 1984.

Trombly, John, "Recent Applications of Computer Aided Vision in Inspection and Part Sorting," *Report MS82-128,* Society of manufacturing Engineers, Dearborn, Michigan, 1982.

Tucker, Allen B. Jr., "A Perspective on Machine Translation: Theory and Practice," *Communications of the ACM,* Vol. 27, No. 4, April 1984, pp. 322–329.

Turner, "Logics for Artificial Intelligence," *Ellis Horwood* (in the UK) and Halstead Press, a Division of John Wiley & Sons (in the USA), 1984.

Uttal, Bro, "Here Comes Computer, Inc.," *Fortune,* October 4, 1982, pp. 82–91.

Waldrop, M. Mitchell, "The Necessity of Knowledge," *Science,* Vol. 223, March 23, 1984, pp. 1279–1282.

Wallace, "Communicating with Databases in Natural Language," Ellis Horwood Ltd. (in the UK) and the Halstead Press of John Wiley & Sons, Inc. (in the USA), 1984.

Walton, Paul, "Hungary Stretches a Hand Out to the West," *Computing,* May 24, 1984, p. 27.

Walton, Paul, "Piggy in the Middle of a Power Struggle," *Computing* (U.K.), May 24, 1984, p. 26.

Walton, Paul and Tate, Paul, "Soviets Aim for 5th Gen," *Datamation,* July 1, 1984, pp. 53–61.

Waltz, David, L., "Artificial Intelligence," *Scientific American,* October 1982, pp. 118–133.

Waters, Richard C., "The Programmer's Apprentice: Knowledge-Based Program Editing," *IEEE Transactions on Software Engineering,* Vol. SE-8, No. 1, January 1982, pp. 1–12.

Waterman, "A Guide to Expert Systems," Addison-Wesley Publishing Company, 1985.

Weiss, S and Kulikowski, C., "A Practical Guide to Designing Expert Systems," Rowman & Allanheld, Publishers, Totowa, New Jersey, 1984.

Weizenbaum, J., "Computer Power and Human Reason: From Judgment to Calculation," W. H. Freeman and Company, San Francisco, California, 1976.

Wilensky, Robert, "LISPcraft," W. W. Norton & Company, Inc., 1984.

Winston, Patrick Henry, "Artificial Intelligence," Addison-Wesley Publishing Company, Inc., second edition, 1984.

Winston, Patrick H. and Horn, Berthold Klaus Paul, "LISP," (2nd ed.), Addison-Wesley Publishing Company, Reading, Massachusetts, 1984.

Winston, Patrick Henry and Brown, Richard Henry (eds.), "Artificial Intelligence: An MIT Perspective," Vol. 1 (of 2 volumes), MIT Press, 1979.

Winston, Patrick Henry and Brown, Richard Henry (eds.), "Artificial Intelligence: An MIT Perspective," Vol. 2 (of 2 volumes), MIT Press, 1979.

Winston, Patrick Henry and Horn, Berthold Klaus Paul, "LISP," Addison-Wesley Publishing Company, Inc., second edition, 1984.

Winston, P. H. and Prendergast, K. A. (eds.), "The AI Business: The Commercial Uses of Artificial Intelligence," The MIT Press, Cambridge, Massachusetts, 1984.

Withington, Frederic G., "Winners and Losers in the Fifth Generation," Datamation, December 1983, pp. 193–209.

Wright, J. M. and Fox, Mark S., "SRL/1.5 User Manual," Carnegie-Mellon University, Robotics Institute, Pittsburgh, 1983.

Yazdani and Narayanan (eds.), "Artificial Intelligence: Human Effects," Ellis Horwood Ltd. (in the UK) and the Halstead Press of John Wiley & Sons, Inc. (in USA), 1984.

Zadeh, Lofti A., "Making Computers Think Like People," IEEE Spectrum, August 1984, pp. 26–32.

Trademarks

AI-BASE, Extended-Streams Interface, LMI, LMI Lambda, Lambda/E, RTime, and ZetaLISP-Plus are trademarks of LISP Machine Inc.

ART is a trademark of Inference Corporation.

Arborist, Business-Pro, NuBus, NaturalLink, Personal Consultant, and Explorer are trademarks of Texas Instruments Incorporated.

C-3PO, R2-D2, and STAR WARS are registered trademarks of Lucasfilm Ltd.

CONSIGHT and KEYSIGHT are trademarks of General Motors Corporation.

DEC and VAX are trademarks of Digital Equipment Corporation.

Dipmeter Advisor is a trademark of Schlumberger, Inc.

Ethernet, InterLISP, Smalltalk, and Xerox are trademarks of Xerox Corporation.

Expert Choice is a registered trademark of Decision Support Software.

Expert Ease is a trademark of Human Edge Software Corporation.

FranzLISP is a trademark of the University of California at Berkeley.

IBM, IBM PC, and IBM PC/XT are trademarks of International Business Machines Corporation.

KEE and Knowledge Engineering environment are trademarks of IntelliCorp.

MacLISP, SCHEME, and EL are trademarks of M.I.T. Artificial Intelligence Laboratory.

M.1 and S.1 are trademarks of Teknowledge Inc.

MS and MS-DOS are trademarks of MicroSoft Corporation.

Multibus is a trademark of Intel Corporation.

RuleMaster is a trademark of Radian Corporation.

Symbolics, Symbolics 3600, Symbolics 3640, Symbolics 3760, and ZetaLISP are trademarks of Symbolics Inc.

UNIX is a trademark of Bell Laboratories, Inc.